PENGUIN BOOKS
# THE BATTLE FOR BIHAR

Arun Sinha is among India's distinguished journalists and has worked for the *Indian Express*, the *Times of India* (Bihar edition) and the *Free Press Journal*. Acclaimed for his path-breaking investigative journalism, he was the first Reuters Fellow from India at Oxford. Since 1993, he has been the editor of the *Navhind Times*, Goa. His scholarly articles have been published in anthologies in India and abroad. His other books include *Against the Few: Struggles of India's Rural Poor* and *Goa Indica: A Critical Portrait of Postcolonial Goa*.

# BIHAR

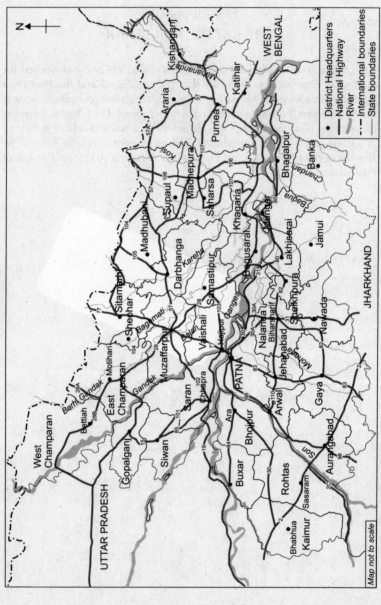

**Legend**
- • District Headquarters
- National Highway
- River
- International boundaries
- State boundaries

*Map not to scale*

The international boundaries on the maps of India are neither purported to be correct nor authentic by Survey of India directives.

# THE BATTLE FOR
# BIHAR

## NITISH KUMAR AND
## THE THEATRE OF POWER

## ARUN SINHA

PENGUIN BOOKS

An imprint of Penguin Random House

PENGUIN BOOKS

USA | Canada | UK | Ireland | Australia
New Zealand | India | South Africa | China

Penguin Books is part of the Penguin Random House group of companies
whose addresses can be found at global.penguinrandomhouse.com

Published by Penguin Random House India Pvt. Ltd
7th Floor, Infinity Tower C, DLF Cyber City,
Gurgaon 122 002, Haryana, India

Penguin
Random House
India

First published as *Nitish Kumar and the Rise of Bihar* in
Viking by Penguin Books India 2011
This updated edition published 2020

ISBN 9780143452065

Typeset in Adobe Garamond by R. Ajith Kumar, New Delhi
Printed at Replika Press Pvt. Ltd, India

www.penguin.co.in

MIX
Paper from
responsible sources
FSC® C016779

*To Purnima,*
*my life partner*

# Contents

# introduction

I am emotionally attached to Bihar because it is not only my land of birth and education but also the land of my explorations as a journalist. My motherland constantly, untiringly, stimulatingly nourishes me and amazes me with unorthodox wisdoms. To many it looks like a chaotic land, but that is because too many revolutions are taking place, the old is giving place to the new and the society is not stabilized. There is chaos because to the people living in a state of subjection for centuries the dream of walking free with their heads held high and sharing existence as equals no longer seems distant and impossible.

Lalu Prasad emerged because large sections of the oppressed majority wanted a hero who could break the dominance of the few and help them grow economically for them to be able to challenge their sway on their own. But he botched the historic opportunity, leaving Bihar in disarray and desolation and Biharis drowned in shame.

But again, deep within the society, the dynamics of discontent never ceased to operate. Dreams did not die. A general sentiment grew that regardless of social station Biharis could not progress unless Bihar was developed. A popular search began for a leader who could make this possible. But the 'backward' sections of society would not trust anyone from the 'upper' castes. He could do things to re-establish and perpetuate upper-caste dominance. That was how Nitish Kumar qualified and was chosen.

A few years into his first term the media started talking of a 'turnaround'. Nitish Kumar had brought Bihar back from the dead. I felt happy for my motherland and was glad for Nitish who was my classmate at the National Institute of Technology Patna (formerly Bihar College of Engineering) and a very intimate friend. That was when the thought of this book first came to me. But, simultaneously, a doubt arose in my mind that the objectivity of the book could be compromised by my closeness to him. It took quite a while for me to resolve the conflict in favour of professional integrity. Nitish separates the professional from the personal. I also decided not to mix the two.

This is an unconventional biography. It is a story of Nitish Kumar interwoven with the story of contemporary Bihar. There are slices of Lalu's story too, without which the stories of Nitish and Bihar would not be complete. However, the book essentially attempts to tell the story of Nitish's life and politics, where he succeeded, where he failed, of his accomplishments together with the mistakes and compromises he made, of his struggles and defeats and how he managed both.

Much of the material in the paperback is based on interviews with political leaders and workers, state government officials and people from various classes of society, articulate and not so articulate, in the towns and villages of Bihar conducted over a period of about two decades. Views on specific issues were gathered with the help of research teams through structured questionnaires. Books on Bihar's contemporary social and political movements and trends, such as backward classes movements and electoral politics, are but few, so as secondary sources I had to often depend on micro studies, mostly PhD theses published as books. A select bibliography is provided at the end of the book.

For Nitish's personal and professional accounts I interviewed him several times during the period of research and writing and was able to cross-check and enrich them with materials gathered in conversations with politicians who were associated with him at one time or another, journalists, friends and family members. Nitish's late mother, brother, sisters and close relations and residents of Bakhtiyarpur and Kalyanbigha helped me a good deal in knowing about his childhood and growing-up years.

# prologue

# an equal honour

May 2018. In less than a year Prime Minister Narendra Modi was to go to war with the Opposition to stop them from seizing his throne. Yet Amit Shah, his party president, his Machiavelli, his general, his political twin, appeared in no hurry to mobilize his allied forces. The allies were impatient to pitch for an increase in the size of their platoons, but Shah seemed to be deaf to their calls. The allies could sense he was playing at being naive: there was an alertness in his indifference, a telescopic eye in his closed door, a plan in the apparent lack of it. He wanted the allies to bake in their own heat before they arrived at his table.

Of all the allies, Nitish Kumar felt the pain of Shah's apathy the most. He had returned to the National Democratic Alliance (NDA) at enormous cost to his political image a year ago; he expected the leading partner, the Bharatiya Janata Party (BJP), to redeem his prestige by giving him an 'honourable' number of seats which, he thought, he deserved in any case because his party, the Janata Dal (United) JD(U), had been the senior partner in Bihar for years, enjoying greater electoral support than the BJP. He did not specify how many of the 40 Lok Sabha seats he wanted. He left it to Shah, hoping he would not be taken for granted because he had come back to them after four years of lone-ranging misadventure disastrously followed by a misalliance.

However, Shah remained unmoved. He had the reputation of being opinionated, inflexible and adventurous. These traits of his personality had become even more prominent with the BJP's gigantic expansion across the states since he took over as party president. He had taken his party closer to its dream of establishing a Hindu nationalist polity. In the climax of this dream, regional parties were to have no place because they were 'parochial', 'divisive' and 'corrupt'. Shah was treating his allies from the perspective of their future foretold, making them feel that the BJP was the giant and they the pygmies.

Nitish wouldn't have it. In a series of indirect messages sent through the media, JD(U) spokesmen conveyed to Shah that he would have to accept the JD(U)'s superiority, as it had larger support than the BJP in Bihar. In the 2009 Lok Sabha elections, the JD(U) had won 20 seats and the BJP 12. In Assembly elections since 2005, the JD(U) had consistently won more seats than the BJP. Even in the 2015 Assembly elections, swimming against the Modi tide, the JD(U) had got 71 seats, while the BJP got 53.[1] From the very beginning of the NDA, Nitish had been recognized as its tallest leader in Bihar. The BJP rode pillion to spread its support among the voters and its presence in the Assembly. Nitish's spokesmen summed it up for Shah: 'You have to give us a seat share befitting our honour.'

Shah didn't respond to Nitish's indirect message himself. But covert hints wafting in from the BJP camp trashed it, saying the JD(U) had got only 2 seats in the 2014 Lok Sabha polls and needed to stop craving for the moon. The BJP had won 22 seats and there was no way they were going to give up any of those. That left 18 seats, and the party had still not decided how to distribute them among its three allies in Bihar: the JD(U), the Lok Janshakti Party (LJP) and the Rashtriya Lok Samata Party (RLSP). The fourth ally, the Hindustani Awam Party, led by Jitan Ram Manjhi, Nitish's hand-picked stopgap chief minister-turned-usurper, had quit the alliance in February 2018, reading the writing on the wall after the JD(U) returned to the NDA.

It so happened that the BJP failed to get the right numbers in the Karnataka Assembly elections in May 2018. That bruised the giant's ego. In the following months, the BJP lost a series of Lok Sabha by-polls. Reports from Madhya Pradesh, Rajasthan and Chhattisgarh, which were to go to polls towards the end of 2018, suggested a surge of discontent against BJP-led state governments. Nitish's camp chuckled, beginning to feel sure that Shah, unsettled by the sight of the receding Modi wave, would now open dialogue with him.

But Shah still refused to descend from the heavens.

Anxiety grew within the JD(U). The party wanted to know clearly how many and which seats it was going to fight for, so they could start making preparations. After all, it was the Lok Sabha elections, and the constituencies in Bihar were huge. Shah's unhurried approach, which was obviously intended to force the JD(U) to take whatever was offered to it at the last moment, could prove calamitous to both.

The JD(U) had the example of Araria before them. A few months after their reunion with the BJP, Mohammed Taslimuddin, the Rashtriya Janata Dal (RJD) MP from Araria, died. Nitish saw an opportunity for the NDA to grab the seat. As a candidate, he picked Taslimuddin's son, Sarfraz Alam, who was a JD(U) MLA from Jokihat, a part of the Araria constituency. Though Alam had been suspended by the party for his reported misbehaviour with a couple in a railway coach, Nitish wanted him to be the NDA candidate for three reasons: one, as Taslimuddin's son, he would get a substantial sympathy vote; two, as a Muslim, he would get some votes on his own, as Muslims made up a large part of Araria's electorate; and three, he would get the votes of JD(U) supporters among the extremely backward castes and Dalits. But Shah showed no interest in Nitish's proposal. According to a top JD(U) leader, when Nitish met Modi and Shah in Gandhinagar, at the time of the swearing-in of the new Gujarat ministry in December 2017, he requested them to take a final decision on his proposal quickly as there was the danger of Alam quitting the JD(U) to join the RJD, which was eager to nominate its deceased MP's son. They did not respond. Finally, after waiting for over three months for a JD(U) nomination, Alam took the RJD offer. Modi and Shah put up a BJP candidate who lost.

Nitish did not want a repeat of Araria. Yet, some months away from the 2019 Lok Sabha polls, he found no change in Shah's approach. The JD(U) was very keen on getting two seats to begin with—Aurangabad and Darbhanga. Aurangabad was important because it was dominated by the Rajputs, and Darbhanga because it was dominated by the Brahmins. The party, which had its base among extremely backward castes and Dalits, wanted Darbhanga and Aurangabad to win the support of the higher castes, to demonstrate that they stood for social diversity.

In an exchange of informal messages between the two parties, the JD(U) was given to understand, according to its senior leaders, that they would not get Aurangabad. The then Union home minister, Rajnath Singh, had told Amit Shah not to give the seat to anyone but the sitting BJP MP, Sushil Singh. Why Rajnath Singh insisted on that only he knew. But the JD(U) would get Darbhanga, though it had lost it to the BJP in 2014. The JD(U) started working in the constituency to mobilize support.

As for the overall seat share, the hints from the BJP camp were ominous. They would not be willing to give the JD(U) more than 12 seats, including the 9 they (the BJP) had lost in 2014. That was not an 'honourable' number of seats. According to senior JD(U) leaders, Nitish wanted more seats than the BJP, or at least the same number. He insisted on the recognition of his equality with Modi in Bihar. Anything less than that amounted to downgrading his political status in the public eye, which he was not going to accept. Yet nothing could be settled until Shah opened negotiations. And he wouldn't.

Nitish decided to administer Shah a little of his own Machiavellian medicine to goad him to come to the table. He dug out his demand for a special status for Bihar. That was clearly rubbing salt on Modi's wound from the Telugu Desam Party stomping out of the NDA over the issue of special status for Andhra Pradesh. Both Andhra Pradesh and Bihar had been bifurcated. They had justified claims. Simultaneously, Nitish dropped another hint: his party would fight elections in Madhya Pradesh, Chhattisgarh and Rajasthan independently of the BJP. The JD(U) did not want to be confined to Bihar! Nitish even gave his party's expansion plan a catchy name: Bihar Plus. To these subtle messages he added a direct one: the NDA must finalize seat distribution among the allies within a month so they could start preparing for the elections well in advance.

His arrows found their target. Shah's office fixed a meeting with Nitish in Patna on 12 July 2018. That day the two had two rounds of talks, one over breakfast and another over dinner, at Nitish's official residence. According to a senior JD(U) leader, Shah assured Nitish, '*Ham seaton ke bantware mein aapka samman rakhenge* [In seat-sharing, we will give you the honour you deserve].'

A few more weeks passed, and Shah would still not tell Nitish how many seats 'honour' translated to. True, Shah had his own problems. All his sitting MPs wanted renomination. Even his losing candidates, such as former minister Shahnawaz Hussain, wanted it. The LJP insisted that it must have all its 6 seats, and the RLSP, which had got 3 in 2014, wanted 4. These minor allies were making a noise. LJP leader Chirag Paswan publicly took positions contrary to the BJP's stance on demonetization and Dalit issues. RLSP leader Upendra Kushwaha complained of Shah not giving him an appointment and threatened to leave the NDA.

The impression that gained ground in the JD(U) was that Shah was working under the presumption that Nitish would accept the 'honourable number' the BJP decided, as he had no option but to stay on in the NDA. Exactly in such an atmosphere there were rumours about Nitish going back to the RJD. There were no such moves from Nitish, though. The rumours, however, were so strong that the RJD had to publicly deny them. Lalu's elder son and former minister, Tej Pratap Yadav, flashed a placard reading: 'No entry to Nitish Chacha' at the gate of his parents' official residence. Yet, in Uttar Pradesh, Akhilesh and Mayawati had come together. Shah could ignore the probability of Nitish realigning with Lalu only to his party's peril. Anything could happen in politics. If the realignment happened, Nitish could even emerge as a focal point of the national Opposition.

According to senior JD(U) leaders, after two months of dilly-dallying, Shah telephoned Nitish to convey that both the BJP and JD(U) would get an equal number of seats, 17 each. A few days later, Modi too called Nitish to confirm the equal seat share. Owing to some superstitious reasons, Shah had made a formal announcement only a month later. Nitish was happy. But the LJP and the RLSP were not. The deal left only 4 seats for the LJP and 2 for the RLSP. However, soon, Kushwaha crossed over to Lalu, which remedied the LJP's grievance.

Though Nitish got 17 constituencies, Shah kept him in suspense over which ones they would be. That meant another series of hard negotiations. Nitish insisted on retaining the only 2 seats his party had won in 2014: Nalanda and Purnia. He got them. He resisted the BJP's attempts to dump all the 9 seats they had lost in 2014 into his basket. The BJP still managed to dump 6 of them. And they went back on their promise to give Darbhanga to JD(U). Not getting it after all the work they had done in the past few months came as a disappointment to the party.

Nevertheless, the seat sharing, despite all the wrangling and uncertainties it created, ultimately proved to be fabulously profitable to the NDA in the Lok Sabha polls during March–May 2019. The alliance hoisted its flag in 39 of the 40 constituencies. Before the elections, no party was sure that the mutually hostile caste blocs, separately aligned with the BJP, the JD(U) and the LJP, would vote together for the NDA's common candidate. But they had done so. The NDA got 53.6 per cent of the total votes polled compared to the 41.6 per cent it had got in 2014.

The vote for the NDA in Bihar was as much a vote for Modi as it was for Nitish. Giving an equal share of seats to the JD(U), which some BJP leaders saw as a bane, proved to be a boon. The BJP's recognition of Nitish's prominence in Bihar greatly boosted his position. It assured people that he would be leading the state government for the fourth term—the first from 2005 to 2010, the second from 2010 to 2015, the third from 2015 to 2020—if the alliance wins the Assembly elections in November 2020.

# I

## ON A SEA OF TURMOIL

# the second coming

The counting of votes for the Bihar Assembly results started at eight in the morning on 24 November 2010. At 1 Anne Marg—Chief Minister Nitish Kumar's official residence in the exclusive precinct of white bungalows the British had built for their top officers between the Governor's House and the Secretariat in western Patna—the mood was buoyant and jovial but not without the nagging apprehension of the wild beast that ballot boxes quite often produced.

Media exit polls had forecast an absolute majority for Nitish, with pollsters differing only on numbers. Yet, the same media before the elections had prophesied a hung Assembly.

When we met Nitish at our common friend Kaushal's son's engagement in Mumbai three days before the day of counting, everybody expressed joy over the 'results foretold', but he wouldn't accept congratulations from anyone. We put it to his ability to be calm to the point of stolidity: he would never, unlike any of us friends, yell, jump up and punch the air at his moments of triumph.

However, when we were alone in his suite, and I told him about the exit polls and how a senior journalist covering elections had junked all crystal-gazing by the media and told me two weeks before the polling ended—'Nitish will get 200 seats, the others will have to fight for a share in the remaining 43. It's going to be a tsunami. People are not telling anyone, the media is not getting the feel'—I could notice Nitish's face glisten with pleasure. '*Yeh kaam ka asar hai* (It's a reward for work),' he said.

But the next moment the glow on his face disappeared. He began to look concerned. 'It's a very huge responsibility. I was going around asking people to give me five more years, but I was also asking myself, "Do I have the energy and capability to deliver what I am promising them? Will I be able to transform the system?"'

Heaving a sigh he said, 'But then, I have to first be sure if people are giving me another tenure. I nurtured a tree. Whether it's going to bear fruits or not depends on nature's mood.' The stoical posture, the impassivity, had returned.

Instructions had been passed on to the security men in grey safari outside 1 Anne Marg not to stop any party men or others who wished to come in to congratulate the sahib on the day of counting. At the same time, inside the two-storeyed bungalow facing big manicured lawns edged with flower plants, its exterior and rooms humble, unadorned and functional just as originally designed in the 1910s, everyone sported a little swagger of certainty but dropped it in Nitish's presence to assume the leader's monkish attitude.

Television sets were on: in Nitish's secretary Chanchal Kumar's room on the ground floor, in CM's chamber opposite it, and upstairs where Nitish's family lived. Everybody was receiving the latest news from sources of their own; every piece was shared with others and cheered or waved away for being stale or inauthentic.

Nearly every result was going in favour of Nitish's party, the Janata Dal (United). The seats not contested by it were going to its ally, the Bharatiya Janata Party (BJP). The leader of the Opposition, Rabri Devi—who had never lost an election since her husband, Rashtriya Janata Dal (RJD) president and '*Gharibon ka Masiha* [Messiah of the Poor]' Lalu Prasad had installed her as chief minister in 1997—was on the verge of losing by several thousand votes in both the Sonepur and Raghopur constituencies. I had got some sense of it when I visited Raghopur during the campaign. I had heard the Yadavs—Lalu's caste-men, the pillars of his electoral edifice— say the Nitish regime was good because *loot-maar* (seizing things by force) had stopped and the bazaar remained open till late in the evening.

All the four close relations (two brothers, two sons-in-law) of Ram Vilas Paswan, the leader of the RJD's ally, Lok Janshakti Party (LJP), were trailing far behind. The state Congress party president Mehboob

Ali Qaiser and the ex-leader of Congress Legislature Party, Prakash Ram, were facing defeat.

Within a few hours, the picture was clear. The lawns were swarmed with JD(U) officials, workers, supporters. Truckloads of laddoos started arriving. In that atmosphere of jubilation, media persons and TV cameramen were barely noticed and were shoved about. Everyone waited with garlands, bouquets, red clay powder to congratulate the conqueror.

Inside the bungalow Chanchal Kumar's room, the waiting lounge next to it and the passages were crowded with Nitish's aides, friends, senior party men and bureaucrats. Nitish's aides were amused to see among the senior civil and police officers streaming in to compliment him a few from the bunch who were suspected to be hatching plots to deny Nitish a second tenure. The bunch allegedly operated in collusion with Lallan Singh, Nitish's overambitious shadow who had turned hostile to him before the elections, and Congress election machinery manipulators in Delhi; Lallan in his heyday had had them placed in key positions. They were so effective in instilling fear in the top rungs of the civil service and the police that the latter would not even resist unwarranted transfers of officers by election authorities based on fallacious complaints. At the end of it, the bunch was sure of the success of their plan. They even wagered bets on the number by which Nitish would miss a majority.

Among the first to congratulate Nitish was Union Home Minister P. Chidambaram. 'He was the first to congratulate me but he won't give me the funds I need,' Nitish told us in good humour. Then Sonia Gandhi called. Other ministers, BJP leaders, chief ministers—the string of calls seemed endless.

In between the calls, Nitish once turned to me and, beaming, said, 'So that journalist was right, after all, wasn't he? The rest have to share among 43. It's not a tsunami. It's a far bigger phenomenon than that.' Incredulity was written all over his face.

Lalu Prasad called. '*Poora sahayog rahega* (You shall have our full cooperation),' he assured Nitish. Just one day before, Lalu had trashed the exit polls, accusing the media of being biased against him, and had boasted, 'The victory is going to be ours.' And Nitish had chortled, 'Lalu has been a poster boy [for Bihar] of the media. No other politician has garnered so much mileage from the media as Lalu has. However, he has done nothing for the people of Bihar, and tomorrow's result will speak volumes. Lalu's worries will only increase after the verdict is announced.'

During the election campaign Nitish's diatribes were directed mainly at Lalu. Nitish's scheme of giving bicycles to girls and boys entering class nine had earned him considerable public goodwill. To give voters a bigger temptation, Lalu made a promise to distribute motorcycles to schoolchildren. Nitish told the people: 'I gave children bicycles to go to school. Laluji wants to send them to jail, as minors using motorcycles are going to go nowhere else because they would be caught for driving without licence.' Lalu stopped making the promise.

When Nitish wanted to emphasize his appeal for a second mandate, he would say: '*Baat bananewale ko pandrah saal, aur kaam karnewale ko bus paanch saal?* (You gave a charlatan fifteen years, and you can't give five more years to a performer?)'

At the peak of his campaign Nitish triggered a kind of amusement nobody had expected him—a staid, sober man obsessed with verbal correctness—to indulge in. At a media conference he recited a parody on the popular song *Jai ho* from the film *Slumdog Millionaire* to satirize Lalu:

> *Jai ho, Kayapalatji ki jai ho/ Jai ho, Railways ka kshay ho/ Jai ho, Bihar me bhay ho/ Atank raj ki jai ho/ Aur is liye Maharaj Kayapalatji ki jai ho.*
> (May Lord Turnaround be victorious/ May the railways be ruined/ May fear reign in Bihar/ May there be a reign of terror/ And therefore may King Turnaround win.)

Lalu hit back with a rhyme:

> *Yeh shasan hai Maharaj Sushasan ka/ Khel ho raha hai kushasan ka/ Barh, sukhar se janata to rulayenge/ RSS ki goad mein baith kar secular kahlayenge.*
> (Bad governance characterizes the regime of Lord Good Governance/ People hit by drought and floods cry in misery/ Mr Good Governance claims to be secular while being a puppet in the hands of the Rashtriya Swayamsevak Sangh.)

The media had nicknamed Nitish 'Sushasan Babu', the Man of Good Governance, owing to some effective measures he had taken to put the state administration back on the rails. Lalu's sarcastic rhyme called him 'Maharaj Sushasan' in retaliation of his description as 'Maharaj Kayapalat' by Nitish. Jolted by the public anger against stagnation and lawlessness that caused him loss of power in November 2005, Lalu promised all-round development of Bihar during his 2010 election campaign. Conscious that few would believe him, he started trumpeting about his fame as the man who had turned around the Indian Railways.

Lalu had demanded and got the railway ministry from the Congress after the 2004 Lok Sabha polls for providing it support of 22 MPs of his party. Presenting his 2007–08 budget to the Lok Sabha, Lalu claimed that the Indian Railways had earned a surplus (income) of over Rs 20,000 crore during 2006–07, the highest ever in its history. He took the entire credit for this upswing. In reality, it was due to a host of factors: officers' initiatives that reduced the turnaround time of wagons from seven to five days; substantial increase in freight volumes due to high economic growth during the preceding years; and arbitrary changes in accounting policy, such as recording the capital component of charges paid by the Indian Railways for leasing rolling stock from the Indian Railways Finance Corporation (IRFC) not as working expenses but as capital expenditure (in other words, as an asset, rather than as an expense).

The railways story annoyed Nitish no end. It made his stint in the railways before Lalu look like a monumental failure. It portrayed Lalu as a man of ideas and him as a pen-pusher. The contrast eminently suited Lalu, and he tried to make it worse for Nitish by dismissing his claim of development under him as *sirf lifafabazi*, sheer illusion, and assuring people he would revive Bihar just as he had done the railways.

Nitish could have allowed Lalu to get away with his tall claims only to his peril. Lalu also seemed to be trying hard to outdo Nitish in the caste algebra. He had the Yadavs and Muslims with him, the Dalits with Paswan on his side and also the upper castes who were angry with Nitish. Nitish was working his own caste algebra to beat this formidable combination. Nitish's caste algebra was working imperceptibly as a result of his positive discrimination policies and programmes directed at the extremely backward castes and Dalits. Where Nitish needed to work hard was to demolish the image of Lalu as a repentant redeemer. For that he needed to hit him hard where he was posing to be the strongest: the magic wand for regeneration.

Nitish broke out of his 'dull Jack' mould to recite the folksy acerbic rhyme quoted above because he decided it was the best way—what with television's reach across the towns and villages, among the schooled and the illiterate—to stop anyone being brainwashed by Lalu. The message Nitish constantly dinned into the ears of his electorate was: 'Don't you believe I have led you out of the tunnel into light? Do you want to go forward or back into the darkness? The return of Lord Turnaround would mean return of the rogue raj. Do you want that?'

But seeing Lalu buried in the debris of the 24 November 'pollquake' Nitish was, strangely, filled with apprehension. It was the kind of result even Nitish had not dreamt of. He felt small and humbled. It did not seem entirely of his own making. People had shown they were the supreme power—the almighty—and could take decisions on the fate of mortals like him. The result was as much awe-inspiring for Lalu as it was for him. Today he was victorious because the ultimate authority wanted him to win handsomely and to sideline Lalu completely. Tomorrow, they could haul him off to the margins. Triumph in politics was as transitory as other things in life.

'I put myself in Lalu's place to feel his pain,' Nitish said. In his responses to media questions at 1 Anne Marg that day, he did not ridicule or belittle Lalu or the RJD. On the contrary, he made every effort to be magnanimous. Over the next few days, he repeatedly urged the NDA (National Democratic Alliance) members not to 'make fun of the defeated Opposition' in the Assembly. 'Nobody should say that the Opposition is finished. Be restrained in your celebrations.'

He was also guided in this by the surplus of shrewdness he possesses. It worked well with his dignified appearance and speech, which were two very important components of his appeal. Apart from other positive things people saw in him, they distinguished him on these grounds from Lalu, who often displayed an earthy, sardonic demeanour. By looking to be compassionate towards his vanquished enemy Nitish was only consolidating his brand.

After Rabri lost in both the constituencies, it looked like only a matter of time when she would have to vacate the bungalow at 10 Circular Road. Few knew that Lalu had been pleading with Nitish for quite some time for passing a legislation providing for lifelong official accommodation to former chief ministers like former prime ministers. 'Every now and then Lalu would call Sahib and say, "*Aye bhai* Nitish, do it as soon as possible, please,"' a Nitish aide said. Nitish procrastinated for long, for it might seem as if he was doing it for his own future comfort, but then got a legislation passed. But it was framed in such a way that only one accommodation would be provided if both husband and wife were former chief ministers.

To the media persons fishing on the issue after the election results Nitish said, 'Rabri Devi and Laluji are free to stay at 10 Circular Road or can move to another accommodation of their choice.'

Lalu's election strategy had relied on pooling of Dalit and upper-caste votes with his Yadav and Muslim constituencies. He got a small section of the Dalit and the upper-caste vote. His support among the Yadavs and Muslims was decreasing but they still remained his strength. Out of the 22 RJD MLAs, 9 were Muslims and 7 Yadavs, making 72 per cent of the party's total strength in the House.

In a relaxed conversation after dinner on the day of results, Nitish said to me, '*Hum bhale jitini hawabaazi kar lain, yeh election kaafi-kuchh jaat ke adhaar par hua hai* (Our tall claims about social transcendence apart, the results of this election were influenced heavily by caste). I don't say people have not voted above caste. But casteism has played a very important role.' The victory of the RJD at Fatuha, Bakhtiyarpur and Maner—the Yadav-dominated constituencies around Patna—provided clear proof. 'Casteism worked as much against us as it did in our favour,' said Nitish, 'because some castes voted as much in solidarity for us as the Yadavs did for the RJD.'

After a moment of silence, he said, 'We will have to fight one more battle against casteist forces—casteist forces in all castes.'

The NDA had won a steamrolling majority. A pervasive sentiment in the JD(U) camp was that the BJP profited more from its alliance with the JD(U) than vice versa. A good chunk of the BJP vote was actually vote for Nitish. For the first time a number of Muslims voted for the BJP because of him. Lalu's Muslim vote was basically a 'protection vote'—a trade-off for safety of life and property. By ensuring Muslims' safety as well as Lalu had done, or better, Nitish broke Lalu's monopoly over the protection vote. Muslims also gravitated towards him because of the several initiatives he took for their educational advancement and skill development. They began to see Lalu as a 'talker' and Nitish as a 'doer'.

On the evening of victory, one of Nitish's aides said, 'We lost some of the constituencies the BJP left for us because they put up independent candidates with a plan to help them win and admit them into their party to increase their number over the JD(U)'s in the Assembly. Their independent candidates divided the vote on Hindu–Muslim lines, scaring away even those Muslims who were inclined to vote for Nitish.'

Nevertheless, the JD(U) camp was happy to note the positive effect of their leader's strong rebuff to the mascot of aggressive Hindu politics and Gujarat chief minister Narendra Modi. Nitish deflated Modi's self-congratulatory ballyhoo in Bihar newspapers about monetary and other aid from his state to the Nitish government after the 2008 floods in north-eastern Bihar. Nitish not only returned the Rs 5 crore Modi had sent to the Chief Minister's Relief Fund but also stopped him from joining the election campaign. He knew the Muslims of Bihar could never accept Modi as he had come to represent annihilating anti-minorityism after the pogrom of Muslims in Gujarat in 2002 by Hindu mobs, apparently unrestrained by any administrative intervention. Muslims disillusioned with Lalu would have gone right back to the RJD.

Nitish said, 'All Lalu had to do was print thousands of posters of Modi and me with clasped hands raised in the air taken at a meeting a few years back in Haryana and put it up across the state to scare away the Muslims.'

Nitish's strong stand against the 'Butcher of Gujarat' succeeded in splitting Lalu's Muslim constituency. 'I'm ready for elections,' Nitish had said to me when I met him at the peak of the controversy triggered by his decision to return the money to Modi. 'Some people in the BJP are saying I have gone too far and it is time the party gave a befitting reply to me for the insult. Do they mean end of the alliance? That may do a lot of good to me as who knows I may sweep the elections with strong backing from the Muslim community.'

And, in the late evening on 24 November 2010, as Nitish sat with his aides to glance over the confirmed final results with a sense of pride, one of them couldn't help sending out a warning to the BJP: 'We must tell them to behave properly. Else, we will break out of the alliance. We are just seven short of a majority of our own.'

I said to Nitish a number of liberals in the country, including newspaper columnists, often wondered why he did not break away from the BJP and turn a Congress ally. Pat came the reply, 'Why don't you make a list of such people? If they together succeed in getting the Congress to grant a special status to Bihar I'm ready to go with them. I will leave the BJP for that cause.' He grinned. He had said it in jest.

A moment later he said, 'Congress displays so much arrogance, it is hard to bear it. They believe they are the only political party in the country, the rest are an aberration. In real fact, it is a party of slaves. The power flows from one family. It provides no room for independent identity. *Yeh desh ki sabse wahiyat party hai* (It is the most worthless party in the country).'

This suggests that his alliance with the BJP would continue in all probability when the NDA makes a bid for majority in the Lok Sabha in 2014. Would he be a serious contender for leadership of the NDA election campaign? The media had hardly any doubt after the 2010 Assembly election results, which had come as a popular certification of his successful performance in bringing Bihar back from the dead. 'If he can revive a corpse like Bihar,' people said, 'he will do wonders for the rest of India.'

Nitish laughed it off. 'I have enough to do in Bihar,' he said. When Kaushal and I were alone with him that night, he said in response to our prodding, 'To me prime ministership is no more than a daydream. From the kind of humble origins I had chief ministership itself was too high a position to achieve. National politics is altogether a different ball game.'

It is difficult to tell what is cooking inside his head. He seems to be in the race for prime ministerial candidature among NDA leaders, of course. It is not clear who else would be competing with him, except Narendra Modi who is a favourite of a large section of the BJP. In terms of mass appeal, he is far ahead of the other two probables in the BJP, Sushma Swaraj and Arun Jaitley. Nitish's insistence on the exclusion of Modi from his election campaign was traced by most media analysts to their rivalry for NDA prime ministerial candidature.

However, Nitish faces several barriers on the road to prime ministership. His party is too small and confined to Bihar; even in the best of scenarios the number of its MPs would be much smaller than the BJP's. As the largest party, the BJP must enjoy the privilege of selecting a prime ministerial candidate from within itself. If the JD(U) and other 'secular' allies do not accept Modi, the BJP could choose someone else whom they would have to endorse. The non-BJP allies are currently not in a strong position to insist on a prime ministerial candidate from among them.

# the inheritance

I do not remember the exact day I met Nitish at the Bihar College of Engineering. The college was a fine example of early-twentieth-century architecture in red stone at the far eastern edge of the long stretch of Patna University on the bank of the Ganga. It was not long after we enrolled in electrical engineering in mid-1968 that we struck a chord. I cannot fathom what bonded us, nor can any two friends scientifically analyse the links that make the chain of their relationship, but I guess it happened naturally because we were both from vernacular backgrounds and were scornful of the *angrezida*, or westernized culture, of the urban elite. We thought they were a stilted bunch, clannish with their own lot but standoffish, even intimidating, to the rest. We often derided them with the common saying, *Angrez chale gaye, aulad chhod gaye* (The British have left their illegitimate offspring behind). We saw them as a continuum of the native elite that ruled as lackeys of the British and still thought they were ruling over India.

Those were days of student radicalism, and our ideas were shaped both by leftist ideological currents as well as our family origins. Bihar was wrecked by zamindari, the British land revenue collection system in which most agricultural land (*zamin*) was permanently settled with thousands of small, medium and big revenue farmers (zamindars) who held hereditary rights to ownership of land. We were strongly opposed to the surviving feudalism of big landlords who had managed to keep large areas of agricultural land even after the abolition of the zamindari system in the late 1950s. This, despite the fact that among the four of us who gelled into a close group in the initial days of college, Narendra

Singh came from a zamindar family in Saharsa whose landholding had shrunk in size due to peasant claims. My family too had a small zamindari but it was gone after the abolition. Kaushal Kishore's family owned land in a village in Jharkhand, but was surviving, like my family, with salaries from jobs in the middle bureaucracy.

Nitish's grandfather was a middle peasant, not well-to-do, but not poor either. Towards the end of the nineteenth century, his great-grandfather Sitaram Singh branched off from his family in Telmar village—now in Nalanda district—to settle a few kilometres away in a small village, Kalyanbigha, in the same district where he bought about six acres of agricultural land. Kalyanbigha formed part of a large tenure of a Muslim zamindar who contracted out rent collection from the village to some big ryots on a commission. Although these ryots, known as *thikedar*s, represented the inequity and injustice of zamindari, they did not indulge in unfair squeezing or harsh penalizing that was the satanic tattoo of the system. Nitish's family carried no legacies of zamindari, so Nitish, who was born in Kalyanbigha but had grown up about ten kilometres north in Bakhtiyarpur town—forty-five kilometres east of Patna, where his father set himself up as an Ayurvedic physician—was expected to have far less personal bitterness towards the system.

Our antagonism to big landholders and the urban elite flowed essentially from our intellectual exposure. The whole atmosphere of the mid-1960s was revolutionizing. Our family status provided the framework for it; in the social hierarchy we could be ranked as middle-middle class, or even lower-middle class, that looked at the traditional upper classes and nouveau riche in villages and towns with disdain. We bore the notion in our subconscious that our families had been well-off and respectable earlier and were in a hard economic situation now because our fathers and grandfathers would not make moral compromises that had become the endemic formula of success in the present system. We had to blow up such a malignant system. Looking back, I can say that our family background provided us the ideological car and our intellectual experience, the fuel.

Nitish's father, Ramlakhan Singh had actively participated in the freedom movement, suffered detention and prison sentence and been a very popular Congress leader in Bakhtiyarpur. If there was one candidate who deserved Congress nomination for the Bakhtiyarpur seat in the first general election based on free franchise to the Bihar Legislative Assembly in 1952, it was Ramlakhan Singh. But the Congress gave it to someone else, with a promise to nominate him in the next election. When he was denied a ticket even in 1957, he quit the Congress, fought on another party's ticket and lost miserably.

In the initial years at college, Nitish told us about his father's alienation from the Congress and his unsuccessful electoral sally, but we never discussed it in any detail. Perhaps friends know about the families of their friends only in scraps, at least initially. Maybe Nitish himself knew little of his father's agony of 1952 and rebellion of 1957 because he was born in 1951 (1 March) and had heard about it only in slivers and snippets from his father, mother, relations and others.

Yet, having observed Nitish at close quarters it became clear to us that much of his original motivation to take up politics as a career could be attributed to his father's determined but partially successful electoral adventure. Somewhere deep in his mind Nitish felt his father had been treated unjustly by the Congress. His father had passed on his political wound to him. And without being aware of it—for when Nitish began to take active part in student politics at the college and at Patna University and went to jail leading engineering undergraduates in the fight for security of employment, his father was not amused. He told him: '*Pehle degree le lijiye, phir aapko jo man hai kariye* (Concentrate on your studies first; do whatever you like after you have finished your education).'

Ramlakhan also bequeathed the trait of simplicity to Nitish, plain living and a lack of craving. In 1934, when Ramlakhan came to set up his practice in Bakhtiyarpur, he was the only Ayurvedic physician in this tiny bazaar town. In a short time he was able to purchase a small single-storeyed house from a semi-bankrupt trader as well as some pieces of agricultural land that were added to his family's landholdings at Kalyanbigha. He bought the pieces at Kalyanbigha not in his name, but in his father's name. Close relations termed it as a folly for, they said, when the family property would be split after his father's death, his elder brother would get half the share of even those lands that Ramlakhan was buying with his money. The elder brother, who never took much responsibility for the family, or interest in the cultivation of family lands, was constantly on pilgrimage to Hindu holy towns and had been nicknamed Pujariji, the Eternal Pilgrim, by the village.

Ramlakhan ignored his well-wishers' advice: the house was one, and he could not think of buying land in his own name, which would look like he was separating himself from the family. His father died four years after Ramlakhan moved to Bakhtiyarpur, so he must have earned well in the initial few years to be able to buy his house and agricultural plots. In the forty years till he died Ramlakhan bought no other properties. Only some years later he added an upper floor to his modest house when his children were growing up.

The house faced the road that had connected Patna to Kolkata along the Ganga for centuries. The Eastern Railway had been built parallel to this route. Houses stood sparsely on both sides of the road, which forked on the outskirts, one leading to eastern Bihar, and further east into West Bengal, another to southern Bihar, and further south into Jharkhand.

Ramlakhan had his clinic in the front room of the house, and the child Nitish would keep popping in from the inner rooms. He was the fourth of Ramlakhan's five children—the first being a daughter, Usha, another also a daughter, Prabha, and the third, a son, Satish—and they acted sometimes benevolent, sometimes dictatorial towards him. As a child, Nitish was not a wild rogue: he would not snatch things from children his age, wrestle or exchange blows with them, never break things or tear papers and books, nor do dangerous things when alone, like playing with fire or swallowing coins or dirty stuff.

He was seen by the family as a quiet type, until they discovered Prabha's bride doll missing one day, mother's sandal-rubbing stone another day, and then father's water pot, Usha's comb and more. Everybody became watchful for the ghost that was scooting with things. At last they caught him when the little spook laid his hand one day on the pincers in the kitchen and was walking stealthily across the courtyard to drop it into the well. Before they ran towards him he had dropped it. A neighbour, Panditji, who was an expert swimmer, was summoned to descend into the well, just to see what else the apparition had flung into it. Everything that had gone missing in the past months was found there.

They admonished the ghost, but he remained unrepentant.

The water in the well was unpalatable and used mainly for washing utensils, floors and sundry things. Everybody in the family went to the Ganga to have their bath before breakfast. Drinking water was brought by water sellers in pots. Nitish's mother Parmeshwari Devi cooked meals after breakfast while his father saw patients at his clinic. After lunch, especially during summer, the family shut the doors and windows to keep out hot winds and had a siesta. That would be the best time for the ghost to come out and drown things.

He could be really stubborn. Once when he was about eight years old a nilgai—a species of antelope once commonly found in Patna district that had started getting rarer—strayed on to the road outside the house. Although groups of people gathered on either side nobody showed the courage of going near it. Nitish came out of his house with other members of the family and watched the spectacle for a while. Then he suddenly ran towards the nilgai and stood facing it with arms akimbo. The antelope did not take long to size up his challenger and butted him out of the way, though not too harshly, letting him go home with just a few bruises.

If that suggested that the child loved adventures, it was to be proven wrong during his growing-up years. At the Sri Ganesh High School at Bakhtiyarpur, co-founded by his father who was the school secretary, Nitish showed no interest in sports. He could go with close friends to watch a local football match and cheer a team on but would never play himself. He did play traditional games, such as marbles or *gulli-danda*, but once in a while and not with obsessive interest. He flew no kites like most Bihari boys did.

When he was small one of his favourite entertainment activities was a ride to the point where the road forked for east and south, popularly known as Biharsharif Mod (turning). His father's patients who came from the neighbourhood on bicycles or in rickshaws or *tamtams* (single-horse carriages) were followed to their conveyance after consultation by Nitish who insisted on being taken to Biharsharif Mod, which formed a sort of public square. But after he joined high school his fascination for the Mod ended. He wouldn't be part of the groups of youngsters hanging around at the square.

He had three or four classmates with whom he spent time at and outside school for recreation. One of them was Munna Sircar who was to take Nitish on his motorcycle for his first election campaign. Yet, Nitish loved his privacy. After all the enjoyable sessions with his friends Nitish liked to retire to his exclusive world. His zealous love for privacy was revealed when, for the first two years in college, he stayed at a lodge because rooms in the college hostel had to be shared with two–three inmates, and he wanted a room to himself. The lodge was not well-kept and located in a messily built area, but he preferred to live there until he was allotted a room entirely to himself—a rare privilege to a student before or after our time.

Perhaps there were a few reasons why a strong sense of individual space had developed in Nitish. His elder siblings recall that he became very quiet and aloof after their mother moved to Kalyanbigha to supervise the family farms. Their father's income had decreased due to his political engagements and the mushrooming of Ayurvedic physicians in and around Bakhtiyarpur. Ramlakhan's uncle, the Eternal Pilgrim, had proven a bad manager and the yield had been declining. Cereals brought in gunnybags in bullock carts from the farms after harvest were a key support for Ramlakhan's burgeoning family in Bakhtiyarpur. At least there was food in the house, if nothing else. Nitish's mother decided to stay in Kalyanbigha to ensure this essential supply to the house.

Being the younger son, Nitish was the darling of his mother. She would forgive him for whatever he did, and she was the one to whom he turned for everything, not to his father, who appeared too big and distant with his public persona. He could say anything to her, ask anything of her. There was constant dialogue between them. His separation from her, which he could not prevent, created a vacuum which Father or his elder siblings could not fill. Usha, the eldest sister, assumed the mother's role but she could never replace Mother. Nitish became formal, reserved, unsentimental and started staying away from others. As he withdrew into a world of his own and spoke rarely the family could sometimes not fathom what was going on in his mind. His behaviour has remained much the same even though he is deep into politics. In an allusion to this trait of his, Lalu Prasad often used to say, with the earthy sense of humour he is famous for, 'Nitish has incisors even in his back.'

Ironically, Nitish's sense of private space in his growing-up years intensified with his family seeing him as a special child. This was primarily because he was the most intelligent of all the siblings. He was always among the top four students in class. The family talked about his excellent academic performance among themselves and to others, making him feel he was unique and different.

Nitish was good at mathematics from primary school. To his good luck, at high school he found a mathematics teacher in Jagdish Prasad who could make even the most difficult of problems seem easy. Nitish reminisces, 'He showed us how to solve a problem step by step, just as a mason builds a house brick by brick. Although mathematics is abstract and formless he made us see meaning in every step, making the science of numbers so enjoyable. If I never scored less than 80 per cent marks in the subject, much of the credit goes to him. And, don't forget, mathematics is so important to get into engineering.' His father's dream was that Nitish take up a medical career, but seeing his son take no interest in biology and remain obsessed with mathematics he decided to let him go for engineering.

Nitish was also fortunate in having a very good Hindi teacher. Shambhu Sharma not only ignited a passion in him for the short fiction of Premchand, Rambriksha Benipuri and Phanishwarnath Renu and the poetry of Nirala, Mahadevi Verma and Pant, but also created interest in reading quality Hindi periodicals such as *Sarika* and *Dharmayug* (now defunct). The greatest contribution this teacher made to the evolution of Nitish's personality was in giving him a very strong foundation for refined diction in Hindi, which was to become Nitish's forte in his political career. Shambhu Sharma taught him a blend of chaste and popular Hindi; Nitish in later years garnished it with Lohiaite innovations.

Nitish's love for simple, expressive Hindi also developed in his high-school years with the reading of classics. Keen on enriching the intellectual world of his children, Ramlakhan subscribed to the Family Library Plan of Hind Pocket Books to acquire low-priced, abridged translations of biographies of extraordinary men and the world's great literature. 'I pored over these books,' says Nitish, 'not only to take in the content but also to derive pleasure in the economical, precise and effective way in which great authors used the language.'

His Hindi in his growing-up years was an imitation of the great authors he read and of Shambhu Sharma whom he admired. His school and neighbourhood friends, more comfortable in Magahi, which was spoken in the family and in social intercourse, sometimes made fun of Nitish's '*shuddh* [chaste] Hindi'. His elder brother Satish recalls the Nitish of school years as a reticent person. 'He was a man of few words, sometimes to the point of being laconic,' Satish says. 'But he was able to communicate with clarity whenever he spoke.'

Although Hindi remains top on the languages he loves, Nitish regrets he could not learn English as well as he desired in his school years. Sri Ganesh High School used to have a headmaster who was passionate about teaching spoken English. Headmaster Mukherjee was accompanied by students eager to learn the language on his way from home to school and back. He insisted on talking to them in English and corrected them when they made mistakes in pronunciation or grammar. In his middle-school years Nitish envied those Mukherjee acolytes who spoke *phataphat angrezi*, fluent English. By the time he reached high school Mukherjee had retired. The English teacher he studied under confined himself to the classroom and the given syllabus.

His craving for lucidity and gracefulness in English writing and speech still remains unfulfilled. When we were visiting him at the start of his second term as chief minister in November 2010, he said, 'I want to learn English.' For him to make a start we brought him an advanced dictionary, a thesaurus and *Oxford Collocations*. He said he had decided to read good books in English as the English in government files had 'corrupted' him.

Self-teaching ran in the family. Nitish's grandfather Kishori Sharan Singh was a self-taught Ayurvedic physician. While managing farming on the family's seven acres at Kalyanbigha, Kishori Sharan collected several books on Ayurveda and pored over them.

Life was not easy for the family then. Of the seven acres, over two acres were rain-fed (*bhitta*), where rice and maize grew, and five acres were a saucer-shaped tract (*tal*) that grew only *masur*, a staple pulse. Masur brought cash for non-food necessities, but for masur to grow the tal needed to be inundated by the Dhoba, a tributary of the Punpun River, during the rains. The inundation killed the pests and brought in silt and other nutrients to leave the tal fertile as the water receded by mid-winter. If the rain failed there was less food and no cash.

Kishori Sharan's fees as an Ayurvedic physician were very low and paid as often in cash as in grains. Sometimes patients from neighbouring villages also called on him as his reputation spread. He learned of newer medicines and lines of treatment from wandering ascetics who sojourned at the temple situated close to his ancestral fifteen-room house. In a way, Ramlakhan's career as an Ayurvedic physician was a legacy.

However, the old man didn't drive Ramlakhan into it. Initially he only wanted his younger son to get educated, to finish school. After Ramlakhan was through the lower primary grade at the village, he sent him to an upper primary school at Harnaut, four kilometres from the village. Primary schools, then intended chiefly for the common people, were poor structures, with low-paid and few teachers and no water and sanitation. Yet Ramlakhan learnt some history, geometry, literature and science. Kishori Sharan, keen to see his son pass through matriculation, got him admitted to a *gurukul*, a school opened by the Arya Samaj at Danapur. Danapur is a small town west of Patna drawing its life from agriculture, a large grain market and a military cantonment. It was at the Danapur gurukul that Ramlakhan was spiritually transformed.

The gurukul was far from home by the standards of the times—about seventy kilometres—but Bakhtiyarpur was connected to Danapur by train. The British had built the Eastern Railway in the late nineteenth century to connect Calcutta, the chief port in eastern India, to the North-Western Provinces—as the Uttar Pradesh state was known then—up to Delhi to facilitate trade and travel. For centuries before the railways came, the Ganga with its tributaries had served as the main highway for trade along the route, also travel, because although a roadway parallel to the great river had existed since ancient times, it had fallen in disuse in many parts and remained undeveloped. Bakhtiyarpur was on the bank of the Ganga and so was Danapur. Both had small ports that served as feeders to the main regional port at Patna. The Patna port, apart from serving trade in south Bihar, also transported merchandise in and out of north Bihar through a grid of rivers, the major ones of which streamed into the Ganga.

With the coming of the railways, river-borne trade gradually declined, and more and more traders and passengers began to flock to train stations instead of at river ports. During the four years in the mid-1920s when Ramlakhan was studying and residing at the gurukul, we can imagine him mostly taking a train to and from Bakhtiyarpur. He may have sometimes taken the river route due to shortage of trains, or even tamtams—the single-horse carriages with a flimsily cushioned, flat wooden seat that took passengers, crammed and constantly in pain from rocking on the hard bench—from Patna to Danapur. And from Kalyanbigha to Bakhtiyarpur he could not have avoided the tamtam even if he wanted to because that was the only transport available, unless of course he decided to take Bus Number Eleven, as they say in Bihar, that is, to use his own two feet.

Exactly why Kishori Sharan sent him to an Arya Samaj gurukul and not to a government high school is hard to know because nobody survives to tell the story. Kishori Sharan, much like many other Kurmis, might have been influenced by the patriotic and caste-levelling ideals of the Arya Samaj. There is no record to suggest he joined the Samaj, although historical records of his time show that a bulk of early Samaj recruits were Kurmis, Yadavs and Koeris—Bihar's three leading intermediate castes. Much like other Shudras, the Kurmis of Bihar were fighting for their social elevation.

A state organization of the All-India Kurmi Kshatriya Mahasabha was formed to campaign for recognition of the Kurmis as Kshatriyas, the warrior caste. A mythology of pristine grandeur of the caste had been invented; it 'proved' that Kurmis had been great warriors and had ruled many kingdoms in the ancient past, when at some juncture the Brahmans and Rajputs defeated them and reduced them to a lower social rank. There was as much evidence for proving that the Kurmis had been rulers as for disproving it.

Everyone knew the battle was for the present, and history was only being used as a subterfuge by the 'Shudra' elite for upward mobility. The battle was for carving out spaces in worlds that were exclusively occupied by the upper castes: classrooms, teaching, government services, the army, the bench and the bar and politics. The British consciously fomented the discontent, for when the Brahmans and Rajputs who constituted the Bengal Army led the Mutiny of 1857—which nearly overthrew British rule almost a hundred years before they actually lost it—they realized that the only way to continue to rule was to break the upper-caste solidarity by the inclusion of soldiers from the 'lower' castes. Accentuating the caste divisions in Hindu society was seen by them as the surest bulwark against the growth of the spirit of nationalism. Outwardly, however, the British played the liberal mediator: they swore they were working only for the uplift of the underclass.

They appropriated to themselves the right to grant Brahman or Kshatriya status to the lower castes. The authority of adjudication was delegated to the census commissioner who enumerated the population by caste decennially. Lower-caste associations submitted petitions to the census commissioner, petitions that drew evidence from the Vedas, ancient treatises, epics, anecdotes from various accounts and cultural practices, legends and symbols of particular castes. This triggered a mass mobilization of the Shudras in Bihar who, while they fought for official recognition as Brahmans or Kshatriyas, began to 'reform' themselves to bring themselves at par with the upper castes.

In its mad zeal, the reform adopted many of the hyper-orthodox practices of the upper castes, such as seclusion of women within the four walls of the home, prohibition of widow remarriage and wearing of the *janeu*—a sacred thread round the shoulder by men—but its general spirit was progressive. It broke down the endogamous walls of the many sub-castes in every caste by campaigning for intermarriage; it bridged the rich–poor gap within a caste by funding education of economically disadvantaged children and founding schools and colleges in small towns and rural districts with community donations; and, most importantly, it directly challenged the authority of the upper castes to demand free labour from the lower castes on their fields and at their homes on an everyday basis, and more so on occasions like weddings, as well as their legitimacy to subject the lower castes to multiple discriminations.

In the perception of the lower-caste associations, however, it was not a movement for *sudhar*, or reform of their community, but for *unnati*, its advancement. Kishori Sharan and Ramlakhan could not have remained uninfluenced by this movement; and the movement among Kurmis was widespread in Patna district, where their population was high and where an educated elite had already emerged in the caste.

The Arya Samaj came with an ideology in tune with this movement, and no wonder this district provided the Samaj the original base, with many Kurmis joining it. Danapur became the nerve centre of the Samaj; and while his father as a cultivator and self-taught Ayurvedic physician at Kalyanbigha was influenced by its ideology, Ramlakhan as a student of the gurukul there got converted to it. Much like Buddhism, the Samaj rejected the principle of determination of a man's social status by birth, which was the edifice of the caste society, asserting that every individual must be judged by his deeds. Its aim was to establish an Arya Samaj, a noble society based on the Vedas, 'the one true source of all knowledge' and 'the original scripture of all mankind', which must be read freely by the castes that had been prohibited by the Brahmans to do so. The Samaj rejected polytheism, idolatry and superstitions and promoted belief in the Vedic principle of monotheism and one formless god. Ramlakhan was greatly inspired by these ideas, and the Samaj's patriotism and promotion of education finally won his heart.

Ramlakhan was to remain a committed Arya Samajist throughout his life. He would worship no gods, even those in the small images in metals and prints on a shelf in his wife's shrine. He would allow the family to observe the holy days of the Hindu calendar and even help them organize a puja, but he would have nothing to do with the devotional rituals, mantras, stalks of *doobh* grass, sacred fire and oblations of ghee.

But he never became an evangelist of the Samaj. He followed its ideas as an individual practitioner. And his individual zeal was not restricted to his faith in a formless god but extended to the social ideals of the Samaj. He became a staunch nationalist and an active supporter of the Indian National Congress that had transformed under the leadership of Gandhi from a pressure group to a mass organization fighting for freedom from

British rule. At the time he was finishing school, the Congress fought
the elections to the provincial councils and Central Assembly under
limited constitutional reforms in 1926, but found that the official
and nominated members who were in majority would always defeat
its proposals. The Congress wanted constitutional reforms that would
guarantee power to elected members, but when the British announced
a commission for the purpose, Congressmen rejected it because it was
an all-white commission from which they did not expect justice.

The visit of the commission led by Sir John Simon to different
provinces faced huge masses of Congress supporters waving black
flags and shouting slogans. When Simon with other members of the
commission arrived in Patna by a special rail coach at 6.30 on a chilly
December morning in 1928, over 30,000 Congress supporters stood
behind police barricades shouting 'Simon, go back!' Determined
protestors had been moving in procession through the streets of the city
and gathering behind the barricades from 3.30 a.m. in large numbers.
Ramlakhan, then a student of the Government Ayurvedic College
in Patna, was also there with fellow students. We can imagine him
somewhere deep in the swarm of demonstrators, shivering in his thin
woollen clothes, teeth chattering, holding a black flag and shouting
slogans, the passion for India's freedom supplying him all the warmth.

Continuing to take part in Congress activities he was put under
police detention not long thereafter, as a consequence of which he was
expelled from the college. He fought his case in court which decided his
expulsion was unjust; he was re-admitted into the college, though he
had lost more than a year. Ramlakhan was married when he was still a
student at the gurukul. His wife stayed with the family at Kalyanbigha
and looked after the house with her mother-in-law and sister-in-law—
wife of her husband's elder brother, the Eternal Pilgrim. She dutifully
remained with her husband's Congress activism and silently suffered the
anguish of his detention and expulsion. Even after Ramlakhan moved
to Bakhtiyarpur his participation in Congress activities continued.

He was a marked man in the Patna district administration's records,
more so because he had formally joined the Congress. This never
deterred him from propagating and mobilizing people for freedom.
Congressmen and fervent supporters would gather at his house and the

conversations could go on for hours. Sometimes district or provincial Congress leaders dropped by at his house for tea when travelling from Patna to other towns or back. He would often engage his patients too in fervent discussion on nationalist issues; and soon, because of his curative successes, Ramlakhan had sick people, not only from Bakhtiyarpur but also from nearby villages, calling on him.

At Gandhi's 'Quit India' call in 1942, asking the British Raj to go home, Ramlakhan suspended his medical practice and plunged into the popular uprising that sought to hinder the colonial government's functioning; he was arrested, accused with heinous charges and sent to jail. It was a terrible phase for Nitish's mother who did not know how to manage the house with her two children, Usha and Prabha, as she had neither income nor savings. Kishori Sharan had passed away four years earlier. Staple cereals continued to flow from Kalyanbigha, but she had to often do with meagre supplies of other stuffs or even without them for want of cash.

The early decades of Ramlakhan's migration from Kalyanbigha to Bakhtiyarpur were also years of very intense struggle of the Kisan Sabha (Peasants Association) against zamindari. Although its leader Swami Sahajanand Saraswati was a Hindu ascetic with Congress sympathies, the Kisan Sabha had among its second- and third-rung leaders and rank and file not only Congressmen but also socialists and communists. Most socialists were ex-Congressmen who, unable to push forward their agenda for radical change in the Congress, formed the Congress Socialist Party at a meeting of their leading protagonists in Patna in 1934; but they too, like Sahajanand, though to a far lesser degree, had Congress sympathies. Yet, together with communists, they drove the Kisan Sabha along more radical lines, always itching for a confrontation with the zamindars, pressing for the abolition of zamindari.

Ryots organized by them defied zamindars in many parts of Patna district, resisting their many extortions through illegitimate levies. Ramlakhan's father at Kalyanbigha and Ramlakhan in Bakhtiyarpur saw eruptions of peasant resistance in villages around and were in sympathy with the socialists and communists who inspired it, but neither of them got themselves to think beyond the Congress and take to a leftist ideology. One of the reasons could be the far less extortionist and repressive zamindari they experienced at Kalyanbigha. Another reason could be the security of land tenure they enjoyed. The third reason could be class interest: they hired farm labourers from the untouchable castes whose cause the leftists, particularly the communists, championed, threatening to make them demanding and rebellious.

In Ramlakhan's case, to all these factors was added his self-engineered elevation to the urban middle class as an indigenous physician in Bakhtiyarpur. Ramlakhan kept his distance from communists—from socialists too, though he was acquainted with most provincial and local socialist leaders because of their old association with the Congress. Eventually the socialists moved from the ideology of revolutionary political and economic transformation in the 1930s and '40s to an ideology of reform of the status quo with social equality as its main focus by the 1950s and '60s. Even as they mobilized the lower castes under their banner—including the Kurmis who had been fighting upper-caste supremacy in various walks of life for several decades—Ramlakhan would stay on as a Congressman and not join them.

Later too, when he quit the Congress to teach them a lesson, he preferred to join a rabidly feudal and right-wing party to achieve his objective, but not the socialists. The switch was not ideological but opportunistic and temporary; it was only a burst of anger against the Congress provincial leadership; after it subsided he returned to the Congress a year or so later.

In contrast to his father Nitish grew up as an unswerving socialist. It was during his high-school years that he began to be slowly attracted to the socialist leader Rammanohar Lohia's ideas on social equality— positive discrimination to backward classes, women, untouchables and tribes—and on primacy of mother tongues over English in education and administration.

The starting point of his attraction was repulsion with the Congress whose ministers both at the Centre and in the state were widely seen as self-aggrandizing and caring little for public interest. Nitish, who knew about it from newspapers and hearsay, sometimes argued with his father how he could go on supporting a political party that had degenerated from an organization of selfless individuals to an association of selfish manipulators. And Ramlakhan, much like his Congressmen friends and acquaintances who would regularly gather at his place, responded with criticism of Lohia's irreverent, 'indecent' statements about the 'phoney socialism' of Nehru and the unruly, militant protests against his government's policies. This would make Nitish more aggressive in the defence of his political icon. Ramlakhan never shut his son up or forced him to toe his political line. He remained a good father to him, caring more about the teenager's studies than his political prattle.

Nitish too loved and respected his father: in matters other than political views he was never disobedient and irreverent. On the contrary, he unconsciously imbibed many of his father's traits: Arya Samaji disbelief in Hindu idolatry and rituals, simple living, frugality, love for neat clothes and living environment, altruism and disdain for idlers.

However, politically, it was the coexistence of two ideological currents under one roof, one formed and steadfast, the other nascent and still vague. Yet the credit for that too goes to his father who followed the principle of tolerance and accommodation very typical of the Congress. This attitude was unconsciously instilled in Nitish and would go on to become a part of his personal and political nature. Nitish, like his father, would never be an extremist, which he only later understood was the sine qua non for conducting politics in a diverse country like India with a fragmented polity.

Following the same principle, his father developed an all-embracing social attitude. In the mid-1940s, when he became the moving spirit behind the setting up of Sri Ganesh High School and Sri Ganesh Sanskrit School at Bakhtiyarpur, he was thinking not only of the children of his Kurmi caste but of all castes, including the Yadavs who dominated the demography of the town and the rural neighbourhood. This, despite the fact that a significant part of the fund for the buildings and the teachers' salaries was provided by Kurmi traders and commission agents (*arhatiyas*) of the Bakhtiyarpur grain market. Teachers were from different castes and so were students. He helped children from poor families, irrespective of caste, to enrol and study in these schools at nominal fees.

Growing up under a father who, though being conscious of his caste identity, kept himself out of the political discourse of his caste,

Nitish too developed an aloofness from caste-centric political and social activities. He wouldn't be hostile to Kurmi partisans but he wouldn't be one of them. The reason in the case of both the father and son could partly be the lack of economic and social insecurity in their lives. They were Awadhiyas, a sub-caste of Kurmis who traced their origins to the British Oudh—present-day Lucknow and neighbouring districts in Uttar Pradesh—and were economically, culturally and educationally most advanced at the time among Kurmi sub-castes in Bihar. While being excellent cultivators as all Kurmis were, the Awadhiyas prided themselves on having several members of their community as lawyers, teachers, even college principals. The Awadhiya elite were envious of the upper-caste elite, but only for not being accepted as a part of it. There was no class conflict, only a sense of rivalry that the upper castes had dominated the landscape and must now 'make room for us'.

The rivalry was there in Bakhtiyarpur and around as well. Nitish could not but have been engaged in it consciously or unconsciously in his growing-up years, at school and in the neighbourhood, with his excellence in studies and sharp wit. This rivalry stayed at the level of academic competition with upper-caste students; he competed with them and they competed with him. But it was free from the hostility witnessed in many rural parts of Bihar where upper castes used intimidating and manipulative ways to keep lower-caste children out of school. Such attempts at deterrence could also not be made by the upper castes in a town where his father had an overarching presence with his social and political profile and his reputation as an educational missionary. The liberal and caste-neutral attitude Nitish had imbibed from his father survived in him due to the absence of any upper-caste conspiracy to deny him education.

The unmistakable yearning of the lower castes to break out of the hegemony of the upper castes that they had borne for thousands of years was, however, difficult to ignore for someone growing up in the 1960s. Having been the principal victims of an unjust Hindu division of labour—in which all manual and menial labour was assigned to them and all mental labour appropriated by the upper castes—they craved for recruitment to positions where they could use their mind to earn their living.

Many scholars tend to see the mobilization of lower castes through caste associations in the early decades of the twentieth century as a cultural movement (sanskritization), but it essentially was an economic movement that aimed to dismantle the oligopoly of the upper castes by dismantling their control over the means of production, primarily land, and knocking down the ossified social division of labour. The cultural symbols—such as wearing of the sacred thread, mythologies of their castes' royal and martial grandeur—were merely used to boost self-esteem, to lift up the spirit, to slowly grind down the fatalism of the subordinate castes; these were tools of being, not the way of being.

The upsurge of the lower castes in the 1960s that Nitish witnessed was not a sudden eruption but a continuity. The upsurge was the third phase of the lower-caste movement, and we were to see many phases in the later decades of the twentieth century. The caste association-led mobilization was the first phase, which lasted from the 1880s to the 1920s. Then came the second phase with political mobilization under the Triveni Sangh in the 1930s and '40s. The proof that the first phase was an economic and political, and not a cultural, movement was provided by the emergence of the Triveni Sangh with the caste associations of Kurmis, Yadavs and Koeris confederating to claim the political space that the Congress had denied them—the first had provided the foundation for the second phase.

Provincial Congress leaders—unlike those of today who are out of touch with the people except for a few months before an election—moved around the countryside very often to mobilize the masses for the freedom struggle. As they saw the lower castes yearning for power, they began to recruit more of them to positions in the party organization, but were still very ungenerous in giving them positions of power in civic bodies, district boards and the provincial legislature or ministries. The lower castes were divided into two streams: one followed the strategy of remaining within the Congress and fighting for wider representation, and the other of staying out and claiming political space independently.

Ramlakhan, who had witnessed the first phase and been indirectly influenced to embrace the Arya Samaj and the Congress, continued in the latter during the second phase, even though large numbers of

Kurmis, Yadavs and Koeris of his district began to sympathize with the Triveni Sangh. Their sympathies only increased in the 1937 elections to the provincial Legislative Assembly with the Congress preferring a Bhumihar, Sheelbhadra Yaji (whom Ramlakhan had defeated in the election for Congress delegates from the district a year or so before), to the prominent local Kurmi leader Deosharan Singh in the nomination to the Barh constituency, which included Bakhtiyarpur. Fourteen years later, Congress was to do a Deosharan Singh to Ramlakhan too by choosing a Bhumihar, Tarkeshwari Sinha, over him for the Patna East seat for the Lok Sabha and denying him even the Bakhtiyarpur seat for the state Assembly. Yet, until that happened, Ramlakhan stayed in the Congress, and like others in the party was overjoyed to see the defeat of all the candidates of the Triveni Sangh in 1937.

In the early years following the separation of Bihar as a province from Bengal, particularly in 1912, the Congress was dominated by Kayasthas, one of the four upper castes and educationally the most advanced among them. The chief skill of the Kayasthas was writing, which made them ideal recruits for recordkeeping, secretarial services, clerical jobs and general administration in Muslim and British Indias. The zamindars, estate managers, lawyers, teachers and students from this caste powered the 'separate province' campaign as well as the initial phase of Congress organizing in Bihar. They constituted the leading group of assistants to Gandhi when he wanted to investigate and record the views of the peasants of Champaran in northern Bihar in 1917. Gandhi wanted to first find out how the European indigo planters were exploiting and oppressing the peasants before deciding on a course of action.

However, nationalism could not have been the monopoly of the Kayasthas. The freedom struggle drew masses and threw up leaders from all castes; by the 1940s Bhumihars and Rajputs displaced Kayasthas from the Congress leadership. The former had two distinct camps in the Congress—the Bhumihars led by Shri Krishna Sinha, who was to become the first chief minister of Bihar after Independence, and the Rajputs by Anugrah Narain Sinha, who was to become the finance minister under Shri—each competing with the other for power.

Shri and Anugrah typified the duality of the liberal breed of Indian politicians who built their edifice of power with bricks of caste. As leaders of government, they often took decisions contrary to the wishes of their caste and in concert where larger interests of society or nation were involved. Yet, they also often resorted to unfair tactics to consolidate their caste support and co-opt smaller factions of the other two upper castes—Kayasthas and Brahmans—as well as the lower castes into their broad factions. Whether established or aspiring, no provincial or local Congress leader could hope for a party nomination during an election without the support of one of the two factions. And the Shri and Anugrah factions chose candidates with the intention to outnumber each other in the Congress legislature party in order to be its majority leader and hence the chief minister.

Ramlakhan was dropped from the list for the 1951–52 election because neither of the two Congress poll war rooms in Patna saw him fitting into its overall strategy of giving 'due representation' to all castes, primarily the upper castes, within its factions across the state. So they struck a deal between each other with a Bhumihar candidate Tarkeshwari Sinha for the Patna East (later Barh) Lok Sabha seat and a Kayastha candidate Sundari Devi (sister of the late prime minister Lal Bahadur Shastri) for the Bakhtiyarpur Vidhan Sabha seat. Tarkeshwari Sinha was very young, in her late twenties, and had been involved in the freedom struggle, but she was selected essentially because she was strongly favoured by the Shri faction. Sundari Devi had been a freedom fighter too, but was not much known in Bakhtiyarpur.

Ramlakhan was terribly hurt. Yet, after being persuaded by faction leaders that he would be given a seat at the next election, he took it as one of the many sacrifices he had made as a Congressman and campaigned whole-heartedly to see that Sundari Devi won—and she did.

He could have left the Congress and fought the election as an independent, like many Congressmen denied nomination did, but he remained a dedicated soldier. As the Shri and Anugrah factions began to draw up their competing lists in the 1957 elections he reminded them of their promise; nobody heard him. Tarkeshwari Sinha and Sundari Devi were renominated. The dam of his patience breached and he decided to teach the two factions a lesson.

He was joined by other local Congressmen including Acharya Jagdish, a Rajput, who too had aspired for a Congress ticket but was rejected. They left the Congress and joined the Janata Party led by the raja of Ramgarh. Acharya Jagdish became the Janata candidate in Bakhtiyarpur, Keshav Prasad in Fatuha Assembly constituency, which was reserved for the Scheduled Castes, and Ramlakhan in Barh. They knew it very well that it was not easy to swing all Congress voters in their favour; the broad masses were still loyal to the party that had brought them freedom. Yet, they wished to work hard to slice out as much of the Congress vote as possible, so that even if they did not win, other parties, not the Congress, won those seats.

In their own perception, they were *vote-katwas*, vote-splitters. And they concentrated on Bakhtiyarpur and Fatuha, because they calculated that it was in these constituencies that Ramlakhan's individual popularity would fetch them most dissident Congress votes. Ramlakhan knew he did not have much of a chance of running away with but a very thin slice of the Congress vote in Barh, especially because Tarkeshwari Sinha had risen greatly in stature as a junior minister in Nehru's cabinet and had impressed everyone with her oratory in and outside Parliament. Two or three meetings in Barh were addressed by the raja of Ramgarh, and Ramlakhan too held a few of his own meetings, but he devoted most of his time and energy to Bakhtiyarpur and Fatuha, where he knew he with his popularity and Acharya Jagdish with the support of his Rajput caste could make a major difference.

The results from the three constituencies were on expected lines. In Barh Ramlakhan got only 5.6 per cent, about 9,500 votes, against Tarkeshwari's 47 per cent, about 79,000 votes. But he succeeded in his mission. Sundari Devi lost in Bakhtiyarpur; the Congress vote split with Acharya Jagdish helping the Socialist Party candidate Shiv Mahadeo Prasad win. And Keshav Prasad won in Fatuha.

Years later, Nitish would avenge his father's defeat in Barh and go on to beat Tarkeshwari Sinha's record of four successive wins with five successive wins in 1989, 1991, 1996, 1998 and 1999. He secured the majority of votes over ten years despite fighting under different party banners: first Janata Dal, then Samata Party and then Janata Dal (United). These parties were of course essentially socialist groupings and regroupings, all drawing their inspiration from the ideas of Lohia and Jayaprakash Narayan.

By the 1980s the Socialist Party of the 1950s, led by Lohia, had ceased to exist; what existed were its splinters that no longer had the militant activism of Lohiaite socialism and had instead become election-oriented, much like other parties. The decline had started with Lohia's death in October 1967, barely a few months after the socialists came to power for the first time in Bihar through what the prominent left historian Bipin Chandra described as a 'promiscuous alliance' of extreme rightists and leftists, with the common objective of ending the eternity of Congress rule.

The socialists were trained in Lohia's school of revolutionary transformation through civil activism in contrast to Nehru's model of planned transformation through state machinery. So they found themselves short of ideas on how to run a state government, which, under the federal system, had to follow the Central government that still remained in the hands of the Congress. Their life soon turned more miserable with infighting between the upper-caste and lower-caste factions and consuming lust for power among those not made ministers within their party—a situation that became hellish with the right-wing and communist partners in government pursuing their own agendas.

The Congress watched the inner squabbles of the United Front government with canny amusement and soon got the opportunity to pull it down when one of the prominent socialist ministers hankering for chief ministership, Bindeshwari Prasad Mandal, defected from the socialist camp with a group of legislators. The Congress announced support for Mandal who became chief minister, though he could not stay in office, thanks to the splintering he triggered, for more than a month.

# political beginnings

We were in the first year of college when the first non-Congress government fell and we witnessed the enthronement and dethronement of B.P. Mandal barely within a month and then of Bhola Paswan Shastri within three months. Nitish, who had joined the Samajwadi Yuvajan Sabha (Socialist Youth Council), a front of Lohia's Samyukta Socialist Party (SSP), during his pre-university year at the Patna Science College, felt embarrassed and found it hard to explain to us.

None of his close friends was a Lohiaite; and we missed no opportunity to make fun of him, citing the 'daily instances' of 'socialist lustfulness'. Nitish was no great fan of the state's socialist leaders himself. He had not yet had any close association with them; and he was not one of those student members who frequented the offices and houses of party leaders and, in their anxious search for a godfather, aligned themselves with one or another. Even as an SYS member, he did not engage himself in the student politics of Patna University as actively as some key leaders of the organization did. He kept himself confined to his college.

Unlike his close friends, Nitish had a father who was an amateur politician, so he was more of a political animal than we were. But he had absolutely no plans till the third year of college to make politics his career. He had a better school board record than us, a performance that had earned him a National Merit Scholarship of Rs 150 a month—a royal sum that made him king the day he received it, with us herding off on his hospitality to movies, restaurants, coffee houses.

Nitish grew fond of watching Raj Kapoor movies during high-school years. He liked the typical village-idiot-in-a-metropolis that Raj Kapoor played as lead actor in his films: the rustic simpleton totally at odds with the unethical, loveless urban environment. Munna Sircar, his school friend, recalls that Nitish would watch a Raj Kapoor movie with rapt attention and get annoyed when urchins made catcalls or whistled or passed comments. Nitish was sort of inspired by the ultimate triumph of the innocent bumpkin against the forces of evil, no matter how powerful.

That said, Nitish also watched romantic films. Our college had no girl student then, and that was one of the most frequent lamentations at canteen caucuses. We, Nitish included, even talked of presenting a memorandum to the principal, pleading for admission of girls on the high grounds of gender justice. 'That, sir,' we thought of telling the principal, 'would also make the boys prim, disciplined and studious.' That would not force them to bunk classes and wander about the neighbouring Patna Science College where every class in every department had a fair number of girls. Or stand like loafers at the college turning to catch glimpses of girls in rickshaws going to or returning from various colleges on the university road.

But who would bell the cat? Eyes would go round and settle on Nitish. 'He is our leader. He can even move a rock.' There would be an explosion of laughter and the subject would change to a film, to tyrannical teachers, political corruption, a friend's eccentricities, funny anecdotes, to the growing power of hooligans all around. And amidst all that, someone would walk in for a glass of tea and hurl a shocker at us: 'Did you know there was a girl in a room in our hostel yesterday afternoon?'

Several of us knitted our eyebrows. It was the peak of Bihari summer, with heat waves shutting up people indoors in the afternoons, even in hostels. The roads were deserted. How could a mysterious woman brave incinerating winds and deserted roads to walk into the hostel? 'He must be talking about the warden's daughter,' Kaushal said dismissively. Everyone laughed. 'I'm not talking of the warden's daughter,' the fellow said. 'Can anyone dare to even glance towards her, even by mistake? Can you? The warden will throw you out in the street. You may have to come to attend classes from the railway platform. When even a glance is prohibited, invitation to a room will bring hanging. Brothers, I am talking of Swayambhu Thakur, our classmate, our sex guru. A young, charming saleswoman came to sell personality development books at the hostel gate, and our guru said it was too hot to talk of a deal outside. "Why not come into my room?" he said to her. And she thought it was not a bad idea.'

Desperate to hear the story straight from the horse's mouth, we spent the whole of that evening hunting for Swayambhu at all possible joints. At last when we got him he would just go on giggling. The entire class knew he had a way with women. But he was also a braggart. We slapped and kicked him. He had made up this story.

Nitish's pre-university year batch at Patna Science College had girls, but the environment on the campus was still conservative. Girls entered class with the teacher, as his tail. They occupied the front benches, the boys the rear ones. Love affairs did blossom but were extremely rare. Ladykillers on occasion went missing from classes, and the others pined. Nitish never chased any girl, primarily because of his reserved nature, but also because he was constrained by his small town background to strike a chord with girls brought up in the capital city.

His friends from Patna Science College said he hardly talked to or of girls, and this inhibition remained with him in his years at the Bihar College of Engineering. He would laugh at our ribald jokes but wouldn't ever tell any. Unlike most of us he never used profane, sexist words to show affection or anger.

But he enjoyed life as much we did: we saw films together, roamed around Patna, ate at small but popular restaurants, took a boat out in the Ganga on full-moon nights. The monthly allowance from parents was over for everybody by the second or third week, and the desperate search began for lenders among friends. Nitish was the richest among us, with Rs 150 from his father and Rs 150 from the scholarship every month. The scholarship money was what sustained his royal life and ours. His fine clothes, aristocratic rides in a rickshaw, movie-going, going out for snacks like samosas and dosas, a library of books and magazine subscriptions were luxuries others could barely afford.

Notwithstanding these indulgences, Nitish was not extravagant. He handled money with great care, unlike most of us who would exhaust it without much thought. He never bought things on impulse. Nitish was the only one among us who was seldom driven to borrow.

We bunked classes, gossiped for hours. The college canteen was where we were most often found during the day. In the evenings after snacks we gathered in a hostel room where we would use a drawing board as percussion and sing Hindi film songs. Most of us sang *besura*, with an atrocious sense of tune or tone, but the very discordant and grating chorus provided us the enjoyment, if not the melody.

It would only be a month or so before the announcement of annual examinations that we would part and confine ourselves to our rooms to begin studying. It would be then, while struggling with the definitions of terms, explanations of concepts and the sea of scorpions of advanced mathematical problems, that we would repent why we had not attended the lectures, performed the laboratory tests as all those who were surely going to do better had done, with full attention. Facing a common fate, we shared our knowledge, whatever we had, with each other, trying to mitigate one fellow's darkness with the dim light of another. It was dangerous to go to teachers for help, for they might ask where you had been all through the year, and it was beneath our dignity to approach serious-minded classmates because we, 'men with broader horizons', looked upon them as livelihood-seeking 'bookworms'.

None of us—Nitish, me, Kaushal or Narendra—was interested in studying engineering because it had been forced upon us by our parents. Left to ourselves we would have pursued other courses: Kaushal, Narendra and I would have preferred humanities and Nitish, physics or chemistry. But we were doing it for the sake of our parents. So we paid attention to our studies only to get above average marks. But inside our hearts the anger against parental authority persisted. 'Why are we doing this? The government is corrupt. The engineers are corrupt. What do our parents want? Go and join the robbers?'

We were against all authority; we wanted to pull down the established order. The parents, the principal, the politicians, the civil servants, the traders and industrialists, the priests in the temples, mosques and churches, the owners of rickshaws who took the lion's share of the rickshaw-puller's blood-and-sweat daily earnings—all of them and more constituted the 'system' we every day swore to overthrow. Although we differed in analysing the causes of the degeneration and its remedies—

Nitish using Lohia's indigenous ideas and Kaushal and I, stray thoughts from Marx and Mao—we never disagreed on our core mission, which was revolution for a new order.

It would be an order in which all will be free, all will be equal, birth will not determine identity, there will be no rich or poor, there will be food and happiness for everyone, there will be no exploitation or oppression of man by man, and English would be banished and mother tongues will rule. In such a system, production and productivity in factories and fields will touch the skies and everyone will get adequate food and education, and India will join the galaxy of leading nations of the world. It all does sound like Utopia now, but these appeared achievable goals to Nitish and us at that fiery stage of our lives.

We devoured anything we could get to read about the student revolt in France during March–May 1968, and I remember Nitish saying one day: 'India needs a revolution of this kind.' We shared his sentiment. General de Gaulle looked almost on the verge of being overthrown. 'The general will against the will of the general' insurrectionary posters said. Rebellion on the Nanterre and Sorbonne campuses turned into a popular revolt. Acting in unison, workers, hugely aggrieved about low pay, went on strike and 'liberated' 122 factories from the 'bloodsucking bourgeoisie'. The Arc de Triomphe was draped with red and black flags. Rebels pulled out cobble stones from the streets and built high barricades piling them over with cars, dustbins, metal posts, logs of wood, whatever they could get. Streets turned into battlefields for days.

The revolt died down by June, but its two features left a lasting impression upon us. One, that a German student, Daniel Cohn-Bendit, was accepted by the students and people of France as their leader. It showed the power of transcending the dragon of 'particularism'. If the French could transcend national chauvinism for the larger goal, why couldn't Indians transcend caste? we thought. 'I think Lohia's dream of a casteless society is not a pipe dream,' said Nitish. And we—who dreamt the same dream but were not convinced it could be brought about by promoting the 'casteism' of backward castes as Lohia advocated—agreed.

The other striking feature was the ideological orthodoxy of the French Communist Party, Parti Communiste Français (PCF). The PCF stayed away from the revolt, denouncing it as 'plain adventurism' mostly of 'sons of the grand bourgeois' who would 'quickly snuff out their revolutionary flames to become directors in Papa's business'. That convinced Nitish that he was right in preferring socialist ideology over Marxism. And it led me and Kaushal to develop greater aversion to the communist establishment in India and more affinity towards radical communism.

However, all our revolutionary ideologies were confined to the realm of thoughts. They expressed themselves largely in our approaches to the environments in the family and in college. We hated engineering because it was thrust upon us and was preparing us for recruitment to a degenerated system. We wanted to be as far away from it as possible.

So, it suited us when some senior students stirred up an agitation for the abolition of terminal examinations that we all had to take to qualify for the annual examinations every year. That would rid us of the burden of studying extra before the annual exams. There was no officially recognized student union at the college then, but there were three or four seniors, all of them upper caste, Rajput or Bhumihar, who played a chief part in everything connected with student affairs and had come to command a following among students for reasons good or bad.

They led us in a mob to the administrative office of the Patna University, blockaded the main entrance and besieged the vice chancellor's office in a gherao—a form of civil disobedience catching on then in which the top official was surrounded and not allowed to move out of the room until he conceded the mob's demands, which the vice chancellor that day eventually did. Nitish and all of us participated in this siege, though not very prominently, only as a part of the mob.

We were in the first year, and it would take at least one more year before Nitish started to emerge as the chief representative of our batch. He was initially quiet, low profile and confined to himself. He was what we in Bihar call a *chuppa* (silent) type—he would not speak in a crowd just to make his presence felt; he would not go out and make friends. But he responded warmly when approached and spoken to. He charmed others with decency in his speech and behaviour.

Friends who visited his room in the lodge, where he stayed for two years until he moved into the college hostel, were astounded by its neatness. The lodge was antiquated and ill-maintained; the lane leading to it was littered with squalor; and the other lodgers' rooms were untidy and cluttered, but Nitish's room looked like it was inhabited—books and magazines carefully arranged on racks, neatly folded clothes, barely any creases on the bed sheet, shoes in a corner.

Much like us he did not have more than a few shirts and trousers and shuffled them around to not seem too wretched to be wearing the same clothes every day, but he was more particular than all of us about the rumples and creases. He loved to wear ironed clothes. This turned into an obsession when he got on to the centre stage of student politics in the college in the third year and started wearing a white kurta-pyjama after college hours. The creases in his clothes had to be as sharp as the edge of a sword.

He was extremely articulate, and whenever occasions arose for representatives of every batch to speak at meetings on students affairs he would be sent up by all of us. A part of the credit for that went to Suresh Shekhar, the state topper of our 1966 school board examinations and his classmate at Patna Science College, who initiated him into the Samajwadi Yuvajan Sabha. Shekhar emerged as the tallest socialist intellectual on the Patna University campus, until Lalu Prasad—an arts student at B.N. College who was also an SYS member—stole the limelight by steering his Lohiaite iconoclasm with his natural instincts for foolery. Lalu fashioned his political persona after Raj Narain, the socialist leader from UP, who became famous for his rebellious antics and gimmicks (Narain would lie down on the floor of Parliament to draw attention to his point).

Lalu, stimulating himself with Magahi paan sprinkled with a liberal pinch of aromatic tobacco, would go uninvited to the Medical College hostel whose residents had a grievance over food served by the contractor in the mess. He would stand on the seat of a cycle rickshaw and start making a speech denouncing the contractor with nasty epithets. Pleasantly surprised, the inmates would come out to see whose was the voice descended from nowhere to champion their cause, and soon there would be a crowd in front of the rickshaw. Even passers-by would stop to hear him—'The youth, Indira Gandhi says, are the backbone of the country. But look at how the mess contractor in her government college serves yellow water as dal and rice with pebbles and stones to transform our future doctor-*bhai*s [brothers] into skeletons. At this rate we will soon have enough skeletons to export for anatomy study to every medical college in the country!'

I had gone to the Patna Medical College Hospital to see a relation under treatment and happened to see Lalu making that speech. He came to our college rarely; Nitish met him at SYS meetings or on the university campus occasionally. Suresh Shekhar often came to our college to meet Nitish and Ebadur Rehman, another SYS leader, two years our senior. Shekhar and Rehman were Nitish's early mentors. They did not think very highly of Lalu because of his profound aversion to serious discussion or reading Lohia literature and the blustery projection of himself over the organization. But they would let him go on with his buffoonery because in a university still dominated by upper castes in the teaching faculties and student population, he had emerged as a magnet for the backward castes.

Nitish, from the second year onward, began to actively participate in classroom and college debates and also speak at student meetings convened on issues to be raised before the college management. His diction, which was unmistakably Lohiaite—an informal, colloquial, folkish version of Hindi—had begun to impress listeners. The diction had come to him through copious reading of Lohia's books and the Hindi weekly *Dinaman* that under its socialist editor Raghuveer Sahay zealously used Lohia's style in its reports and commentaries.

He began to be noticed by high-caste student leaders as a good motivator. They probably saw him as a useful tool in maintaining student solidarity. They did not see him posing any threat to their leadership because Nitish kept a low profile—a junior who was like other juniors except for his oratorical and motivational abilities. Also, in the traditional student hierarchy at the college the seniors enjoyed superiority, power and authority over the juniors—more so in a professional college where greater knowledge bestowed a higher position in the profession. As scholars, the juniors had to show respect and be tame and conformable to the seniors because as professionals in later life in government or private sector jobs they would have to work under them.

We were aware of the demerits of the high-caste leaders and saw them doing many things essentially motivated by personal interest—one of them engineered a class boycott for ten days a few months after his wedding because he had to go bring his wife formally to his home, a custom called *vidai*, or 'second marriage'. However, we discussed this only in private, in cafés, hostel rooms or at the canteen when no ears were listening. Until Nitish, much to the amazement of us all, turned the tables.

We knew something was happening but had no idea of the strategic game Nitish had decided to play in concert with some key seniors and juniors at the college student union elections in 1969. Outside our crony circle Nitish had become a part of two circles: one of socialist students and another of backward castes. He never consciously built the backward-caste circle, for he hated being identified as a Kurmi, but with his growing recognition in student affairs he was beginning to draw support from other Kurmis in particular and the backward castes in general in the student community. He would not spurn the support, either, for it was coming in handy for building his strength and stature.

The challenge to the undisputed position of the three or four Rajput and Bhumihar student leaders in 1969 was the first election Nitish would fight in his life, without being a candidate. A panel of candidates drawn from various batches was set up to oppose the panel of the high-caste leaders, and Nitish was one of the key strategists behind the scenes. The backward castes alone could not win the game for him, so he set up alliances with other castes. Secret meetings for building alliances took place in hostel rooms at night. The strategy, helped in no small way by the general disenchantment with the high-caste leaders, led to the defeat of the entrenched leaders. It was an unbelievable win, and we, his cronies, began to realize that Nitish had something of a remarkable political strategist in him. Without the alliances woven by him we would not have been able to wreck the *mahanthi*—the stifling oligarchy of the higher castes.

With Nitish assuming leadership, we started taking up student issues. Among the first agitations was a hunger strike against the principal D.N. Singh who had acquired notoriety for his ruthless treatment of students on flimsy grounds. We were able to force him to withdraw several of his decisions. Then we hijacked a government bus and kept it within the college campus until the authorities met our demand of providing a special bus for students who travelled from home to college from western parts of Patna (I being one of them) every day. Nitish would often joke, pointing at me, 'We did it for him. But he never threw us a party.'

The second half of the 1960s were years of acute unemployment for engineers due to economic stagnation and there was widespread concern among engineering students across the state over their future. That became the grounds for a joint agitation of students of all the engineering colleges of the state for government assurance to create jobs for them. Even though Nitish was not interested in a career in engineering, this provided him a good opportunity to graduate to a larger canvas of student activism. He participated in and addressed several rounds of meetings of students from various engineering colleges. He insisted that any agitation must be peaceful and there would be no arson or vandalism. When the authorities did not respond till the evening after our hijacking a government bus, someone suggested we set fire to it to force their attention. Nitish and all of us kept up a vigil around the bus, consuming cups of tea throughout the night in order to prevent anyone from damaging it.

The agitation for jobs finally drew the attention of the government, which was headed by Karpoori Thakur. Every day seventy to eighty students marched to the police barricade shouting slogans and courted arrest. Nitish and Kaushal were among those arrested. Within a few days the Patna Central Jail was full of engineering students, and the prison officials did not know how to find room for so many, especially because they were given the status of the higher rung of prisoners who could not be placed with ordinary undertrials and convicts.

Karpoori Thakur was forced by the agitation to take decisions that would mitigate unemployment among engineers. He announced a policy entitling unemployed engineers to first preference in bids for government contracts. He set up a joint committee of officers, unemployed engineers and engineering students under his labour secretary I.C. Kumar to make a list of technical vacancies in all departments. The irrigation department after a review recruited about 8,000 civil and mechanical engineers.

Although the mainstream of student politics in Patna University was broad and liberal, powerful clannish and factional undercurrents flowed beneath. You could be baffled by examples of naked partisanship and liberality going hand in hand. The coexistence of the liberal and the sectarian gave the average student a dual character, leaving nobody sure about his behaviour when his inclusive side was put to an acid test, such as during the elections. This was true of all castes and communities: upper castes, backward castes, Hindus and Muslims.

Sectarianism based on caste and religion in the university was not as dogmatic and rigid as in the larger society but it was still heavily influenced by the reality outside. And the politics of the 1960s, with the ascendance of the backward castes, only rocked the shaky edifice of flexibility and openness that progressive forces from all castes and communities were beginning to build.

However, caste as a question wasn't thrown up suddenly in Patna University. It dated back to the initial decades of the university, the 1920s and '30s, when other castes found that Kayasthas numerically dominated both the student and teaching communities.

When other castes woke up to higher education they found themselves in a minority at the university, because they entered slowly and in small numbers, having to tackle the resistance from the Kayasthas who resolutely guarded entry to their fort. That led to competition and formation of cliques among castes in the teaching faculties and student community, a segmentation that was identifiable and open because those were the decades when castes were advancing their interests through caste associations. By the time we reached the university, caste had long gone underground and had therefore become more slithery and dangerous. No student leader made an open appeal to his caste. For a few years before Nitish got recognition as a student election strategist in Bihar College of Engineering, Ranjan Yadav, Lalu Prasad, Sushil Kumar Modi, Ravi Shankar Prasad and Ram Jatan Sinha were established as leading figures in Patna University's student politics. It is a remarkable coincidence that all of them later became leading figures in state politics. The university proved a training ground for them, a political laboratory where they could carry out their tests, watch the results, modify their approach, add a material or two to their mix to overcome their weaknesses.

They would compete with each other by taking up student issues in other colleges and their own, convening meetings, making speeches and leading delegations to college and university heads of administration. They fought for acquiring seats of student representation wherever the university provided them: in the decision-making and deliberative bodies, the university senate and the syndicate and in various committees. They belonged to youth wings of the different political parties: Congress, Jan Sangh, Samyukta Socialist Party, Communist Party of India or Communist Party of India (Marxist).

Their supporters could be grouped in three categories: ideological supporters, who were few; caste supporters, who were numerous and provided the core; and ordinary supporters, who were the largest in number and swung in favour of or in opposition to them according to their perception from election to election.

During elections to the Patna University Students Union (PUSU), in which Lalu Prasad would be a candidate for the post of general secretary or president, Nitish would work hard to mobilize support for him in his college. There were but a handful of SYS members or sympathizers in our college and students were informally grouped in castes, yet Lalu would get the most votes, thanks to Nitish's vigorous campaign. In 1973, when Lalu won the PUSU president's post—an event that proved to be a turning point in his political career—Nitish was responsible for mobilizing 450 of the 500 votes from our college for him.

Nitish was able to convince even friends like us who did not subscribe to Lohia ideology and considered Lalu a buffoon undeserving of the support of those who seriously wanted social change. Students not only from the backward castes voted for Lalu, but also most from the upper castes because they had turned against the Congress—much like the majority of voters in the parliamentary politics of Bihar—and wanted the strongest candidate from the Opposition parties' youth wings to win.

The SSP had emerged as the most preferred party in the Assembly elections in 1967 for people opposed to the Congress but not in favour of the Hindu chauvinist Jan Sangh or the 'anarchist' communist parties, the CPI and CPI(M); the SSP continued to hold strong despite desertions by groups and individuals. The student preference for Lalu Prasad was to an extent a reflection of the popular preference for the SSP. With all that plebeian ancestry, appearance and accent that he proudly flaunted and all the folksy metaphors of dark wit he laced his speeches with to hit out at the imagined or real monsters afflicting the student community, Lalu would have been no more than an outstanding jester to entertain students had he not been associated with the SSP. This association helped him to be seen as a political personality because of the currents that were flowing through the social and political mainstreams.

Lalu's rustic profile fitted into a pattern. He was raised by a father who lived with his family in a one-room thatch-roof hovel and made his living by selling milk from the one or two buffaloes he owned and supplementing it by hiring himself out as a farm labourer. The numbers of such first-generation scholars from villages had increased in Patna University, with the growing awareness of education as a tool for upward mobility among the lower castes. All of them were not as poor as Lalu; many of them were from families that owned land that produced enough food for them and even a surplus. After the abolition of zamindari in the 1950s, peasant proprietors had emerged and they had come into their own by the late 1960s. Lower castes formed the majority of this group, who were investing to the extent they could in their children's education.

Towards the end of the nineteenth century, the backward castes—watching the rise of the upper castes who claimed English education first—were convinced that a school or college degree was the gateway to social respect, steady, good income and power through employment in government. Professions such as law or medicine also brought social respect and reliable income but no power. In the British days, even the lowest officials down to the constables and orderlies wielded power over the masses.

The race for jobs in government departments that began in the late nineteenth century became tougher after Independence, with the Shudra mindset spurred by the inclusive approach of free India's polity towards everyone, from franchise to education to economic growth. The approach proved to be self-destructive for the urban elite led by Nehru that had conceived and engineered it. The rural elite drew strength from their landholdings and caste coalitions, were less educated, were impatient and militant and prided themselves on representing the 'real India'. They rose like a typhoon by promoting their peasant-proprietorial and caste interests almost indistinguishably from each other.

The essentially high-caste Congress elite were stunned by the genie from the bottle they had released. For several decades before and after Independence they had successfully met challenges by following a strategy of 'co-opt and rule': they had lured in icons of adverse social and political currents to eliminate threats to their leadership. In our political conversations at the canteen, Nitish often characterized the co-option as the 'opium Congress has long used to keep the backward castes in slumber'. These were the times when backward-caste parties and icons had begun to challenge the Congress co-option policy and set themselves up as independent powerhouses. The ground for their emergence was ironically provided by the Congress. By the mid-1960s, the Nehruvian left-of-centre boon to peasants, backward classes and the poor had turned out to be a farce. The underclass had waited for equality and prosperity for twenty years after Independence in vain.

In Bihar and UP, Lohia's SSP rose like one such major powerhouse during this period. The socialist elite had a rural, homespun, middle-caste, militant, iconoclastic, artless and acerbic profile, and in the Patna University of Nitish's political growing-up years, Lalu best represented that profile. Nitish represented the same current, though with an urban sophistication and less of militancy or bitterness.

The SSP's rise in Bihar in the mid-1960s had been powered by a string of local and national factors. Misery pervaded rural life in the state with two successive near-famines in 1965 and 1966. Prices soared. The poor starved, and not only peasants but also urban lower middle classes had meagre meals for days without the staples, rice or wheat. 'We had to eat rotis made of *madua* and other coarse grains, which in normal days was considered fit for consumption only by paupers,' says Nitish who was preparing for his final school board examinations at Bakhtiyarpur then. The story was the same in my home and in Kaushal's.

Massive assistance flowed in money and kind to the state. Jayaprakash Narayan headed the Bihar Relief Committee. There was genuine effort at various levels to mitigate the misery, but the country did not seem to have enough resources. The food shortage was severe. The country used to wait for US wheat ships to feed its population. India earned fame across the world as a 'begging bowl'.

Nehru's state-driven economic development model had, after the initial burst in post-Independence years, led to falling rates of growth in agricultural and industrial production as well as of exports in the 1960s: India had neither food nor money to buy food or capital machinery to run factories; and the two wars, first with China in 1962, then with Pakistan in 1965, had drained a substantial part of its resources and demanded more in terms of defence expenditure. The country was in terrible distress, with high unemployment, acute shortage of food and low national self-esteem when Indira Gandhi's surrender to US pressure—abetted by the World Bank and the International Monetary Fund (IMF) controlled by it—with devaluation of the rupee by 35 per cent in 1966 turned the public distress into anger against her.

Nitish was in Patna Science College then, I in B.N. College where Lalu also studied. The Congress failures, combined with the rampant corruption in its state government led by K.B. Sahay, triggered spasmodic student protests. Officials of the student wings of SSP, Jan Sangh and CPI and CPI(M), with encouragement and support from party leaders, took the lead. In November 1966 a joint committee called United Students Front (USF) comprising student wings of communist parties, SYS, Progressive Students Union (Naxalite group), Bihar Rajya Chhatra Kalyan Samiti (Bihar State Students Welfare Group) and representatives of the PUSU held a convention which gave a call of general strike in all the educational institutions on 9 December. The USF charter of demands included a check on rising prices and corruption and better student facilities. The real purpose, we as freshers came to know, was to overthrow the Sahay government.

The USF leaders took upon themselves the task of visiting different towns to address students meetings to mobilize them for demonstrations, processions and rallies throughout the state. When the Sahay government issued prohibitory orders to stop the protests, the USF asked students not to allow Sahay or any of his ministers to address public meetings. Police repression followed and the USF decided to give a call for student strike and organized a massive march to Sahay's official residence, which ended in police firing and arson and violence by retreating student mobs.

Lalu and Nitish were with the agitation but as a part of the crowd. Lalu had just begun as an SYS member; Nitish was yet to join it. Hardly six months had passed after Nitish took admission in Patna Science College that the agitation broke out. He was still coming to terms with his personal environment, going through the pangs of transition from a rural town to the capital city. He had no friends in other colleges, and even in his college he knew his classmates, and even among classmates but a few because of his introvert nature.

But he recalls going to the Gandhi Maidan, Patna's favourite public meeting ground, to hear Lohia's speech one of those days. 'He was my icon. I could have missed anything but his speech that day,' says Nitish. 'This was perhaps the last big public speech Lohia gave in Patna before he died,' says Nitish. 'I was mesmerized by his oratory. His depth of knowledge showed. His words oozed with love for the marginalized classes. The way he analysed the failures of the Indira government was so convincing. He ripped "Nehruvianism" apart. He was aggressive without being offensive. Hearing him as a part of the outer ring of the huge crowd I couldn't help telling myself I was not wrong in choosing him as my ideological guru.'

In north India, particularly in Bihar and UP, Lohia attracted people of all classes disillusioned with the Congress. Of course the middle and lower castes formed the core of his growing support owing to his relentless campaign for special opportunity for them. But the general anger of the mid-1960s also gravitated towards him, making him the centre of anti-establishment forces.

Lohia had refashioned socialist politics. In his view, the socialist politics of pre-Independence and early post-Independence years was no more than 'leftist nationalism'. Then it was split into two streams: one stood for aligning with the 'nationalist' Congress to drive it towards radical changes, the other for making a clean break with the Congress and building an independent political vehicle to bring about socialist transformation. Broadly, the work-within-the-Congress stream was represented by the PSP, the Praja Socialist Party led by Asoka Mehta, and the independent stream by the SSP. They split. But at several junctures they reunited. They separated again. They split, merged and parted ways so many times in a decade or so, their mergers came to be seen by the public as a farce.

Lohia struggled throughout to build a 'real' left-of-centre alternative to the 'phoney' left-of-centre Congress. In Lohia's writings and speeches the focus of attack was on the bogus socialism of Nehruvian economic policies—such as the structure of the public sector that was 'no different from the corporate sector', salary disparity and goals.

In a few years Lohia emerged as the tallest figure in the Opposition. But despite his relentless efforts he failed to create a socialist alternative to the Congress. In order to weaken the Congress by defeating Nehru he fought the election against him in the Phulpur Lok Sabha constituency in UP in 1962. He lost by a huge margin.

That was a turning point in Lohia's politics. He no more considered it possible to build an alternative to the Congress without aligning with the parties with whom he had fundamental ideological differences. In the Farrukhabad Lok Sabha by-election in 1964 he gained support of the 'Brahmanist' Jan Sangh, now Bharatiya Janata Party, to defeat the Congress.

In a great irony, Lohia thus followed the very model of broad coalition that the Congress had hitherto used, with the aim of displacing it from power. Lohia's coalition gathered all parties of the left and right under its umbrella, even on occasions, the work-within-the-Congress PSP whose *sarkari samajwad*, establishmentarian socialism, he had always railed against. His disciples followed in his footsteps. Lalu, who boasts of his secular credentials like nobody else, twice won offices in the university students' union in alliance with the Jan Sangh's student front Akhil Bhartiya Vidyarthi Parishad (ABVP).

The Congress-style broad coalition of the Opposition fathered by Lohia was to appear in scores of forms in the later decades in the states and at the Centre. Even the Bihar Movement of 1974 led by Jayaprakash Narayan—that caused Congress ouster from power at the Centre and in Bihar in 1977—adopted the same broad coalition pattern. However, the Opposition model nearly always proved to be what it was: an imitation.

The Congress had created and consolidated a broad coalition of the leftist, centrist and rightist streams within its organizational fold through debates, struggles of ideas and an accommodative character in pre-Independence years. In contrast, the Opposition broad coalition emerged as fronts formed on the roadway to power, mostly before elections. The Opposition coalition was external, whereas the Congress coalition was internal. The Congress coalition remained intact despite the Nehru family's central control—largely because while never letting control slip out of their hands, all the heirs had followed the Congress model, rather than breaking away into an absolute monarchy.

Most parties in the Opposition were formed with specific ideologies—left, left of centre, Hindu supremacism, Muslim protectionism—that found the Congress model of broad coalition stifling and obstructive to the progress of their constituencies. Then there were parties that were, in reality, groups under a key leader who had left the Congress when they did not get the positions of power they wanted. Specific ideologies and specific groups formed as a negation to the Congress's coalitional model were by their very origin non-accommodative of each other's ideologies and interests. The spirit of non-accommodation was only accentuated when many of the Opposition parties and groups were controlled by one leader. So whenever the Opposition coalition achieved power, the leaders of the parties and groups invariably got into a bitter quarrel over key offices; and the dirty confrontation ended with the collapse of the coalition, usually within months, at best in over a year.

Although the SSP was the largest party in the Opposition coalition that replaced the Congress in Bihar in the 1967 elections, Lohia, despite his strong preference, could not have its legislature group leader Karpoori Thakur elected as the coalition leader and hence as chief minister, because another state SSP leader, Ramanand Tiwari, also staked his claim. The Karpoori–Ramanand rivalry divided the MLAs of the SSP along caste lines, the upper castes backing Ramanand and the middle and lower castes, Karpoori. All efforts of Lohia to persuade the Ramanand group to climb down failed as they said it had to be either Ramanand, or neither Karpoori nor Ramanand but someone from another party in the coalition.

In order to avert a split, Lohia consented to the name most partners agreed upon—Mahamaya Prasad Sinha—at least he used to be a socialist once, even though a work-with-the-Congress type. Some years ago Mahamaya, like many other key Praja Socialists, had joined the Congress but left it to set up a new party, Jan Kranti Dal (People's Revolution Party), for better bargaining prospects in politics.

The problems for the new coalition didn't end there. B.P. Mandal, a big Yadav landlord from Saharsa in northern Bihar, had been elected an SSP member of Lok Sabha, the polling for which was held simultaneously with the state Assembly, but he insisted on an office in the state coalition ministry. Lohia, who had publicly declared that no MPs would be allowed to join a state ministry, refused to budge. Mandal—who was to become famous for the chairmanship of the second Backward Classes Commission, the implementation of whose recommendations by a non-Congress coalition government at the Centre was to take the anti-upper caste politics to new heights in the 1990s—also refused to budge. During the Karpoori–Ramanand battle, Mandal had been eyeing the chief ministership: not succeeding there, he decided he would be a minister in the Mahamaya government first and then continue making efforts to get to the highest executive office.

Mandal had no socialist background; he was part of the Congress, co-opted as a key figure from the Yadav caste, when K.B. Sahay, the Congress chief minister from 1963 to 1967, brought in another Yadav leader, Ramlakhan Singh Yadav, and made him virtually number two in his cabinet, marginalizing Mandal. Soon, Mandal left the Congress to join the SSP, his hopes to gain an important position of power aroused by the lower-caste mobilization under Lohia's leadership. The very first opposition coalition ministry in the state offered an opportunity he wanted not to miss, even if it meant embarrassment to Lohia for bending his own rule. Lohia fumed and fretted at Mandal's unseemly greed, but fearing that if unsatiated it might cause a good deal of trouble in his party, even a split, he eventually acquiesced, swallowing the insult to his authority.

To Mandal, a ministerial office was only a stopover: his eye was set on the chief ministerial chair. The coalition had troubles from the very beginning: specific ideologies and groups disagreed more than agreed on policies, programmes and issues. People who had voted for the Opposition parties, particularly the SSP, were disappointed seeing the new government set as many different priorities as different partners in the coalition. The government had no direction, and the basic problems that people had identified the Congress regime with—stagnant agriculture, low growth of industry, unemployment, corruption of ministers and officers, mounting food prices—remained unmitigated.

The students across the state who had voluntarily worked for the Opposition candidates to see the Congress out of power felt let down. You could sense chagrin in conversations at homes, teashops, social gatherings and in our college canteen. Nitish was dismayed at the high-caste prejudicial antagonism that prevented Karpoori from becoming chief minister; among the SSP leaders he held Karpoori in highest esteem for his moral integrity, ascetic persona and ideological sophistication. 'Socialist politics is the reigning metaphor for chaos in unity,' we often pricked him. He smiled in approval, though he was not ready to lose all hope.

The Mahamaya ministry had not even passed a year in office when Mandal used popular disappointment to walk out of the SSP with thirty-odd party legislators who coveted ministerial offices. The Congress instigated the 'revolt' and announced support for a ministry with Mandal as chief minister. Only a month later, however, the Congress withdrew support to Mandal, ushering in a party ministry headed by Bhola Paswan Shastri, an MLA from an untouchable caste. The coalition saw it for what it was: a tactic of the Congress to grab power by luring away its MLAs after having failed to get a majority in the House by a popular mandate.

There was no law then to check defections of a lawmaker from one party to another, and the Opposition too, like the Congress, took advantage of that to bring down the Shastri ministry in a little over three months. Prime Minister Indira Gandhi responded by placing the state Assembly under suspension and imposing Central rule, which continued for a year until fresh elections were held in June 1969. The elections brought back Shastri as chief minister, but he could not last beyond a month. With no party or coalition in a position to carry a majority with it, the state had to remain under Central rule again for eight months, until the Congress managed to pull off enough numbers for the next eight months when the Opposition, aided by factional rifts in the Congress, brought it down.

This time Karpoori manoeuvred to get himself into the highest office, but the Congress outmanoeuvred the coalition in six months and came back to rule with Shastri—no more in the party—as a puppet chief minister for the next six months. At this time Indira Gandhi, riding the popular wave for 'break-up' of Pakistan and creation of Bangladesh, went for fresh elections in the state, which brought the Congress back to power. The Opposition coalition had collapsed, and the myriad, desperate and disparate alliances did not help.

The Congress learnt quickly how to decimate Opposition coalitions—within the first few months of the first coalition taking office in 1967. The ideological fissures in the coalition were all too obvious, and so were the fissures within fissures of factional, personal ambitions. All that the Congress had to do was to work on the separation of one major part, with a promise to make its key element chief minister.

Destabilization became the pattern the Congress was to later follow to demolish an Opposition coalition at the Centre whenever and wherever it assumed power: pull out a factional leader and help him run a new ministry until he had discredited himself; then withdraw support to him to force fresh elections. The Congress would then approach the electorate with a promise to provide a stable government. It demolished the Janata Party government in 1979 and United Front government in the mid-1990s.

But the failure several times of the Lohia model of a broad Opposition coalition based on anti-Congressism between 1967 and 1972 in Bihar, and of the similar JP model in 1979, was not due solely to Congress demolition tactics. The fragmentation of the Indian polity was also a reflection of the social fragmentation as all sections of society mobilized themselves for the advancement of their particular interests.

Everyone seemed to have a grievance, from the prince to the pauper. The Nehruvian 'socialistic' rhetoric of the Congress antagonized the rightist forces—the maharajas, the lesser landlords, the business class—and aroused high expectations among the peasants, the middle class and the poor. They all mobilized themselves to decide what India's freedom should mean to them as a class. Exploiting the groundswell of sectional and sectarian sentiments, and stirring it up to a surge with their particularist extremities to beat the competition, arose the myriad political parties that were to band together into coalitions, only to fall apart under the weight of their incongruity.

Leftist historians infatuated with Nehru's Fabian socialism refuse to see the Bihar Movement of 1974 as a milestone in the progress of India's democracy; Bipan Chandra portrayed it as no more than an 'unconstitutional and undemocratic' agitation through which the 'non-left' parties 'trounced' in the elections of 1971–72 wanted to 'acquire credibility' as an alternative to the Congress. This view shuts out many significant features of the movement.

The Bihar Movement must find its rightful position in the continuous struggle of the Opposition parties to forge a stable coalition of their own. Their efforts to build a bipolar polity had ended miserably between 1967 and 1972; but they had learnt from their failures and not given up. The movement of students in Bihar in early 1974—inspired by the recent student agitation of Gujarat that forced the resignation of the Congress government in the state and the dissolution of the Assembly—offered them an opportunity to coalesce again.

The Bihar Movement was not started or guided by political parties, but by students in the youth wings of the Opposition parties. It began with a two-day conference of student union leaders from colleges and universities of the state on 17–18 February 1974 in Patna. They deliberated on major issues agitating students in particular and people in general and decided to set up a Chhatra Sangharsh Samiti (Students Struggle Committee) to launch a statewide agitation to put pressure on the Congress governments in Bihar and at the Centre to resolve them.

Students had spasmodically organized anti-government agitations in Bihar in the past, in the mid-1950s and mid-1960s. In 1972 students revolted against the Congress government and were joined by teachers and other sections of society. Opposition parties, including the CPI, came out in the streets in their support. For two months in early autumn there were rallies, demonstrations and processions almost every day. The police assaulted them during their protest on campuses and outside the Assembly. The students built barricades around the Gandhi Maidan and Ashok Rajpath, the university road, and showered rocks at the policemen who tried to clear the blockade.

As the president of the college union by then, Nitish organized students from Bihar College of Engineering to join several of these protests. We were not among the students pelting stones but we stood behind them in solidarity. We were a part of the 5,000-strong mob that gheraoed the Patna University vice chancellor Sachin Dutt's office for three hours and forced him to resign. 'The student revolt of 1972,' observes Nitish, 'ripped off the populist façade of Goddess Durga that Indira Gandhi was portraying herself to be after the creation of Bangladesh.'

All student revolts in Bihar had an identical pattern: they started as an outrage against the campus administration and ended up as a revolt against the government. The 1972 rebellion was triggered by the appointment of bureaucrats as vice chancellors of universities. Often the initial charter of demands included better student facilities such as bus fare concessions, improvements in hostel amenities and food, hike in scholarship stipends and adequate student representation on the universities' decision-making bodies. Soon these issues went into the background and the issues of corruption, police brutality, rising prices and unemployment came to the fore.

The Chhatra Sangharsh Samiti too started with student issues but on a broader canvas: it wanted changes in government policy to provide employment-oriented education, security of employment for the educated unemployed and a monetary allowance during the period of their unemployment. It soon turned into an agitation against rising prices, corruption and democratic rights.

The prime movers of the agitation were officials of the student wings of Opposition parties, chiefly the SSP and Jan Sangh, but the larger number was made up of politically conscious, non-party students. Student leaders of the Opposition fronts from Patna University played a stellar role, among them Lalu Prasad and Sushil Modi. Nitish was also among them, having taken part in the deliberations at the 17–18 February 1974 conference where he was named as one of the twenty-four members of the steering committee of the Chhatra Sangharsh Samiti, but was still not in the front line of the leadership. Among socialist youth-wingers Lalu was the undisputed leader: he was the face; Nitish was close to him but in his shadow.

Lalu was president of the PUSU when he, along with others, convened the conference. Lalu had been elected for 1973–74; his term was ending and he wanted to do something to stay in the limelight.

'*Kuchh hudadang karna chahiye* (Let's stir up some trouble),' one of his close associates claims having heard him say often during that period.

Lalu was desperate as he had not got a break in his political career in the past few years. He had managed to get himself elected as general secretary of the PUSU during 1970–71, but his attempt to get to the presidency, the highest office of the union, was foiled the next year by a Congress candidate. Lalu would have no more chances as he would graduate with a Bachelor of Arts at the end of the year. He nearly gave up thinking of politics and, with the responsibility of a family from an early marriage pressuring him, began to work as a casual clerk in Patna Veterinary College.

His political itch, however, returned to him in 1973 when he, with the help of his friend Ranjan Yadav—who had been a cabinet member of the PUSU—got himself enrolled as a law student at Patna Law College to be able to fight the upcoming students' union election. We were in the final year of engineering then and often saw Lalu riding the pillion of Ranjan Yadav's scooter to college campuses to build support for his candidature for the president's post.

Nitish canvassed for Lalu among the students of our college. Yet, Lalu's chances did not seem bright until an alliance was struck between the SYS and the ABVP, according to which he would fight for the president's post and Sushil Modi for general secretary's. Both he and Modi won.

The agitation started on 18 March 1974 with a rally in front of the state Assembly in Patna on the inaugural day of its budget session. Most of the prominent student leaders had gone into hiding for a few days before the rally to avoid the preventive arrests Chief Minister Abdul Ghafoor had ordered. Lalu and Nitish found shelter in the houses of relations, friends and acquaintances, constantly shifting from one place to another. One of Nitish's safest hideouts was his eldest sister Usha's house at Raja Bazar in western Patna, where he would find shelter also during the Emergency.

A huge number of students from across the state turned out for the rally that threatened to break through the heavy police barricades at the main gates to the British-built secretariat complex with an aim to disrupt the opening day of the Assembly. Lalu and other student leaders gave fiery anti-government speeches, building up excitement among participants, which soon led to a ding-dong battle between rock-pelting protestors and club-charging police. The Ghafoor government decided to end the battle by firing gunshots into the mass of students, causing several casualties and forcing them to take to their heels. The indignation triggered student violence in other towns in the state over the next few days, and the Ghafoor government dealt with them all in the same manner, inflicting more casualties, generating broad public sympathy for the student agitators.

Public disappointment with the Congress had been growing; the stability for which they had been voted back into power at the Centre and in the state had come to mean stagnation in growth, unchecked inflation, corruption and state tyranny. Indira had lost much of her radical halo with her failure to carry out her promise of faster development with the state takeover of banks and of eradicating poverty. Topping this was her authoritarianism and open promotion of her son Sanjay—whose conclusive proof came when she imposed an internal Emergency in June 1975 that continued till March 1977, during which period Sanjay emerged as the most powerful man after her.

The Opposition parties—except the CPI that still thought the Congress was the most radical bourgeois party to deserve the support of all 'progressive' (read 'secular') forces—sensed in the Bihar student agitation the potential to channelize the popular disenchantment into an electoral wave, but they were not sure whether students could do it alone. Battered in the last election, they were also unsure whether they could pull it off by taking a direct lead of the agitation, because people might see their motivation too plainly. They needed a camouflage.

And seventy-one-year-old Jayaprakash Narayan, popularly known as JP—who had been living in virtual retirement in his home in western Patna after decades of socialist politics and then of saintly politics—proved to be an excellent one. He still remained the country's tallest political figure after Nehru in public memory, with a strong image as a rebel saint. He was not in very good health but had kept in touch with the country's major issues, occasionally commenting on them through measured, persuasive statements to the media.

Various people claimed to have talked JP into leading the agitation, most prominently, Nanaji Deshmukh, a prominent leader of the Rashtriya Swayamsevak Sangh (RSS), the Hindu nationalist organization that patronized the Jan Sangh, and Ramnath Goenka, the media baron who loved courting trouble with the political establishment by championing 'national causes' such as the fight against Indira's authoritarianism through publications in his *Indian Express* chain of newspapers. But JP made it clear as soon as he took over the leadership that the student and people's committees that would conduct the agitation would have no association with political parties. JP was aware that several members of the steering committee of the Chhatra Sangharsh Samiti that had chosen him leader had distinct affiliation with the Opposition parties, but he also saw that the majority of students and people who had spontaneously joined the agitation were motivated by the cause and had no political tie-ups.

JP's iconic image as a non-partisan, selfless reformer pulled tens of thousands of ordinary men, women and youth out of homes into his processions and rallies, turning a student agitation into a people's movement.

# the grind

The Bihar Movement had unmistakable features to suggest that JP fashioned it on the model of the Gandhi-led non-cooperation movement of 1921 against the British. Gandhi wanted the British to grant India freedom within a year, and called upon people to build up pressure for it by refusing to cooperate with the colonial government in any of its institutions and operations. He asked students to pull out of government schools and colleges and people not to go to courts but settle their disputes outside. He motivated Congress workers to picket at liquor shops to bring down sales so government got less income from excise duties. JP got the students and people in Bihar to implement similar ideas. He even added a 'constructive programme' to eradicate caste, making the movement a complete replica of the three-pronged non-cooperation movement: agitation, boycott and social reconstruction.

JP's focus remained on the radical transformation of society based on the principles of 'Total Revolution' enunciated by him, even though he articulated the dominant view of the Chhatra Sangharsh Samiti members that the Congress government was 'the problem' and must go. Public anger had built up against the Ghafoor ministry and the 'root of the problem', Indira. This was like a dream come true for the Opposition parties, but JP saw the ouster of the Congress governments in the state and at the Centre as only a means to an end. He saw the Bihar movement as a revolutionary movement and the change of the party in power as only a small part of it.

Over the years JP, who starting out as a Marxist saw Indian society in terms of unequal classes, had begun to realize the importance of caste in the political dynamics. He had come somewhat closer to Lohia's thought that the social system that had depressed the lower castes for thousands of years must be broken and special opportunities given to them to rise to equal levels in every field.

He took several initiatives towards 'social revolution' in the course of the Bihar Movement. The upper castes had a prominent presence among the Chhatra Sangharsh Samiti and Jan Sangharsh Samiti (People's Struggle Committee) leaders. He started consciously patronizing and projecting backward-caste members of the Chhatra Sangharsh Samiti, prominently Lalu; JP would later on also encourage Nitish.

JP started a *janeu todo andolan*, a campaign to motivate the upper castes to discard the sacred thread they wore round their shoulder as a sign of their high status and ritual purity, and encouraged lower castes to wear one by way of assertion of their equal status. He persisted with the campaign despite resentment and resistance by the Hindu nationalists among members of the student and people's committees as well as those in the Jan Sangh.

JP's central idea was to make India's democracy truly a people's democracy. Representatives elected by the people and governments formed by a majority of representatives could not claim to have legitimacy if the electorate found them working against public interest, he said: he wanted a law to give the voters a right to recall their representative any time during the term if they were dissatisfied with his/her conduct and, in the absence of such a law at that time, demanded dissolution of the state Assembly on the strength of the popular will manifested in the mass movement he represented.

Unlike the Opposition parties that backed the dissolution demand with the expectation of riding the popular wave to power, one coalition replacing another in yet another electoral game, JP aimed at making Indian democracy as embedded as the US democracy with strong public opinion, a free press, a free judiciary and an independent intelligentsia. Such democratization was possible only by building strong foundations of *jana shakti*, people's power. One of the most radical ideas he tried to implement was to set up committees of non-partisan members in every Assembly constituency. These constituency committees would select candidates in elections or back the best candidate available in the field who, when elected, would be responsible to the electorate through these committees. If the committees judged the performance of their representative as unsatisfactory they would have the right to recall him and elect another representative in his place.

One of his radical ideas, much on the lines of the local 'arbitration courts' and 'panchayats' of the non-cooperation movement, was to set up *janata sarkar*, a people's government, which would have committees at local levels to settle disputes without referring to any institution of the state. The janata sarkars in many places also conducted raids on food hoarders, seized their stocks and distributed them at fair prices to people.

Like most of the other student leaders, Nitish never engaged himself passionately and deeply with JP's revolutionary plan for creating a 'party-less democracy' based on people's power; he was a socialist partisan after all, and set on winning a party nomination for election sooner or later. But he says, 'I could not help being influenced by JP's passion for making democracy truly a rule by the people.' Many of the initiatives he was to take as chief minister were inspired by the ideas of JP as much as of his original icon Lohia.

For Nitish, there was still a long way to go. He had become a member of the Chhatra Sangharsh Samiti by virtue of being the president of BAMSU (Bihar Abhiyantran Mahavidyalay Students Union), his college students' union, whereas Lalu owed it to his status as the president of the PUSU. Patna was the capital, and the PUSU central to the Chhatra Sangharsh Samiti, so these two factors made Lalu the most prominent student leader across the state.

Nitish was small compared to him. Nitish was also overshadowed by other prominent student leaders and JP's disciples from 'Sarvodaya', literally meaning Everybody's Welfare, a movement to establish a borderless global community based on unselfish individuality. Nitish participated in the meetings the Chhatra Sangharsh Samiti members held with JP to discuss issues and decide on the course of the agitation. He was there in the lead ranks in all the street processions, city and state shutdowns, sit-ins and other programmes of the agitation, but he was still in the second or third line of the samiti leadership. 'I was initially no more than a *shamil baja*, a drone player in the band,' recalls Nitish.

And that proved to be trying at times. Not achieving prominence in the movement only increased the weight of the responsibility he very clearly felt towards Manju Kumari, whom he had married on 22 February 1973, as well as towards his father and mother who hoped to see their son start off as an engineer. After we graduated in October the same year, Nitish travelled along with us to Bokaro to register himself with the steel city employment exchange. No calls ever came from there to any of us and none of us cared because our minds were set on careers of our choice.

But within a couple of months, Nitish received a letter from Bihar State Electricity Board to join as a trainee engineer in its Ranchi division; in those days you had to do one year as a trainee to be recruited as assistant engineer (then designated as engineer assistant). Nitish travelled to Ranchi and joined as a trainee but never worked for a day after that. He did not want to get stuck in a job; the passion for politics drew him away. He felt his father should have no complaint as he had done his moral duty of getting a degree. Father did not press him to retain the job, which he soon lost and had to depend on pocket money from his father, close relations and friends.

Manju, the eldest daughter of Krishna Nandan Sinha, a well-off farmer and the headmaster of the secondary school in his native village Sheodah in Harnaut, was traditional, soft-hearted, understanding and ready to go along with Nitish in whatever he wanted to do. She was distantly related to Nitish's elder brother's wife Geeta who liked her for her keen interest in studies and fine culinary skills. Nitish was in the final year then and Krishna Nandan was happy marrying his daughter off to an engineer.

Nitish's family knew of his resolve to take up politics as his career, but this ambition was not broadcast to relations. During negotiations for marriage Nitish's father did not forewarn Krishna Nandan about his son opting out of a career in engineering, largely because he was still hoping that Nitish's angularity would smooth out after he passed out and was forced to earn a living. Ramlakhan wanted to give his son two persons to feed instead of one, thus leaving him no choice.

A photo of Manju was shown to Nitish by the women of the family when he went home on a weekend. He didn't look at it hard, and blushed and giggled with a mixed sensation of excitement and embarrassment. One of Nitish's most sorrowful and annoying moments of life was when he was lodged in the Gaya jail during the Bihar Movement and Manju came to see him. He was lodged in the jail under the MISA (Maintenance of Internal Security Act)—Indira's hated law of preventive detention without trial—from September to November 1974.

'The superintendent of the Gaya Central Jail was a brute,' Nitish recalls. 'He allowed visits of prisoners' relatives only once a week. And he would not allow anyone to come inside the gate. The visitor had to stand outside an iron-meshed window, and the prisoner inside. Manju came to visit me once a week but he refused permission even to the wife to come inside the gate. The sadist had had the mesh made so fine in that heartless window I could not even touch Manju's finger to live with that memory until we met again a week later. Imagine; we were young and had married just one and a half years before.'

But back then, even after his father accepted the marriage proposal in the winter of 1972, Nitish wouldn't have the courage to go and see Manju at the Magadh Mahila College of Patna University where she was pursuing her graduation in sociology. He hesitated to go to the G.D. Women's Hostel where Manju stayed, despite the fact that Nitish's younger sister Indu was also an inmate there. Kaushal, Narendra and I taunted him about his jitters every day: 'You threaten to dare all the demons of the world and tremble at the thought of going to see your future wife! You are a phoney, man.' But he wouldn't do it despite all our exhortations. Then one day, without telling him, we took a rickshaw and loitered around G.D. Women's Hostel for hours to get a glimpse of her. We had seen her photo. When we at last spotted her she knew by our smirks what we were there for. She flushed scarlet with embarrassment and was hurrying away when Kaushal flung a remark at her: 'Do not run, you may trip!' Responding with a smile she sprinted out of our view.

Returning to college we sought Nitish out and told him we had seen his wife before he had and she was sweet and beautiful. 'Her smile makes her seem even more beautiful,' Kaushal said. Nitish laughed heartily at Kaushal's remark. He said, still laughing, 'What more do I need! Now I have a certificate of excellence from the Three Musketeers.'

The following week, however, the marriage proposal ran into rough weather. It was going to be a traditional Hindu wedding and Nitish's father had agreed to take a cash dowry of Rs 22,000 from Manju's father. Nitish had taken a silent vow not to accept dowry for his wedding. And he was totally against the elaborate rituals of a Vedic marriage. That was incompatible with his Lohiaite commitment to a crusade against Brahmanism. I remember him agonizing for days over how his father, with his adherence to the principles of Arya Samaj which advocated simple marriage, could agree to a wedding conducted by Brahman priests around a sacrificial fire.

He declared he would do nothing except exchange garlands with Manju. No rituals, no festivities. The marriage would take place in a public hall in Patna. His father and Manju's father eventually succumbed. The Lala Lajpat Rai Memorial Hall close to the Gandhi Maidan was packed for the wedding. A large number of socialist leaders and workers had turned up. There were speeches attacking the cancer of dowry and opium of ritualism and applauding the 'revolutionary marriage'. Every young man of Bihar must follow the example of Nitish, the speakers said. In order to spread the message far and wide, the famous socialist journalist Jugnu Shardeya published an interview on the marriage with Nitish in the popular Hindi weekly *Dharmayug*.

Shortly after we passed out of college, we went our own ways. Narendra decided to become a public works contractor, Kaushal joined the Bihar State Housing Board at Ranchi, I became an apprentice in a news agency and Nitish entered the political world. He lived with Manju in Bakhtiyarpur but regularly travelled to Patna to meet socialist leaders and student leaders such as Lalu—to be in touch, to build relations.

Manju was fully supportive about his choice of political career and never complained about him not taking up a job, but her father and brothers often advised him, though very discreetly, to do something for a livelihood. 'You can also do politics side by side,' they said. Nitish would always smile away their suggestions.

Manju, on the contrary, egged him on. There was a period during his youth idealism when he decided he would not fight elections. Manju told him one day, 'What is the point in being in politics if you are not in electoral politics?' That comment worked like a 'spark' in his life. He felt Manju was right. It altered the course of his career.

The determination to pursue his passion was, however, sometimes shaken by self-doubt. He was not the kind who believed in aggressive self-promotion. He saw Lalu doing that in the course of the Bihar Movement, at meetings, in protest programmes, in the media. Lalu wore his assertive backward caste image on his sleeve, always did something dramatic, repeated JP's catchphrases and invented a few of his own, delivering them in Bhojpuri folk lingo with sparkles of dark humour. All this helped him stand out in any gathering of student leaders. Lalu avoided intellectual debates, but he had the knack for quickly identifying catchphrases and using them to effect.

Nitish marvelled at Lalu's self-promotional ability, respected him as a senior in the socialist stream, but was too constrained by his own character to follow in his footsteps. Nitish's first role model was his father, a principled fighter, and his youth icons were Lohia and now Jayaprakash. He wanted to be a serious, thinking politician. His readings of Lohia and post-Lohia socialist commentaries had built his intellectual foundations and helped him understand JP better. He felt a natural kinship with JP because of his socialist background, which was only beginning to deepen with his new leader's ideological tilt borne out of his rethinking of Lohia's theory of social revolution. Being in the movement did not demand jettisoning of Lohia's ideas, and Nitish had retained them all.

With JP beginning to see the importance of breaking the caste hierarchy, Nitish's belief in Lohia's core formula of *sainkra saath*, 60 per cent representation for backward castes, tribals, women and religious minorities in all fields for establishing their equality with the upper castes, was strengthened. Nitish had inherited from his father an aversion to think in terms of caste, but at the same time he saw the backwardness of the non-upper castes as a reality. He became a follower of Lohia because he alone among epochal leaders advocated the primacy of social revolution, of levelling up castes. Also because Lohia held the view that by bringing up the depressed castes in every field, caste will lose its association with social status and hence disappear from any reckoning.

Yet, Nitish's elevation on the scale of prominence depended as much on his individual endeavours as on JP's commendation. His feeling of ideological kinship with JP was still one-sided; it took time before JP noticed him. Nitish's father, who had reconciled to Nitish's decision, was also concerned about it, if not for the sake of his own dream, then for his son and daughter-in-law's future.

Without letting anyone know, Ramlakhan one day travelled from home to Patna and waited on JP, who knew him distantly from his association with the freedom struggle and later with electoral politics during the first decade of Independence. Ramlakhan told JP that he had stayed with the Congress for much longer than him but had been alienated from it because the party's governments had betrayed the ideals of the freedom struggle, and he supported with full heart the mass movement led by JP. Then he mentioned that although he was not an active participant, his son was. 'He is an idealist too. I have come to seek your blessings for him,' Ramlakhan told JP.

No matter how strongly Nitish felt that his work in the movement alone and not anybody's commendation should earn him JP's favour, he thought that his father had after all behaved like any other father—concerned about setting his son up—and had only a respectful gratitude for his good word to JP. Nitish's choice had shattered his father's dream of seeing his son as an engineer, but in his private moments Nitish felt he was only working to realize his father's own dream of seeing himself as a lawmaker. If he became a politician with a difference and yet became successful he would think he had fulfilled his filial duty and done his father proud.

It was uncertain though how much his father's good word influenced JP. JP was overburdened with so many things in the movement—thinking ideas, devising strategies, fighting deviations, addressing meetings, conversations with numerous callers, framing responses to derisive statements from Indira Gandhi down to Chief Minister Abdul Ghafoor, and fulfilling all these demands with the plethora of demands of his ageing body. He could not allow himself to pay too much attention to a personal request from a father for individual guidance to his son. JP was too high for that and too just-minded. He could have distantly noticed the boy, and his look of remote favour could be seen as a result of the boy's backward caste, but JP would not be partisan to anyone except on merit. Let the boy prove his worth.

JP had given a call to the students to keep away from classrooms for a year and work for the movement: that would signify a rejection of the existing meaningless education system and also give students an opportunity to actively participate in the building of a new India. The boycott had been an initial success, but soon a strong opinion built up among the students that this might jeopardize job prospects for them and they started going back to classrooms in increasing numbers. Patna set the tone, and JP was worried that if students of Patna University returned to classes, students in the rest of Bihar would too. He gave a fresh call, asking students to make a year's sacrifice for the nation, but he was not heeded. There were stray efforts by movement activists to bring students out of classrooms at Patna University that weren't working. Most of the leading members of the Chhatra Sangharsh Samiti were in jail.

It was in these circumstances that Nitish went from college to college, addressing a knot of students here and a small gathering there to motivate them in favour of the boycott. Nitish remembers the day vividly. It was his first experience of having to confront so many students, from unyielding to sceptical to hostile, in so many colleges, not to speak of disapproving administrators and teachers, all on his own. It was a test of his oratory, of his grit to field all kinds of questions, of his leadership skills.

At the end of the few hours of his persuasion, over a hundred students followed him to the office of the vice chancellor, where he delivered a speech denouncing the university administration for threatening to penalize students for boycotting classes and examinations. He dared the vice chancellor Devendra Nath Sharma to come out and talk to the students: finding the crowd determined not to leave unless he did so, Sharma came out and told the students to return to their classes, which triggered a heated argument between him and Nitish, who pooh-poohed the vice chancellor's warning that continuing boycott would harm their career and future on the grounds that the students' future was already in darkness because of the faulty education system and wrong economic policies of the Congress government.

The successful motivation of students for a boycott that day won

Nitish appreciation from JP, which proved to be a turning point in his political career. Looking back, Nitish thinks that though he had been a part of the Chhatra Sangharsh Samiti it was that day that JP acknowledged his presence. From that day on, Nitish would no more be just one of the many members of the samiti but an outstanding one in JP's eyes. He was thrilled to see JP addressing him after that by name during meetings of the samiti and paying attention to his suggestions. From a shamil baja, the drone player in the band, he had become an important player, almost a *dholakia*, the percussionist. His elevation in JP's eyes was noticed by other samiti members who also began to look upon him with more respect. That added significantly to Nitish's belief in himself, driving him to work his way further up with redoubled effort.

Nitish began to tour districts and address larger meetings. Doing it every day, interacting with local activists, giving speeches, he began to see his strong and weak points, to see what worked with the activists and the people and what did not, and constantly improved his articulation.

Alongside, he tried to understand JP better, his ideas as well as his personality; he read more, argued more, listened more. He started winning the respect of the student and citizen activists at Patna and in the districts, acquiring fame by word of mouth. Adding to his political image was his personal image. He kept his life simple: he had no addictions, ate largely vegetarian meals, was satisfied with bare accommodation, did not need more money than would fulfil his basic requirements.

On many of the district tours he accompanied Lalu who, being on top among student leaders, did not feel threatened by the growing prominence of his socialist junior. Their bond was strengthened by their common approach towards advancing their political careers. They believed in making the movement strong and successful enough to cause dissolution of the state Assembly when they could stake their claim for a ticket in fresh elections.

They also had a similar attitude in dealing with the silent manoeuvres of the student leaders from the Hindu nationalist stream. They knew JP was a former socialist and secularist and was opposed to the ideology of Hindu nationalism, but JP had accepted Hindu nationalists and their student activists as part of the movement. He often lauded them as 'patriots' and maintained a close relationship with some of the national leaders, so the socialist student leaders had to keep a constant vigilance to prevent them from owning JP.

The Hindu nationalist student leaders, however, did not indulge in any manoeuvres to discredit Lalu, get him out of JP's favour, or secretly promote their organization and themselves, even though they resented his conduct. But Lalu felt threatened by them—if he ever did by any force—and kept socialist student leaders, particularly Nitish, close to him to keep looking strong.

Lalu and Nitish were two different characters, but Nitish would keep Lalu's company because it slowly helped him gain the space next to him—the man who wore the crown of the movement's youth leadership. Lalu needed him, he needed Lalu. Although they were seen by others in the movement as senior and junior, nobody saw them as unequal because Nitish had his own personality and was a student leader in his own right.

They were involved in several dramatic episodes together during the movement. In one such the police arrived to arrest them while they were holding a meeting in a town in Gaya district and they fled the scene and went on running and running, until they faced a high wall. The chasing policemen would have surely got them had they not climbed the wall with great difficulty and jumped over to the other side to start running again without pausing for breath.

Although it all seemed very romantic and revolutionary, one of the reasons why Lalu fled was that he hated going to jail and spending days in deprivation. When he was thrown into the Patna Central Jail during Indira's Emergency under the draconian MISA, he grew restless very soon and had himself shifted to a room under guard in the Patna Medical College Hospital. There, he managed to get the sympathy of junior doctors and nurses who allowed him to stay on in spite of finding him in perfect health as they were among the silent supporters of the movement.

Nitish had no problem with going to jail: after all, his father had gone to jail twice fighting the British. Imprisonment for a cause was a part of the occupational hazard of a political activist. What was better, it brought honour, public recognition and reward in terms of political elevation. He went to jail under the MISA during the movement and also during the Emergency. And his only reason to run or hide from the police was to enable the movement to stay afloat.

Indira swept about two hundred thousand leaders and activists of the movement, including JP, into jails across the country within a few days of the imposition of Emergency. Nitish was among the few leaders and activists in Bihar who managed to go into hiding to evade arrest. Indira proclaimed the state of Emergency by misusing an article in the Constitution that provided for suspension of all civil liberties and elections and entitled the state to unbridled powers under the extraordinary circumstance of a 'serious threat to national security'. It sent waves of repulsion through a nation that had built strong foundations for democracy despite being largely illiterate and poor. But people kept their mouths shut, even though they saw Indira using it for crushing political opposition, sending her police to raid offices and homes and snoop around in disguise with intelligence men for the 'enemies of the state' at railway stations, bus stands, river jetties and crowded bazaars.

Every day, news of someone picked up from here, another one pounced upon there came to the people in whispers. The newspapers, which were censored by officials before going to print, carried stories and speeches only extolling the remarkable achievements of the government and nothing about the repression. There were individuals in every walk of life known to be critical of Indira who turned overnight into her supporters under her reign of terror, and a current of suspicion ran through society about her agents and informers being everywhere.

With people blind to what was really happening in the state and the country, the immediate task that Nitish and other unimprisoned activists had to undertake was to bring out information bulletins and circulate them with the help of trustworthy sympathizers. They had to do it with great discretion and caution—nobody was to know where they were staying, how they were disguised, where they met, how they dispersed and where they went after the meeting. They kept off the movement's offices and usual meeting places and from their own and relations' homes, kept shifting from place to place in order to dodge any blackleg or eavesdropper. Nitish avoided even his elder sister Usha's place at Raja Bazar where he had hidden many times during the movement before the Emergency; he avoided the places of even his close friends, such as Narendra who was staying in the engineering college hostel. He met Manju two or three times at safe places.

Narendra was the contact man through whom Nitish's wife and parents used to get sporadic news about him. Narendra was not an active participant in the movement so he was not under surveillance, and that made his hostel room a safe place for hiding or meeting for many of the activists. Ram Vilas Paswan, the socialist youth leader who was to emerge as an important Opposition leader and hold ministerial offices at the Centre for many years, hid in Narendra's room for eight days. Narendra helped activists find safe stay also in the homes of some acquaintances, among them a state government officer who had bought a flat in eastern Patna but was not occupying it. It was the activists he helped and was in touch with who gave him bits of news about the activities of Nitish, whom he hardly met.

Nitish continued to circulate underground literature, sometimes just cyclostyled and not printed—photocopiers had not come in yet—and to hold clandestine meetings for a few months after the imposition of the Emergency, when he began to see that people were becoming less fearful of the Emergency as the days advanced. The news of JP suffering kidney failure under detention had sent a fresh wave of anger through the nation against the barbarity of the Emergency. Adding to it was Indira's younger son Sanjay's hyper-Malthusian drive to curb India's population by forced sterilizations, which found easy victims among the rural and urban poor. People gradually became less fearful and more resistant in indignation. The atmosphere of resentment, even though still highly subdued, encouraged Nitish and other activists to hold meetings in villages to organize people against the autocracy. People would be informed of a gathering by word of mouth and the meetings held by night, with seemingly innocuous lookouts—children, women or old men—watching for police or stool pigeons at village entry points.

It was at one such nocturnal meeting, at Dubauli village in Bhojpur district on 9 June 1976, that Nitish fell into the hands of the police. It happened because the young boy who was watching the top of the pathway to the village left his post for some time to attend to some call from his mother or grandmother—who out of discretion had not been told why the boy was there—giving a chance to the police to get in. Before they knew it, the gathering was surrounded by armed policemen. There was no option for Nitish but to allow himself to be taken into custody and be taken to the Ara police station. From there the police, quickly finishing the paperwork, drove him under armed escort fifty kilometres to Buxar Central Jail.

Narendra heard of the arrest in the morning and rushed along with Manju, Usha and her husband Devendra Singh to see him. Manju was extremely concerned: she had no problems with his political activities, no problem even with his imprisonment, but was prison not a horrible place with dangerous inmates and savage officials? Wouldn't he have but an abnormal, disturbed and miserable life, with tasteless routine meals and a naked floor to sleep on, crowded with the others? Nitish gave her an intrepid, smiling look. 'I am here not forever. The dictatorship won't last long,' he assured her.

Manju was not convinced. She had been completely distanced from politics, but she was now a part of the movement as an associate of her husband's. Her husband's future was linked to the future of the movement. She could only hope for the dictatorship to be overthrown at the soonest. 'I would pray for that to happen,' she said, 'morning and evening.'

For six months until Indira ordered fresh elections to Parliament in March 1977, Manju and family regularly visited Nitish in jail. The Buxar Central Jail was one of the better-administered jails in the state, with jail officials taking special care of the political prisoners: Nitish had no complaints. Everything he wanted within the rules was made available to him: newspapers, magazines, pen, paper, clean clothes and towels, proper food. He kept no prison diary: he has had very little interest in writing. But he kept himself abreast of what was happening outside from reading between the lines and meeting visitors including his family, Narendra and movement sympathizers. One or two prison officials too sometimes provided him clues to developments outside through casual remarks.

That is how he came to know that the four Opposition parties whose student and youth activists were actively involved in the movement—the Socialist Party, Jan Sangh, Bharatiya Lok Dal and Congress (Organization)—had decided to merge into a single political vehicle with JP's blessing and name it Janata Party. The formation of a single party came with the shared understanding that any combination as a united front on the 1967 pattern was bound to result in failure as it had all these years. A grand Opposition coalition could not work unless it made itself into a single unified entity with intra-party divergence of ideas and approaches but within a strict code of organizational discipline, much like the Congress.

The formation of the Janata Party in January 1977 fitted also with the mood of a very large number of people—particularly in northern Indian states where the JP movement had gained wide sympathy—who wanted a strong alternative committed to civil liberties, a free press and judiciary and fair elections. Indira had ordered elections because her intelligence agencies had assured her a clean sweep through the nation. If her intelligence agents had failed to see any sign of the storm coming, a large amount of credit should go to the ordinary people who kept their 'Indira *hatao*', 'Oust the Dictator', plan strictly confidential. No stirring, no loud proclamations, no angry processions, no sloganeering: people just waited for the polling day and delivered their verdict.

Nitish was being mentioned in the Janata Party circles as one of the two student leaders (the other being Lalu) who deserved nomination for parliamentary elections. Lalu had been released from jail and got nominated from Chhapra—a constituency separated from Patna by the Ganga. But Nitish's release got delayed because prison department officials took longer to process his papers. There was apparently no intention behind it: it so happened that soon after the elections were called, Nitish, for some reason, was transferred from Buxar to Bhagalpur Central Jail. Even the policemen escorting him were nice; when they missed the late evening train to Bhagalpur at the Patna railway junction, Nitish asked them if they would mind spending the night at the house of his in-laws at Kankarbagh in south-eastern Patna and they said they wouldn't.

Manju was overjoyed to see Nitish at home. She made some delicious dishes for the policemen and comfortable beds for them to sleep in.

Nitish had no handcuffs, nor did the policemen object to the hearty conversations he enjoyed with Manju and family. They knew here was not a prisoner who would escape. And the atmosphere had changed and he would soon be released. His relations thought the same, so did Nitish. He hoped he would get a ticket but did not talk about it with anyone. It was all in the hands of big party leaders.

But bureaucratic delay marred his chance. The prison department wanted papers from both the central jails, Buxar and Bhagalpur, for completing the file, and that took time. Despite Narendra's repeated visits to the inspector general of prisons he could not manage to get the release papers and present it to the jail superintendent at Bhagalpur to have Nitish freed before the Janata Party finalized its selection of candidates. But there were other factors working: although Nitish's name was being seriously mentioned as a deserving candidate from among student leaders for Barh, his native constituency, none of the former socialist leaders who were now in the Janata Party insisted on his name, partly because unlike Lalu he had not propitiated them. They gave Barh to Shyam Sundar Gupta, a businessman based in Kolkata who sympathized with the movement and had helped with money and provided shelter to several leaders and activists during the Emergency. Even a clod of earth would have won on a Janata Party ticket in the parliamentary elections of 1977, considering the public sentiment, and no wonder Gupta got 76 per cent of the total vote and Lalu 86 per cent.

Nitish had to wait. His family and friends were disappointed. Manju felt sad but left it to destiny: he had come so close and lost it because that is how *uparwala*, the Almighty, wanted it; he would get his chance. Nitish was vexed with the bureaucratic delay, but also felt that had Narendra stuck out longer in the inspector general's office he could have got his release papers in time. Narendra felt that had the selectors really wanted no one else but Nitish for Barh they could have got him out on bail to enable him to file his nomination papers. Dogged to pursue a political career, Nitish quickly shrugged it off. Elections to the state Assembly won't be long.

## repeated failures

'After the Janata Party nominations in March 1977, there was no time to think of the eligibility or non-eligibility of candidates,' recalls Nitish. 'The popular upsurge against Indira was so powerful that I, like everyone else in the movement, plunged into the election campaign to work for the victory of every Janata Party nominee including Gupta.'

Thousands of students and youth who had participated in the movement spontaneously joined the campaign of Janata Party candidates across constituencies in Bihar. Nominees were overwhelmed to see bevies of them going about villages and towns canvassing for them, without ever being asked to, without being paid anything for the expenses of their travel or food.

They were joined by a large number from the intelligentsia—college and school teachers, lawyers from lower courts to the state's high court, poets and journalists—and from the trading classes, lower bureaucracy, peasantry and landed gentry. It was the greatest uprising in Bihar's history after the Quit India movement of 1942, with two distinctions: 1942 aimed to throw out the British Crown, 1977 to bring down Dictator Indira; in 1942 public anger burst out in violence in many places, in 1977 it would be expressed solely through the ballot.

The Congress was decimated in Bihar; it also suffered heavy losses in other states of north India. The Janata Party won a brute majority in Parliament.

Trouble began when it was invited by the President to form the first coalition federal government in India. Election of a leader proved more difficult than electoral conquest, with every dissolved constituent of the

Janata Party projecting its own old chief for the office. Unable to reach a consensus they left the choice to JP who picked Morarji Desai for his impeccable integrity and long administrative experience. Morarji, a prominent figure in the freedom movement from Gujarat, had served as a senior minister in the Nehru government and lost bids for succession as prime minister after Nehru's death to Lal Bahadur Shastri and after Shastri's death to Indira Gandhi. Though Gandhian in his conduct, he could never rein in his craving for the country's highest office.

But his dream turned sour no sooner than it came true. Within a few months of his assumption of office, the other prime ministerial aspirants in his cabinet began to torment him. He tried to contain them, only to make matters worse. The predicament both he and his gravediggers faced was that they could not approach JP for mediation as they had stopped going to him for any advice after taking over office.

The people, who had voted for better governance, watched with dismay. Both Morarji and his rivals swore day in and day out by JP's ideas but would not make laws or policies to implement them. India had come very close to joining the community of failed postcolonial democracies under Indira: JP's singular achievement was the rescue of democracy from her deforming clutches. People saw him as the country's second liberator after Gandhi. He had made them sovereign again and revived hopes for India continuing as a robust democracy.

Yet, restoration of democracy with a free press, civil rights, independent judiciary, free and fair elections and embedded restraints on misuse of the Constitution by the ruling party could not be an end in itself. In JP's eye, democracy must serve as a means to establish a morally right, socially and economically egalitarian, people-centric, not politician-centric, polity. The aim of the Bihar Movement was transformation of society, not mere replacement of an authoritarian regime by a democratic party. JP and millions of supporters of the movement were disappointed to see Janata Party leaders behaving as though the struggle for transforming the system ended with their assumption of power. They were fighting for loaves of office.

With his failing health—emaciation, constant dialysis to purify his blood, diabetes, complications—JP could only hope that the student and youth activists of the movement carried on with the work for social and economic transformation. In the months following the March 1977 parliamentary elections, activists were distinctly divided into two camps. One comprised those with political affiliation who now were in Yuva Janata, the Janata Party's youth wing. The other was of those without political affiliation who formed a new student-youth organization, Chhatra Yuva Sangharsh Vahini, as a vehicle of social transformation directly under the command of JP.

Nitish was in Yuva Janata but, like many in it, continued to also be a part of the Chhatra Sangharsh Samiti, which was in a standstill situation after the March 1977 elections. Those were days when he and others in Yuva Janata did not know which way they should go: Should they follow JP down the road to social transformation? Should they shape Yuva Janata into a strong pressure group to make the Morarji government fulfil the ideals of the movement? Or should they wait for the government to dissolve the state Assembly for a fresh election and fight for a major quota for themselves in the Janata Party nominations?

Nitish decided not to join JP's movement for social transformation as a full-time worker because he was not made that way. He had never had any inclination at any stage of his life to be a 'revolutionary' working outside the parliamentary system. His mind was set on electoral politics from the very beginning, even as he remained sympathetic to the major aims of the movement.

He felt changes could be brought about from within the parliamentary system. No evidence of this was coming from the performance of the Morarji government, but, as he had set himself the goal of becoming a lawmaker, he had no other way but to tell himself that he would be different from others. His idealism was subordinated by his desire. For a few weeks after he missed the opportunity of getting a parliamentary ticket he did go along the idealist stream. But his mind was set on the next chance, which came to him when the polls were announced and he was nominated as Janata Party candidate for the Harnaut constituency, closer to his home town Bakhtiyarpur.

However, he was soon to realize the folly of seeing electoral politics as a universe independent of social currents. A few days before the polling day, at Belchhi village in Harnaut constituency, a large group of landowning Kurmis, armed with illegal guns and other lethal weapons, attacked the quarters of the poor, overpowered eleven recalcitrant farm labourers and dragged them out into a fallow plot. Trussing them up, they made a heap of pieces of wood and set it alight. They tossed the farmers into the flaming heap and fired at them, fiendishly jubilating while they struggled and screamed till their burning bodies went cold.

The incident caused revulsion throughout the nation, as much for the sheer savagery as for the majority of victims being from the untouchable caste of Dusadhs, also known as Paswans. The Kurmis of Harnaut, nay the whole district of Nalanda, however, did not see it in human terms. They saw it as a war against the 'insolence' of the Paswans who had been 'harassing' the Kurmis no end. While the rest of the country had a gory view of the Belchhi massacre, the Kurmis saw it as a milestone in their campaign for the restoration of Kurmi pride.

Rural Bihar witnessed dramatic changes in the three decades since the British left. One of the most epochal changes was the liquidation of zamindari. The big landlords, rajas and maharajas lost their power over the peasantry, their success through legal manipulation in holding on to parts of their estates notwithstanding. The zamindars were predominantly upper caste: with the loss of their control over the chief means of production, they also lost their political control.

The second remarkable change, a socio-political reaction to upper-caste feudal dominance, was the rise of the backward castes. They constituted the bulk of the tenant farmers tilling for the zamindars. Now they were landowning peasants, entitled to all that was produced in the land and free to sell any surplus they got from it. There was a growing solidarity among them as peasants to prevail upon the state to get the best terms for their trade. At the same time, they were in a race as separate castes for shares in employment in government departments and undertakings, colleges, schools, political party recruitment and for the membership of hundreds of committees, statutory or temporary, that were formed for everything.

In the race, the three middle castes, Yadavs, Kurmis and Koeris, pushed ahead of others. They were not only numerically much larger than most of the backward castes but also owned more land than they did. The Kurmis and Koeris had great traditions of excellence as peasants. The Yadavs had traditionally been a pastoral, cattle-rearing caste, but many of them had taken to agriculture, even though most who owned cattle and sold milk in villages and urban neighbourhoods were still Yadavs.

The peasants of the middle castes worked their land with fine skills. They valued land the most and there would be rare cases in which a Kurmi, Koeri or Yadav would sell his agricultural land. On the contrary, they would keep looking for opportunities to buy more land. They bought land from Muslim families who emigrated to Pakistan after Partition in the late 1940s and from former zamindars short of cash after the abolition of zamindari in the 1950s.

They also bought land from big landowners who, alarmed by the ceiling on agricultural landholdings in the 1960s and troubled by the 'land grab' campaign of the landless led by socialists and communists in the 1970s, sold off the 'most vulnerable' portions of their land—usually those leased out to sharecroppers who had to pay 50 per cent of the produce as rent. The big landowners were happy with whatever price they got for these plots, for sooner or later either the state or the same sharecroppers, with the backing of those 'leftist hooligans', threatened to seize it. The big landowners also sold plots of land when they needed big cash for a wedding in the family or for funding their sons' professional education in engineering or medicine in an institute outside the state.

Then there were upper-caste families or branches of a family that settled in towns and sold their holdings to the highest bidders. Less than 10 per cent of Bihar's population lived in towns by the end of the 1970s, a significant percentage of which was upper-caste owing to their dominance in education and employment; but we can safely assume that a majority of the upper castes still lived in their native villages. However, the fact that the upper castes did not actively engage themselves in agriculture, and the fact that their standards of judging individual progress were largely urban, drove them into towns more than the backward castes. The latter still remained deeply rooted in their native villages. That was why the politics of Charan Singh—the Jat leader from western UP who rose to be prime minister for five months during 1979–80—and of the socialist parties that drew strength from the backward castes, looked so rural.

The rise to power of the three middle castes that followed the fall from power of the upper castes in rural Bihar was characterized in its initial years by an assertiveness that bordered on perversity and lawlessness. They often acted like the upper-caste zamindars they condemned, using force to get what they wanted. Mahavir Mahato, the main accused in the Belchhi massacre, had seized public (*gair mazarua*) properties—lands, ditches and tanks—in the village. He had influence with the local block office and police station. He had retainers with unlicensed firearms. Over a period of some years he imposed his will on everyone, harassing and battering villagers from all castes, including his own, until a young, strong-willed farm worker from the untouchable Dusadh caste, Singhwa, moved to his in-laws at Belchhi and started organizing villagers to fight Mahavir's tyranny, paying eventually with his life for his defiance.

With the rise of the dominant peasant castes, the state witnessed growth in rights consciousness among the landless farm labourers too, most of them from the untouchable castes. They wanted higher wages and homestead and cultivable land. And they wanted to be treated with respect. Being at the bottom of society they were treated inhumanly both by the shrunken-in-power-but-still-entrenched-as-landowners upper castes as well as the assertive, ascendant middle castes. Their demands met with indifference from both the upper- and middle-caste landowners. That forced them to organize themselves.

In the rural Bihar of mid-1970s, the labourers were fighting for their rights under five broad kinds of political organization: first, spontaneous, village-based, led by a gallant youth from among them; second, socialist, very scattered survivals of the 'land grab' campaign started in 1971 in which the SSP and CPI jointly encouraged landless labourers to seize plots of land held by landowners in excess of the ceiling on agricultural holdings; third, the CPI; fourth, the CPI(M); and fifth, the CPI (Marxist–Leninist).

The CPI(ML) movement, which developed strong roots across the southern Bihar plains, resulted in a great deal of senseless bloodshed by its activists, allowing a 'morally justified' alliance of the landowners and the state to decimate the 'anarchists' through mass murders of unarmed labourers, men, women or children, whoever fell in the way of the sudden charge on the huddle of their hutments. But it had changed the way the landowners looked upon the landless and poor peasants. The wanton days of landowners when they treated labourers like cattle and took liberties with their women were gone.

The organization of the poor and landless peasants of Belchhi oppressed by the landowner-tyrant Mahavir Mahato under the leadership of Singhwa was spontaneous. Singhwa had never been to school and did not have any association with any political party, right or left. Yet the mobilization by him changed the scene. He led his group to resist Mahavir's cruelties—preventing him from forcibly occupying someone's land, compelling him to pay proper wages, protecting labourers against physical assault—causing a contraction in the bully's image.

Mahavir found that he could no more face the challenge of the Singhwa group on his strength alone. He sought the help of the independent MLA, Inderdeo Chaudhary, who had won largely with the support of his Kurmi caste-men from Asthawan, a constituency contiguous to Harnaut. The Singhwa group was seen as a threat to the collective self-respect of the Kurmis. It was identified with the string of spontaneous or political organizations of farm labourers in the district. The Kurmis felt the Paswans were getting an upper hand. The Singhwa group's triumphs over the Mahavir-led Kurmis showed it very clearly. It was to extinguish the spark that could cause a conflagration to end Kurmi hegemony that they gathered from various villages in large numbers and carried out the Belchhi massacre, in which Singhwa and his active associates were killed.

Belchhi caused a clearer antagonistic divide between Kurmis and Paswans in the district. More and more Kurmis were swayed by the casteist propaganda that the 'Kurmi nation is under threat'. They saw Mahavir Mahato, Inderdeo Chaudhary and other Kurmis who were arrested on charges of involvement in the massacre as heroes. They believed they alone could 'salvage the Kurmi pride'.

When the Assembly elections were announced, the Kurmis of Nalanda district decided to back only those Kurmi candidates who would lead their campaign for restoration of their pride. In Harnaut they picked Bhola Prasad Singh, who had helped many of them get gun licences. Bhola also assisted a number of them in getting an electricity connection. He was a patron of the Kurmi caste organization. During floods in the Mohane River in 1976 he had personally organized relief in the constituency.

Bhola had quit the SSP in 1974 to form a party called Indian Socialist Party because he disagreed with party leader Karpoori Thakur's view that all party legislators resign to force dissolution of the state Assembly, as JP and the student leaders of the Bihar Movement wanted. He incurred the wrath of student leaders owing to his disassociation with the movement, so much so that when he organized a condolence meeting for the slain Koeri leader Jagdeo Prasad at Gandhi Maidan, Nitish with others stormed on to the dais, threw about things and flung down the mike.

Bhola, famed for Raj Narain-style antics, became a member of the state Legislative Council in 1962 and was elected to the Assembly from Bakhtiyarpur in 1972. As an SSP candidate, he was supported by Nitish, then in the fourth year of engineering college. Bhola's campaign office was right in front of Nitish's house.

The Bihar Movement drew a good deal of support from the backward castes. Bhola lost sympathy of a sizeable section of Kurmis, including that of Nitish, by not participating in the movement. He would have lost by a heavy margin had Belchhi not taken place. Bhola had for years been the biggest leader of Kurmis from Nalanda district. Belchhi provided him a god-sent opportunity to harvest Kurmi votes with his open advocacy of the 'innocence' of the accused. He blatantly spoke out in their support at public meetings.

That was to assure the Kurmis that he would be the best man in the Assembly to fight for their interests. And the Kurmis did need a voice up there, perhaps as many as they could, because in their view the state under the Janata, much like under the Congress, favoured the untouchable castes and was prejudiced against Kurmis, as the 'state repression against us' after the Belchhi incident showed.

Nitish was seen by the Kurmis as an honest and intelligent candidate; the engineering degree added its own special touch to his respectability. The part he had played in the JP movement had drawn the Kurmis' attention towards him. Some glory was also reflected on to him by his father who was held by the Kurmis in high esteem for his excellent healing skills and initiatives in the spread of education.

The Kurmis also had sympathy with him because Seodah, Manju's native village, was a part of the Harnaut constituency. Some extra respect also accrued to him from his father-in-law being the headmaster of the Seodah high school. Manju, who had joined as a home science teacher at her father's school, campaigned vigorously for Nitish along with her family. But all this came to mean little when the Kurmis looked for an assurance from Nitish about protecting them in their war for restoration of Kurmi pride. Nitish talked of larger issues but never of issues directly threatening the life, liberty and dignity and pride of the community—he was not a good candidate to represent their interests.

The belligerent local leadership of the Kurmis endorsed Bhola. Most Kurmis in Seodah, including two uncles of Manju, supported him because Bhola also hailed from their village. Caste backing meant that Bhola would have no dearth of men and money to manage his election campaign. Armed Kurmis would be there to scare away voters of other castes and even of the Kurmi caste who were inclined to vote for Nitish.

Compared to the number of vehicles and canvassers and the volume of expenditure on workers' food and entertainment in Bhola's campaign, Nitish's campaign looked poor, miserable and amateurish, with hardly any vehicle and hardly any money to engage workers. And he engaged no armed groups to resist Bhola's rigging gangs as he was fighting for clean, 'value-based' politics.

Narendra, who was one of Nitish's key campaign managers, recalls that the fund for the campaign trickled in in very small amounts from odd places: relations, Nitish's father's friends, sympathizers of the JP movement. Many of Nitish's friends from college like us and many juniors who were in jobs made small contributions to his campaign that added up to a few thousand rupees.

Nitish's closest schoolmate Munna Sircar joined him with his motorcycle, taking him on his pillion to villages and towns. Towards the end, despite great handicaps, Nitish emerged as a serious contender for the seat. The majority of the upper castes, Rajputs and Bhumihars, and backward castes other than the Kurmis, such as Yadavs, supported him because of their continuing strong sympathy with the Janata Party. The few Kurmis who supported him were among the Bihar Movement supporters, his father's acquaintances and close relations such as Manju's immediate family. Nitish lost to Bhola by about 5,900 votes. The gap of slightly under 8.5 per cent between them was caused by the Kurmi endorsement of Bhola.

Looking back, Nitish campaigners feel that he would perhaps not have lost if the Janata Party had given a ticket to Inderdeo Chaudhary for Asthawan, where he had fought and won again as an independent candidate. That would have assured the Kurmis that they had someone in the Janata Party to 'protect' them. They would have identified with the Janata Party and voted for Nitish on those grounds, even if he did not project himself as a caste leader.

Even though they had sensed it coming, the members of Nitish's family were aggrieved by his defeat. Manju was especially sorry for Nitish. She had also worked hard to mobilize support for him, even though she kept her distance from politics and had no craving to be known one day as a lawmaker's or a minister's wife. She was the traditional wife who would have loved her husband doing a regular, stable job. But she never argued, never complained, never cried over her fate. She had felt the deep yearning for a political career in Nitish's heart and she prayed daily for the fulfilment of his dream.

What would Nitish do now? Should he try and get a job as an engineer? How would he support himself and the family if he wanted to pursue a political career? Wouldn't it be wiser to give up politics?

Those were trying times. As many as twenty-nine student activists of the movement had been elected as Janata Party MLAs—most far smaller in stature than him and far less articulate—but he had lost. The loss vexed his nerves in solitary moments and kept posing a question to him: 'Can you ever win an election without money, goondas and caste support?'

His mother, brother and sisters decided politics was not the place for a noble person; sometimes Manju was also influenced by their views, though she never discouraged him. His father's example was before them.

Nitish refused to give up. He decided he would keep trying until he succeeded or was ruined. Soon after the dust of the election storm settled he resumed his visits to the villages of Harnaut where he met people and listened to them. A homespun bag strung round his shoulder, he became a frequent passenger on the ramshackle Bakhtiyarpur–Harnaut buses, and knowing who he was the conductors often refused to charge him any fare.

During his interactions, villagers told him of their common and personal problems. He took up the issues with the officials or ministers concerned and tried to resolve them as quickly as possible. Sometimes his visits met with barbed and dismissive remarks from staunch supporters of Bhola Singh: 'Our MLA has done a lot for us and is doing it continuously.' They wanted to put him off, but Nitish surprised them with a smile. 'I took it as a part of the competitive game that is politics,' Nitish told me. He told Bhola's supporters, 'Look, I am a politician. A politician is a social worker and I am only doing my job.'

To Nitish's bad luck, while he tried to consolidate his vote and win over a good slice of Bhola's Kurmi solidarity vote, the Janata Party was dipping in popularity. And Nitish wondered if there could be a more luckless legislative aspirant than him! The Morarji government had failed to fulfil its promise of reining in the prices of essential commodities which were making life difficult for ordinary people, while the ministers of his government lived in luxury at public expense as the Congress ministers used to, breaking their vow of austerity.

Karpoori Thakur led a no better government in the state. People noticed no change in the quality of governance under the Karpoori regime: the bureaucracy was as circumlocutory, bribe-driven, arrogant and oppressive as under the Congress regime. There were as many as eight places where the police opened fire on crowds in four months of the Karpoori rule, proving his regime to be the most repressive in the state's political history with one police firing every second week.

Civil rights had been the most important issue in the Bihar Movement. The movement's activists and sympathizers, who had been victims of police repression under the Indira regime, had hoped that the Janata government would create a strong legal and policy infrastructure for truly democratic governance in which the police would not be allowed to use firearms to kill people assembled on any issue. There could still be some justification for the police using firearms against armed criminals or radical communists, but not against unarmed processions and gatherings.

Police firings in the Karpoori regime followed the Congress pattern: police lathi charged a pressing crowd; some from the angered mass would start pelting stones; this provided the police with an excuse to open fire in 'self-defence'. What lethal threat could the small pieces of bricks or concrete rubble pose to the policemen to justify firing in self-defence? People expected that the police would be civilized under the Janata regime and directed to deal with excited gatherings without resorting to guns. There had been demands raised by civil rights campaigners during the JP movement and before for allowing the police to use only non-lethal rubber or plastic bullets even in extreme situations of crowd control. It was not discussed any more under the Janata regime.

On being reminded in the Assembly by a member of his statement that there would be no police firings in the Janata raj, Karpoori denied having ever said anything like that. He also refused to give any promise that there would be no more police firing. He told another member he could not think of making such a foolproof policy as would prevent police firings from taking place. 'But if you have a better idea, give it to me, I will implement it,' he told the member, his tone laced with sarcasm.

Soon Karpoori was to reap a fresh harvest of public resentment with his order of 7 January 1978 prohibiting any demonstrations, sit-ins or hunger strikes by government employees and others outside the houses of ministers and officers. The very next day, the police cleaned up all tents of protestors from outside ministers' residences.

The first tent to go was where groups of unemployed engineers and engineering college students sat on hunger strike outside Karpoori's residence demanding jobs. Nitish happened to be there to express his support for the engineering protestors when the police were pulling down the tent. 'They are carrying on a peaceful protest,' he told the magistrate leading the policemen, 'why are you removing them from here?' The magistrate said haughtily, 'They will have to go. This is a government order.'

'People are outraged by the deeds of the Kapoori government. Has it forgotten the Bihar Movement?' Nitish wrote in an angry commentary in *Samayik Varta*, a Hindi fortnightly brought out from Patna by the eminent Lohiaite ideologue Kishan Patnaik. 'The use of force to remove tents of protestors from outside ministers' residences shows that the government has no respect for the language [of non-violence] of the Bihar Movement . . . Ministers are treating the big houses officially allotted them as their private houses. And they do not want any disturbance to their contented life.'[1]

Nitish's commentary reflected the mood of growing public disappointment with the performance of the Janata governments at the Centre and in the state. The mood was apparent the previous year, in November 1977, at the three-day conference of about 500 youth activists of the Bihar Movement in which members of the Yuva Janata and the Chhatra Yuva Sangharsh Vahini and several organizationally non-attached youths participated. There was unanimity about the failure of the Janata government to fulfil the promises made in the party's election manifesto. On behalf of the Yuva Janata, Nitish moved a political resolution, which was seconded by Anil Prakash of the Vahini and approved by the delegates. The resolution said:

When the Bihar Movement was creating the base for total revolution by mobilizing people's and youth power a state of emergency was proclaimed, and the whole energy of the movement had to be directed toward saving democracy. The struggle had to be suspended during the elections. We were never under any illusion that the Congress government would be replaced by a revolutionary government. We hoped the new government to be collaborators in revolution . . . That [such collaboration] would give a fillip to the popular movement, and the government too would be able to fight the pressures of the bureaucracy and feudal and capitalist forces with the support of people's power . . . [However] the Janata Party government's performance has been dismal. It is walking the Congress path.[2]

JP made a long inaugural speech at the conference despite the terrible difficulty he faced in speaking loudly and at a stretch due to his weakness. 'The atmosphere for social transformation created by the Bihar Movement has turned somewhat cold after the elections,' JP told the delegates. 'Today, at this conference, you have to work out how the movement can be revived. If not in other states, let the bugle of total revolution blow in every village of Bihar.'

At the end of its deliberations, the conference issued an ultimatum to the Janata government to fulfil the promises made in its election manifesto within six months or face mass agitation. The delegates wanted the government to act immediately to repeal the Maintenance of Internal Security Act (MISA), the article in the Constitution guaranteeing right to property and laws that provided scope for authoritarian rule; to enshrine the right to employment in the Constitution; to make declaration of assets compulsory for ministers and other lawmakers; and to free the national broadcasters, All India Radio and Doordarshan, from government control.

The conference was imbued with an eclectic melange of ideas of Gandhi, Lohia and JP. It was organized by Lohia Vichar Manch (Forum for Lohia Thought), a small group of followers of Lohia's ideology scattered across the country, whose central figure at the time was Kishan Patnaik. Socialists in general, and those attached to this forum in particular, held Patnaik in great esteem because he had the most comprehensive and clear understanding of Lohia's thoughts among all his associates. He was a failure in electoral politics; he had dissociated himself from party politics and engaged himself with the forum when JP's takeover of the leadership of the Bihar Movement drew him to Patna to lend his intellectual support to it.

Patnaik shared with JP an active socialist past, failure in and disillusionment with electoral politics and a passion for the moral cleansing of Indian polity. He saw the Bihar Movement as a part of India's social revolutionary continuum from Gandhi to Lohia to JP. That is why he had brought Lohiaites as well as JP followers together at the conference: to make them work in cohesion guided by what he described as the 'ideological trinity of Gandhi, Lohia and Jayaprakash'.

It suited JP too. He needed a strongly motivated youth force to 'complete the unfinished task of the movement'. He wanted to re-energize the citizenry to work for social transformation. He had been a crusader all his life and would not let the matter end just with the removal of authoritarian Indira from power.

Yet, the question that stared in his face was: had he done enough to make the movement truly revolutionary, to prevent it from being appropriated by the Opposition parties which later coalesced into the

Janata Party? The answer was yes and no. There was no ambivalence in JP's mind (though there was plenty of ambiguity in his concepts of Total Revolution) about the parliamentary route being a revolutionary one. Where he wavered during the pre-Emergency phase of the movement was to give more importance to the parliamentary struggle than to the fight for social transformation. By directing the movement towards the goal of removal of authoritarian Indira, JP let the few transformational initiatives taken by him recede to the background.

For instance, the initiatives to end casteism with the discarding of the sacred thread by the upper castes, inter-caste marriages and representation of the lower castes in institutions: after the initial burst, virtually nothing was heard of them. Then there was the janata sarkar (people's government) with a *jan adalat* (people's court) in villages for settlement of disputes outside the courts of law. They worked in very few villages, for a very short time and on very few issues. The core of the infrastructure for Total Revolution was to be made up of *jan samitis*, people's committees in electoral constituencies, that would drive all change, from the selection of the right persons for representing voters in elective bodies—from the panchayat to the Parliament—to cultural revolution to development with equity. The jan samitis never got going.

Talking about 'rebuilding' the transformational movement was fine, but did JP ever start building it? Did he have the scope to build it? The student movement primarily drew its strength from people's anger towards the state Congress government and would have faded out had Indira agreed to dismiss the Ghafoor ministry and dissolve the Assembly as in Gujarat. But Indira, after having succumbed in Gujarat, saw a chain in the attack on the Congress government in Bihar and refused to yield any more, resorting to harsh methods to put down the movement.

It was with her harsh methods that Indira helped a state movement build into a national movement. The highly unscrupulous ways she used to remain in prime minister's office—after her disqualification as a member of Parliament on the charge of malpractices in her election by the Allahabad High Court—added fuel to the fire. JP could maintain the mass movement only by keeping the focus on the removal of Indira. As long as this focus was sustained, everybody, from the Opposition parties to their youth wings to the urban intelligentsia and farmers, allowed him his 'revolutionary indulgences' such as encouraging inter-caste marriage and sacred-thread disavowal, even though most had serious objections to them. It was not surprising that they all left him after Indira was removed.

JP admitted in a newspaper interview in August 1977 that no leader of the Janata governments at the Centre and in the state had sought his advice on any issue since they took office; during the movement they all regularly met him and took his advice. The architect of the 'revolution' that had brought them to power had turned irrelevant.

The conference organized by the Lohia Vichar Manch was one of the several meetings that politically unaffiliated activists were to have with the Lohiaite youth to deliberate on how to use the energy generated by the Bihar Movement for social transformation. Much of it was just idle talk: there was no activity to revive it.

If there was any group that wanted to build on the gains of the movement it was the politically unaffiliated activists enrolled with the Chhatra Yuva Sangharsh Vahini. The members of the Yuva Janata who participated in these deliberations were divided into two broad camps: one of Nitish and others who had lost the election and considered such conferences an important part of their political activity until they got a ticket at another election; and another of those who wanted to commit to Yuva Janata to stay away from electoral politics and work for the realization of the goals of the Bihar Movement.

Nitish remembers the period as his 'idealist phase', with a conscience turned towards carrying forward with the good things of the movement, with a greater influence of the 'socialist saint' Kishan Patnaik over his ideas, but never losing sight of the next election. And most members of Yuva Janata thought like him.

So, who would stay on with JP to revive the movement? Not the Janata leaders, not the Yuva Janata, not the youth-wingers of the former Jan Sangh who had set up their own front, the Janata Yuva Morcha, not the urban intelligentsia nor the farmers—a majority of whom would be sceptical and scared of JP's radical ideas on caste-levelling and farmland redistribution. JP seemed a castaway in his Patna home.

JP failed to revive the Bihar Movement. But a powerful current was sweeping Bihar's society in an entirely unforeseen direction. It was a current that had started building up towards the end of the nineteenth century with the cultural movement of the Shudras to seek equality with the bipolar elite of the Brahmans and Kshatriyas. Of these Shudras, the Kayasthas and Bhumihars achieved recognition as upper castes early on the strength of their economic status, education and political influence. The Congress in the state was overwhelmingly composed of these four upper castes.

Vying for equality with the upper castes were the Yadavs, Kurmis and Koeris. After Independence, their first major victory was the abolition of zamindari. Their next major victory was the stonewalling—in concert with farmers from the upper castes—of all other government measures of land reform. These reforms aimed to place a ceiling on the size of farmland holdings, acquire the lands held in excess of that ceiling and redistribute them among landless agricultural labourers, and also legally secure the tenancy of sharecroppers who leased land from farmers. Their third major fight, again in solidarity with the upper castes, was for maximizing the flow of public resources into agriculture.

Although 'farmer' was a caste-neutral identity, increasingly over the years it was the dominant peasant castes that appropriated it in Bihar and UP. People in north India use the same word—*kisan*—for peasants and farmers, distinguished here as those who work on their lands and those who do not. Although the upper castes also were kisans, most of them considered working on their fields below their dignity. Rarely did a Brahman or Kayastha kisan guide a plough or plant or transplant paddy on his farmland, no matter how poor he was. A large section of Rajputs and a small section of Bhumihars also shunned farm work. In general the upper castes perceived themselves as *zaminwale*, landowners, and not as kisans, which connoted a rustic identity, evoking images of turbaned men behind ploughs and digging up earth with a spade.

The dominant peasant castes had no such snobbery; on the contrary, they took pride in their peasant traditions and skills and constantly looked for opportunities to enlarge their landholdings and farm yields. By the mid-1960s a heterogeneous group of middle castes in Bihar, UP and Haryana emerged on the political scene with a dual identity:

one as kisan (peasant) and another as *pichhde* (backward castes). Both as peasants and backward castes they had serious grievances against the state. As backward castes they had a serious case of exclusion against democracy and as peasants they had a serious case of discrimination against development. Mobilizing their large numbers behind SSP and Bharatiya Lok Dal, they had brought coalitions led by them to power in elections in 1967 in Bihar and UP.

The Congress, which became more solicitous of the three dominant middle castes in Bihar after they started organizing under the Triveni Sangh in the 1930s and '40s, began to follow a conscious policy of accommodation towards them in the 1950s and '60s. Key leaders from the three castes were brought up to higher levels in the organizational and ministerial hierarchies to serve as iconic magnets for voters of these castes.

It did not help the Congress to any significant extent because both its organization and ministries continued to be dominated by upper castes. The party's policy of accommodation towards middle castes in practice proved grist to the factional mill within the Congress where every upper caste, with an identified leader, was forever plotting to appropriate the largest number of positions of influence and power, even jobs in the government, at the cost of other upper castes. In order to gain wider influence for itself, every upper-caste faction picked up one or two key leaders of the three middle castes and gave him an important position.

The three dominant middle castes, described as 'upper backwards', were not very enthused by the Congress policy of co-option, because they saw it for what it was: their caste leaders playing cogs in the party's factional wheel. They had no independent standing or power to be able to promote their dual interests as peasants and backward castes in the mechanisms of the state. The old social structure with upper-caste predominance was crumbling; the upper backwards established their dominance in agriculture very quickly, and had a growing presence in the higher professions as lawyers, college teachers, engineers and doctors.

Their increasing share in the economic sphere was, however, not accompanied by a matching growth in influence in the political sphere— party organizations, legislature, ministries, local self-government and bureaucracy. In other words, the institutions of state power were still in upper-caste hands.

The upper backwards had tried to gain a share of state power through the Congress for over four decades but had been terribly disappointed. The Congress had come to rely on the support of the upper castes, the untouchable castes and the Muslims; it did not need more than small segments of backward-caste votes to win seats, which it managed by co-opting one caste leader here, another there. The party had failed to feel the pulse of the backward castes who wanted nothing short of a share in state power. The neglect hurt them.

Upper-caste factions in the Congress made it worse by plotting to remove Daroga Prasad Rai, the first backward-caste Congress chief minister of Bihar, within less than a year in 1970. With Rai's nomination as CM, not only the Yadavs, his caste-men, but the other backward castes too had felt a glimmer of hope about the Congress at last beginning to give them prominence in state institutions. The appointment by Rai of a State Backward Classes Commission in 1971, under the chairmanship of a senior Congressman Mungeri Lal—to identify socially and educationally backward classes in the state and recommend measures including reservations in government jobs for their amelioration—only boosted their hopes. However, with Rai's removal their hopes were dashed. They turned away from the Congress and never went back.

But they had no good political alternative. In the early 1970s their choice was confused and dispersed: while the core of them continued to be with the socialists, particularly the SSP, others lent their support to parties or individuals according to their local situations.

They saw a prominent leader emerge in Jagdeo Prasad, a Koeri, who earned the nickname of 'Lenin of Bihar' by virtue of his charismatic appeal among the Koeris, other backward castes as well as Dalits. His public meetings attracted thousands of people. He became a thorn in the side of upper-caste landowners, particularly in central Bihar, the principal battlefield of the upper backwards for political equality with the upper castes. On 5 September 1974, when the Bihar Movement was at its peak, Jagdeo Prasad was killed by the police while leading a peaceful crowd of about twenty thousand for pressing some demands at Kurtha in Gaya district.

There was widespread suspicion among the backward castes that Jagdeo Prasad had been killed at the instance of a Bhumihar minister in the Congress government. His 'martyrdom' was to sharpen the sense of alienation of the backward castes from the Congress and give a huge impetus to their 'crusade' against upper-caste hegemony in the state.

The backward castes supported the Bihar Movement not only because it aimed to dislodge the Congress from power but also because JP's ideas held a promise of social restructuring for their empowerment. In the middle of the movement, a new party called Bharatiya Lok Dal (BLD) was formed by the merger of the SSP led by Karpoori with the Bharatiya Kranti Dal (BKD) led by Charan Singh, twice chief minister of UP and a towering champion of the causes of peasants. Hailing from the middle caste of Jats, a community of excellent peasants with a significant population in UP and Haryana, Charan Singh represented the peasant–backward dual identity of the lower castes as no politician of his time did.

The Emergency made the upper backwards more hostile to the Congress with Indira's authoritarian state announcing a more pronounced patronage to Dalits and the lower backwards, by freeing debt-bonded labourers, gifting pieces of land to them for homestead and cultivation and raising the minimum wages for agriculture. This pronounced patronage also made the upper-caste farmers hostile to the Congress. The Janata Party's electoral triumph owed to the anger both of the upper-caste and the upper-backward farmland owners as much for muzzling civil and democratic rights as for 'pampering' the Dalits and the lower backwards.

Both the upper castes and upper backwards inevitably hit out aggressively at the Dalits and the lower backwards, attacking and perpetrating massacres in many villages, no sooner than the Congress was replaced by the Janata Party in Delhi in March 1977. The first such gory retaliation took place at Belchhi in May, followed by about a dozen other massacres largely across central Bihar. A majority of the mass murders were carried out by the upper-backward landowners aided by caste outlaws and local police. The reason behind this was that the upper backwards were an acquisitive, rising class of peasants who hated to see themselves shackled in their onward march by demands from labourers. They were already facing strong hostility from the upper castes who would like to see them where they were before. Facing hostility from above and resistance from below, the upper backwards became increasingly militant.

In the Janata Party, both at the national and the state level, the upper backwards, who were represented by the BLD and the socialists, soon got into a confrontation with the upper castes, who were represented by the Jan Sangh and the Congress(O). It was a fight for the 'ownership' of the Janata Party, and for more than a year the upper castes let the upper backwards have their way to avoid a split that could bring back the Congress. In Delhi, Morarji Desai continued to absorb shocks and swallow insults from his home minister Charan Singh and the Lohiaite gadfly and health minister Raj Narain. In Patna the upper-caste Janata MLAs accepted Karpoori as chief minister and allowed him to give the largest-ever representation in any Bihar ministry to the backward castes (42 per cent against 29 per cent to upper castes).

Upper-caste indulgence, however, failed to keep Charan or Karpoori quiet and contented. Charan openly declared his ambition to be prime minister and exploited his iconic image to mobilize huge upper-backward peasant rallies in Delhi in his support. Charan and the socialists began to press for quotas on the pattern of Scheduled Castes and Tribes for the 'other backward classes' (OBCs)—backward classes other than the untouchable castes and aboriginal tribes listed in the national Constitution who together had 24 per cent reservation—in order to consolidate the support of the backward castes for them.

Towards the end of 1978, both the Central and Bihar governments announced quota-related decisions that were to reshape the state and national politics. Morarji set up the second Backward Classes Commission under the chairmanship of B.P. Mandal. Mandal, who was then a senior Janata leader, was asked to identify OBCs and suggest measures, including reservations in Central government services and educational institutions, for their development.

In Bihar, Karpoori dug out the Mungeri Lal Commission report that had been submitted to the Congress state government in 1976 but not implemented; he announced his government's acceptance of its main recommendation for 26 per cent reservation in government jobs for OBCs in early 1978.

Within weeks of his announcement, Bihar's society seemed split in two. In the government departments, universities, political parties, trade associations, on buses and trains, there emerged mutually hostile sections of 'forwards' (as the upper castes were popularly known) and 'backwards'. A new group called the Forward League formed by some upper-caste youth, with the blessing of upper-caste lawmakers across party lines, claimed to lead the forwards and an old organization called the All India Backward Classes Federation, the backwards.

The League and the Federation organized rallies and counter-rallies in Patna, whipping up anti- and pro-reservation sentiments through the state. The confrontation scaled into mob violence and there was hardly a day for almost eight weeks when the anti-quota protestors did not burn a bus or derail a train or attack a government office and destroy things, or the pro-quota agitators did not publicly hurl abuses at JP, who had only said that the quota must benefit only the economically depressed sections within backward castes, or physically clash with the anti-quota protestors.

Upper-caste Janata MLAs and ministers wanted Karpoori to put off implementation of his reservation policy to an indefinite date, and set up a campaign for his removal when he refused.

Although Nitish was too small to make an impact on the scene, he came out with a new reservation formula that slowly gained appreciation and acceptance in political circles. Nitish, who was a member of the national executive of the Yuva Janata, convened a meeting of concerned citizens at Gandhi Museum Hall in Patna in collaboration with a fellow Lohiaite Bajrang Singh and presented a document on reservation which was unanimously accepted.

The document, a product of Nitish's youthful idealism, suggested four major amendments to Karpoori's reservation policy: one, the economically better-off segments of the backward castes must be excluded from the benefits of reservation (the segments that were to be described as 'creamy layer' by a nine-member constitution bench of the Supreme Court in its landmark judgement in the case, *Indira Sawhney v. Union of India*, on the Mandal Commission in 1992); two, the poorer section of the upper castes must also be given a share in the quota; three, the right to employment must be enshrined in the Constitution (to assuage the fear of the upper-caste youth); and four, higher government assistance and attention must be paid to enable the backward castes to be educated enough to be eligible to avail of the quota.

Nitish's suggestions were aimed at bridging the forward–backward chasm created by Karpoori's quota announcement. His formula took care of the three major concerns of the upper-caste youth: one, that there were economically backward people among the upper castes; two, that with unemployment already very high, the Karpoori quota would further reduce job opportunities for them; and three, that the quota would benefit only the elite section of the backward castes. The first concern would be met with a quota for the economically backward among the upper castes, the second with a constitutional guarantee of employment to everyone and the third with an income ceiling for eligibility.

The document never became a subject of deliberation in the Janata Party organization or cabinet, nor was Nitish ever called by Karpoori for any high-level policy consultation, yet just by word-of-mouth circulation and its publication in the *Samayik Varta* it came into the reckoning of the chief minister.

JP found himself in agreement with Nitish because he wanted the quota to benefit the genuinely needy among the backwards and also stood for constitutional guarantees for the rights to education and to employment. The ideas that had guided Nitish's suggestions were not entirely his own: they were taken from his readings of Lohia and understanding of JP. It was only in the fashioning of them into a formula that assuaged everyone's concerns that he showed himself to be thoughtful and innovative. In the revised formula announced in November 1978, the state government eventually imposed an income ceiling for OBC beneficiaries, reduced the OBCs quota from 26 to 20 per cent and gave 3 per cent quota to the economically backward sections of the upper castes and 3 per cent to women.

Karpoori's quota policy agglomerated the lower castes under the leadership of the upper backwards; but it sent out a negative message to the polity at large, and the upper castes in particular, that he had announced the policy to divert people's attention from the main issues— such as soaring prices, low agricultural and industrial growth, high unemployment and police atrocities—which the Janata government had failed to resolve. The policy subdivided the already divided organization of the Bihar Movement along forward–backward lines, though many in the Yuva Janata including Nitish tried their best to contain the fissures. Nitish was among the leaders of a procession taken out by Yuva Janata through the streets of Patna on the fourth anniversary of the movement on 18 March 1978, with members drawn from all castes, to express commitment to a casteless approach to social revolution. However, the forward–backward divide was complete and such processions could only play a symbolic role.

Upper-caste Janata MLAs wouldn't rest until they had thrown Karpoori out of chief minister's office. At the national level, Karpoori drew his strength from the patronage of Charan Singh who seemed to be losing out in his fight for pre-eminence against Morarji. By the time the Janata government completed two years in March 1979, a split was looming large over it. Taking advantage of the caste divisions in the national government, the upper-caste Janata MLAs struck up an overarching alliance with the Dalit and tribal MLAs to reduce Karpoori's support in the party legislature group to a minority, forcing him to resign in April 1979.

The upper-caste MLAs propped up a Dalit, Ram Sundar Das, as new chief minister. Das did not jettison Karpoori's reservation policy but immediately announced an amendment to it, which enlarged the quota percentage to include even those from the OBCs who were recruited in open competition. For instance, if there were twenty jobs, four (20 per cent) would be reserved for OBCs. If two OBC candidates were recruited in the reserved category and two in the general category, the quota would be deemed to have been filled.

Clearly, the Das amendment was designed by his upper-caste puppeteers to restrict the share of the OBCs in all government jobs to 20 per cent, irrespective of economic status. That would veritably ensure the perpetuation of upper-caste control over the bureaucracy, the second most important organ of the state after the legislature, with 53 per cent share of jobs to them (all of 50 per cent general category plus 3 per cent quota for the economically backward among them). The upper castes could also add much of the 3 per cent quota for women to their favour (at least 75 per cent of it, or 2 per cent quota), taking their total representation in the bureaucracy to 55 per cent, because most women going for higher education were from their communities.

Das's boat rocked very hard in only three months when Charan and Raj Narain led the former Bharatiya Lok Dal and Socialist Party out of the Janata parliamentary group, bringing down Morarji. This left no option to the President but to invite Charan to take over as prime minister but on the condition that he prove his majority in the Lok Sabha. The Janata legislature group in Bihar split too, with Karpoori joining the Charan–Narain formation, Lok Dal (on election records, Janata Party [Secular]). Karpoori started working right away to instigate another split in the Janata legislature group and to negotiate support from other parties, including the Congress and the CPI and CPI(M), to gather a majority to become chief minister again. But they all gave him a cold shoulder.

The split forced most members of the Yuva Janata, including Nitish, to cast their lot with the Lok Dal where anti-establishment socialists, the SSPites were dominant rather than with the Janata Party headed by Chandra Shekhar, which largely comprised former members of Jan Sangh, former Congressmen and former establishmentarian socialists, the PSPites.

The second half of 1979 proved to be a highly unscrupulous period in Indian politics, with Charan and Narain, 'sworn' enemies of Indira, supplicating her support to prove their majority. Indira had already begun to see the chance of a comeback with the Janata split; she played along with Charan till he was discredited in the public eye as a Congress puppet, and eventually refused to support him, forcing him to resign and obliging the President to declare fresh national elections in January 1980.

Indira won two-thirds majority with her slogan 'Vote for a Government that Works' against the background of Janata's preoccupation with personality clashes, factional intrigues and the coalition's ideological fissures that did not allow the historic first non-Congress national government to take the country ahead with a democratic and progressive vision, which the people had expected it to do. Her party, which had drawn a blank in Bihar in the 1977 election, bagged 30 of the state's 54 parliamentary seats. The anger of the people, particularly the upper castes, against the Janata splitters was so fierce that even the student hero of the Bihar Movement, Lalu Prasad, who had won from Chhapra by a huge margin in 1977, lost. Upper-caste voters supported the Janata Party (now shorn of its anti-establishment socialists) candidate as a bloc while the backward-caste vote got divided, with the Congress candidate, Budhan Yadav slicing away a substantial Yadav vote.

Eager to take advantage of the popular swing, Indira got all the state assemblies dissolved where her party was not in power, including Bihar. The announcement of state Assembly elections in June triggered more de-alignments in the Janata camp. The members of the former Jan Sangh came out of the Janata Party to revive their old organization with the new name of Bharatiya Janata Party (BJP). Their aim was to claim the Janata legacy with their old and sound constituency at its core, backed by the new segments of urban and rural population they had won with their 'immaculate' conduct as leaders and participants in the JP movement. Raj Narain, the eternal dissident, broke away from Charan Singh with a tiny group and decided to field candidates in almost every constituency in Bihar and UP with the bravado of coming to power with a majority.

A majority of former socialist youth-wingers, including Lalu and Nitish, stayed with Charan when Raj Narain left him, and they were rewarded with party tickets for the June elections by the state party leader Karpoori Thakur. The multiple splits had scattered 'winnable' candidates over the disintegrated Janata camp; with a short supply of such candidates in Lok Dal, Lalu and Nitish faced no opposition to their selection. Lalu decided to move away from Chhapra where the upper castes had mauled him and the backwards were not all behind him either and try his luck at Sonepur, closer home. Nitish chose to fight from Harnaut again.

In the preceding three years Nitish had built up a base for himself in Harnaut constituency. People had seen he was regularly interacting with them and making a sincere effort to get their issues resolved.

The Kurmis saw him as a very promising leader of their caste. However, they were unhappy with him for suggesting exclusion of the better-off sections of the backward castes in his job reservation formula.

Kurmis dominated the demography of Harnaut, and the Kurmi elite decided which way the community should vote—and the elite would not vote for a man who advocated denial of job quota to them.

The Kurmis of Harnaut were a part of the statewide pro-reservation mobilization. Bhola Singh addressed pro-reservation gatherings opposing the Nitish formula of economic criteria.

Nitish was indeed in a sorry state. He lost the support of the upper castes he had enjoyed in 1977 because Karpoori's reservation policy alienated them. They were aware that Nitish's formula addressed upper-caste concerns, but they were not ready to support him because he was Karpoori's candidate, and Karpoori was at that point the most hated man to the upper castes.

Then there was a third problem. The pro-reservation campaign brought about solidarity of backward castes under the leadership of the upper backwards. With that happening, the upper backwards—the Kurmis, Yadavs and Koeris—began to fight over the mantle of leadership. Old social rivalries between them were accentuated.

In Harnaut, this rivalry helped the selection of Braj Nandan Yadav by the Congress (Urs)—a new national party formed by a group of prominent Congressmen who left Indira in 1978. Most of the Yadavs backed Braj Nandan. To Nitish's misfortune, the Congress(U), which had fought the January 1980 elections to the Lok Sabha in alliance with the Lok Dal, decided not to share seats with them in the Assembly elections.

Also, the Kurmis did not seem to have come out of the Belchhi fixation. They had backed Bhola Singh the last time because he had openly supported their demand for withdrawal of criminal cases against the Belchhi accused. In the weeks following Karpoori's announcement of the reservation policy, Bhola organized rallies in concert with other backward leaders, voicing support to the policy and asking the state government to release the Belchhi accused. Bhola's message to Karpoori was that he could not claim to be a champion of the well-being of the backward castes without 'ending the injustice' of 'framing' the members of these castes 'without any evidence'.

Bhola had moved to a neighbouring constituency, because this time in Harnaut the Kurmis were backing Arun Kumar Singh, one of the main accused in the Belchhi case, who stood as an independent. The word of mouth sent by the heads of the Kurmi community was: 'The government is bent upon sending Arun to the gallows. Let us save him by electing him MLA.'

The appeal touched Kurmi hearts because the Congress, which prided itself as a protector of Dalits, appeared most likely to return to power in the state. If Belchhi had come into national focus portraying the Kurmis as 'scoundrels', much of the credit went to Indira who paid a visit to the village in August 1977, five months after she lost power. She made the visit to revive her old constituency of Dalits, and she succeeded in her mission despite the fact that she did not stay but for a few minutes in the village and did not talk to any of the relations of the victims who had waited the whole day to tell her of their gruesome experiences.

There was no metalled road from Harnaut town to Belchhi, and the dirt track was waterlogged or muddy from the recent flooding caused by heavy rainfall. After a few kilometres by jeep, Indira was helped on to the back of an elephant which took her to Belchhi. The picture of her on an elephant that appeared in the media the following day drew the nation's attention to the troubles the 'maharani' had taken to meet the poorest of the poor. She made it even better by paying a long visit to the ailing JP at his Patna house the following day, signifying her apology for the Emergency that had proved harsh to the nation and personally to his health. It worked for Indira. But it was going to 'ruin' the Kurmis.

The paradox of Nitish's identity in the election was that while the upper castes and the Yadavs saw him as a Kurmi, the Kurmis did not see him as a Kurmi. They saw him as a liberal who would not stand for the interests of the community. The aggressive elements among the Kurmis campaigned against him and even went to several villages with arms on the day of polling to rig the vote in favour of Arun Kumar Singh. Some of Nitish's election managers wished they too had armed groups to counter those of the rivals. Narendra recalls:

> Nitish had taken the plunge in electoral politics in the mistaken belief that he would be able to win popularity as a good man. But the 1980 election showed us how foolish he and his campaign managers like us were. You can gain popularity as a good man but you cannot win an

election purely on the strength of your goodness. The example of JP was there before us: the man who was the nation's second most popular man after Nehru in the early years of free India lost so traumatically in elections he gave up electoral politics. Saints make poor politicians. Having seen the free play of arms and muscle and total lack of scruples during that election, we were forced to think that no matter what name you give to it and what forms of it you use, a little bit of sinning is necessary even by a saint to be a lawmaker.

Nitish lost the election by about 5,000 votes to Arun Kumar Singh. The second defeat in the elections came as a heavy blow to him. His belief in himself was shaken.

Lalu had pulled it off in Sonepur. In a triangular contest, he had beaten the sitting MLA, Ram Sundar Das, who had played the upper-caste puppet in the coup against Karpoori in the Janata legislature group in July 1979, as well as a strong Congress candidate, Jawahar Singh.

# 6

## the ladder to power

In 1980 the Congress returned with a tally of 169 in a 324-member House—a wafer-thin majority but remarkable nevertheless, compared to 57 in the typhoon of June 1977—in one of the bloodiest elections in the state that claimed at least a hundred lives, mostly of ordinary supporters of political parties. The party enormously profited both from the overall public disappointment with the Janata and the particular indignation of the upper castes directed at the Lok Dal for making the OBC quota their holy grail. A majority of the upper castes voted the Congress; the rest were divided between the Janata Party and the Bharatiya Janata Party.

The most striking thing about the election was that quota politics failed to bring the Lok Dal into power. The underlying assumption of quota politics was that the OBCs formed a numerical majority in the state. Some Lok Dal leaders put the figure at 52 per cent, others even higher. The election, which was virtually a referendum on Karpoori's OBC quota, busted the illusion of quota champions of depending on the simple arithmetical equation that demographic majority equals parliamentary majority.

Only 42 of the 254 candidates of Lok Dal, that is, under 17 per cent, won; as many as 132 of them forfeited their security deposits for not getting the bare minimum vote set by the Election Commission. The party received only 15.63 per cent of the total vote, which clearly suggested that the majority of the OBC vote was shared among other parties.

Also, the 1980 election proved once again that an alternative to the Congress could be built only with a conglomeration of left–right–

centrist parties in the Opposition and not by a single party identifying itself with a single segment of society. While it was true that popular disappointment with the Janata Party created a favourable environment for a Congress victory, what tilted the balance in its favour was the splitting of votes among the many Janata avatars.

In the 1977 state election, the Janata Party had received 42.68 per cent of the total vote; in 1980, Lok Dal received 15.63, BJP 8.41, Janata 7.21 and the others together 1.67 per cent, which added to 32.92 per cent. The number of seats this aggregate percentage brought was 77, which was far higher than the 57 the Congress had got in 1977.

Had the Janata avatars fought as a conglomerate, they would have won many more seats as they would have avoided splitting the vote. This went to show that there was a huge electoral base out there for a non-Congress polity, provided you knew how to perform on the political stage to get it. The Lok Dal leaders—Charan Singh at the national level, Karpoori at the state level and emerging ones such as Lalu and Nitish—understood this very well but they had their own difficulty: in a conglomerate they were inevitably dwarfed and repressed by upper-caste leaders. They were not averse to working with the upper castes, but they had to come before them.

It was with the objective of charting a political course independent of the upper castes that the Socialist Party–BLD group leaders had pressed ahead with quota politics. The aim was more psychological than actually transforming the character of the bureaucracy through OBC representation. There were very few jobs offered by the government annually, but the thesis advanced by quota politicians was that the appointment of even one from a backward caste would make the whole community feel proud.

Although the Lok Dal leaders were disappointed by the results of the state election they were determined to persist with their quota politics. They were driven by the optimism that drawing support from the history of cultural, economic and political movements of the backward castes they would be able to build a strong constituency for gaining a parliamentary majority and power in the coming years. The second Backward Classes Commission headed by Mandal submitted its report to Indira Gandhi towards the end of 1980. One of its chief recommendations was 27 per cent reservation in national government services and educational institutions for the OBCs.

The Lok Dal demanded implementation of the Mandal recommendations, but Indira kept putting it off. The early 1980s witnessed mounting pressures for its implementation. Charan Singh addressed a huge rally of backward castes at the Boat Club near Parliament House on 18 February 1982. The Congress, said Charan Singh, had not implemented the recommendations of the first or second Backward Classes Commission because it wanted to perpetuate upper-caste domination over backward castes.

Despite persistent demands from the Opposition, Indira procrastinated on Mandal. She did not want to do anything to hurt the upper castes who had come back to her after voting against her in 1977 in anger over her authoritarianism and pro-Dalit actions during the Emergency. Indira knew that the upper castes, comprising most of the rural gentry and urban intelligentsia, formed the head of the Congress voter base, and the Dalits and Muslims its body.

The upper caste–Dalit–Muslim alliance—a 'coalition of extremes', as American political scientist Paul Brass puts it—was not invented by Indira. Its architect was Mahatma Gandhi. In the middle of its anti-colonial struggle the Congress realized that upper castes dominated its national and state organizations, forcing Dalits and Muslims, the two pariah communities, to build their own organizations to represent their interests. The British were taking advantage of these social fissures with what popularly came to be known as the 'divide and rule' policy. Gandhi, the supreme leader of the Congress, developed unique strategies—such as a campaign to eradicate untouchability, reservation of parliamentary seats for Dalits and support to the Khilafat movement—to bring Dalits and Muslims into the party and present a united India to the British.

Indira wrecked the coalition of extremes during her extra-radical tilt (by Congress standards) towards Dalits during the Emergency and paid dearly for it. Her Dalit welfare programme made Congress supporters in the upper-caste rural gentry feel that the party is no more what it used to be: that is, relying on social rhetoric and stray action against untouchability and never pressing the Dalits' economic issues. Dalits incurred the wrath of the rural gentry by petitioning for the benefits offered by Indira—such as homestead land, payment of minimum wages and freedom from bonded labour—and they were attacked for their 'insolence' in many villages even during the Emergency.

She made amends in 1980 by returning to the soft line on Dalit issues. She also went an extra mile to please the upper castes in Bihar by giving them a major share in the state cabinet and making a Brahman, Jagannath Mishra, chief minister. Three years later, when Mishra had to bow out as a result of factional and personal rivalries within the party's state legislature group, Indira chose a Rajput, Chandra Shekhar Singh (of the Congress), as his successor.

Rajiv Gandhi was to follow his mother's high-caste appeasement policy in Bihar during the Assembly's next term from 1985 to 1990. He appointed four chief ministers, due to exigencies caused by factional wars, who were all upper caste—three Brahmans and one Rajput. The Congress had reduced the chief minister's office to a game of musical chairs with participation restricted to the upper castes: this feeling was to grow like a prairie fire among the upper backwards. It dropped like a gift of god into the lap of Lalu Prasad when he became chief minister in March 1990.

Congress did not realize its blunder until the full blast of the backward-caste storm hit it in the 1990s. Its efforts to keep itself in power with its historical coalition of extremes headed by the upper castes had resulted in the alienation of the backward castes. The tragedy of the Congress was that its efforts to retain even its Gandhian coalition had failed. This coalition had 'worked' during the three decades from Independence to Emergency largely as a barter of security for vote. The Dalits in the villages were too poor, weak and helpless to defy the upper-caste landowners, who were their employers and lent them grains when their families had nothing to eat and money when they had a wedding or illness or funeral in the family. So, they did what the 'masters' asked them to do in the polling booth: stamp on the Congress symbol. There was no open defiance, of course, but the masters gave no scope for secret defiance, either: as the organs of the state always favoured them, the polling booths were located far away from Dalit streets, in quarters under the control of the upper castes.

Dalits were left with no choice but to vote for the Congress, as high-caste bullies would watch them even though the vote was supposed to be secret. It was also not uncommon for the upper castes to ask Dalits not to 'take the trouble' of leaving their work to queue up at the booth, because the polling officials would allow the upper castes to vote in their names.

The coalition of the upper castes and Dalits that stood the Congress in good stead during pre-Emergency years was thus involuntary. It was merely a political extension of the upper-caste control over the economic life of Dalits.

A number of factors were motivating Dalits to break out of the involuntary coalition—growth of education and representation in the bureaucracy and legislature; participation in left campaigns for freedom from bondage, fair wages, secure sharecropping tenancy and cultivable land; armed struggles against landlord tyranny by the radical left; the passing of stricter laws in their favour; the hyper-Congress rhetoric.

Indira's opportunistic attempt to provide some 'real' economic benefits to Dalits catalysed the rupture of the coalition. If the landowners had no economic control over Dalits they could no longer have any political control. Indira after her comeback in 1980 whittled down her Dalit radicalism, which had a calming effect on the Congress locomotive, the upper castes, but a disjunctive impact on its carriages, the Dalits. This, together with the alienation of the backwards, as well as that of the Muslims, was to virtually reduce the Congress to the margins of Bihar politics in the 1990s and 2000s.

The coming of the backwards on to the centre stage of politics in Bihar in the 1990s would have been but a wild fantasy even for the most ardent champions of quota politics in the early 1980s. The main actors on the 1990s' centre stage, Lalu and Nitish, were still in an incubatory stage, one training as a legislator, the other struggling to be one. Lalu had a head start over Nitish with more than two and a half years as an MP and with the Sonepur victory, but in the state Lok Dal hierarchy he was in the third or fourth line, with Karpoori at the top, followed by elder socialists Hukumdeo Narain Yadav and Anup Lal Yadav.

In the years immediately following his first defeat in 1977, Nitish was seen to be associated more with 'idealist' politics than 'practical' politics. He spent a lot of time with his mentor Kishan Patnaik at the spartan office of *Samayik Varta*. JP was still alive, and issues raised by the Bihar Movement were still being discussed and pursued.

By the early 1980s, the Bihar Movement was extinct, the *Samayik Varta* had folded up, JP had passed away and Kishan Patnaik had moved out of Patna.

Pragmatism instead of idealism was in the air. The Lok Dal in Bihar, as in the other states, was carrying on a campaign for the implementation of the Mandal Commission recommendations. Nitish organized meetings in support of the demand. His interactions with Lalu increased during these years. They both participated in a Lok Dal national rally in Delhi.

But in 1982 the Lok Dal split. Several leading figures, including Devi Lal, H.N. Bahuguna, Biju Patnaik and Karpoori Thakur were 'expelled' from the party by president Charan Singh for opposing his ideas and suggestions and 'conspiring' to remove him from the leadership. The expelled leaders claimed they were the real Lok Dal and elected Karpoori as president. Two years later, the Lok Dal (Karpoori) and Lok Dal (Charan) reunited as Dalit Mazdoor Kisan Party (DMKP), which within a few months was renamed Lok Dal.

Whatever the name, the cohesion was missing. 'What have I got myself on to, a disintegrating ship?' Nitish thought. For some months he stayed away from Karpoori and joined the Janata Party headed by Satyendra Narain Sinha. Lalu joined Lok Dal (Charan). Nitish was moving from party to party: from SSP to BLD to Janata to Lok Dal to Lok Dal (Karpoori) to Janata to DMKP back to Lok Dal. The graph of his political career had moved as much up as down, leaving him in the early 1980s as a man without any title in the party, legislature or society. How would he introduce himself to others: as a jobless engineer, twice loser in Assembly elections, an important student leader of the extinct Bihar Movement?

Of course, his crisis to create a socially respectable identity was not his alone: it was shared by Manju, who had begun to find her feet in Patna as a home science teacher at a school in Gulzarbagh in a far-eastern part of the city. She had been staying with her brothers at a modest house her father built at Kankarbagh in near-east Patna since the late 1970s. A son was born to her on 20 July 1980, bringing joy to Nitish and her, but also greater demands on her time and purse—and increased moral pressure on Nitish to set himself up quickly to be able to bring home an income. Manju continued to manage her expenses with her meagre salary as a schoolteacher. Her parents and brothers could not help suggesting to Nitish every now and then that he do something for a living; he must give a decent life to his wife and son. Manju's family was economically better-off than Nitish's. Sometimes the advice from her parents and brothers was tinged with snobbery, which hurt Nitish; this was one of the reasons that strained his relations with Manju.

A man who had failed twice to win an election and was a jobless husband and father did not have anything to depend upon except determination to reach his destination. There were nights when anxiety wouldn't allow Nitish to sleep. He was not even carrying out the duties expected of a son. His family had fallen on bad times. His father had passed away at his Bakhtiyarpur home in 1978 when Nitish was in the midst of a Bihar Movement youth camp at Serai in Vaishali district. After his father's death, the family found it difficult to find cash that used to be available from his fees. The Kalyanbigha farms provided the family food round the year and also some cash from sale of surplus but not much.

Nitish remembers how he used to commute between Bakhtiyarpur and Patna in the crowded coaches of ordinary passenger trains that carried milk and vegetable vendors, lower-grade government officials, litigants, the ailing, students and pickpockets every day. Quite a few of them travelled without tickets, preferring to risk being caught in a sporadic inspection and paying a fine than paying for tickets daily. Nitish never did so, even though he would not have much left after buying his ticket and a morning newspaper for reading through the hour-long journey. There were days when he would travel standing, though it was rare because someone or the other would recognize him and offer him their seat.

Rail commuters in Bihar enjoy arguing on current issues: it tells of their ingenuity in mitigating the discomforts of the travel as well as of their high political consciousness. With a professional politician in their midst, the passengers around him would get even more excited to debate issues. And that would provide a good opportunity for Nitish to launch into expository sessions. He took it as constituency-building.

Nitish's visits to Patna were to keep himself politically active—and politically visible. Whether it was deliberations in the party or Yuva Lok Dal or any of their protest activities, he put all seriousness in what he did.

There would be quite often long or short idle conversations with Yuva Lok Dal officials or younger MLAs such as Lalu in a room in the MLA Club. Nitish frequently met Karpoori—who was leader of the Opposition in the Assembly and also the party's national president—on issues or just on a courtesy visit.

More than once, Karpoori offered Nitish help in getting some job as an engineer. 'You can do the job temporarily, just to tide over the present economic difficulties, until you get a break in legislative politics,' Karpoori told him. Nitish said he wanted to do nothing but politics and was ready to go through difficulties until he achieved his objective.

Nitish had to visit Delhi now and then in order to go round and meet the top leaders—Devi Lal, H.N. Bahuguna, George Fernandes, Sharad Yadav—to keep himself abreast of what was happening and also to cultivate them. He also had to go to Delhi to attend the Yuva Lok Dal national executive meetings. For all his travel and other expenses—daily to Patna and occasionally to Delhi—he got nothing from the party.

For about a couple of years after losing the election in 1980 he could somehow manage with the savings from the election funds he had been able to collect. But then he completely ran out of money. The period between 1982 and 1984 was when he was virtually penniless. 'On many days during the period,' Nitish reminisces, 'I had to skip lunch.' Forever in want of money but reluctant to ask anyone for help, he would sometimes very embarrassedly accept a few hundred rupees with a return train ticket to Delhi from his eldest brother-in-law Devendra Singh who was a ticket reservation clerk at Patna railway station.

Devendra Singh, who had sympathies with the CPI(M), often in good humour teased Nitish as a *phaltoo*, good-for-nothing fellow, but both he and Usha were actually very fond of him and treated him as guardians would. They were the ones who often provided him the cash to buy kurta-pyjamas or jackets, to travel to Delhi and to move about in Patna in cycle rickshaws. Narendra, who had become a contractor, also helped Nitish at times, as did other friends.

Nitish visited his father-in-law's house at Kankarbagh frequently to spend time with his wife and son, but he would not reside there at a stretch. It would have been more convenient for him to carry on his political activities in Patna if he stationed himself in the city. But he decided to stay at Bakhtiyarpur for three reasons: he would be closer to his constituency; he could take care of his widowed mother; and he could avoid being a *ghar jamai*, a permanent resident at his wife's natal house—a pejorative in the cultural milieu of Bihar.

Some good things were happening though, in the midst of Nitish's personal and political blues in the early 1980s. The Jagannath Mishra government was earning unpopularity on many scores. I was stationed in Patna as a roving correspondent of the *Indian Express* towards the end of the year 1980 when I was told of a gory police campaign in Bhagalpur to blind criminal suspects by puncturing their eyes with a needle and then pouring acid into them—a deterrent to bring down the crime graph in the district. I made my investigations and exposed it in a series of reports in the paper. The nation was revolted by it: Indira, who was trying hard to rebuild her credentials as a democrat, howled at Mishra for allowing such open disregard for the rule of law and human rights. She tried making it up by expressing regret in Parliament: 'The nation's head hangs in shame.'

The superintendent of police of Bhagalpur at that time happened to be Vishnu Dayal Ram, an incorruptible officer and a close friend of Nitish, Kaushal and all of us from university days. My reports put him in a bad light, and following the suspension of several junior police officials of the district, departmental action against him too seemed to be in the offing. I met Nitish and Kaushal—who was then regional head of an insurance company in Patna—twice or thrice during the period, but neither of them ever made even a discreet or indirect suggestion that I restrain from reporting anything further that could go against Ram.

Even though Nitish believed the media may have overdone it, he preferred to leave it for a fair inquiry to settle the accountability for the horrid chain of blindings. The political fallout of the exposé benefited the Opposition of which he was a part. When he spoke to the media on the issue he, like other Lok Dal leaders, presented it as proof of the Congress's disregard for the rule of law.

Nitish had always been very good at cultivating the media; in the early 1980s he strengthened his contacts. This was the time when the media was gradually turning against the Mishra regime. Mishra too was very unhappy with the media. He lost his patience when a local newspaper published reports implicating him for having obtained loans from the Bihar State Urban Co-operative Bank against forged documents. Working on an overdrive, Mishra's law department drafted a Bihar Press Bill with provisions for fine and imprisonment for the publication of 'scurrilous' reports. The media reacted to it with protest meetings and processions, not only in Bihar but across the country.

The Opposition presented the bill as one more proof of the Congress's lack of faith in democracy. Nitish was a prominent voice in the Opposition in support of scrapping the bill. He led protests and addressed meetings; he was arrested and was imprisoned for about a month.

Mishra was finding it difficult to cope with not just the Opposition attacks but also factional assaults within the party. He had to constantly fight off the intrigues of his cabinet colleagues and MLAs. The consequence was a complete absence of cohesion on approaches to the pressing problems of the state. Indira sacked Mishra after the Congress lost a by-election to the Assembly in Chandi in Nalanda district to a joint candidate of the Opposition in May 1983.

The assassination of Indira by two of her Sikh bodyguards on 31 October 1984, bringing in Rajiv as prime minister, however, turned the situation once again in favour of the Congress. In the Lok Sabha elections less than two months later, Rajiv won with a landslide majority riding on national sympathy. Of Bihar's 54 seats, the Congress took 50, with the Lok Dal, Janata Party, Congress (Jagjivan) and CPI getting one each. In 1980 the Lok Dal, then fighting as Janata Party (Secular), had won five seats.

In Chhapra, Lalu Prasad as Lok Dal candidate came third with 28.27 per cent of the total votes polled, trailing behind Ram Bahadur Singh of the Janata Party (35.91) and Bhism Prasad Yadav of the Congress (30.20).

Nitish chose not to fight the Lok Sabha election. Going by the emotional upsurge in favour of Rajiv that brought a virtual sweep for the Congress in the constituencies of Patna and neighbouring districts, Nitish could only thank his sixth sense for not falling to the temptation as Lalu did and thus saving himself the shock and embarrassment of yet another defeat.

Nitish was preparing himself for the Assembly election in June 1985, but Rajiv, buoyed up by his thumping majority, advanced it to February. That gave Nitish too little time. He hardly had the funds to quickly set up a campaign. The Lok Dal gave him the Harnaut ticket, a jeep and Rs 1 lakh—in an election where leading candidates spent Rs 10 lakh on an average.

I remember meeting him at the MLA Club around that time. We chatted about this and that for a while when I asked him, despite an inner warning that I was touching a raw nerve, what his prospects this time were. 'Don't know. A hundred factors work in an election,' he replied. Then he flashed me a beatific sort of smile and said: 'I have told Manju: Let me try just one more time. If I fail I shall retire from electoral politics.'

At the back of his mind he was already picturing himself as a castaway in electoral politics. He had the examples of his icons JP and Lohia before him. But the harsh reality was that he did not know where he would stand in politics without being elected a lawmaker. He had nothing of the charisma of his icons. He would just be marginalized and forgotten. Without a position and a salary he would fail to command respect in society, in his and Manju's families. The dread of all that made him stretch himself to the maximum in this election campaign.

Manju was bowled over by Nitish's vow to renounce electoral politics. She wanted him to win. She kept his spirits high by appearing cheerful, optimistic and cooperative. And she helped him with money. She poured out all her savings from her school salary to his election kitty: twenty thousand rupees. Not a royal sum, but a huge emotional boost to Nitish.

Politically, the Congress seemed invincible across the state. But there were some factors in Nitish's favour in Harnaut: appreciation for his work towards resolution of their problems; wearing out of the caste frenzy among the Kurmis generated by Belchhi; and a feeling among several voters—Kurmis and of other castes—that the man they had rejected twice deserved to be given a chance.

At one of his large public meetings in Harnaut, Nitish said that this was the last time he was asking them to vote for him, and if they did not elect him he would never again fight an election in his life. 'When I made the announcement,' Nitish recalls, 'the gathering was stunned into silence. I could see the eyes of some of those sitting in front turn moist. It had touched their emotional chord.'

Kaushal and I spent a day with Nitish during the campaign and saw the sympathy for him among the voters. As we took leave of him in the evening, he said in Magahi, beaming, shaking our hands warmly, '*Abri jeet jaibau* (This time I'm going to win).'

The one thing many voters had come to like about him was that he had not dropped out, not stopped visiting them and always been there to take up their issues during the past eight years. He looked unaffected by his defeats and never discriminated against those who didn't vote for him: he was seen as sincere, hard-working, focused. And the greatest thing, unlike other politicians: not interested in money. A simple, straight, spartan fellow with a determined soul.

Yet, elections are not won solely on good image. The armed groups that took control of several booths and rigged polling in the last two elections in favour of the patrons of Kurmi militancy were still out there, ready to be provisioned and paid. The young men who constituted these groups lived in different villages; most possessed illegal guns. On the eve of polling, they would collect at a prearranged point to be assigned target booths by their leaders who dealt with the election managers of the candidate who hired them.

Nitish had lost a large number of votes in the booths captured by Kurmi armed groups in 1977 and 1980, and his campaign managers were keen that they be stopped from doing so this time. But how? There were three ways it could be done: one, Nitish's voters put up resistance to rigging; two, the armed gangs were prevented by the administration; and three, Nitish hired hooligans to deter them.

Voters would not be ready to risk their lives for a vote, so no resistance could be expected from them. However, to Nitish's good luck, the superintendent of police of Nalanda district that time, Ram Chhabila Singh, who had jurisdiction over the Harnaut constituency, happened be a close relation of Narendra who was managing his election a third time. Two days before the polling day Narendra met Singh to tell him about the armed groups planning to capture booths for Nitish's rival. Singh wanted precise information. Late in the evening Nitish met Singh at his official residence with a detailed list of the names and addresses of the key members of the armed groups.

Singh's intervention was swift. Within twenty-four hours most of the goons were arrested and their illegal arms were seized. Some subordinate police officials who were colluding with them had no choice but to go after them when their district chief instructed them. In two or three sensitive places, Ram Chhabila Singh led the raiding police party himself. Some hooligans fled the constituency to avoid arrest. The plans of Nitish's rival—Arun Kumar Singh, the Kurmi caste hero from the Belchhi massacre who had defeated him as an independent in 1980—went haywire.

However, Nitish's campaign managers took no chances. There were men with licensed and unlicensed guns even among ardent supporters of Nitish, but neither his campaign managers nor the gun owners had ever thought in the last two elections to make use of this armed power. This time they decided to keep them in readiness as a deterrent to booth looters. Not sure whether Nitish would approve of such marshalling of arms, even if just for deterrence, his campaign managers kept the plan hidden from him.

Hush-hush meetings were held to set up 'booth defence squads' in what were seen as 'sensitive' booths, but then the question arose: what if they had to open fire? The licence holders were given a certified number of cartridges for use in their self-defence; they could be caught if they used them to shoot at booth looters.

And the unlicensed gun owners had firearms but only a few cartridges for their personal defence: when it came to an exchange of fire they had to have a large number of cartridges. Extremely tight and economical on funds, Nitish's campaign managers would not have liked to spend a good amount (about Rs 5,000) on buying rifle cartridges via the contraband route. But they had no other option.

At one of those review meetings with campaign workers that Nitish held usually in the late evenings at the campaign office after spending the day delivering speeches and touring from village to village, he came to know of the 'booth defence squads'. Nobody gave him any detail, nor did he ask for it. And the matter was passed over, his campaign managers interpreting his studied indifference as his silent approval.

Police superintendent Ram Chhabila Singh made the Nitish camp's task easier by asking his subordinates to keep a special eye on the 'sensitive' booths. There was intensified police patrolling in those areas, creating the first line of deterrence to the booth looters. And the result was that Arun Kumar Singh got just 1,500 votes, or 1.6 per cent of the total vote, in the election. Nitish came out the winner with 50,000 votes (53 per cent), with the runner-up, the Congress candidate Vrijnandan Narain Singh, getting 28,600 votes (30.5 per cent).

There was wild dancing and singing outside the counting centre at Biharsharif. Jubilant workers hoisted Nitish over their shoulders, rending the sky with their boisterous chant, *Nitish Kumar Zindabad, Long Live Nitish Kumar!*

Tearing himself away from the celebrations, going on till well past midnight, when Nitish arrived at his home in Bakhtiyarpur, his parents welcomed him with tears of joy. An enraptured Manju waited behind his parents, gazing at him; they smiled as their eyes met, as though telling each other: 'We got there at last.' Nitish bowed to touch his mother's feet who blessed him by marking a red tilak on his forehead. Manju laid out a special dinner of *alu dam*, puris, *kheer* and *pua* that she had prepared for him.

The Congress returned to the state Assembly with a colossal strength, 196 in a House of 324—an increase of 27 seats from 1980. On the Opposition side, only the Lok Dal defied the Rajiv sympathy avalanche to improve its tally from 42 to 46. The BJP shrunk from 21 to 16, the CPI from 23 to 12 and CPI(M) from 6 to 1; and the Janata Party could barely maintain its tally of 13.

Although the Lok Dal emerged as the largest party in the Opposition—which helped Karpoori Thakur become leader of the

Opposition once again—its tally of 46 represented more the failure of his quota politics than its success. Karpoori had announced 26 per cent reservation for OBCs without preparing the ground for it, that is, without mobilizing the 'sainkre saath', or 60 per cent of the state's population supposedly composed of backward castes, Dalits, tribes, Muslims and women.

In any case, it was Lohia's revolutionary Utopia to weld the five social segments together. The impossibility of the lower-backward castes fraternizing with the upper-backward castes was obvious, because the former were economically and socially closer to Dalits. And Dalits could not fraternize with the upper backwards who shunned them socially and exploited them economically. The tribes saw all non-tribals as their exploiters, backward castes included.

The Muslims had no social meeting grounds with the Hindus. What was more, the backward castes and Dalits nearly always formed the mobs that looted and killed Muslims at the outbreak of a riot. The women had no consciousness as a class; upper-caste women would not have a feeling of sisterhood towards women of the backward castes, and neither of them towards Dalit or Muslim women.

The chariot of the socialist movement charging through the social battlefield of Bihar, with Karpoori's quota flying as its pennant, had managed only to federate the three upper-backward castes, the Yadavs, Kurmis and Koeris. These were numerically the largest among the OBCs and right behind the four upper castes in terms of agricultural landholdings, education, employment, entrepreneurship and political muscle. The federation of the 1980s was far more powerful than the federation of the 1930s—the Triveni Sangh—because over four decades of Independence a large number of upper backwards had improved their economic status and now wanted a reflection of it in their political status.

It was riding on the strength of the increased numbers of the upwardly mobile backwards that the socialists in their new avatar as the Lok Dal were charting an independent course. For decades, backward-caste leaders had served as adjuncts to upper-caste leaders. They had not been allowed to take the centre stage. The desire to get out of the confines of adjunction and gain autonomy was growing among them. In going through their myriad avatars, the socialists had reduced the presence of upper castes among themselves. Men from upper castes in the socialist camp were liberals who believed as much in Lohiaite social revolution based on reverse discrimination as their colleagues from the backward castes did. Yet, they were treated as an auxiliary group, supplemental to the backward-caste command. The Lok Dal of the early 1980s represented the infancy of the upper backwards' political autonomy movement, and the Lok Dal of mid-1980s its growing-up years.

Karpoori was nurturing it. He was from the caste of *nais*, barbers, a lower-backward community with a very small population, and had, metaphorically speaking, acted as the midwife to the autonomy movement with his reservation policy of 1978.

It was only when he started losing power to the Yadavs within the Lok Dal in 1987 that he realized he had created a Frankenstein. The Yadavs ganged up to remove him as leader of the Opposition in collusion with the Speaker of the Assembly and a senior Congress MLA, Shiv Chandra Jha, who despised Karpoori. Karpoori enjoyed the support of the majority of the Opposition members and challenged Jha's 'arbitrary' ruling by parading them before the Governor. But Jha did not reverse his ruling. Karpoori was terribly aggrieved by the conspiracy hatched by the Yadav MLAs who had the single largest number (in the Lok Dal legislature party, 19 of the total 42 MLAs, about 45 per cent).

Nitish held Karpoori in great respect. Karpoori had always encouraged the younger generation in the party. He appreciated Nitish's work and made him president of the state Yuva Lok Dal in 1987. Nitish resented Jha's action as he felt Jha had pulled Karpoori down because he had a rivalry with the Congress chief minister Bindeshwari Dubey with whom Karpoori had developed a close working relationship. But Nitish could do little to prevent it, nor could any of the remaining 16 non-Yadav backward MLAs.

Yadavs as a group had begun to assert themselves within the Lok Dal in the mid-1980s. They wanted to be the decision-makers in the party as they represented a caste with the single largest population (11 per cent) in the state. They turned hostile to Karpoori who stood for a fair representation of all castes, particularly the lower backwards, to which category he belonged. Their hostility grew to such an extent that they conspired to defeat him in Samastipur in the Lok Sabha elections in 1984–85. The Yadavs, who made a large segment of the electorate in Samastipur, voted for Karpoori's opponent.

Karpoori became so fearful of the Yadavs that in the 1985 Assembly elections he moved from Samastipur, which he had won in 1980, to Sonbarsa in Sitamarhi district. During the selection of Lok Dal candidates in 1985, Yadav leaders opposed nominations of lower backwards, commending names from their caste. 'You are not interested in giving representation to the poor,' Karpoori lamented, shaking his head in incredulity.

Nearly half of the Lok Dal men elected to the Assembly in 1985 were Yadavs. In the House and the party organization they worked as a pack to undermine Karpoori's position. They had obviously made a plan to oust him and take over the party leadership. Karpoori's supporters remember him commenting after the Yadav MLAs toppled him in collusion with Speaker Jha: 'I would not have faced such humiliation if I were born a Yadav.'

Karpoori was shattered seeing his dream of bringing all the backward classes under one umbrella turn into a nightmare, with the Yadavs lusting for power and disregarding its adverse effect on OBC solidarity. Soon after he was removed from leader of the Opposition office, he fell ill. His diabetes grew worse and started causing complications. He died in February 1988 at the politically young age of sixty-four.

Anup Lal Yadav succeeded Karpoori as the leader of Lok Dal legislature party; the Yadavs had sounded the bugle of their arrival. Being the single largest caste, the Yadavs had been predominant in all socialist avatars. And they had become the deciding force not only on their numerical strength but also by their assertive disposition.

First, the Yadavs, Kurmis and Koeris fought the upper castes. When they managed to edge out the upper castes they quarrelled among themselves. The Yadavs sidelined the Kurmis and Koeris and took over the leadership. Now the Yadavs began to fight Yadavs. Alliances last in politics as long as the war against the common enemy: once the common enemy retreats every constituent returns to its tent in the coalition camp, with the terrible urge to now plant its flag across the camp.

Soon after Anup Lal Yadav took over as officiating leader of the Opposition he began to realize that not all Yadav MLAs were in favour of endorsing him. He was double-crossed by another Yadav—Lalu Prasad. Anup Lal was a socialist of the old school—morally upright and straightforward to the point of being abrasive in speech and dismissive in dealings, showing no regard to who it hurt and not caring for its fallout. Many of the Yadavs, and others in the legislature group too, did not think they could have a way with him if he became leader of the Opposition. They wanted a Yadav who would be pushy, adroit and pugnacious to put the Congress government on the defensive and at the same time be approachable, amenable and flexible to party MLAs.

Lalu had been at it for quite some time. He was among the Yadav MLAs who barely concealed their aversion to Karpoori. He despised Karpoori because he always tried to counter-balance the Yadavs with the other castes in the party and never revealed his plans to anyone. He nicknamed Karpoori Thakur '*Kapati*' (foxy) Thakur.

In the beginning Lalu had no supporter among the Yadav MLAs, except one. There were four or five senior Yadavs who were vying for the post. The dilemma of younger Yadav MLAs was that they did not want Lalu but they also did not want any of the older MLAs to take over.

Nitish decided to back Lalu. They both represented the young generation in the Lok Dal, with their ambitions set high. Despite the fact that Nitish and Lalu were poles apart in attitude, Nitish felt he was the best choice under the circumstances.

He talked to the 16 non-Yadav backward MLAs in the party and convinced them that there was no option but to give primacy to Yadavs in a party wedded to backward-caste politics. Secondly, he told them, they must endorse Lalu despite all their reservations about his eligibility because he represented the younger lot in the party. 'My strategy,' says Nitish, 'was to bring the younger generation into a leadership position. If we had elected an older MLA as our leader we would have had to wait for a long time to emerge on our own. It was aimed to gain a quantum jump in terms of our political careers.'

And so it was that with Nitish's mobilization of non-Yadav MLAs, Lalu staked his claim to the leadership of the Lok Dal legislature group. Arun Srivastava, a journalist, recalls having met Lalu and Nitish in a room at the Assembly at the time. Lalu said to him: 'I have a choice to be the party president or leader of the Opposition. What do you think will be better for me?' Srivastava said, 'Your guru, Nitish, is sitting next to you. He is the best person to give you advice.' Lalu gave a short, amused laugh, and then said, 'Look, my brother, it is power alone that matters. Nobody looks upon you with respect unless you have power. Who even cares to remember a party president's name? That is why I think I should be leader of the Opposition. I will have the rank of a cabinet minister and a beacon-fitted car.'[3]

Lok Dal president H.N. Bahuguna, who was a former Congressman and a Brahman, could not afford to be authoritarian in a party dominated by Jats and Yadavs. He personally preferred Anup Lal for his honesty and integrity, but soon after he arrived in Patna with party leaders Devi Lal and Sharad Yadav, to help the members of the state legislature group formally elect their leader, he sensed that both his colleagues were in favour of Lalu Prasad. Sharad Yadav, a socialist youth-winger like Lalu and Nitish, came into prominence in his state Madhya Pradesh with his victory in a by-election to the Lok Sabha from Jabalpur in 1974. He saw Lalu as a non-serious character and Nitish as just the opposite. He also liked Nitish for his ideological understanding and organizational zeal. Nitish pleaded with him to back Lalu for leadership. Sharad Yadav's own assessment of the situation in the state legislature party also drove him to back Lalu. Devi Lal was ready to support anybody who would not tail behind Bahuguna.

Thus did Lalu jump on to the first step of the ladder to power.

Lalu's further climb could be credited more to the environment created by Congress's misgovernance in the 1980s than to his political dexterity. In the first place, Congress failed to provide a stable government during both terms, 1980–85 and 1985–90, despite enjoying a comfortable majority in the Assembly. Factional bickering pulled down a chief minister before he could do anything meaningful; there were five in all, with an average tenure of two years.

People were left wondering if it wasn't pointless electing the Congress with a formidable majority. Lalu, Nitish and other Lok Dal leaders described the internal coups in Congress in their speeches as *bandar bant*, a distribution wrangled over between upper-caste monkeys, with backward castes denied any piece of it; and it sank in, because among the five chief ministers three were Brahmans and two, Rajputs.

But in the Bihar of the 1980s, land was as much intertwined with politics as caste was. For over two decades after Independence, the Congress had to face serious electoral opposition from the maharajas, rajas and big landlords of the state—who formed their own parties or set up strong lobbies in existing ones, including in the Congress—over the abolition of zamindari. After it succeeded in abolishing zamindari, the Congress, over the next few decades, worked on land issues, such as ceiling, redistribution and tenancy, in a very slow, inoffensive, spasmodic way so as not to alienate the landowners.

The last spurt was witnessed during the Emergency (1975–77) when Indira tried to push harder on land issues and burnt her fingers. Realizing that her comeback had been powered by the mercy of the landowners, and that she could remain in power only if she did not return to her 'communist' ways, she placed upper castes as chief ministers—a policy Rajiv continued.

The 1980s thus marked the decade when the Congress abandoned all land reform programmes that had the potential of alienating the landowning upper castes in Bihar. There was no redistribution of land assets.

During 1983–84 nearly half of the state's population lived below the official 'poverty line', the highest incidence among all states; and landless farm labourers, with marginal cultivators/sharecroppers, formed the bulk of this half-fed population. Labour migration had a very old tradition in Bihar with shiploads transported to plantations in Mauritius and the West Indies, starting from 1834. It had revived in the 1970s, with large numbers going to meet labour demands in the green revolution belt of Punjab and Haryana, and picked up in the 1980s as it had not done in any decade post-Independence.

It was largely owing to the remittances of the migrants, who sometimes worked fourteen hours a day, to their families that as much as 10 per cent of the state's population ate better and managed to climb above the poverty line in a matter of just three years, by 1987–88. So much so that Bihar could feel happy it had now only the second highest incidence of poverty among states, the first being Orissa.

Other factors were also at work to mitigate poverty. The rural poor, comprising landless and marginal peasants, were getting organized in several districts under the banner of radical communist groups. Each group had a 'red army' that was broken up into squads for 'action'; and the 'action' usually involved 'annihilation of class enemies', who could be a tyrannical landowner or an informer from among the poor. The boldest actions were attacks on police stations to loot arms and to engage in several hours, sometimes several days, of combat with the police.

The rural poor demanded social respect and economic justice. Jolted by their armed rebellion, landowners became circumspect and began to treat them more humanly—no more beating for flimsy reasons, no more routine humiliation, no more liberties with their women. On the economic side, the landowners were forced to make concessions to the rural poor on wages, debt recovery and harvest sharing on leased lands. A study observes:

> The rise in real wages [in Bihar] has been really phenomenal between 1970–71 and 1988–89. [As much as] 56.1 per cent increase took place in the case of male labourers, 7.8 in the case of female labourers, which [is] quite impressive in comparison to other states—both high wage and low wage states. The rise in real wages has been particularly pronounced during the 1980s. There are a number of factors behind this rise. Apart from the relatively better performance of the agricultural sector, changes in rural labour market conditions due to out-migration of workers as well as state intervention through wage employment programmes have been the major factors behind it. Besides, in large parts of the state radical movement of the agricultural labourers has been a very important factor behind the rise in wages.[4]

The radical movement not only shook the socio-economic structure, it also made the state realize that it could not just bet on the strong—a rethinking that reflected in the Congress state government's thrust for improvement in life conditions of the rural poor. One of the mantras it adopted came from the party's supreme leader Rajiv Gandhi, who as prime minister represented the youthful, technology-savvy, modern face of India. He had fired people's imagination with his six technology 'missions' that aimed to end underdevelopment in basic areas with the application of science and technology. These missions were: drinking water to every village, total literacy, immunization of children and pregnant women, white revolution, adequate edible oil and telephone connection in every village.

Rajiv began to push the country on to the fast track by accelerating the process of liberalization and modernization of the economy begun by Indira. Since agriculture formed the core of the economy, he urged the instruments of state to increase the coverage of green revolution so that farmers got higher incomes and farm labourers got work, with rise in cropping intensity, round the year. In order to provide employment to farm labourers for lean seasons until the green revolution took place in agriculturally backward areas, he introduced a scheme, Jawahar Rozgar Yojana—the government would hire unemployed farm labourers on daily wages to execute minor public works in rural areas (a road, a culvert, a pond).

The Rajiv years (1984–89) proved to be good both for agricultural growth and poverty alleviation in Bihar. Foodgrain production increased from 10.3 million tonnes in 1984–85 to 14.5 million tonnes in 1988–89. Fertilizer consumption increased from over 200,000 tonnes in 1980–81 to over 600,000 tonnes in 1988–89. Pesticide consumption jumped from 175 tonnes in 1985–86 to 3,000 tonnes in 1987–88. Because of higher growth in agriculture, Bihar's GDP grew at 5 per cent in the Seventh Five-Year Plan (1985–90), 1 per cent higher than in the Sixth Plan (1980–85).

However, this growth was uneven, unstable and temporary, because the state had only pushed things slightly harder and done pretty little to overcome infrastructural, institutional, technological or ecological constraints on agriculture. Irrigation, power and credit, the three main pillars of infrastructure, remained in short supply. By the end of the 1980s, only 38 per cent of area under foodgrains was irrigated. The demand for power was 1,500 MW and the supply only 900 MW, turning private tube wells non-functional with shortage, bad quality or unavailability of energy.

Most farmers still borrowed from private moneylenders because commercial banks were cagey and cooperative banks were captured by a well-ensconced corrupt Congress veteran who got himself chosen as its head at every election. The institutional reforms to establish secure tenancy to sharecroppers or consolidate the scattered holdings of one owner had been given up. The new agricultural technologies were not applied as a system. And initiatives for prevention and control of floods had not gone very far.

For the first two years of Rajiv's reign, Lalu and Nitish had difficulty building support for issues the Lok Dal considered important because people wanted to give Rajiv time to do something. They raised those issues inside the Assembly whenever opportunities arose, but the eagerness in people to hear the Opposition leaders was still missing.

But from mid-1987 onward, the beginning of the disenchantment with Rajiv was palpable. The Congress was butchered by the Lok Dal led by Devi Lal in June 1987 in Haryana state Assembly elections. Over the following months, some of Rajiv's closest colleagues, estranged by his compromising decisions on several issues, left the Congress to form a group called Jan Morcha (People's Front). The leader of the Jan Morcha was Vishwanath Pratap Singh, the former raja of Manda, a small estate in UP, who had donated his entire estate for distribution among the landless to the Bhoodan movement. He was used by Indira as a magnet for Rajput votes and made chief minister of UP and later commerce minister in her cabinet. He had earned reputation as a strong-willed, upright administrator who loved fighting for causes with the passion of a gallant knight.

He was obliged to Indira for giving him opportunities and remained fully loyal to her. When Rajiv took over, his work profile began to change. Rajiv moved him from commerce to finance, where he began to rummage through the income tax statements of the country's top businessmen and to book them for evasion. He cleverly kept leaking news about income tax raids in the media to build up his image. When he ordered the arrest of the leading businessman L.M. Thapar for tax evasion and threatened similar action against Ajitabh Bachchan, elder brother of the Bollywood superstar Amitabh Bachchan, both of whom were close to Rajiv, Rajiv moved him to defence.

There he dug out two deals—the HDW submarines purchase from West Germany, which implicated the late Indira as defence minister, and the Bofors howitzers purchase from Sweden, which implicated Rajiv—and ordered an inquiry into the 'heavy underhand commissions' paid by the supply companies to 'top politicians'. Finding it too much, Rajiv threw him out of the ministry in April 1987, and out of the Congress in July.

V.P. Singh became a national hero. Leaders of the splinters of the 1977–79 Janata Party—barring the BJP that insisted on maintaining a separate identity—who had been trying to reunite saw in him the linchpin of the Opposition wheel. And as in 1967 and 1977, so in 1987, almost like a prophetic decennial avatar, the grand Opposition coalition—left, right and centre—would be reincarnated with the common aim of pooling their fragmented constituencies into a ramming whole.

The four powerful state leaders of Janata splinters—Devi Lal and Karpoori Thakur of Lok Dal (Bahuguna) and Ramkrishna Hegde and Biju Patnaik of Janata Party—fully endorsed the proposal for the formation of a single party. One of the reasons why efforts at reuniting the Janata splinters had not succeeded before the arrival of V.P. Singh on the scene was their disagreement on who would be the leader—the same old persistent question that had ripped the party apart in 1979. The Opposition went for a prominent Congress dissident as they had done in 1967 and 1977: V.P. Singh would be the president of the Janata Dal, the party formed with the merger of the Janata Party, the two factions of the Lok Dal and the Jan Morcha.

Chandra Shekhar, who had been the president of the Janata Party for almost a decade, tried his best to gain leadership of the Janata Dal but accepted V.P. Singh in view of the overwhelming support for him. Soon the Janata Dal set up an alliance, the National Front, with three regional parties—Telugu Desam of Andhra Pradesh, Dravida Munnetra Kazhagam (DMK) of Tamil Nadu and Asom Gana Parishad (AGP) of Assam—and a very minor Congress dissident group, Congress (Sarat), led by the former chief minister of Assam, Sarat Chandra Sinha.

When parliamentary elections were announced for November 1989, V.P. Singh, flowing with the trend of regionalization of Indian politics, gave a lot of autonomy to state leaders in the selection of candidates.

With Charan Singh, Karpoori and Bahuguna dead, Devi Lal took full control of the party in Haryana and Lalu Prasad in Bihar. Chandra Shekhar had succeeded in getting a loyalist Brahman, Raghunath Jha, chosen as the state president of the Janata Dal. But Jha, who started out as a Lohiaite and had moved in and out of various parties, proved an abject failure as a leader and had to be removed in three months. That created space for Lalu and Nitish (who had become secretary general of the Janata Dal) and others of the younger generation to strengthen their hold on the party organization. Lalu and Nitish often made trips to Delhi to meet the party's national leaders and cultivated V.P. Singh and Devi Lal more than Chandra Shekhar.

The Janata Dal's election strategy was to swing the kisan–pichhda, peasant–backward-caste constituency created by the Charan Singh–Socialist Party coalition in the 1970s, in its favour. The party promised to allocate half of the budgetary resources to agriculture and 60 per cent of political offices and electoral nominations to the backward classes, Dalits, tribals, women and Muslims as Lohia had envisaged. However, the motor of the Janata engine was powered by the energy generated by V.P. Singh.

V.P. Singh succeeded in building an image of himself as a great redeemer who had arrived on the scene to liberate the country from the clutches of a prime minister who 'took bribe from foreign companies' and protected unscrupulous big businessmen and had proved himself 'incompetent and vacillating' on critical issues. Although he failed in his efforts to place himself in the popular psyche as a saint in the lineage of Gandhi and JP, he came to be widely seen as a messenger of 'value-based politics'.

Freedom from corruption proved a good cloak for the body of kisan–pichhda politics. The state Janata Dal used the veil (and V.P. Singh's policy of regional autonomy) to distribute more than 80 per cent seats in the 1989 parliamentary elections to the 'backward' classes, a majority of which were upper backwards. Lalu decided to fight for Chhapra and Nitish for Barh. While Lalu had been both MP and MLA, it would be Nitish's first attempt to enter national politics.

Nitish had nursed an ambition to be an MP from the day he decided to join electoral politics. He was forced to fight for an Assembly seat in 1977 because he failed to get a Lok Sabha ticket that year. In 1980 a senior and respected Kurmi leader, Dharmvir Singh, was given the Lok Sabha ticket from Barh as a candidate of the electoral ally Congress(U) by the Lok Dal; Nitish had campaigned for him. In 1984–85 too, Dharmvir Singh contested the seat, though he lost. In 1989, however, the field was clear for Nitish: Dharmvir Singh had passed away, and Nitish had broadened his support by his work in the constituency.

Charan Singh's crusading pro-peasant stands had a heavy influence on Nitish. After all, he had a peasant ancestry. He still was eating out of his fields; his whole family was. Then, most of the communities in his constituency, Harnaut—upper, upper-backward, lower-backward or Dalit—were peasants. And the most important thing, peasant was a secular identity shared by cultivators of all castes. Fighting for peasants, Nitish reckoned, would win him sympathy and support from all castes, which would make the chances of his success better at the next election.

His search for a good peasant cause led him nearer his home and constituency to the Mokama–Barahiya group of tals after he was elected MLA. The tals (tal, a Bihari Hindi term meaning accumulation) made a unique agro-ecological region, a 1,000 sq km, basin-shaped, low-lying area separated from the Ganga by its natural southern levee. The region remained waterlogged from the backwaters of the river during the monsoons (July through September) because the natural drainage systems via the smaller rivers in south Bihar did not reach up to it.

The four-month inundation meant that the owner–cultivators of plots in the tals could sow just one crop in a year. The soil was fertile after the floods receded, and especially very hospitable to pulses—black gram, lentils, peas. 'The region has the potential to become the pulse bowl of Bihar,' a state agricultural document said. But it was beset with problems. The region had been described and discussed in official documents of the state government, but the various ministries had paid virtually no attention to its problems. Leave aside taking measures to improve drainage to prevent its flooding and turn it from mono-cropped to double- or triple-cropped land, governments had introduced none of the interventions associated with the green revolution, such as improvements in technology, agricultural research and extension services to this region.

Nitish saw here an opportunity to make a fundamental contribution to the development of agriculture in the region. He knew something of the problems first-hand because a part of his family farmland at Kalyanbigha was tal, where only lentils grew. Bakhtiyarpur, where he lived, also had a good part of its land as tal. Overall, 15 per cent of agricultural land, or over 30,000 hectares, in the Patna district was tal. He convened a meeting of local political workers in 1986—from the Lok Dal and Yuva Lok Dal and those personally loyal to him—at Bakhtiyarpur and said to them: 'During my tours of the tal region I have found that the peasants face a host of problems. Their condition is pitiable. And it seems to be nobody's concern. There is an urgent need for the tal peasants to get organized and raise their voice so the government can hear.'

He travelled through villages of the tal, sometimes on the pillion of his schoolmate Munna Sircar's motorbike, to find how the peasants reacted to the idea of organizing. The response was positive and warm. Within a few weeks, Nitish convened a meeting of peasants to know how they looked at the problem and the possible solution. The bitterness from government's neglect was palpable in the peasants' speeches. Nitish found no difficulty in getting them to agree to form an organization to fight for state intervention for development of tal agriculture—Tal Sangharsh Samiti. At his initiative, another organization, Nalanda Navnirman Samiti, was also formed for the repair and revitalization of the old zamindari dams over the rivers in the district.

Local leaders and activists of all parties, the Lok Dal, BJP, CPI and CPI(M), joined the two organizations individually. Meetings were held in different parts of the tal region to build up a strong organization. Local branches of the organs of the state, from agriculture to police, began to pay more attention to the complaints of tal peasants. Nitish often led peasant delegations to officers who were baffled by the sharpness and shrillness in the peasants' voices. Nitish encouraged the peasants to speak; he wanted the officers to hear them in order to appreciate their predicament. The list of peasants' grievances was so long it seemed endless.

And you could hardly blame them. They were able to get just one crop from their land in a year and the yield of even that single crop was very low. They were forced to use traditional seeds, because the government did not care to provide them high-yielding seeds. The agriculture department never gave them a demonstration of yield-raising technologies.

Nitish's organizing efforts culminated in a huge rally of tal peasants at the public maidan in Biharsharif, where a resolution was passed demanding that the government solve their problems. Nitish in his speech warned that if no action was taken by the Congress government the Tal Sangharsh Samiti would mount an agitation.

In the Lok Sabha election of 1989, the Lok Dal was helped by several local factors across Bihar, apart from the national issues of Rajiv's corruption, incompetence and indecision. The open wars between the Congress factions resulting in frequent replacement of chief ministers led many people to think they would behave the same way if given a majority; secondly, the Congress would never make someone from the backward castes chief minister.

Upper-backward elites of Bihar were already competing socially, educationally and economically with the upper castes. They had grown self-confident of their talent and traditions and were no longer subordinate to the latter. The reflection of this attitude in politics was inevitable, and this is what the Janata Dal phenomenon represented.

Karpoori Thakur in his second avatar as chief minister (1977–79) and subsequently as Lok Dal president symbolized the change in the upper-backward elites' attitude from appendage to autonomy. V.P. Singh's new avatar as a champion of 'social justice', with the promise of positive discrimination for backward castes in every walk of life, was intended to capitalize on their autonomy sentiment. Lalu put it across in a more direct, earthy, unalloyed, provocative language to the backward castes.

The autonomy sentiment worked well for both Lalu and Nitish. Lalu regained Chhapra after two defeats. Nitish vanquished the tallest backward-caste leader in the Congress, Ramlakhan Singh Yadav, suggesting that the backward castes had transferred their loyalty from the Congress to the Janata Dal.

At the national level, Nitish was seen among the three or four top leaders of the Janata Dal from the state. He had earned the recognition of V.P. Singh. Knowing his work among the peasantry, Singh made him minister of state for agriculture.

In the state, the Janata Dal won 31 of the 54 parliamentary seats. It was not entirely on the strength of a backward-caste upsurge that the Janata Dal had triumphed over the Congress, however. A significant section of the upper castes had voted for the Janata Dal, particularly Rajputs for whom V.P. Singh was the iconic magnet. Rajiv's tactic to reduce Singh's magnetic effect by replacing the Brahman chief minister of Bihar, Bhagwat Jha Azad, with a Rajput of feudal ancestry, Satyendra Narain Sinha (now back in the Congress), eight months before the election fell through. A section of Congressmen had pleaded for a backward-caste successor to Azad but their plea was ignored. Lalu and Nitish, as most other Janata Dal candidates, profited from the support of Rajputs in their constituencies as well as segments of other upper castes, votes that significantly added to their total whose core was made of backward castes.

Another major local factor, which actually sliced away Congress votes in other states too, was the communal violence at Bhagalpur that started a month before the election and continued uncontrollably for almost two weeks. The violence between Hindus and Muslims erupted over the disputed passing of a 'Ramshila' procession through a Muslim-dominated street in the east Bihar town famous for its handloom silks.

Hindus from different states were carrying 'consecrated' bricks to Ayodhya to lay the foundations of a Ram temple on the Babri mosque site. Ramshila (*shila*, foundation) processions, as these marches were called, had sparked communal violence in Sitamarhi, Hazaribagh and a few other towns in the state earlier. Rajiv, in order not to let the entire Hindu vote swing to the BJP, played soft on the issue, with the result that the local administration in Bihar, as in other Congress-ruled states, appeared to the Muslims to be 'cooperating' with the organizers of Ramshila processions. The Muslims of Bhagalpur alleged that the local police joined Hindu mobs to kill Muslims and plunder and burn their houses. Of course, there was violence from the Muslim side too, but most of the nearly 1,000 dead and 45,000 looted or uprooted were Muslims.

Most of those who died were poor Muslims: weavers, rickshaw pullers, bangle sellers, wage labourers. One of the most macabre incidents took place at Logain village. According to eyewitnesses, a mob of about four thousand Hindus, armed with swords, knives and clubs and accompanied by a group of policemen, led by an assistant sub-inspector, with guns ready, attacked the village with a large Muslim population at seven in the morning on 27 October and killed 115 of them within a few hours.

They did not run away after the massacre. In order to confound investigators, they hauled the bodies of the victims to a tank near the Muslim street of the village and dropped them into it. The bodies floated. They pulled them out and carted them to a well and threw them into it. Fearing that the stench of the bodies might still give it away, they pulled them out of the well and carried them to a piece of fallow land. They scooped out the earth down to a couple of feet, buried the bodies in the shallow pits and covered them with earth. Over the following weeks, they hurriedly made beds in the field plot and planted cauliflowers in it.

It was about six weeks later that the administration said it came to know of it and dug out 108 bodies from the 'cauliflower bed'.

The state government called in the army to control the situation; Rajiv flew over to Bhagalpur; but it was too late to repair the damage done to the Congress. Astounded by the government's direct and indirect complicity in the massacres, the bulk of the Muslim community transferred its support to the Janata Dal—and to communist parties where their candidates were stronger—in the 1989 parliamentary elections. The communists, all groups taken together, had never garnered so much support in any parliamentary election before: even the Indian People's Front, the open front of the underground Communist Party of India (Marxist–Leninist Liberation group) won a seat for the first time and huge support in the ten other constituencies it contested.

At the same time, the BJP registered a fantastic growth: from no Lok Sabha seat from Bihar in 1984, they had 9 in 1989. Even in its earlier avatar as Jan Sangh, the party had never won more than 2 parliamentary seats in Bihar. Its rise was attributable to three factors: increased share of upper-caste vote; growing solidarity of Hindus against Muslim 'intransigence' on the surrender of the Babri mosque site for 'reconstruction' of the Ram temple; and rising support for a separate state for tribals of south Bihar.

Bihar set the national pattern: the Congress was trounced, but the Janata Dal encountered a strong presence both of leftists and Hindu nationalists. V.P. Singh, who had conspired with Devi Lal to eliminate Chandra Shekhar in the race to the leadership of the Janata Dal parliamentary group, could claim a majority only with the support both of the left parties and the BJP. As a result, Singh avoided taking decisions or making announcements that would alienate either of them. Inside the party, he was hemmed in by an ambitious Devi Lal, his deputy prime minister and minister for agriculture, his sworn enemy Chandra Shekhar and numerous prima donnas. Elections to six state assemblies were due in less than three months since he took over, and Singh wanted to play safe until he consolidated his position with favourable results.

Within four days of V.P. Singh taking over as prime minister, Rajiv replaced Satyendra Narain Sinha with Jagannath Mishra as chief minister of Bihar. Mishra had good pro-minorities credentials and his return was expected to bring Muslims and Dalits back to the Congress. It was also intended to lead to better management of the internal conflict in the party, because Mishra himself had been a major cause of it for some years. Mishra's Muslim appeal could be traced back to his announcement within two days of taking oath as chief minister in June 1980 that Urdu would be made the second official language in Bihar.

Mishra's announcement came as a fulfilment of the promise the Congress had made in its election manifesto, a promise that was made to pull back those Muslims who had gone over to the Lok Dal with Karpoori Thakur's decision as chief minister in September 1977 to provide 'free scholarships' (exemption from fees) to school and college students of the backward classes among Muslims at par with those of lower backward classes among Hindus. Mishra followed up his announcement with the enactment of a law in December 1980 to enable Muslims to submit applications and petitions in Urdu to state government offices in the districts.

For Dalits though, Mishra held no such special appeal. Probably in Rajiv's eye, he best symbolized the old patron–client coalition of Brahmans, Dalits and Muslims. Mishra could more easily be identified with Indira's 'pro-Dalit' political inclination as he had worked as her party's chief minister during her time than Satyendra Narain Sinha, who had migrated back to the Congress after some years in the Janata Party. Besides, in the raging conflicts between upper-caste and upper-backward landowners on the one hand and landless Dalits on the other in the Bihar countryside, Kuer Sena, the militia of Rajputs (Sinha's caste-men), was in the forefront.

In the past three decades, Dalits had shifted their support to left parties. In the 1989 parliamentary elections, the Indian People's Front (IPF) garnered substantial votes in all the 11 constituencies it fought, largely with the support of the Dalits. In popular perception, the IPF was a 'Dalit party'. There was very little chance of Dalits returning to the Congress, especially when the post-1980 Congress had been wary of not doing anything as radical as speedy land reform during the Emergency. Empty promises could hardly work any more, but the Congress was relying self-deceitfully on the assurances alone. A commentator said:

> Among the first announcements of Mishra after taking over was that his government would acquire surplus land from the big landlords of the state and would distribute it among the landless. A month after his announcement [Hindi daily] *Hindustan* reported on January 7 that the Mishra government is committed to implement land reform but since the file containing the list of big landlords is missing from the secretariat it is unable to do so.[5]

During the first two and a half months of its rule at the Centre, the Janata Dal lost some of its sheen owing to the gulf between V.P. Singh's promises and his actions as a consequence of his dependence on the left parties and the BJP. Yet, the Janata Dal had no choice but to follow the Central model in the Assembly elections in eight states including Bihar. Though it had no official alliance with the left parties or the BJP, it decided not to set up party candidates in 11 seats in which the BJP's winning chances were high, and left 25 seats for the CPI and 8 for the CPI(M).

For all the drumming in later years about its 'secular' credentials, the Janata Dal in the February 1990 state Assembly elections was extremely vague and diplomatic, and not straightforward and emphatic, on issues such as the temple-over-the-mosque-site demand the BJP was using to charge up the Hindu psyche. The strident pro-Muslim oratory for which Lalu was to become famous in the later part of the 1990s was absent. In his election speeches Lalu cleverly avoided any tough posturing against the 'fascists' (as he would call them later) and poured all his venom on the Congress. Nitish followed the same tactical line during the campaign.

The Janata Dal also openly compromised its professed commitment to 'value-based' politics by nominating more than fifty men with criminal antecedents, most of them from upper-backward castes, as party candidates. Lalu's associates recall that he had by then taken full control of the state party. He got their names cleared by others in the selection committee on the plea that these were men who were a terror in their constituencies and were supported by their caste-men; they had the money and muscle to capture booths and have the election results their way, so it was better to have them on the party's side. In answer to media queries, Lalu justified it by arguing that his candidates were only facing charges and that 'it is unfair to describe anyone as a criminal until his conviction by the lower courts has not been upheld by the Supreme Court of India'.

Nitish went along with Lalu in the nomination of the suspect elements. Although he did not directly interact with them or indulge them as Lalu did, he approved of their selection in terms of realpolitik, maintaining that in the constituencies allotted to them they were the strongest possible candidates for the party.

People were bewildered to find Vishnu Das Chaudhury, one of the main convicts in the Belchhi massacre case, as Janata Dal nominee in Asthawan (a 'fort' of Belchhi heroes from the time of Inderdeo Chaudhary). Still more baffling was the nomination in Harnaut at Nitish's instance of Bhola Singh who had defeated him by swearing patronage to the Belchhi accused in 1977. Their nominations stood out as major compromises made by Nitish with the hooligan forces of his caste from his ancestral district.

Harnaut had been won by Nitish in 1985—he was the sitting

MLA—so Bhola's nomination from there was widely seen as a gift from him. Nitish's calculation obviously was that such elements must be accommodated in order to win absolute support from the Kurmis. However, people can sometimes be shrewder than politicians. They voted out both Bhola Singh and Vishnu Chaudhury.

The Janata Dal election strategy was intended to garner support of the backward castes, the Muslims and a section of the upper castes. Working within this overall strategy, Lalu played his own game of making himself stronger by nominating about 100 of the 270 party candidates from the Yadav caste. This was a highly disproportionate allocation (37 per cent) to a caste that had a total share of 11 per cent in the state population. It exposed the duplicity of the party in attacking the upper castes for enjoying 40 per cent or more share in the Congress with a population share of less than 15 per cent.

Lalu's Yadav candidates included old and young socialists, their relations, new recruits, hooligans and former bureaucrats. It was like *Shivji ki barat*, the mythological wedding procession of Lord Siva that comprised an odd mix of characters. Lalu's arbitrariness sparked a chain reaction in the party, with the upper castes—particularly the Rajputs who thought they made the head of the party with V.P. Singh on top—threatening to walk out, and the other two upper-backward castes, Kurmis and Koeris, demanding larger shares.

Nitish, reluctant as in the past to directly identify himself with his caste, would not be among the vocal Kurmi advocates for a higher caste-quota, but could not keep himself completely out of it. For, after all, caste identity mattered in elections, and he could not be so foolishly self-righteous as not to admit that he had benefited from it in his election to Parliament from Barh. When he pleaded with Lalu, Nitish made it more a case of fair distribution, rather than Kurmi advocacy. He did succeed here and there, but Lalu was able to push most of his list through the selection process.

Ever since the Janata Dal came to power in Delhi, upper-caste students and youth in Bihar started organizing demonstrations to pressurize the V.P. Singh government not to implement the Mandal Commission recommendations. The demonstrations, which were held under the banner of an anti-reservation front in major towns across the state, were supported by the Congress and BJP student and youth organizations. On 15 December 1989, upper-caste students of colleges in Patna boycotted classes and blockaded roads for many hours in the city. In the following weeks, anti-quota mobs attacked government offices and properties and set them on fire in some places.

V.P. Singh avoided making a categorical statement that he was going to implement the Mandal Commission recommendations here and now. The Mandal Commission, in its report submitted to the Indira government in 1982, listed 3,743 communities as other backward classes (OBCs), noting that they made up 52 per cent of the country's population. It recommended 27 per cent reservation for the OBCs in the Central government services, considering that the Scheduled Castes and Tribes already had 22.5 per cent reservation, both adding up to the 50 per cent ceiling on quota fixed by the Supreme Court of India. Neither Indira nor Rajiv took any steps during their prime ministerial tenures to act on the commission's advice.

On the insistence of former socialists, the Janata Dal included this among the promises it made in the 1989 parliamentary election manifesto. In speeches at his nearly forty election campaign meetings in Bihar, V.P. Singh made it a point to assure the OBCs that he would implement the commission's recommendations if voted to power.

During the Assembly election campaign, Lalu made his party's Mandal promise a key part of his speeches. More than his official speeches, what mobilized a major section of the backward castes, both upper and lower backwards, in favour of the Janata Dal was their perception that the Congress was a party of the upper castes and hostile to the advancement of the backward castes. The Assembly elections, much like the parliamentary elections, turned out to be anti-Congress. Congress presence in the Assembly was reduced from 196 to 71, its vote share dropping from 39.30 to 24.78 per cent.

All the Opposition parties benefited. The BJP increased its tally from 16 to 39, the CPI from 12 to 23 and the CPI(M) from 1 to 6. Contesting Assembly elections for the first time, the IPF won 7 seats. In 1985 the Janata Party and Lok Dal (B) together had won 59 seats. In 1990 the 'reunited' Janata Dal won 122, more than double.

For the Janata Dal, Bihar's Assembly elections presented a situation similar to the parliamentary elections: it emerged as the single largest party but 41 short of majority. The BJP and the two communist parties agreed to provide 'outside support' to a Janata Dal ministry as at the Centre, giving it a comfortable majority. The problem arose, who would lead the ministry.

Officially, the Central leaders left it to the party MLAs to elect their leader. But behind the scenes, they backed their own candidates. V.P. Singh picked up the senior socialist Ram Sundar Das, a Dalit, who had served as chief minister of the Janata Party government for ten months (April 1979–February 1980) after Karpoori was forced to quit.

V.P. Singh's preference for Ram Sundar Das suggested that he had no immediate plan of engineering the 'social revolution' of Lohia's dream and his ex-socialist colleagues' obsession yet. His plan seemed to be a Janata replica of the Congress coalition model with upper castes, Dalits and Muslims. In this model, the backward castes would have to play subordinate roles, but be projected as leaders.

Devi Lal favoured Lalu. Over the past few years, Lalu had taken all decisions in tune with the changing psyche of the upper backwards who wanted a leadership role in positions of power. And behind the façade of his buffoonery, he had used every opportunity to project himself as the most promising and deserving candidate for a top role. There were many in the younger socialist brigade, including Nitish, who were solidly behind him. This brigade primarily drew strength from the ascendancy of youth power in the Bihar Movement. They had won their first battle for the generational shift through the election of Lalu as leader of the Lok Dal legislature group and their second battle through his election as leader of the Opposition. His election as leader of the Janata Dal legislature group was a continuum of the same battle.

Most of the socialist MLAs were aware of Lalu's inadequacy as a chief ministerial candidate. In their eyes, he just did not have the intellectual or administrative ability to qualify for the post: he was a man lacking in discipline and application, a man who hated working within a system. How could such a man deliver as chief minister?

When Nitish visited MLAs to canvass support for Lalu, at least eighteen of them, mainly from the Lok Dal, told him: 'Why do you want to make Lalu chief minister? Why don't you become CM instead?' Nitish would smile away the suggestion, arguing, 'We need to carry forward the social revolution and Lalu alone could be its face in the given situation, where we have to galvanize not only the upper backwards but other backward castes as well.'

Three election observers arrived in Patna from Delhi to conduct a fair election on behalf of the party's Central leadership. Two of them, Ajit Singh and George Fernandes, were V.P. Singh's close lieutenants, and they tried their best to get Ram Sundar Das elected unanimously. The third observer was Sharad Yadav, who was Devi Lal's man, there to build up support for Lalu. All the three election observers were playing a partisan role behind the façade of neutrality. For three days, together and separately, they 'interviewed' party MLAs to 'know their minds'. Ajit Singh and Fernandes called Lalu to tell him that only an MLA would be eligible for candidature. Lalu argued that if elected he would resign as MP and get himself elected as a member of any House of the bicameral legislature within six months, as the law demanded. All their efforts to persuade Lalu to back out of the race failed.

There was a stalemate for almost a week. V.P. Singh's emissaries wanted a unanimous choice and no election. Lalu was, however, bent upon forcing an election—if he was not the unanimous choice. Both the camps feverishly campaigned among the party MLAs, going to their houses, meeting them in groups, giving them assurances of reward of ministerial berths or other positions of power. At night, Lalu, Nitish and other prominent members of the camp would sit with a list of party MLAs and tick or cross out names to see if the arithmetic was working in their favour. They made three categories: supporters, opponents, 'wobblers'. They found that the opponents and wobblers could together defeat them.

Lalu's strategy to give 80 per cent of party nominations to backward castes, mainly Yadavs, was paying off. Upper-backward MLAs were backing him. Barring a few, upper-caste MLAs were opposed to Lalu; so were Dalits and some lower backwards. In a straight fight, Lalu would have lost to Das.

But to his good fortune, Raghunath Jha stood as a third candidate. Contrary to the general perception that he was set up by the Lalu camp to split the Das votes, it was Chandra Shekhar who, wanting to see anything in the world but V.P. Singh's man take over as chief minister, sponsored Jha, a Brahman. Shekhar knew very well that Jha had no chance of winning. He would be there just to take a good chunk of the upper-caste vote—mainly of Rajput supporters of Shekhar—away from Das, and that will help Lalu, who had the OBC bloc solidly behind him.

Interestingly, Nitish was chosen by the Central observers to conduct the election, because Das, who was state party president, and Jha, who was chairman of the parliamentary board, were both candidates. The result of the election by secret ballot was close: Jha pulled away 12 votes from Das, leaving him with only 56. Lalu got past him with 59 votes.

Lalu had arrived.

# the rebellion

Lalu wanted to look different from other chief ministers. And he wanted common people to identify him as 'a man from our midst'. He took his oath of office in Gandhi Maidan, Patna's historic public ground, in the presence of thousands of ordinary citizens, and not at the Raj Bhavan, Governor's House, where chief ministers were customarily sworn in before 'distinguished guests'.

Lalu, who was to grow as a political Robin Hood, shaped Bihar's social environment as much as he was shaped by it. He happened to be in the right place at the right time with the right slogans. The upper castes and the lower castes had related to each other as master and servant for ages. No matter how much education or income a low-caste man had, at his slightest error, even of the kinds that are human, the upper castes would snigger at him, '*Jaat kahin chhupti hai?* (Can anyone hide one's low birth?)'

Low-caste people had to face sneering remarks, innuendoes, stage whispers, double-meaning epithets from childhood, because birth determined it all. The caste of your parents stuck to you like a branding on your forehead; suffering humiliation and injustices every day was your inescapable destiny.

A minor illustration, as narrated by a young man from the intermediately ranked Koeri caste: he was (when much younger, thirteen or so) playing carrom one afternoon at a place run as a kind of open public club, with a few newspapers and a carrom board and a chess board. The club was close to his village, which fell within a sub-district dominated by upper-caste Bhumihars. With three others, he was in the middle of a round on the carrom board when a few Bhumihar boys arrived at the club, and one of them, without saying anything, reached over the shoulders of the players and picked the striker off the board. Then, the players sitting around the board were quickly motioned to leave: 'Be off. We are going to play now.' The Bhumihar boys then took the quietly vacated seats, jerked the coins out of the corner pockets and settled down to play.[6]

With the abolition of zamindari and other developments, the economic basis of the master–servant relationship between the upper and lower castes ceased to exist. After Independence, the lower castes, particularly the peasants, had come up economically and educationally. So the social humiliation and injustices hurt them. They no more considered it their fate. The gulf between their economic mobility and social immobility had to be bridged.

They longed to be free. And Lalu struck the right chord. His aggressive and hectoring speeches against the upper castes were music to their hearts. They fell in love with the haranguer.

It was something that had happened in the states of south India in the 1960s and '70s. The backward castes of Bihar arrived at their moment in the early 1990s when they said: 'Step aside, upper castes. We have the land. We have the numbers. We are awakened and united. Stop oppressing and ill-treating us. We are now going to rule.'

Lalu connected with the backward castes splendidly with his emotionally arousing slogan—*Vote hamara, Raj tumhara/ Nahin chalega, Nahin chalega*—that warned the upper castes that their days of enjoying power with the vote of the backward castes were over.

The announcement by V.P. Singh in both Houses of Parliament on 7 August 1990 of his government's decision to accept the Mandal Commission recommendations and provide 27 per cent reservation for OBCs in Central government jobs came as a boon to Lalu.

Lalu and Nitish were part of the pressure group that had kept nudging Singh for enacting the reservation. However, in certain respects their approaches were different. Lalu was opposed to the inclusion of Jats in the OBC category, as demanded by the deputy prime minister Devi Lal, but

Nitish supported it and wrote a letter to V.P. Singh, before he made the announcement in Parliament, urging him to include Jats and Marathas. However, Nitish was not in favour of holding up the announcement until Jats and Marathas had been included.

V.P. Singh came under pressure from his allies, the BJP and the Left Front, to incorporate economic criteria into the reservations. They wanted him to modify the Mandal recommendations according to the 'Bihar formula', the quota system Karpoori Thakur had implemented in November 1978. The Bihar formula had three distinct features. One, instead of providing reservations for all OBCs it broke up the category into EBCs (extremely backward classes) and BCs (backward classes), giving them 12 per cent and 8 per cent quota respectively; it prevented the upper backwards, who were placed in BCs sub-category, from running away with all the quota jobs. Two, it excluded the children of income-tax-paying parents. Three, it also treated the poor among the upper castes as a backward class and provided 3 per cent quota to them.

There were some Janata Dal leaders who supported Mandal's implementation according to the Bihar formula, Nitish being the most enthusiastic of them. He had a special reason to back the idea since the Bihar formula devised by Karpoori was closer to the formula he had suggested at the peak of the forward–backward confrontation in 1978, which had come to be known as the 'Nitish formula'. Just as in his equation, the creamy layer was excluded in the Karpoori formula.

Nitish backed the idea also because he thought Karpoori had proven himself a visionary by sub-categorizing OBCs as EBCs and BCs. Nitish had not realized the importance of this sub-categorization in 1978. 'When I look back, I feel I was young and immature,' says Nitish. 'I was not seeing what Karpoori could see with his vast knowledge and experience—that the EBCs would never benefit from positive discrimination without a quota within quota. They were far, far behind the upper backwards in education and personal resources. They would never be able to catch up.'

However, the majority in the Janata Dal, particularly the socialists, opposed any classification of the OBCs as EBCs and BCs, any income ceiling for eligibility or any share to the economically backward among the upper castes. Lalu was prominent among them. Under the given circumstances, after pondering over it for a while, Nitish decided not to press for sub-grouping: the topmost priority was the implementation. The overriding concern was empowerment of the backward castes as a class against the fierce resistance of the upper castes. The need of the hour was solidarity of the OBCs, an objective that would certainly be defeated with sub-categorization. Nitish joined Lalu as a co-driver to steer the Mandal juggernaut in Bihar.

With the Mandal announcement, a tornado of upper-caste anger hit the state. Mobs attacked and destroyed and burnt to ashes government properties as well as shops of the backward castes. Mobilizing themselves with Lalu's tacit support, the backward castes marched through towns and fought the upper castes that came to destroy their properties. Lalu gave orders to his policemen to treat the anti-Mandal agitators toughly. His objective was to inspire fear among the upper castes, to keep doing and saying things to feed their hatred of him, so that the lower castes felt euphoric and rallied behind him. He wanted to be seen by the lower castes as their knight, redeemer, messiah. Twelve upper-caste youths were killed by the police in different towns in the state.

Soon, the confrontation spread to rural areas. The animus, the loathing between the forwards and backwards in 1990 was deeper than it had been in 1978. The social intercourse between them seemed to have completely frozen. The forward youths took Mandal as a life-and-death issue in those days of high unemployment, and the backward youths saw it as their right to take what they had been denied for centuries.

Instead of mediating and making peace between the forwards and backwards, Lalu gave speeches that widened the chasm. Political profit could be maximized only in a conflagration. This was the time when Lalu ranted most vituperatively against the upper castes and turned into a Pied Piper for the backward castes.

Nitish had serious disagreements with Lalu's provocative approach, but, under the circumstances, went along with him. Together with Lalu he got V.P. Singh to address several Mandal rallies in the state. At Singh's rally in Nitish's constituency Barh, upper-caste protestors hurled shoes and slippers towards them on the dais.

Amid the ongoing fracas over the Mandal decision, BJP president

L.K. Advani announced his *rath yatra*, a Hindutva crusade across the country that would culminate at Ayodhya where he would lead devotees to start the construction of a Ram temple on the site where the sixteenth-century Babri mosque stood.

Lalu demonized the BJP because it opposed Mandal. This struck a chord with the backward castes. Against the Hindutva offensive he set in motion a secularism juggernaut. He succeeded in swinging the backward castes to his view that the BJP's Hindutva crusade was aimed at perpetuating the predominance of the upper castes. The Muslims were already alarmed by the BJP's aggressive Hindutva stand and looking for a strong political anchor. Lalu's moves against Hindu supremacism thus won him the support both of the backward castes and the Muslims.

Nitish's speeches were also highly critical of the BJP but without the acerbity and contemptuousness of Lalu. 'Advani's rath yatra is nothing but a conspiracy to stonewall Mandal,' he said at a Mandal rally at Gandhi Maidan in Patna on 8 October 1990. 'The BJP represents the social diehards who attack Mandal because they want the old social system based on injustice to continue. Mandal has fulfilled the aspirations of the oppressed classes and given them social esteem. There is no way anyone can turn back the clock of social justice.'

It was a real epochal moment for the backward castes. Using Mandal as a war cry they were forging ahead to wrest away political leadership from the upper castes. And they had to foster a sense of solidarity. The close companionship of Lalu and Nitish represented this cohesion better than anything else because Yadavs and Kurmis, the forwards among backwards, had traditionally been antagonistic towards each other.

As Advani's rath yatra progressed, riots between Hindus and Muslims broke out in several towns. In Bihar, the horrors of the Bhagalpur massacre caused by the Ramshila procession in 1989 were still fresh in the Muslims' memory.

V.P. Singh decided to stop Advani reaching Ayodhya. Advani was driving through Bihar on his way to Ayodhya when Lalu was directed by Singh to stop his rath yatra and take him under detention. Advani's arrest on 23 October 1990 at Samastipur in north Bihar did truly seem an act of political chivalry, considering the massive swell of Hindu fervour. Stopping Advani amounted to stopping the Hindu 'giant' in its tracks when it was leaping forward to 'trample' the Muslim 'pygmy' under its feet. Although Singh mainly deserved the accolade for daring the tempest, it was Lalu who ran away with the knighthood. He became a 'hero' to Muslims.

On 7 November 1990, the BJP withdrew support to the V.P. Singh ministry. Lalu's chief ministership came under threat. BJP's withdrawal meant the loss of 39 votes. The silver lining was that all the left parties—CPI (23), CPI(M) (6), Marxist Coordination Committee (2) and the IPF (7), total 38—backed him as they did Singh. But that alone would not help. Lalu had to do some desperate negotiations to garner support of the Jharkhand Mukti Morcha (19) and the independents (30). He sought Nitish's help in bringing around Bashishth Narain Singh—a key leader of 17 Janata Dal MLAs with Bihar Movement background who had fallen out with Lalu because they could identify no clear direction in his policy and administration and had been thwarted by his imperiousness in their push for any change.

Lalu survived by expanding his 11-member cabinet to 69. Lalu's open compromises did not affect his growing popularity among the OBCs and Muslims. On the contrary, they celebrated it as an act of gallantry: everything was fair in the drive for political domination over the upper castes. To capitalize on the sentiment, Lalu described his victory as the victory of social justice and secularism.

Even though the tension over Mandal subsided with the Supreme Court stay on implementation of its recommendations following a plea from an upper-caste plaintiff Indra Sawhney, Lalu kept making speeches intended to heighten it. His rant against the upper castes turned more blistering and vitriolic. He told his charmed audiences that the upper castes had monopolized the state bureaucracy and were engaged in a conspiracy to perpetuate their monopoly. And why wouldn't they believe him? Eight out of ten IAS officers in the state were high-caste. They wanted Lalu to end this monopoly.

In September 1991 Lalu got the Governor to issue an ordinance providing for fine on and imprisonment of officers (read, upper-caste officers) who were found ignoring the provisions of reservations for Scheduled Castes, Scheduled Tribes and other backward classes while making recruitments to state government services.

In 1992 Lalu revisited Karpoori's reservation formula, in force for thirteen years, to remove the 3 per cent reservation for the economically backward among the upper castes and reduce the quota for women (which he suspected benefited largely upper-caste women) from 3 to 2 per cent. He distributed the withdrawn 4 per cent quota between the backward classes and extremely backward classes, raising their percentage of reservation from 8 to 10 and from 12 to 14 respectively. In 1993 he got a legislation passed (Bihar Panchayati Raj Act) extending the 26 per cent reservation to the elective posts of the panchayati raj institutions in the same proportion (EBCs, 14 per cent; BCs, 10 per cent; and women, 2 per cent).

Quota in public services was a shortcut to the OBC voter's heart. It was actually a great deception played on the OBC masses. Quota created opportunity but no capability. Even the Mandal Commission had warned that the real progress of the OBCs can come only with the change in their economic conditions. Lalu showed little interest in implementing even the existing programmes of the state and Central governments for the economic and educational uplift of the poorer classes, what to speak of inventing new ones. In his political perception, propaganda attracted larger following than welfare schemes. He used Mandal as a propaganda tool rather than an instrument for fetching material gains for the OBCs.

He was quite aware that Mandal and the revised Karpoori formula combined could at best bring a few thousand jobs to the state's OBCs in a year, which could only create a very tiny oasis in the desert of OBC disability. And then the jobs were shrinking, not growing, in number. He knew the farce of Mandal quota providing OBCs jobs in government in a fast liberalizing economy—the quintessence of which was pruning of state power and downsizing of the government.

The novelty and uniqueness of Lalu was that he took Mandal beyond quota jobs: he converted it into a psychological machine. Through his decisions, speeches, appearance and public behaviour he was able to portray himself as *apna admi*, 'one of our own', to the masses. The only other politician of Bihar before him who had been

identified by the poor as 'apna admi' was Karpoori Thakur. Lalu
went beyond Karpoori. Whereas Karpoori positioned himself as a
great benefactor of the poor, Lalu positioned himself as the poor
man's king entrusted by history with the task of taming the rich. He
depicted his election and tenure as chief minister as a triumph of the
downtrodden, making them feel it was actually *gharib raj*, rule of
the poor.

Lalu's regime was the culmination of a great shift. This shift entailed
the movement of the upper backwards in politics from a subordinate
role to a leading role, which had begun in the 1960s and had its first
climax in the election of Karpoori as chief minister in 1977. Lalu built
his superstructure over the structure made by Karpoori. With an agenda
for equality with the forwards, Karpoori inspired the backwards. Lalu
took the battle to a higher level: he would settle for nothing less than
their domination over the upper castes.

Lalu's greatest success lay in creating the illusion of overturning
existing patterns of governance. Hitherto, the organs of the state had
functioned in a shameless nexus with the big and the mighty: Lalu
showed himself to be working to break this nexus and provide protection
to the weak. In order to make this illusion work, he constantly warned
and exhorted his officers to ensure that no injustice was done to the
poor and protection given to their life and assets.

With his triumphal roars rousing the poor, the upper castes began to
fear risking trouble with their old ways. The transformation was evident
especially in the small towns and villages, where the lower castes were
the most oppressed. The upper castes turned wary, circumspect and
unadventurous. They would avoid rather than engage in a conflict with
the backwards, particularly the upper backwards, and among the upper
backwards, particularly the Yadavs. The Yadavs were the spearhead of
the Lalu revolution.

The demonizing of the upper castes and open patronage to the
backward castes by Lalu accentuated the social churning. The backward
castes began to assert themselves everywhere—in villages, offices,
associations, everyday dealings with upper castes. They were the ones
now seen hovering around block offices instead of the upper castes. In
Mithilanchal, the Brahmans became wary of prominently wearing the

traditional tilak on their forehead when they walked the streets. The very term 'backward' came to be associated with awe: police stations showed reluctance in registering any complaint against a Yadav.

The retreat of the upper castes had a profound effect on the minds of the other castes. They began to gain self-respect and self-confidence. And this was true not just of upper backwards but also of lower backwards and Dalits. They loved the psychological game in which Lalu had subdued the upper castes.

And then there were Muslims who had never seen a chief minister so doggedly on their side. He was the ruler of their dreams. Lalu had already won the Muslim heart by reversing the prejudice of the state. Till then, more often than not, the police openly showed their bias in favour of Hindu attackers during communal riots. Lalu raj was virtually riot-free. Even when communal riots broke out in several cities in the country following the Babri mosque demolition on 6 December 1992, Bihar remained peaceful. Muslims in Bihar felt safe and protected. It was the least they had expected of all previous governments. They had never got that from any.

This helped Lalu consolidate the OBC–Muslim coalition. Mandal was not an 'employment scheme' but an 'empowerment scheme', V.P. Singh had said.[7] Lalu went beyond Singh. He infused the empowerment campaign with bellicosity. He led the backwards in a socio-political combat with the forwards. The quota formed just a corner of the battlefield. Mandal was merely a means, not the end. Lalu's idea of empowerment of backward castes was disempowerment of the forward castes.

So much so that he appropriated the entire credit for the social transformation that had taken place in the state as a result of socialist and communist struggles over the past fifty years. The CPI had socially and economically empowered lower-caste sharecroppers and labourers in Madhubani and Darbhanga—Mithilanchal was the cradle of the communist movement in Bihar—through militant campaigns. The singular achievement of the CPI-ML (Naxalite) movement in central Bihar was *izzat*, social dignity, for the backward castes and Dalits.

Lalu appropriated the radical language of the Naxalites, the communists and socialists without taking any steps to empower the lower castes in the real sense. 'In my raj, the upper castes can't dare to maltreat the poor and molest their women'—this was one of the key elements of his self-propaganda that turned him into a heroic myth, despite a series of massacres and rapes perpetrated against the rural poor under his regime. As many as 147 of them killed in seventeen massacres by landlord militias or the police during Lalu's first tenure (1990–95) had invited severe criticism of his hypocrisy in the media.

Governance under Lalu was temperamental, desultory and aimless. Politics took precedence over policies, programmes and rules of business. Officers were nettled by his impulsive actions and announcements. One of the best examples of his thoughtless actions was Charwaha Vidyalaya, primary schools for graziers. He lamented that many young boys from poor peasant families could not attend school because they had to graze their cattle; and that he knew their problem because born a Yadav he had herded cattle himself.

At Lalu's prodding, as many as 113 Charwaha schools were started across the state in 1991–92. Most of them were situated in government's neglected agricultural farms, where the cattle were to graze while the young boys learnt basic grammar and mathematics. Lalu made the scheme even more grandiose: while the agriculture department that owned the farms would do overall management, the department of human resource development was directed to build the school and provide the educational infrastructure, teachers, uniforms, mid-day meals; the department of environment and forests was to construct a boundary around the school and plant trees in its compound; the animal husbandry department would grow grass in the farms and provide fodder to the cattle; and the fisheries department was to dig water tanks for pisciculture. It demanded exceptional synergy among so many departments that was never really obtained.

But first, where were the students? Bihar had no specific cattle-herding community such as the Gujjars in Jammu and Kashmir. Families that owned cattle sent them out for grazing with anyone who was free at the time. It could be young men of all ages, not necessarily primary-school age, or even older men, often the parents. And there were no specific hours during which all the graziers came out with their cattle.

It showed how little Lalu actually cared to understand of the realities of the rural Bihar he claimed to represent. But assuming that at least a few young graziers were available at particular hours, with keen interest in the novel schooling, where were the teachers? No teachers were recruited for these schools. Two teachers from the nearest government school were deputed to each school, and there being no supervision or surprise inspection, most of them enjoyed it as paid vacation.

Baffled at first by Lalu's impulsive style of functioning, the bureaucracy soon got used to it. While the administration generally moved at its most slothful pace ever, officers at all levels learnt to expect a sudden flurry of activity at the bidding of the 'king of the poor' occasionally. 'I would describe Lalu's governance as reactive,' says a senior IAS officer who worked with him. 'That was natural in him. He could be suddenly driven onward in reaction to what he saw or heard, irrationally, thoughtlessly.' He could order officials to do things for which there was no provision in the budget. During his visits to sites of occurrence, such as a massacre of poor villagers by a landlord militia, he would make announcements—such as allotment of agricultural and housing plots, loans and grants—that made absolutely no sense because the officers could not make them a part of any government scheme.

Lalu's preoccupation with political engineering to retain his elephantine new vote bank caused the state's economy to shrink. Development administration was virtually crippled as the instruments of planning, policymaking, decision-making, implementation and monitoring turned dysfunctional. Cabinet meetings were held in an unprepared, casual manner. Review meetings were rare. The result was that failures were uncovered in late stages when little remediation was possible—such as Lalu himself discovering at a review meeting with district magistrates in October 1993 that not even 10 per cent of the funds allocated for rural development had been spent.

Lalu was never an organization's man. He would be the last person to be bound by rules. From the days in student politics to the chief ministership, he was his own man, relying on his antics and sharp tongue to build his popularity. His spontaneous actions were nothing but political showbiz, a display of the king's zeal to right the wrongs, an exhibition of his benevolence and love for fellow human beings. His justice-delivering, humane adventures in his initial years earned him fulsome praise not only of the underprivileged but also of the middle class including the upper castes. Even though they all were soon disappointed with the waves of sudden excitement, the disillusionment took long because in their living memory no other chief minister had treaded those paths, even if momentarily. Nevertheless, the massive support he received in the early 1990s was even beyond his own expectations.

The JP movement had mobilized the youth and citizenry on the three principal issues of corruption, unemployment and an unimaginative education system. With Lalu—the main face of the youth leadership of the movement—in command of the government, Nitish and his other associates from 1974 expected him to make a focused, determined endeavour to introduce structural changes in the system to curb venality, create jobs and refashion higher education. But Lalu showed no interest in addressing any of these issues. On the contrary, the situation in these areas was turning from bad to worse.

The party he belonged to lost its relevance to him. He began to believe that the Janata Dal was there because he was. Others in the Janata Dal had no role to play, except do whatever he thought needed to be done to keep himself in power. He needed only assistants. He wanted no advisers for deciding strategies, tactics or policies. That is what was to force Nitish to part ways with him in April 1994.

As an MP and as Union minister of state for agriculture Nitish tried, among other things, to push his proposals for saving the tal farmers from the scourge of inundation, using various organs of the Central government. The proposals—which included improvement of drainage in tal and other such critical areas in the country, establishing a research institute devoted exclusively to pulses at Mokama and the inclusion of *masur* dal in the government's minimum support price regime—did not receive much support in the Central government until the late 1990s and early 2000s.

For over two years since he became chief minister, Lalu tried to engage Nitish in almost everything he did. He valued his companionship and advice. When Parliament was not in session and Nitish was visiting

Patna, Lalu would send a car to bring him over to his official residence at 1 Anne Marg; the two could be seen in the upstairs living room of the bungalow, chatting for hours. Sometimes, the conversation stretched till 2 a.m.

'Most of it was idle talk,' reminisces Nitish. 'Lalu has irregular habits, no discipline, no routine. He has no fixed time for breakfast or lunch. Sometimes he took his dinner at one o'clock in the night. I hated his regime . . .' Nitish received little response from the Lalu government to his initiatives on improvements in tal agriculture.

Contrary to the public perception that Nitish was the 'Chanakya' and influenced every decision Lalu, the 'Chandragupta', took, Nitish, since he became an MP and later the minister of state for agriculture, directed his attention to establishing himself in Delhi. He was a beginner in national politics and was trying to find his feet and make a mark.

His wife Manju had joined him with their ten-year-old son Nishi, but not without a sour brush with the media. As his wife worked in a government school in Patna and he did not want her to quit her job— 'Politics being a risky profession I wanted her to continue as that alone could provide some financial security to the family,' he says—he got her transferred to Delhi on deputation as an employee at Bihar Bhavan, the state's official lodge. Stories appeared in the media suggesting Nitish had bent the rules to bring her over which hurt him so much that the couple decided Manju would not take up her new post and go back to Patna to resume as a schoolteacher. She stayed with him for a while and then returned.

No matter what the truth of his 'close association' with Lalu was, the latter exploited it fully by telling everyone he regarded Nitish as his *chhota bhai*, younger brother. 'It was very considered and deliberate,' says Nitish. 'He wanted to show that I was very close to him and at the same time, smaller than him. When I heard people talking about it, I started referring to him as *bada bhai*, elder brother, in sarcasm. "Go and ask bade bhai," I would sometimes tell others. The media clung to these phrases because it simplified things for those who didn't want to go into the complexity of our relationship. Our relationship was never so intimate or deep as those phrases would suggest.'

However, Nitish could not always keep his distance. The two knew each other well since the days of the Bihar Movement. Nitish's late mother once told me: 'I remember Lalu visiting our Bakhtiyarpur home several times and dining with Nitish.'

They were seen as a pair by party men, political rivals, the public and the media, and incidents ended up confirming the perception. Lalu was a man who loved crowds; he would often be addressing rallies, meetings, conferences; and he would invariably have the town pasted with posters in advance. Most posters for rallies or meetings during the first two years of his chief ministership carried pictures of both Lalu and Nitish. Nitish shared the dais with Lalu and invariably made a speech.

Nitish began to notice a change in Lalu's attitude within the first few months of his taking over as chief minister. Although Lalu maintained a close companionship with him, he started ignoring most other former socialists among party colleagues who had been with him through thick and thin. He started taking decisions without consulting them, and sometimes even Nitish. He hogged all the limelight for social justice and communal harmony, pushing his colleagues into the shadows.

Worse, he derided his colleagues. He seldom had a word of appreciation for any of them. Nitish recalls personally having warned Lalu several times, in conversations and through letters, of the risks of excluding everyone from decision-making. A team leader, Nitish told him, had to see the positive attributes in everybody and use them to achieve his goal. But Lalu paid no attention. And Lalu was extremely partial to his caste.

Lalu developed feudal traits. He set up a durbar of close relations, sycophants, fixers and hooligans who were neither in the Janata Dal nor any political party and were answerable to no one. Under his patronage Rabri's two brothers, Sadhu Yadav and Subhash Yadav, emerged as extra-constitutional centres of power. Very often in the evenings, on the lawns of 1 Anne Marg, Lalu entertained himself and other members of his clique with song and dance.

Nitish and other party colleagues could perhaps have ignored these indulgences if he were delivering well as a ruler. But the case was just the opposite. The clique around him developed networks across the state for misappropriating funds from the public exchequer and also extorting money from private entities and well-heeled individuals. Led by

Rabri's brothers Sadhu and Subhash, they seized control of the contract and commission businesses in public works, bus and auto-rickshaw operations and liquor sale outlets. 'In road construction contracts,' a former ministerial colleague of Lalu says, 'Sadhu and Subhash used to decide who will get the contract even before the bids were opened. It was because of their conspiracy with their favourite bidders to loot most of the allocations for the contracts that roads were never constructed under the Lalu regime.' A few Muslim thugs also shared the loot.

One of the networks drew hundreds of crores from the state treasury against fake supplies of fodder to poor peasants, a loot that became popularly known as the Fodder Scam, and in which strong evidence of Lalu's involvement surfaced during his second chief ministerial tenure in 1997, forcing him to resign. Income tax officials seized huge piles of cash from the homes of veterinary department officers and fodder suppliers and, in one case, from air travel baggage. State vigilance officials recommended criminal suits against several senior veterinary department officers. The files were sent to Lalu for action; he showed little interest in pursuing the cases.

Nitish saw the patronization of the plunderers of the state treasury by Lalu as a clear betrayal of the agenda of the JP movement whose number one priority was ending corruption. 'I was saddened to see that the Janata Dal government had proven no better than the Congress regimes of the past,' recalls Nitish. He tried to bring Lalu to think of the ideals of the JP movement and the commitments of the Janata Dal, but in vain. Lalu appeared to be interested solely in perpetuating himself by constantly instilling fear in the minds of the backwards, Dalits and Muslims that they would lose everything if they let him lose the crown. He continued to accumulate financial resources for political and personal providence as long as they were in his enchanted thraldom.

Some of Lalu's disappointed colleagues started working towards an alternative early on. Shivanand Tiwari says he pleaded with Sharad Yadav back in 1991 at a Janata Dal meeting in Munger to replace Lalu with Nitish. The Mandal movement had created a political environment in which only a backward could be thought of as an alternative to Lalu, because the aroused downtrodden communities would not accept anyone from the upper castes.

Sharad refused. He thought a change of leader might derail the 'social justice movement' and send a negative message to the Janata Dal electorate. Shivanand and others continued their effort to push Nitish as an alternative to Lalu. Nitish knew what was happening, but as it was not in his nature to get disappointed quickly he wanted to give himself a longer time to see if things would change. 'I take time to decide but once I have decided there's no going back,' says Nitish.

And his moment of decision came with Lalu's announcement, following the Supreme Court endorsement of V.P. Singh's Mandal decision towards the end of 1992, that his government would implement the Mandal Commission recommendations in the state. Nitish saw through Lalu's dirty game. This would mean end of the quota within quota for the extremely backward classes that Karpoori had created to provide opportunities in public services for several small communities in that category.

Implementation of the Mandal recommendations in Bihar superseding the Karpoori formula was going to mean that the small and much poorer EBCs would have to compete with the larger and much advanced BCs for government jobs within the overall 27 per cent quota and be inevitable losers. This was a bonanza Lalu wanted to give the upper backwards who were powering his OBC–Muslim coalition.

The EBC leaders in the Janata Dal and the politically conscious sections of the EBCs were troubled by Lalu's announcement. Nitish advised Lalu not to go ahead with his supersession plan. It would be grossly unjust, he argued, to shut off job opportunities to the EBCs, which they had been enjoying for the past fourteen years in the state, when the need of the historic moment was to take social justice deeper to improve the life of those at the bottom of the spectrum. 'We should appreciate that the EBCs need special attention,' he told Lalu.

Lalu had been openly favouring Yadavs in the ministry, the party, the bureaucracy, business, local self-government and various committees set up by the government from state to village level. Yadavs were cornering the largest chunks in recruitments to the lower bureaucracy within or outside the OBC quota. Under these circumstances, it was obvious who from among the upper backwards would appropriate the quota. This was causing concern even among the Kurmis and Koeris. Many

prominent Kurmis in the Janata Dal put it across to Nitish, urging him
to fight against 'Yadavization'. The Janata Dal leaders who had been
backing Nitish as an alternative to Lalu for over a year also egged him
on to take a public position on the issue.

Nitish found himself in a predicament. On the one hand, he saw
the Janata Dal as the vehicle for the historic social justice movement
and did not want it to be impaired; on the other, Lalu's insistence on
implementing Mandal and the growing indignation in the party over
his autocratic, casteist ways nudged Nitish to come out in the open and
play the antagonist. On top of it, there was the personal relationship
with Lalu he had to consider. He also had to assess if he could politically
survive ploughing a lonely furrow outside the Janata Dal. He had to
weigh in all the costs.

Sometimes Nitish would be so distressed he would stop visiting Lalu
for days. Sensing his hurt, Lalu would make phone calls. Nitish would
not answer them. Sometimes Nitish would tell his aides to convey that
he was not there. There were occasions when Lalu sent Sadhu Yadav
over to Nitish's place to fetch him. Sometimes Lalu personally came
over to cajole him.

But Lalu took no steps for remediation of the issues Nitish raised.
The divergence only grew and grew. The monopolization of all spaces
by the Yadavs continued unabated under the garb of empowerment of
backward castes. The battle cry of the movement, which was triggered
by Mandal, was: '*Bheekh nahin hissedari, satta mein bhagidari* (We want
no charity but share in power).' It was an announcement of the arrival
of the backward castes. Adjunction had consummated in autonomy. But
whose autonomy was it? Who benefited from the social transfer of power?

By the end of 1992 Nitish had almost made up his mind to raise a
banner of revolt against Lalu's misrule. But he had to see who he had
with him. The promise of the largest chunk of popular support had
come from his caste-men among whom he had emerged as an icon.
Prominent Kurmi social, political and business leaders had been making
persistent appeals to him to confront the monopolization of spaces by
the Yadavs in Lalu raj.

But Nitish consciously shunned any association with caste politics. He never allowed his political image to descend to the level of a 'Kurmi' leader. He would not work exclusively for the benefit of Kurmis—least of them Kurmi vote intermediaries—but only by aggregating them with the other castes, whether it was the question of reservations, development of agriculture, political empowerment or personal issues.

Even though there was general disappointment with Lalu's performance in the Janata Dal at the national level, Nitish was not sure how many of them would walk out with him. Among leaders with electoral constituencies in Bihar, George Fernandes, Sharad Yadav and Ram Vilas Paswan shared his chagrin but none of them was ready to come out in the open. Only one party MP, Brishen Patel, was resolutely with him.

He had the closest relationship with Sharad Yadav; he met him almost daily and conveyed his disappointment with Lalu. Sharad would agree, but would not make any moves to rein Lalu in. Sharad, who had initially not liked Lalu, had developed a fondness for him, not only because he was a Yadav but also because he thought he was making a significant contribution to consolidating the backward castes' position in politics. Sharad wanted to re-establish the rapport between Nitish and Lalu, so did V.P. Singh. But Nitish was not interested any longer.

A fair number of state Janata Dal leaders too were disappointed with Lalu, though an overwhelming number were likely to stay with him: some because they were enjoying ministerial offices or other positions of power, some because they feared Lalu could ruin their political future with his governmental and political power if they rebelled, others because they felt he was creating a strong electoral base for the party; the remaining were undecided.

Rebellion against Lalu entailed the risk of self-destruction. But the other option before Nitish was to be party to Bihar's destruction. Had he joined politics, rejecting the prospect of a comfortable life of an engineer, had he remained steadfastly committed to principled politics not taking the road to self-aggrandizement only to be a mute spectator to the ruin of all ethics and of a state that was already at the bottom of the ladder? If the state was delivered from Lalu's incompetent regime with his effort he would be the happiest person; but if he did not succeed and fell by the wayside he would take it as his destiny and leave it to someone else at some other point in political history. He had to take a leap in the dark.

And he did, using Lalu's decision to replace the Karpoori equation with the Mandal formula as a trigger. At a meeting for the remembrance of Karpoori held on his sixty-ninth birth anniversary on 24 January 1993 in Patna, where several party leaders shared the dais with him, Nitish issued a warning to Lalu that if he got the Karpoori formula superseded by the Mandal formula 'we shall come out in the street and oppose it tooth and nail'. It was a declaration of war which stunned quite a few in the gathering.

Lalu, who was also supposed to attend the meeting, was out of town and only came to know of Nitish's declaration on his arrival later in the day. He made several direct and indirect overtures to Nitish to reopen a dialogue on the issue but he would not budge from his stand.

Nitish had taken the risk of antagonizing some of the Kurmis by opposing Lalu's announcement because if not as much as Yadavs they could hope to get a substantial piece of the cake by virtue of having a proportionately larger educated population. Lalu increased Nitish's risk by dinning into the ears of Kurmis that while he wanted to create greater employment space for them in public services, Nitish wanted to narrow it.

There were murmurings against Nitish's stance in certain Kurmi circles. At the instigation of Lalu's agents provocateurs a section of Kurmi students of Patna University took out a procession in the state capital denouncing Nitish's 'betrayal of the social justice movement'. Nitish remained undeterred.

And he did not lose caste support after all. Two factors worked in his favour. First, an overwhelming majority of Kurmis wanted to demolish the near-absolute power the Yadavs enjoyed and the dethronement of Lalu was on top of their agenda; they saw Nitish as their only hope for achieving it. Second, quota was not a life-and-death issue for the Kurmis as an increasing number of them were getting college admissions and private and public jobs on their own merit in open competitions.

Yadav monopolization had also alienated the Koeris, who were more numerous than Kurmis. Nitish began to mobilize them through their leaders inside the Janata Dal. A 'brotherhood', borne out of old myths, was sought to be established between Kurmis and Koeris as descendants of Luv and Kush, the brave twin sons of Lord Ram. Nitish had already started winning support of the lower backwards with his resolute defence of the Karpoori formula.

The upper castes, many of whom had voted for the Janata Dal, felt a deep sense of anger over their demonizing and marginalization by Lalu, and they looked upon Nitish's revolt with growing interest. Lalu, fearing that his decision to replace the Karpoori formula with the Mandal formula could trigger a storm that could sweep him off his feet, quietly buried the idea. Perception grew that Lalu was growing weaker and a strong opposition could push him out of power.

It was in this atmosphere that a huge rally of Kurmis was held on 12 February 1994 at Gandhi Maidan in Patna at which Nitish was the star speaker. The idea of organizing a Kurmi Chetana Maha Rally (Great Rally for Kurmi Awakening) was first thought of by a group of officials of various caste associations of Kurmis. The idea received support from leaders belonging to the Kurmi caste in all political parties—Janata Dal, Congress, BJP and CPI—who had not failed to note the growing sense of betrayal in the Kurmi community against Lalu. 'We fought shoulder to shoulder in the battle for Mandal. We were cheated,' was the common Kurmi refrain. When Madhu Singh, a Janata Dal MLA, mentioned Lalu favourably in his speech at the rally the gathering exploded with anger and forced him to stop speaking further.

The Kurmis had found immediate provocation in the absence of their caste from the list of backward classes released by the Central government for Mandal reservations and by the Lalu government for panchayat elections. More than three thousand of them protested with a sit-in at JP Circle in Patna. Although both lists were admitted as errors that were quickly corrected, the simmering anger did not subside. The drive to get all the Kurmi leaders on to one platform to fight for a fair share in political power got a boost.

In Lalu's OBC–Muslim coalition the OBCs themselves were a coalition. It was a coalition dominated by the three upper-backward castes. With Lalu brazenly promoting only one of those, it now stood ruptured.

The tempo for the Kurmi Chetana Maha Rally was built up by a preceding Kurmi Chetana Rath (Chariot of Kurmi Awareness) that was driven by a large number of Kurmi youths through various parts of the state from 2 January to 8 February 1994.

When the organizers had first approached Nitish for addressing the Great Rally he found himself in a dilemma. He had never in his political life associated with any caste organization; he had zealously guarded himself against associating even with 'Kurmi leaders', politicians known for undisguised patronizing of their caste. Would his participation in the rally not damage his socially transcendent, secular image? Would it not lead to his identification as a 'Kurmi leader' in public perception?

His conscience would not approve of it, but the compulsions of rebuilding his politics on the foundation of caste were too strong to ignore. The social mutiny sparked by V.P. Singh's Mandal announcement and fuelled by Lalu's virulent diatribes against the upper castes had created an environment which propelled every backward caste to demand a share in power. It was as though power snatched from the hands of upper castes lay out there as a trophy which could not be allowed to be taken away by any single backward caste and must be broken for each one to get a piece of it.

In order to express their solidarity and demonstrate their strength, every backward caste organized rallies in Patna's Gandhi Maidan, many of them addressed by Lalu. Koeris, Dhanuks, Lohars, Kumhars, Vaisyas, Nishads and others had had their rallies before the Great Rally for Kurmi Awakening was planned. The scene, with caste associations coming out in the open to demand their place in the 'egalitarian' political dispensation, was reminiscent of the early decades of the twentieth century when caste leagues fought for political representation.

To an urbane mind like Nitish's, it was a throwback to primitivism. However, a realistic assessment drove him to think that at this crucial juncture of socio-political history the Kurmis were as determined as other castes to grab their share of power; and if he did not claim their leadership it would be the biggest political blunder as they would replace him with someone else. Moreover, it was absolutely necessary to start with the advantage of caste support, on a solid base, when he was engaging as powerful a foe as Lalu in direct combat.

Nitish gave up the initial reluctance and attended the meetings of the rally organizing committee. He made changes and improvements in the issues to be raised at the rally, proposed resolutions, slogans and posters. The word *chetana* was added to the rally at his instance.

In his speech at the rally Nitish said:

> The sea of people at Gandhi Maidan today has sent out a clear message to the occupants of the throne[s] in Delhi and Patna—If you neglect them you will face terrible consequences. The Kurmis feel betrayed. Nobody can hope to stay politically alive if he does not care for the Kurmis…The Kurmis must come forward to take the leadership of the social justice movement. No power on earth can deny job reservations to Kurmis. We have to fight for job reservations also in the private sector. But Kurmis should not fight for social justice only for themselves. They need to form a broad coalition with the OBCs and EBCs for their own political survival.

Lalu's narcissism and unscrupulous governance had aroused concerns even among the top leaders of the Janata Dal. Nitish had conveyed to them from time to time his growing disgust over the systemic collapse in Bihar. But the top leaders were in a fix: they could not think of replacing Lalu because they feared he would walk out with a large number of party MLAs, causing a split that would weaken the social justice movement.

With no option left, Nitish one day in April 1994 told Sharad Yadav he and Brishen Patel were going to leave the party. Sharad tried to dissuade him, in vain. Shortly thereafter, at a meeting of the Janata Dal parliamentary party in Delhi, Nitish spoke out against Lalu. His criticism was reported in the media. George Fernandes called him to his residence and told him Lalu wanted to make a compromise. 'It's too late,' Nitish said.

Fernandes's face brightened. He was testing Nitish's will. Fernandes had long been convinced that Lalu was ruining Bihar as well as the social justice cause. Fernandes convened a meeting the following day of the

12 other Janata Dal MPs who supported him. He personally fetched them to his residence for the meeting where they unanimously decided to break away from the Janata Dal. They signed a letter to this effect and submitted it to the Lok Sabha Speaker Shivraj Patil. A minister in Lalu's cabinet, Sudha Srivastava, also joined them. On 21 April 1994, they formed a new party, Janata Dal (George), with Fernandes as its president.

Organizationally, their separation was a minor ruffle to the Janata Dal, but politically it seemed an event of great significance. 'Why would Lalu's closest confidant for two decades come out in the street with a vow to dethrone him unless he saw a catastrophe in his continuance in power?' Nitish's supporters asked the common people, and it stuck. In the kind of political culture the Congress had bequeathed to Indian democracy, parties did not make personalities; personalities made parties. Lalu had practically turned the Janata Dal into his personal vehicle. Nitish was out to create his own.

Some more key men in the Janata Dal, including another Lalu minister, Bashisth Narain Singh, joined the rebel group. They formally launched Samata Party in October 1994 at a public rally dissolving Janata Dal (George), again with Fernandes as president.

Nitish, with Fernandes and other MPs, started touring the state and addressing rallies and meetings to arouse public opinion against the Lalu regime soon after they broke away in April 1994. They had their eye on the Assembly elections of March 1995; they hardly had time. In the initial months, they did not attract much attention; even the media gave very little space to their meetings and speeches. But as the elections drew nearer, the size of the crowds became bigger and bigger.

Nitish was seen as the focal point of the anti-Lalu rebellion. People paid more attention to what he was saying than what others said. It caused some heartburn among some of the MPs of Samata Party, but nobody made it an issue.

In his speeches, Nitish focused on the abyss Lalu had thrown the state into. 'Kidnapping, extortion, intimidation and collapse of roadways, schools and canals are what people have got from this government,' he told the people. 'The Janata Dal talks of social justice. I want to ask them: does social justice mean reign of terror? Does it mean ruin of Bihar? . . .

The Janata Dal got a mandate for five years. It could have used the huge public support for transforming Bihar. But it [Lalu] wasted it away in buffoonery. Nero was playing the flute when Rome was burning. The government [Lalu] concentrated on creating a social commotion for votes, while we were set on our mission to metamorphose Bihar.'

In his election address on television Nitish declared law and order as the top priority of the Samata Party. 'Our party promises to re-establish law and order within three months of coming to power. We shall either end loot, kidnapping and extortion or be finished in the process. Only by re-establishing law and order and by building roads and other infrastructure we could expect flow of investments which will pave the way for the all-round development and creation of adequate employment in the state.'

The second priority, he said, was resource mobilization for development. 'The public treasury of Bihar is empty. There is no money even to pay the salaries of the government staff.' He blamed it on the wasteful expenditures on Lalu's *ayyashi* and revelry. Third, he promised to bring agriculture back to life and create employment to stem the tide of migration of agricultural labourers to other states: 'Villages are a picture of desolation today.' The fourth priority was to rebuild the infrastructure for education. 'Thousands of students are forced to move to Delhi and other cities for education. Students from poor families cannot afford to go elsewhere, which is ruining their career.'

Lalu portrayed Nitish as a proxy of the upper castes who, displaced by Lalu from power, wanted to end the gharib raj, the rule of the poor, and restore their old system of exploitation and oppression. The upper castes were also backing the BJP, so that when they would 'snatch power from me [Lalu]' they would slaughter Muslims with impunity. Capitalizing on the fears and insecurities of the backward castes, Dalits and Muslims was at the core of Lalu's electoral strategy.

The differences in the vote-seeking approaches of Nitish and Lalu were sharp and clear. While Nitish worked on the material aspirations of broad sections of people, Lalu played with the psychological impulses of the underclass. Nitish addressed the hungry stomach, Lalu conversed with the angry and fearful mind.

Nitish's biggest problem was that large sections of the backward castes, Dalits and Muslims were ready to pardon Lalu a thousand sins because he had 'given' them social esteem and security. He had not created a paradise for them: massacres of Dalits were taking place with even greater frequency; lower-backward sharecroppers fighting for security of tenancy were far from getting justice; Muslims were losing their lives and properties (riots had taken place in thirty towns of the state leading to the death of about two hundred Muslims in Lalu's five-year tenure).

Yet the power of the Lalu illusion was so overwhelming that it swept all his failures and follies aside. Dalits did not leave him even though they were dying and suffering everywhere in his raj. The lower backwards did not desert him even though he had wanted to take away their quota and was denying them representational opportunities. Muslims did not turn away from him even when his police never arrested the chief perpetrator of the Bhagalpur massacre, Kameshwar Yadav; they stuck with him even when he admitted Kameshwar into the Janata Dal.

So no wonder Lalu delivered a crushing defeat to the Opposition in the elections of 1995, leading the Janata Dal into the Assembly with a majority of its own, something the party had not been able to achieve even in 1990 despite V.P. Singh's charisma and all-caste support. Nitish, who had dreamt of winning a majority and dislodging Lalu from power, was petrified by the near-total rejection: 303 of his party's 310 candidates lost, 270 of them forfeiting their security deposit for not being able to get even one-sixth (16.66 per cent) of the total valid votes cast in their constituencies. Twelve more managed to save their security deposit but remained quite low down in the ranking results. Twenty-one of them became runners-up in their constituencies, but the margins by which most of them lagged were quite high. Of the 7 who won, 3 were from Nalanda district—the 'Kurmi country'—including Nitish who got about 40,000 votes against 27,000 of Vishwa Mohan Choudhary of Janata Dal in his old constituency Harnaut. Two of the other winners were Koeris, one a Brahman and one a Dalit from a constituency reserved for Dalits.

The Samata Party received about 7 per cent of the total vote and the Janata Dal about 28 per cent: the difference was gigantic. Nitish went through a despairing phase. The horrid conditions prevailing everywhere in the state, the political environment, the phenomenal rise in his popularity, the mammoth gatherings at his public speeches, the sympathetic media—all of them had pointed to a sure downfall of Lalu but Lalu had emerged triumphant. What had gone wrong? Why did not all those favourable factors translate into votes?

First, circumstantial factors went against Samata. The party had to face an election only a few months after its formation, leaving it hardly any time for preparation or selection of good candidates. Many of the candidates were poor in every respect: personal appeal, organizing ability, funds.

Another factor was the overstretching of the elections. Chief Election Commissioner T.N. Seshan minced the elections in far too many phases. 'We had neither the organizational resources nor the financial resources to sustain our campaign through the endless Seshan schedule,' says Nitish. 'The energy and enthusiasm of both our candidates and workers dropped to a low level as a result of prolongation.'

The Samata Party's internal analysis showed that while most Kurmis and Koeris voted for it, the bulk of the Yadavs, Muslims, lower backwards and Dalits did not. Lalu's propaganda that Nitish was a proxy for the upper castes worked wonderfully with the lower backwards and Dalits. Nitish had expected the lower backwards to support him for defending their share of the reservation quota and publicly revolting against Lalu on the issue. Among the upper castes, only a marginal proportion supported the party, the greater number dividing their patronage between the Congress and the BJP.

Nitish needed to rework the social arithmetic. The primary thing he learnt from his drubbing was that he could not win power all on his own. He had overestimated himself. The vote against Lalu showed multipolar behaviour; the Samata Party, the BJP and the Congress earned fragments of it.

Having been politically brought up on a platform of anti-Congressism he would rule the Congress out for any alliance; but he started working towards a partnership with the BJP, which would fetch him votes of the upper castes. He was so desperate to get upper-caste votes that he also allied with virtually a one-man organization, Bihar People's Party, led by Anand Mohan Singh, a Rajput don.

His second important lesson was that the cult following Lalu had built up among the lower backwards, Dalits and Muslims remained solid and unshaken: he had underestimated the power of the Lalu illusion. Lalu won even though his revolution had no economic gifts in its package for the lower castes and Muslims. But the social and political power he had given to the lower castes and the protection of life and property he had provided to the Muslims were far more important than economic benefits, for which they felt indebted to him. Two, in many cases the power and protection themselves generated economic benefits. Three, they gave him an absolute majority with the hope he would now be able to bring about real economic changes. Four, the Opposition did not offer a credible alternative.

Nitish needed to pull the lower backwards and Dalits out of Lalu's spell. He surmised his political approach towards them was still right: they were suffering under Lalu's regime from under-representation and oppression; only, his message to them had not sunk in and he would have to work harder to convince them. To increase the depth of his reach to them he decided to provide them significant representation in the party organization and candidate nominations in future elections, so that the recruits became his evangelists among their communities.

As far as Muslims were concerned, he could count on his own strong secular image; and he would declare publicly that his covenant with BJP was not an 'ideological alliance' but only a 'tactical alliance'—an alliance to dislodge an evil regime and not to promote the agenda of Hindu chauvinism. He could also hope to win over Muslims by accentuating the sense of neglect the community was feeling due to Lalu reneging on many of his promises—such as speedy prosecution of the accused in the Bhagalpur massacre and speedy distribution of relief to its victims; adequate representation in public services; promotion of Urdu as second official language; and adequate financial assistance to traditional craftsmen in the handloom and silk industries.

The next challenge was the parliamentary election in April–May 1996. Though initially acclaimed for bold economic reforms (1991 onward), the national Congress ministry headed by P.V. Narasimha Rao lost its credibility in the later part of its five-year tenure due to a number of scandals. Two Opposition formations were in the race for power: the National Democratic Alliance, comprising the BJP, the Samata Party and some others, which had declared Atal Behari Vajpayee as its prime ministerial candidate; and the United Front, comprising the Janata Dal and the communist parties, which did not yet have a prime ministerial candidate.

Public sympathy seemed to be swelling in Bihar as across the country in favour of Vajpayee. Lalu, on whom politics was centred in Bihar, towered over others in the Janata Dal with his spectacular performance in the Assembly elections and his cult image among the backward castes; he was elected the party's national president in January 1996. He was instrumental in the formation of the United Front and even appeared in public perception to be one of the front runners for prime ministership.

But the exposure of the Fodder Scam and allegations against Sadhu Yadav and Subhash Yadav of accepting bribes for plum postings of officials and forcibly occupying public and private properties undermined his messianic image.

The impact of the negatives showed in the results. The Janata Dal won only 22 of the 54 seats as compared to 33 in 1991. Its vote slipped from 34.1 in 1991 to 31.9 per cent. Lalu's negatives also cast their shadow on the communist allies. The CPI could retain only 3 of the 6 seats it won in 1991. The CPI(M) could not even retain the lone seat of 1991. In contrast, the BJP won 18 seats with 20.5 per cent votes. The Samata Party won 6 seats with 14.45 per cent vote, up about 7.5 per cent from 1995 Assembly elections.

Nitish won the Barh constituency the third time, trouncing Vijay Krishna of the Janata Dal by 65,000 votes, a margin big enough but much smaller than the 1,74,000 by which his Congress rival had trailed behind him in 1991. He got 59 per cent of the total valid votes cast in 1991, which dropped to 51 per cent in 1996. The fall in his vote percentage was because of the division of the Janata Dal vote.

Barh has four castes—Rajputs, Bhumihars, Yadavs and Kurmis—in substantial numbers. Traditional social rivalry for dominance usually drives Rajputs and Bhumihars to back rival candidates; and the same is true of Yadavs and Kurmis. As the candidate of an undivided Janata Dal in 1991 Nitish had received support both of the Yadavs and Kurmis as well as of the Rajputs. In 1996 the bulk of the Yadavs voted the Janata

Dal, as did the bulk of Rajputs because the party's candidate was a Rajput. That brought about a swing of the Bhumihar vote in favour of Nitish, in addition to the vote of the Kurmis who were solidly behind him. Nitish also picked up important small chunks cutting across caste barriers on the strength of his image as an incorruptible and principled crusader against Lalu's wicked regime.

As far as the 'Kurmi country' was concerned Nitish was the political king: George Fernandes won from Nalanda largely with Nitish's backing. Of the 15 seats Samata lost, it was runner-up in 10, third in 4; and compared to the 1995 elections when 87 per cent of its candidates forfeited their security deposit, only 4.5 per cent of them did in 1996. With the 1996 parliamentary results, Nitish's political stature grew considerably. He gained also from the support of the upper castes who were beginning to see him as the politician with the greatest potential to 'emancipate' them from Lalu. The Samata Party's alliance with the BJP also increased the comfort level of the upper castes with him, doubly facilitating their tilt towards him. These elections saw a significant switch of the upper-caste vote from the Congress to the BJP, throwing the Congress traditional electoral arithmetic haywire and jostling the party to the margins.

Nitish's dream of making Samata a national party, however, came crashing down. The party contested 86 seats spread over twelve states besides Bihar—Andhra Pradesh, Gujarat, Haryana, Kerala, Madhya Pradesh, Maharashtra, Manipur, Orissa, Rajasthan, Tamil Nadu, UP and West Bengal—and the two Union territories of Delhi and Chandigarh and could win only 3 seats, 2 in Madhya Pradesh and 1 in UP; 71 of them (82 per cent) forfeited the security deposit. The Samata appeared destined to be confined to Bihar. But neither Nitish nor George Fernandes were overly disappointed, because politics in India was getting fragmented into regional polities and a party could still wield a lot of national influence if it managed to remain strong in its home country.

In the overall results, the BJP for the first time in political history emerged as the single largest party in the Lok Sabha with 161 seats, the Congress gathering only 140. However, the BJP failed to persuade other parties to join it to make up the required majority of 271 to form the government. With the tactical support of the Congress from outside, a minority coalition of parties with the United Front took over government with Deve Gowda, a Janata Dal regional leader in Karnataka, as prime minister.

Lalu expected Deve Gowda to help him avert the sword of the Fodder Scam hanging over his head, but he didn't oblige him. Lalu tried to influence I.K. Gujral who succeeded him. Gujral was sympathetic, but he could offer no help after the CBI presented strong evidence against Lalu to the state Governor and asked permission for Lalu's prosecution on 10 May 1997. Gujral advised Lalu to resign; so did Sharad Yadav. Seven of Lalu's ministers and 21 of the 167 Janata Dal MLAs also wanted Lalu to quit.

Lalu was politically isolated. But he refused to quit. In June 1997 the Governor gave permission to the CBI to file the charge sheet against him; yet he remained stubborn. Lalu organized processions through the streets of Patna as a demonstration of his formidable popular support. One of the processions put up an angry show in front of the high court in which several lawyers were roughed up. Nitish and other state NDA leaders took out counter-processions in Patna in response to Lalu's mobilization. Mob power ultimately did not help Lalu: the Governor, with the obvious consent of Gujral, granted sanction to the CBI for his prosecution on 17 June.

Election to Janata Dal presidency was scheduled in early July and party leaders favoured Sharad Yadav. Lalu wanted the party to re-elect him as president if they wanted him to resign as chief minister. Sharad would not agree. Lalu refused to withdraw, ignoring appeals from party leaders, including Gujral.

Lalu knew if he was not party president he would not be able to influence the selection of his successor in Bihar. He had enjoyed power for seven years and did not want to let it slip out of his hands. On 5 July, he organized a 'national convention' of his supporters in Delhi where he announced the formation of a new party, Rashtriya Janata Dal (RJD). He proved himself stronger than the other leaders, drawing away 18 of the 45 Janata Dal MPs in the Lok Sabha to his new party. Of the 167 Janata Dal MLAs, 137 switched over to the RJD.

He still needed 25-odd MLAs for a majority in a House of 324. He struck a deal with the Congress, according to which it would join his government with ministerial offices to most of its 30 MLAs. This was the point when the Congress began to be identified with Lalu and lost its moorings in Bihar completely. The CPI (26) and CPI(M) (6) backed Lalu for his 'secular' credentials. The Jharkhand Mukti Morcha (19) stayed with him with the hope for a separate state. That left 26 independents who Lalu could manage with a variety of temptations.

Even after the split, Lalu refused to resign. He took the litigation route for his rescue, filing appeals in the CBI special court, Patna High Court and the Supreme Court. Patna was witness to a high drama, with Nitish and BJP leader Sushil Modi leading several processions through Patna demanding Lalu's resignation. Rejection after rejection of Lalu's appeals by courts added to the swell of public pressure on him to resign.

When all of Lalu's options to evade arrest were closed, he got his wife Rabri Devi elected as his successor. On 30 July 1997 he was sent on judicial remand for 134 days and was released on bail on 12 December the same year.

Lalu had relied entirely on his manoeuvring to broaden his support base, and with the 1995 'hurricane Lalu' he appeared to have fully convinced himself that he could go further up only that way—the collapse of governance, the takeover of institutions and resources by the corrupt, the epidemic of thuggery and the 'Yadavization' of power counting for nothing in his eye. With Rabri, a traditional housewife till yesterday, in the chief minister's office, and Lalu away, occupied with his fight against CBI prosecution, even the semblance of governance took a long holiday.

Lalu's growing unpopularity was to show in the results of the 1998 parliamentary elections in which the BJP–Samata alliance won 29 seats, 5 more than in 1996, 4 of them going to the Samata Party that raised its tally from 6 in 1996 to 10. The alliance got almost 39 per cent of the total vote, 4 per cent more than earlier. Lalu's RJD won 17 seats, 5 less than the undivided Janata Dal won in 1996. The Janata Dal, with Sharad Yadav as president, could win only 1 seat, its sole winner being Ram Vilas Paswan.

Nitish won again from Barh, defeating his 1996 rival Vijay Krishna who had joined the RJD. However, the fight was much closer this time: he won by a margin of only 15,000 votes against about 65,000 in 1996. The reason was that the anti-Lalu votes got divided between him and Braj Nandan Yadav, the candidate of the Janata Dal, who took away over 34,000 votes. Nitish managed to win but many of the Samata candidates could not. This led Nitish to a realization that such a division must be avoided to marginalize Lalu in future elections.

The 1998 parliamentary elections saw a phenomenal rise in the vote across the country for the BJP: it won 182 seats with 25.59 per cent of the total vote, almost equal to the Congress's. The Samata Party got 12 seats—Bihar 10, UP 2—with a national vote of 1.76 per cent. With just 194 members, the BJP–Samata alliance was short of 69 members to make up a simple majority. Negotiations brought 22 other parties, mostly regional and small, on board, taking the number to 265, just above simple majority. A government led by Atal Behari Vajpayee was formed with a very large ministry in order to give representation to all the constituents of the NDA.

Vajpayee named Nitish as cabinet minister for railways, a recognition of his performance as an MP and minister of state for agriculture and cooperation for a brief stint in 1990. As a minister of state he had not had much room to show individual initiative, but what was appreciated by his ministerial colleagues and officers was his focus, attention to detail and going beyond the practical solutions for issues. As an MP he had earned a reputation for studying the subjects on which he spoke and the clarity and sophistication with which he presented his views. Another factor that influenced Vajpayee in promoting him to cabinet rank was his crucial role in Bihar in steering the political campaign for the dethronement of Lalu. The Vajpayee government had tried to remove Lalu from power by imposing President's rule on 12 February 1999 on the grounds of 'total breakdown' of law and order in the state. But the move had backfired and it had to reinstall Rabri as chief minister within less than a month. That convinced Vajpayee and other NDA leaders that the only way to dislodge Lalu would be to strengthen Nitish's position and project him as the alternative. It hardly surprised anyone when Vajpayee handed Nitish the ministry of surface transport as an additional charge, a month after he was given railways.

Meanwhile, Nitish pushed for a merger of the Samata and the Janata Dal for consolidation of the anti-Lalu vote in Bihar. Fernandes and Sharad Yadav also strongly favoured it. Within a few months the two parties merged to form a new party, the Janata Dal (United). But before the new party could sprout wings and fly the Vajpayee ministry lost the majority owing to withdrawal of support by AIADMK (All India Anna Dravida Munnetra Kazhagam) on 17 April 1999, necessitating fresh elections.

To the advantage of the JD(U), however, Lalu further lost support. The two communist parties, which had parted ways with him in 1998, remained steadfast in their refusal to join his election front. The Jharkhand Mukti Morcha also broke away. That left Lalu only with the Congress. Also, Lalu's election propaganda was centred on playing on the insecurity of the backward castes, Dalits and Muslims: 'Defeat the feudal forces and Hindu demons that are planning to butcher you, torture you and re-subjugate you.' Not believing in doing anything to address the politico-economic needs of the poor, he was hardly aware that his model of psychosocial politics had become meaningless.

His party won just 7 of the 17 Lok Sabha constituencies it had bagged in 1998. The most humiliating and demoralizing defeat was his own at the hands of Sharad Yadav in Madhepura. Rubbing salt on Lalu's wounds came Nitish's victory, fifth time in succession, at Barh. Barh had witnessed the maximum mobilization of Lalu's forces and resources— government machinery, campaigners, money, arms, hooligans—because defeating Nitish would have been like hacking the Opposition's head. Lalu nearly succeeded, too; the results showed Nitish losing by a few hundred votes. Had Nitish not forced a recount of a booth he would have been declared the loser. With the recount, Nitish's total went past the RJD candidate (Vijay Krishna again) by 1,335 votes.

The BJP–JD(U) alliance won 42 seats, 13 more than the BJP– Samata alliance got in 1998 in Bihar. Nitish was happy to see the increasing endorsement of his alliance with the BJP. The merger of Samata and the Janata Dal banded the Kurmis and Koeris behind the alliance and also drew substantial support from the lower backwards and Dalits. The spectacular success of the BJP–JD(U) alliance showed the growing estrangement of the Kurmis, Koeris, lower backwards and Dalits from Lalu because of the Yadavs claiming the whole pie. Through their overt and covert election propaganda, the alliance leaders and canvassers worked hard to deepen the estrangement. Other factors worked: more upper-caste voters turned away from the Congress to the BJP and Ram Vilas Paswan proved a pull factor for Dalits.

One of the most significant things to note about the 1999 election results was the rise of Nitish's outfit from a junior partner to almost an equal one. In the 1996 parliamentary elections, Samata had got just 6 seats against BJP's 18; in 1998, it got 10 against BJP's 19; and in 1999 it got 18 against BJP's 23. The exponential ascent of Samata/JD(U) was, apart from other factors, also attributable to the growing pull of Nitish's personality among the masses.

Although no talks or deliberations had been held on who could be the alliance's chief ministerial candidate in the Assembly elections in 2000, it became obvious after the 1999 results that Nitish was the front runner. Most of the senior leaders of the JD(U) as well as of the BJP thought that in the current socio-political environment only a backward-caste leader could drive Lalu out of power and Nitish fitted the bill. With his party's exponential growth, Nitish had already swept a number of Lalu strongholds away from him. His success showed in Lalu's downward graph in the parliamentary elections: 32 in 1991, 22 in 1996, 17 in 1998 and 7 in 1999.

The 1999 parliamentary elections was the second time after 1977's Janata Party triumph when a non-Congress party or front won a clear majority (298 seats). After having been prime minister first for thirteen days (in 1996), then for thirteen months (1998–99), Vajpayee settled down for a full tenure of five years (1999–2004). These five years could be said to be NDA's 'golden period'.

In the first allocation of portfolios, Nitish got surface transport, but within a month Vajpayee moved him to agriculture where he could find greater engagement as he had experience as a minister of state in 1990 and as chairman of the Parliamentary Committee on Agriculture from 1993 to 1996. Nitish also wanted agriculture in order to be able to introduce schemes for boosting agricultural productivity in Bihar, where the collapse of governance had led to a deceleration in the process of making modern inputs and credit available to farmers. He could also address the problems of farmers in the tal region, one of his major concerns since his initiation into electoral politics in the late 1970s.

However, Nitish could hardly settle into the agriculture ministry as the elections to the Bihar Assembly were slated for February 2000.

# building an alternative

Lalu seemed to have lost his hypnotic grip over the masses, and everyone—the media, intelligentsia, social scientists, the grapevine and even some of his party men—predicted his defeat in the 2000 Assembly polls. It was hard to say whether even at this stage he realized that he and he alone was responsible for the massive erosion of his vote base. His popularity had been corroded because of his casual attitude to governance. He had been favoured by fortuity so many times in life that he had turned into a great believer in serendipity. He was relying in 2000 on the same stock-in-trade that he had used in 1990—rustic persona, dark humour, prophesy of an apocalypse for the backwards and Muslims if they didn't follow him in the war to vanquish the 'Brahmanist' demons, grandiose proposals and lavish promises, top-class political skullduggery—highly optimistic about the constellation of stars bearing him a handsome gift again.

However, most of his ardent supporters now saw that he lacked the vision to take his psychosocial revolution to a higher stage. The house of revolution he had promised to build appeared to be a mirage. The society was like a theatre where in the past the stage and the front rows were permanently reserved for the upper castes; the other castes took the back rows or were not allowed entry at all. In Lalu raj the stage and the front rows were filled by the BCs, EBCs, Muslims and Dalits and the upper castes were relegated to the rear. However, the larger masses of the depressed classes discovered that the front rows had been occupied by opportunists from their communities who were not interested in the common good of the communities but in their own rapacious accumulation. The poor felt that 'our own king' was not truly working for change in their life conditions.

This feeling grew not only among other communities but also among Yadavs and Muslims who were the two main pillars of Lalu's fort and who saw lumpen and criminal elements from their communities enjoying his patronage. Among Muslims, there was an added grievance: many felt that Lalu had showered favours only on high-caste Muslims (Sheikhs, Syeds, Pathans) and neglected the backward Muslims (Ansaris, Momins, Kulhayyas). He had extracted most of his protection vote from backward Muslims, who usually suffered in riots. Now they wanted promotion, not just protection.

In the NDA camp, a victory in sight triggered internal conflicts over who should get maximum seats in the Assembly. Sharad Yadav and Ram Vilas Paswan wanted more seats for their own men from the dissolved Janata Dal than Fernandes and Nitish thought they deserved. Much of the JD(U) vote in Bihar was actually what the Samata had earned after years of work, Nitish said. But Sharad and Paswan were insistent, the latter because he wanted to be projected as as chief ministerial candidate. Sharad was fiercely backing him, though the BJP did not want him.

'I felt a terrible sense of hurt and insecurity,' Nitish recalls. 'I thought I had worked so hard to prepare the ground for an alternative to Lalu, and here was somebody trying to appropriate it without having done anything to deserve it.' He prevailed over Fernandes to pull the Samata out of the JD(U). The Samata Party would remain a constituent of the NDA, however, as would the JD(U).

During seat-sharing negotiations at L.K. Advani's residence in Delhi differences resurfaced. Fernandes and Nitish wanted 122 of the 324 seats, arguing that it was the Assembly constituencies that formed the Lok Sabha constituencies from which the Samata had won in 1999. The BJP, the JD(U) and the Bihar People's Party were ready to give much fewer seats to the Samata. In course of the meeting, Advani passed on a chit to Nitish on which was written '108'. That was the number of seats the Samata should expect. Nitish was not happy. Further arguments brought the number down to 90, which Nitish thought was absurd, because Samata was the biggest party in terms of parliamentary seats in Bihar.

Although the NDA released a common manifesto, the fissures

showed. Its constituents were arrayed in open or surrogate contests against each other in 74 constituencies. The BJP set up candidates in 168 constituencies, Samata in 120, JD(U) in 87 and Bihar People's Party in 23, adding to 398 fighting for 324 seats. The NDA did not conduct a joint campaign. Each party organized public meetings for its own leaders and candidates.

During the election campaign Nitish presented himself as a man of today and Lalu as a man of yesterday. Ever since Nitish broke away from Lalu he had been emphasizing the need for development. Lalu ruled with twin mantras: social justice and secularism. Nitish told people these two ideals were also very dear to his heart, but he placed Bihar's development at the top of his agenda, arguing that true social justice and true secularism could only be achieved through economic progress.

The Lalu camp again portrayed Nitish as a puppet of the forwards who were bent upon regaining power under the camouflage of development. Nitish had to fight hard to demolish the Lalu doctrine that development was antithetical to social justice—a diversionary tactic to derail the process of empowerment of the downtrodden. He had to convince the poor that development and social justice were complementary to each other. And two factors came in handy for him: one, the awareness across classes of the opportunities offered by liberalization; and two, the spread of resentment against 'Yadavocracy' and 'Yadavization' among extremely backward classes. The message Nitish delivered was that his development would be focused on the inclusion of the 'neglected' and 'discriminated' castes within the 'Mandal family'.

He had to fight the hardest to keep clear of the daubs of black paint Lalu incessantly hurled at him for his party's alliance with the communal BJP. Nitish had to repeatedly reassure people that his party's alliance with the BJP was not an ideological alliance but a tactical one. He openly expressed disagreement with the BJP's aggressive Hindutva agenda. Before the elections, three major items of this agenda came into focus: a move by the Vajpayee government to set up a commission to review the Constitution; permission by the BJP-run Gujarat government to government employees to join RSS activities; and revival of the campaign to build a Ram temple on the ruins of the Babri mosque at Ayodhya. Nitish strongly, publicly disapproved of these moves, to the

point of dropping a hint that the Samata could walk out of the NDA
if the BJP insisted on implementing those proposals. Arguing through
several meetings between the BJP, the Samata and the JD(U), at Delhi
and Patna, Nitish eventually succeeded in persuading the BJP to
de-emphasize their Hindutva agenda in Bihar and agree on projecting
development as the central concern of the NDA. The NDA, in its
manifesto for the 2000 Assembly elections, declared its fundamental
mantra as 'development, development and development'.

Eventually, the NDA made huge gains on its development plank,
but fell short of a majority. It won 122 seats: BJP, 67, Samata, 34, and
JD(U), 21. The number showed a phenomenal rise from the 48 the
BJP–Samata alliance had got in 1995, a two-and-a-half times boost.
But that was still way behind the number (163) they required for a
majority. Lalu returned with 124 seats, a drop of 43 from 167 five years
ago, supported by the CPI(M) with 2 seats. The NDA needed 41 more,
and the RJD–CPI(M) alliance, 37 to establish majority.

Looking back, Nitish could not but blame his blunder—he calls
it 'immaturity, emotional reaction, needless anxiety'—of pulling the
Samata out of the JD(U). His confidants feel that although Paswan
desperately wanted to be chief minister he had very little backing in the
NDA. Nitish was the front runner for the post and would have got it
no matter how many seats the Samata won. 'Even a donkey could have
seen a clear NDA victory on the horizon,' Nitish reminisces. 'Lalu would
not have come back to power if we had stuck together on seat-sharing.
Instead, we ended up having a hung Assembly.'

With the results unclear, Nitish pleaded—and several other NDA
leaders endorsed it—that the NDA should not stake its claim to form
a government: one, because the chances of getting 41 more MLAs for
making the majority were not very good; two, even if support was
managed it was unlikely to be durable; three, Lalu would find it very
hard to gather support for himself without making compromises that
would discredit him further, thus expanding support for the NDA; and
four, if Lalu failed to garner enough support, a fresh election would
become necessary, which would help the NDA.

However, many NDA leaders also felt they should not allow Lalu
another stint in power; 'we have come thus far and should not lose the

opportunity of ridding Bihar of Lalu'; and there was a good possibility of the Congress (23) splitting in case the party's Central leadership insisted on supporting Lalu. The NDA was banking on at least 8 Congress MLAs led by Veena Shahi breaking away from the party to support an NDA government. Even Intelligence Bureau reports corroborated this.

The NDA also looked sure of getting the support of the Jharkhand Mukti Morcha (12) because of its constituents' clear commitment to the creation of a separate tribal state, unlike Lalu who had said, 'Jharkhand can be created only over my dead body.' There were other parties—CPI (5), CPI(ML–L) (6) and Bahujan Samaj Party (5)—that would not go with the RJD because they too had fought the elections on an anti-Lalu platform. Then there were 20 independents who could be won over through tactful negotiations.

Deliberations followed within the NDA on who should be their legislature party leader. The BJP was a divided house with at least three candidates, so it decided not to stake the claim. That left Nitish and Paswan in the field. Paswan did not have much support within the NDA; also, most alliance leaders thought he would not be acceptable to the parties or breakaway groups whose support was necessary to form a majority. That left only Nitish, but Paswan was strongly opposed to his name. Two days passed after the announcement of results without the NDA deciding on Bihar leadership.

On the third day, Nitish was at the Indira Gandhi airport at Delhi waiting to board a flight to Patna when he was requested by an NDA leader on the phone to come back to attend an urgent meeting. At the meeting, all top alliance leaders were there: Vajpayee, Advani, Sharad, Paswan, Fernandes and Digvijay Singh. In order to make a show of grandeur, Paswan had quietly reached an understanding with BJP leaders that they should propose his name and he would decline. Accordingly, at the start, Vajpayee proposed Paswan's name and Paswan refused. Then Nitish's name was proposed and accepted by all.

Nitish was initially hesitant. But eventually he decided to take it up as a challenge. After all, it was the fruition of his hard work of nearly seven years; he had got so close to ousting Lalu from power: why lose the opportunity now? A meeting of the NDA legislature party in Patna on 27 February elected Nitish as its leader.

Conventionally, the Governor of a state invites the party or pre-poll alliance that wins the single largest number of seats first: thus, the RJD deserved to be invited first. But Governor Vinod Pande, clearly under direction of the Vajpayee government at the Centre, ignored Rabri's claim and invited Nitish to form the government. He had him sworn in as chief minister on 3 March and gave Nitish seven days to prove his majority.

NDA negotiators were in touch with Congress MLAs. The Congress sought mandate from the people for ending Lalu's 'jungle raj'. During her election campaign Sonia Gandhi had expressed her apology to voters for supporting Lalu. The NDA believed the Congress would not go against its professed stance. And if it did, the Congress legislature party would split, the resolutely anti-Lalu section switching over to the NDA.

Lalu was in Delhi begging the Congress to support him when Pande invited Nitish to form the government. Hundreds of RJD workers assembled outside the Raj Bhavan in Patna, pelted stones inside and tried to climb over the gates, shouting: '*NDA ka dalal Pande hosh mein aao! Wapas jao!* (NDA stooge Pande, come to your senses. Go back!)' The state witnessed street violence and arson for three days. Lalu called for a Bihar bandh on 5 March in which his supporters caused considerable damage to railway tracks and properties. That day he led a protest march in Patna and courted arrest with senior party men.

Lalu sought CPI and CPI(ML–L) support for re-establishing solidarity to 'stop the communal forces from taking over power'. 'The fascists already have UP in their hands. They want to seize Bihar too. Let us not allow that to happen,' he pleaded with them. He had used the same plea before the elections, but the Congress, the CPI and CPI(ML–L) had rejected it, accusing him of using 'secularism' as a shield to defend himself from all-round attacks for the total collapse of governance in Bihar. Their pre-poll rejection notwithstanding, Lalu kept on chanting the 'secularism' mantra post-poll to get them to back him. And he had two big leaders in his favour: Sonia and CPI(M) general secretary Harkishen Singh Surjeet.

But the problem Lalu faced was that Sonia could not deliver full Congress support, because at least 8 of her MLAs thought associating with Lalu would be suicidal for the party. Several of the dissenting MLAs were from the tribal region. They had the ready offer of ministerial offices and a legislation for creating a separate tribal state from the NDA negotiators.

Lalu was alarmed. He desperately wanted to herd all the Congress MLAs off into one place and sever all their communication with the outside world, so the NDA negotiators could not reach them. Top Congress leaders connived with him in shutting in those MLAs in rooms of the Hotel Pataliputra in Patna. The task of preventing them from escaping or NDA negotiators from establishing contact with them was entrusted to Mohammed Shahabuddin, the thug and RJD MP from Siwan. A journalist who visited the hotel on one of the days of their confinement recalls:

> I was not stopped by any of Shahabuddin's goons who were watching the lobby and the corridors. One of them pointed me to the room where the 'boss' was. I walked in and found Shahabuddin sitting relaxed in a chair dressed in a vest and lungi. He knew who I was and asked me to sit down. 'What's up?' I asked in a half-knowing, half-curious, cajoling voice. 'Anything to stop Nitish grabbing power,' he said matter-of-factly. I came out and hung around the place for some time and saw glimpses of the MLAs in his captivity. I saw Ram Jatan Sinha and Jagdish Sharma (independent). Most of the Congress MLAs were tribals. Suddenly, I noticed Jagdish Sharma and a few other MLAs walking down a corridor and in a flash Shahabuddin, a cocked gun in each hand, and his gang members rushed to stop and herd them back into their rooms. 'Don't try that again,' Shahabuddin warned them. 'It may prove costly.' I went to the Assembly where I found Nitish in his chamber. I told him what I had seen at the Hotel Pataliputra and asked him if he should not be asking the police chief to raid the place and free the captive MLAs. Nitish said, 'Saryu Rai [state BJP leader] is handling that part.' I was astonished by Nitish's response. I think his soft approach was what pulled him down.[8]

Not that the NDA was a house of saints. It had in its ranks Narendra Kumar (alias Sunil) Pandey, the Samata MLA from Piro, and Suraj Bhan, independent MLA from Mokama. They were both notorious thugs and had together mobilized ten more hooligans who were elected as MLAs into a front to back Nitish. Most of them were in jail, including Suraj Bhan: they had contested from there and won with caste support and through intimidatory tactics.

When NDA negotiators contacted the undertrial MLAs they said they were ready to hand over their letter of support to Nitish if he came over to the prison gate. Nitish was astounded to hear this; he said under no circumstances would he do so. 'You can call it a sham,' reminisces Nitish, 'because after all I was ready to accept their support. It was like, as the Bihari proverb goes: *Gul khaye gulgula se parhej* (One who eats sugar abstains from sweets). But I just thought at that time that going to the jail gate was going to do far more damage to my image than accepting their support would. Eventually, the seniormost BJP leader Kailashpati Mishra went to the jail gate to receive their letter.'

There was no running away from thugs for Nitish though. Sunil Pandey, his party MLA out on bail, was working hard as two journalists found:

> About 40 members of the incoming Bihar Assembly have criminal cases against them. On Wednesday, March 2, the NDA state leadership was in a huddle at Nitish Kumar's residence in Patna's North Srikrishnapuri area. The discussion was interrupted by the ringing of Samata Party MLA Sunil Pandey's phone. 'Dhumalji?' Pandey said excitedly, '*Aap kahan hain? . . . Thik hai. Aap rukiye, aadmi ja raha hai.*' (Where are you, Shri Dhumal? I am sending my men to escort you here.) In a few minutes Dhumal arrived – to express his solidarity with the NDA. Another Independent MLA had been won over . . . To veteran Bihar watchers, Pandey and Dhumal need no introduction. Pandey faces many criminal cases in central Bihar. He is linked to the Ranbir Sena, a private army of largely Bhumihar landlords, and is a sworn foe of the Naxalites from the day they killed his father. Manoranjan Singh (alias Dhumal Singh), who won from Baniapur (Saran district), faces a staggering 174 criminal cases, including a few for murder. His most infamous (alleged) involvement was in the murder of an associate of Dawood Ibrahim in Mumbai's JJ Hospital.[9]

Lalu feared Suraj Bhan and Sunil Pandey might coerce the MLAs he had won over or was hiding. He was further unnerved by the permission from the court the NDA leaders managed, obviously with government connivance, for Suraj Bhan and three other imprisoned thugs—Rajan Tiwary, Munna Shukla and Rama Singh—to attend the members' oath-taking in the Assembly. The four were brought in a prison van from the Beur jail in western Patna to the Assembly. The NDA members thumped the desks when they took oath. After oath-taking, seven of the thugs, including these four, visited Nitish in his chamber, shook hands with him and assured him their support. Nitish joined his palms in response and said, 'Many thanks.' No further words were exchanged.

Nitish distinctly remembers the moment: 'These seven were smarter in public relations than me. They came in followed by press photographers, so their picture with me could be there on television and in the morning newspapers. That brought honour to their image and dishonour to me. But it couldn't be helped.'

Lalu won support from Sonia who was more concerned about weakening the NDA nationally than strengthening her party in Bihar. Sonia's backing ensured the support of a majority of the Congress MLAs. Even otherwise, most Congress MLAs, though they would have been happy seeing Lalu not regain power, were reluctant to leave the party and join an NDA government. Lalu's secularist posturing also got him CPI support.

The vote of confidence for Nitish to prove his majority in the house was to take place on 10 March. When the MLAs gathered one day before to elect the Speaker who would conduct the vote it was clear that Lalu had won. Lalu put up a Congress MLA, Sadanand Singh, as his candidate for Speaker, and Nitish had no choice but to allow him to be elected without any contest, 'with a consensus', because Nitish did not have enough backing of any single party. That evening Nitish decided he would not seek a vote of confidence. It was pointless hoping for a miracle or a mysterious twist at the last minute to achieve something they had failed to achieve during the week. Rather than going down as a loser in a vote, it would be more honourable for him to submit his resignation. That would be an acceptance of defeat—without the humiliation of being outvoted.

The truth was Nitish had not been outvoted but outmanoeuvred. There was no means that he did not use that Lalu had: muscle, money, inducements, warcries, tactics. But Lalu just seemed to have more of everything. Lalu's superiority could be attributed to his experience and to his attitude towards politics that was 90 per cent realpolitik and 10 per cent morality. Nitish's attitude was just the reverse. Lalu was a specialist in realpolitik; he had almost become a pro with his experience of ten years in absolute power. Nitish was an amateur, having decided to use thugs to defeat Lalu's thugs in certain constituencies for the first time. He would not know how to use people like Sunil Pandey or Suraj Bhan as Lalu did Shahabuddin. Nor would he have liked to.

Lalu was back in power with Rabri as chief minister. One of the terms of the pact between the Congress and the RJD post-2000 elections was that Lalu would support the Bihar State Reorganization Bill the Vajpayee ministry had proposed for the creation of Jharkhand. As many as 11 of the 23 Congress MLAs were from the tribal region. Lalu was in a fix, but he was not the type of politician to lose power for principles; he acceded, but with a proviso that he should not seem to have accepted it as a quid pro quo for power, that he should not be forced to make any public statement at that moment in support of the bill.

Less than six weeks later, on 25 April 2000, RJD members in both the Houses of the state legislature voted with members of the NDA, JMM, other parties and independents to ratify the Bihar State Reorganization Bill, paving the way for the bifurcation of the state. On 2 August, the Lok Sabha passed the bill and on 11 August, the Rajya Sabha, following which the President granted his assent to it on 25 August.

The entire mineral wealth, nearly all major industries along with their ancillaries and three-fourths of the forests went to Jharkhand, leaving Bihar largely an agricultural state with its annual revenue—mining royalties, excise, commercial taxes, forest levies taken together—reduced to one-third of the normal collection. And with 55 per cent of the area and 75 per cent of the population in its share, its land would have to take care of more people: Bihar's rural population rose from 86.86 per cent to 89.25 per cent (all India, 74.29 per cent).

Agriculture was already in a poor state; it was going to get worse with reduction in public investments and incentives. There was no alternative employment. Most electricity generation plants went to Jharkhand, crippling Bihar with acute power shortage. This further created a major constraint on the state's ability to mitigate its industrial deprivation with new private investments. Bihar was deep in the morass of poverty; with the bifurcation, it seemed destined to sink deeper.

The plight of Bihar drew the unanimous concern of Bihari MPs in all parties; they demanded a gigantic financial compensation package from the Central government in the form of a grant or long-term assistance for the huge loss their state had suffered.

Lalu and Nitish were one on this common cause. Lalu had come on board only after he was forced to support the creation of Jharkhand for the survival of the Rabri ministry. Nitish was, from the very beginning, part of the discussions within the NDA and the Union cabinet on the drafting of the first avatar of the Bihar Reorganization Bill. That bill lapsed with the fall of the second Vajpayee ministry in early 1999. Nitish held the railways and surface transport portfolios then and was among the leading advocates for an adequate financial package to Bihar in the event of division. He told Vajpayee and Home Minister Advani that the creation of Jharkhand and sanction of financial package to Bihar must be considered simultaneously and given equal importance. At his initiative, the Samata Party made the financial package a precondition to bifurcation.

With MPs from all parties supporting the financial package demand, a provision was made in the Bihar Reorganization Bill for setting up a special unit in the Planning Commission. This unit would identify plans essential for Bihar's development and provide for additional funds for them. Following the assurance given by Advani who moved the bill, a special cell was created in the Planning Commission to draw up a blueprint for the financial package. Less than two weeks after Jharkhand was formed on 15 November 2000, Bihari MPs of all parties submitted a joint memorandum to Vajpayee, making a strong case for the financial package. The memorandum did not mention the amount of financial compensation needed, but Lalu somehow arrived at a figure of about Rs 18,000 crore and kept pushing for his claim from the Centre.

With the bifurcation, significant shifts took place in Bihar's political scenario as well. Both the BJP and the Congress lost nearly half of their MLAs to Jharkhand; they became important players, along with the JMM, in Jharkhand, but in Bihar they suffered a reduction. The division came as a blessing in disguise for Lalu as his party's strength rose from 38 per cent of seats in the 324-member House of undivided Bihar to 47 per cent of seats in the 243-member House of new Bihar; by way of numbers he had needed 39 members more for a majority in the old House but now he needed only 7. He could even do without the Congress with Bihar divided. The bifurcation thus improved Lalu's bargaining position with the Congress.

The political shift in the Opposition camp was even more dramatic: the BJP was reduced from a senior partner to a junior partner in the NDA in Bihar. The combined strength of the Samata Party and the JD(U) in the new House came to 47 against BJP's 35; it had been 55 versus BJP's 67 in the undivided House. This proved to be an important turning point in Nitish's career, for as the undisputed leader of the larger party he could set the priorities and determine the political road map for the alliance.

9

the road to victory

Soon after Nitish rejoined the Vajpayee cabinet as minister of agriculture in May 2000, he revived the idea of consolidating the Opposition vote—a rectification of the folly that had driven him to lead the Samata Party into an independent campaign in 2000, offering another term to Lalu–Rabri on a platter.

With the BJP already an ally, he was concerned about the fragmentation of the socialist/Janata vote. The Samata Party and the JD(U) had to merge to dislodge Lalu. The Janata constituency, which comprised voters from the socialist movement, the JP movement and the Mandal upsurge, was split in three camps represented by the Samata Party, the JD(U) and the RJD. Lalu's vote was a vote of social revenge, a vote of historical correction, as it called upon the insecurities of communities under threat and the Yadav vote bank. A coalescing of the Samata and the JD(U) camps alone could provide a credible and viable alternative to the RJD, because the mass of lower-caste voters who were disenchanted with Lalu would place their faith only in a party that was genuinely interested in their emancipation, empowerment and prosperity. That was the only way to regain the socialist legacy stolen away by Lalu who wore it as a fig leaf.

The reunification move was boosted by the exit of Paswan from the JD(U) to float his own outfit, Lok Janshakti Party (LJP). His exit brought Nitish and the JD(U) president Sharad Yadav closer. At a crucial meeting in New Delhi on 15 October 2000, Fernandes, Nitish and Sharad agreed in principle to amalgamate the two parties.

9

191

They decided to meet in January 2001 to finalize the blueprint for reunification but meanwhile 6 of the 12 Samata MPs in the Lok Sabha raised a banner of revolt. They were led by Raghunath Jha, the Brahman who had split the votes for Ram Sundar Das in the 1990 bid for Bihar chief ministership, leaving the field open to Lalu, and had later joined the Samata. The rebel MPs said a merger would go in favour of Lalu because Sharad Yadav was a 'liability' and the JD(U) only the 'B team' of the RJD. Their argument was that Samata should build on its own assets. They concentrated their attack on Nitish as he was the originator of the idea. They publicly accused him of 'autocratic behaviour', alleging that he wanted to force the merger ignoring the views of dissident colleagues.

They met Fernandes who gave them an assurance—possibly under certain constraints—that the reunification move would be put on hold. Nitish was bothered by Fernandes's acquiescence.

Nitish had an uneasy relationship with Fernandes. Fernandes had backed him as an alternative to Lalu in Bihar. The support was as much ideological and tactical as it was personal, for Fernandes depended on Nitish for winning a Lok Sabha seat from Bihar. It was a relationship of mutual benefit: Nitish got a great patron of national stature to build his way up under his tutelage, and Fernandes, a junior of great promise to depend upon to have at least one state where his re-election would be assured. Yet, all was not cosy in this relationship.

It seemed Fernandes was getting afflicted by Nitish's growing stature owing to his performance as a minister and his persuasive skills in Parliament. Fernandes therefore wanted to clip Nitish's wings; but whatever he would do to restrain his ambitious junior he would do it subtly, all the while appearing to be his greatest well-wisher.

The six rebel MPs wanted to have their own man elected as the party's Bihar unit president. This was aimed to curtail Nitish's decision-making powers with regard to party affairs in the state. Nitish wanted Fernandes to stop the rebels; instead, Fernandes gave them an ambiguous assurance: 'The issue will be amicably settled.'

Nitish could see the game slipping out of his hands. Fernandes had surrendered to the blackmail of his enemies, obviously to keep the party's parliamentary strength intact in order to maintain his own political prestige. Nitish decided to use his trump card. He wrote out his letter of resignation as minister for agriculture to the prime minister and sent it across to Fernandes.

The message Nitish wanted to send out was that if the rebels did not mend their ways and Fernandes showed a leaning towards them he could walk out of the party with his formidable Bihar base. That would leave him free to chart his organizational expansion plan—starting with a realignment with the JD(U)—and Fernandes without an assured Lok Sabha seat. Nitish's clever move forced Fernandes to distance himself from the rebels.

In the early months of 2001, the internal revolt against Lalu also picked up momentum. The early 2000s saw no change in Lalu's attitude to governance. People were hoping the 2000 election setback would jolt him out of his indifference and drive him to accelerate development of the state, but he belied their hopes.

The bureaucracy in the state, not known for efficiency even in pre-Lalu years, dipped to a new low in the Rabri years. The main reason of course was the pervasive apathy of the political leadership to development. Rabri proved to be even more apathetic to development than Lalu, never failing to remind the world that the office was thrust upon her by circumstances. She often refused to take any blame for the slow pace of development, arguing she had assigned the work to her officers and it was their lapse. Besides, she said, there were some officers (probably insinuating the upper-caste officers) who wanted to bring a bad name to her regime.

In her post-2000 avatar she stopped going to her office in the secretariat and stayed most of the time at home with her children. She engaged herself less and less in deliberations over government proposals, showing no interest in understanding or finding out what their provisions or implications were. She did not visit the sites of massacres or other incidents as often as she had done in her earlier tenure. Certain leftists and feminists tried very hard to prove why Rabri must be seen as a milestone in the battle for egalitarian India and how she had come into her own as a ruler,[10] but this was an overly romanticized portrayal of a woman who took office as her husband's rubber stamp and felt bound by tradition to remain so.

Rabri Devi never took independent decisions. She was happy with

Lalu acting as the de facto CM. Lalu always sat alongside her when officers wanted her formal approval or signature. He also took full advantage of Rabri's traditional docility and did not allow her to grow out of his shadow. At one public meeting when Rabri, after reading out her short, prepared speech, launched forth on her own, Lalu, who was sitting on the dais, said loudly: 'Enough. You can stop now.' And she did.[11]

Rabri's indifference bred general apathy in the administration. No officers were appointed to a number of key posts. In road construction and rural engineering—the two departments responsible for providing Bihar urban and rural road connectivity—all the posts of engineers-in-chief and chief engineers were vacant in the second half of Rabri's post-2000 tenure. Of the ninety-one posts of superintending engineers in the two departments, eighty-one had no occupants.[12]

In the absence of key officers, it was common for one officer to look after two or three posts, compelling him to delay the reviewing of files. Making it worse were the whimsical and motivated transfers that allowed many (usually good, efficient and intelligent) officers short and uncertain tenures.

Delay in initiation and implementation of programmes resulted in lower resource utilization as well as a curtailment of Central allocations. A Planning Commission estimate found fast decline in the capacity of the state government to plan and absorb funds during the Rabri years. In 1997–98, the first year of the Rabri rule, the state spent 75.45 per cent of the total plan outlay; in 2000–01, the fourth year of her rule, the expenditure dropped to 56 per cent.

There was poor accountability within the system. Accountability could not be expected to be enforced in the bureaucracy when there was none for the political leadership. The state government was answerable to the legislature (that is, the people) for its failure to spend the allocations for plans approved in the annual budget. Despite the non-fulfilment of its responsibility year after year, the Lalu–Rabri government got away with it, because the majority of the legislators from his party did not ever question the government, leave aside denying further approvals.

Several standard economic indices hit rock bottom or were on a downslide in the Lalu–Rabri regime. However, some aspects of the state economy were not entirely bleak. There is increasing evidence that Lalu was totally blind to the positive features of the Bihar economy that had been globally denounced for economic collapse. He allowed himself to be beaten on the Nitish-led Opposition propaganda because he did not capitalize on those positive features in his political marketing campaigns.

The average annual growth rate of the state GDP between 1993–94 and 2004–05 was over 5 per cent, which was substantially lower than the national GDP growth rate of 6.5 per cent during that period, but this does not suggest stagnation or regression. Agricultural growth in Bihar during the period averaged 4 per cent, which was higher than the national average of under 3 per cent. In 2000–01, construction grew by 11.63 per cent, communication by 21.64 per cent, trade–hotels–restaurants by 7.62 per cent and banking and insurance by 10 per cent. In all these sectors the state recorded lower growth between 2001–02 and 2004–05, but it was positive growth.

Beating the stereotype of gross rural poverty, the rural deposits of the scheduled commercial banks (SCBs) in Bihar were much higher during Rabri's 2000–05 tenure than those in Congress-ruled Maharashtra. From Rs 9,067 crore in 2000–01, the rural deposits of SCBs in Bihar rose to Rs 13,328 crore in 2004–05 (making 6.3 per cent of the total national rural deposits), whereas in Maharashtra the figure made about 3.9 per cent of the national deposits.

The total deposits of SCBs in Bihar rose from Rs 26,800 crore in 2000–01 to Rs 41,007 crore in 2004–05, nearly by 65 per cent (higher than the neighbouring West Bengal and UP). In terms of percentage share in total deposits, Bihar ranked very low, yet an average of 16 per cent growth in SCB deposits did not suggest complete collapse.

Even more interesting was the credit–deposit ratio, an important indicator of the level of economic activity and credit absorption capacity of a particular state; this did not register much increase in Bihar during the 1990s, but rose during Rabri's tenure from 20.7 per cent in 2000–01 to 31.4 in 2004–05. The credit–deposit ratio of the five Regional Rural Banks' 1,466 branches in the state was 44.77 per cent, much higher than that of commercial banks.

These positive features of economic growth possibly go on to prove that the government is not the only driver of growth. Despite the frigid approach to development strategies and lackadaisical implementation of poverty alleviation programmes by the Rabri government, the economy did not crumble.

The market was at work, both in the state and in the rest of the country, to add to the low and slow state-driven growth in the overall economy. The positive indices were largely a result of high growth in agriculture, retail, communication and migrant remittances. The people of Bihar, middle class as well as the working class, had found their own way to survive and grow.

However, in comparison with the rest of India, Bihar looked ready to sink. Industrial growth was very low, roads were in a terrible state, power shortage was acute, hospitals looked desolate, population growth was at its highest. To top it all, total lawlessness prevailed, nobody feeling secure for their life or property.

Some ministers in the Rabri cabinet—Shanker Prasad Tekriwal and Jagadanand Singh—started to publicly lament the indifference of the state government to development. Resentment also grew among senior party men due to the increasing influence of the members of Lalu's and Rabri's families in government decision-making.

Lalu's eldest daughter Misa had been known for getting ministers and officers to pass orders and do things she wanted. She did not take active part in the political activities of the RJD. Nor did Lalu or Rabri ever take her along to public functions to project her as their successor. Yet it was in the air that Rabri faced the threat of being arrested in the Disproportionate Assets case filed by the income tax department and in that event would have to quit the chief minister's office, just as Lalu had to do, and then Misa would take over.

Lalu was fully aware of the increasing influence of his and Rabri's family members. He was also aware that they were speaking directly to ministers and officers for jobs they wanted done. An officer recalls: 'One day Lalu asked me whether I receive phone calls from his elder brother Prabhunath Yadav for favours. When I said, yes, I do sometimes, he said, "Next time he calls you let me know what he wants. Only if I tell you do it, you oblige him, otherwise not."'

A year after he led Rabri again into the chief ministerial chair, Lalu was in a dilemma whether to placate his family or his senior party men.

But this dilemma did not last long. For he knew the main target of the rebels directing their fusillade towards the family was Rabri. They had not wanted her as chief minister in 1997 and they had hoped that at least after the 2000 elections one of them would be given a chance but that too was dashed.

Ranjan Yadav emerged as the rallying point of the dissidents after he fell out with Lalu. Ranjan had been Lalu's favourite because of their association from the university days during most of his first tenure. He influenced Lalu's decisions in candidate selections for ministerial offices and party nominees for elections to the two Houses of legislature. But a stage came when Lalu's vanity got the better of him and he began to ignore Ranjan's advice. Sadhu and Subhash, helped by some party leaders, also worked behind the scenes to edge Ranjan out of Lalu's inner circle. Ranjan turned hostile and began to nurse the ambition of succeeding Lalu and even talked to RJD MLAs and MPs to build support for himself.

By 2001 a large number of party MLAs and MPs were feeling unhappy with the performance of the Rabri government. Nagmani, one of the MPs, said openly to the media: 'After the bifurcation the state requires able leadership, which Ranjan Yadav alone can provide and not a "gentle" woman like Rabri Devi.' At least five other RJD MPs, including three Muslims—Anwarul Haque, Mohammad Shahabuddin and Mohammad Taslimuddin—who were once close to Lalu, echoed Nagmani's sentiment. Ministers Tekriwal and Jagadanand criticized the government. 'Nothing has been done for Bihar during the past ten years,' Tekriwal told the media. 'We want attitudinal change in the leadership.'

The Opposition saw a great opportunity in RJD dissidence not only to dislodge the Lalu *parivar*, his family, from power but also to wreck the party. Getting Lalu out using dissidents would be a much better way than the disgraceful attempts the Vajpayee government had made twice in the late 1990s through the imposition of President's rule.

Ranjan and Nagmani had been in touch with leaders of the BJP, the Samata, the JD(U) and the LJP for some months, and they had all pledged these two full, unconditional support. These parties had altogether 83 MLAs in the Assembly: BJP 35, Samata 29, JD(U) 12 and LJP 7. This number—added to the 39 RJD MLAs (one-third of the total RJD strength) who had to leave the RJD in order not to be disqualified under the anti-defection law—could make up the majority required in a House of 243.

However, Ranjan and Nagmani failed to muster enough support from RJD MLAs despite the discontent. Lalu expelled Ranjan from the party on 28 April 2001, taking the wind out of dissidents' sails.

Fernandes—his troubled relationship with Nitish notwithstanding—remained committed to the consolidation of the Opposition forces in Bihar to create an alternative to Lalu who he believed was ruining the state. Public disenchantment with Lalu was growing faster with Rabri in the chief minister's chair.

Fernandes and Nitish initiated moves in September 2001 for a merger of the Samata, the JD(U) and Paswan's LJP. Several rounds of meetings took place and by the end of 2001 Nitish announced to the media that the three parties had agreed in principle to merge and steps were afoot to arrive at a final agreement in writing. However, the plans got stuck with Paswan leading the LJP out of the NDA ministry in protest against the pogrom of Muslims in Gujarat in March 2002.

Nitish refrained from taking a strong position on the Gujarat pogrom. He supported Vajpayee's view that Narendra Modi should resign. But he did not make it a critical issue. How does he explain his ambivalence during that period? 'My target was Lalu,' says Nitish. 'Quitting the NDA on the Modi issue would have in no way helped me achieve my goal. The vote in Bihar was going to be on governance in that state, not in Gujarat. Also, it was not possible to remove Lalu without taking the BJP along in Bihar.'

During the subsequent months, when Nitish needed to consolidate the other political forces against Lalu, he noticed the dirty beast of factionalism within his own party reawaken. The party was divided broadly into 'Fernandes' and 'Nitish' factions.

At one stage, Fernandes decided to cut Nitish to size by excluding him from NDA protest programmes in Bihar. In January 2003 a spontaneous agitation broke out against the Rabri government in reaction to the killing of three innocent youths in a suburb of Patna in a fake encounter by the police, who claimed the deceased were 'hardened criminals'. The killings in Patna followed similar killings of innocent citizens in Begusarai and Rohtas. The upsurge showed people's accumulated anger against a police force and a government that was indulgent towards hardened criminals and targeted innocent citizens instead. It struck a chord throughout the state. Lalu was shaken.

The NDA saw a great opportunity to harvest public anger. As NDA national convener, Fernandes set out to also achieve his private aim of reducing Nitish's importance in the anti-Lalu mobilization in Bihar. On a few occasions earlier as well, Fernandes had participated in NDA programmes in the state to which Nitish, who was NDA state convener, was not invited. And everyone noticed that Nitish was excluded from all NDA meetings and activities held in solidarity with the popular upsurge of 2003.

It set off speculations of a split in the Samata Party, and these speculations received a boost from Nitish's decision to mobilize his supporters to set up his own platform for expressing his solidarity with the angry public. He addressed a rally in Patna (to which Fernandes was not invited) in which he attacked the Lalu raj for police brutalities and vowed to mobilize forces to end it.

Fernandes could not sustain his game of isolating Nitish in the Opposition politics of Bihar for long. The grass-roots swell was in Nitish's favour. The upper and lower backwards who were getting disenchanted with Lalu would, despite all the suffering in his raj, not be inclined to repose their faith in a leader who was not from among them. They were zeroing in on Nitish because he too had been associated with progressive politics and was from a backward caste. And he had been a close friend of Lalu's who had separated from the latter on principle. They were beginning to realize that Lalu was leading them up the garden path, which Nitish had seen much earlier, and they drew closer to Nitish, gaining an appreciation for his sense of judgement.

The surprising part about the Nitish–Fernandes stand-off was that by the middle of 2003, the BJP had arrived at a very clear conclusion that no one but Nitish Kumar could lead the anti-Lalu front to victory. It was clear from a press interview Sushil Modi gave to *Frontline* in 2003:

[Question]: Can you think of building an alternative to Lalu without internalizing the backward caste assertion that he symbolizes?
[Modi]: No. The alternative to Lalu has to be another leader representing the same constituency. This change in the political stable of Bihar is irreversible. The assertion by the OBCs is here to stay.
[Q]: In this context who among the NDA leaders could be projected as the leader of the combine?
[Modi]: Nitish Kumar has emerged as the leader of the NDA in Bihar. He was chosen to be the chief minister and remains the convener of the NDA. He will remain the NDA's candidate for chief ministership in the next elections too.[13]

However, Modi's own party would not declare Nitish the leader formally and officially yet. That was because the Samata Party had not yet declared him its leader either. Fernandes was playing sometimes subtle, sometimes explicit games to keep Nitish on tenterhooks.

Before the 2005 Assembly elections the NDA and Lalu were to test each other's strength in the Lok Sabha elections in 2004. The number of RJD MPs from Bihar had shrunk in the last three elections. Development had collapsed in Bihar under the Lalu–Rabri government. In contrast, the Vajpayee government had a lot to show in terms of economic growth. The NDA decided to fight the elections across the country on its 'India Shining' slogan.

In order to keep its focus on the development agenda and also to provide an alternative to Lalu in Bihar, the NDA projected Nitish as *vikas purush*, Man of Progress: *Vikas ke mazboot kadam, Asha ki swarnim kiran, Nitish Kumarji ke saath aagey badho* (Let us march forward with Nitish Kumar, the golden ray of hope, with strong steps towards development), said NDA election posters carrying a full-size Nitish image.

Nitish had very consciously built his image as 'vikash purush' over the years in order to set himself in contrast to *vinash purush*, Man of Destruction—Lalu. As minister of agriculture and railways at the Centre he had awarded a number of projects to his base area of influence, comprising the Barh and Nalanda parliamentary constituencies in particular, and Bihar in general. In Parliament, Nitish and other ministers who represented the constituencies of Bihar never missed an opportunity to emphasize that they were formulating and financing schemes for development whereas the Lalu–Rabri regime was failing to utilize them. Once in 2003, even Vajpayee presented a long list of Centrally funded schemes that were allocated to Bihar, quite a few by way of compensation for the loss resulting from the bifurcation.

However, the public mood did not seem to favour the NDA in Bihar as it had done in the last three Lok Sabha elections. The Muslim vote was strongly opposed to the NDA; it could have been prevented to some extent if Vajpayee had got Narendra Modi to resign. There was strong scepticism within the NDA whether the 'India Shining' campaign and the vikas purush mascot of Nitish Kumar would take them all the way.

Added to this was the scary prospect of division of the 'Janata parivar' votes between the Samata Party, the JD(U) and the LJP. There was no hope for the LJP coming back to the fold, as Paswan had moved closer to the Congress. At least the Samata Party and JD(U) could merge.

Nitish was the prime mover of the Samata–JD(U) merger that took place about six months before the 2004 Lok Sabha elections, with the wholehearted support of Fernandes, Sharad Yadav and an overwhelming majority of the members of the two parties. The new party would be known as JD(U) and have the election symbol of an arrow (of old JD[U]) and the green flag of the Samata Party. Paswan joined the RJD-led alliance.

Nitish was preparing himself for his re-election from Barh when Fernandes sprang a surprise on him. Fernandes moved his constituency from Nalanda to Muzaffapur with the obvious intention of proving to the country, and to Nitish, that he could win a Lok Sabha seat without Nitish's backing. Fernandes had won from Muzaffarpur in 1977.

In the JD(U) candidates' list, Nalanda and Barh constituencies were left blank. As it was too late to find and establish a new candidate from Nalanda, Nitish decided to fight both the seats.

Unlike in other states, the NDA campaign in Bihar used a twin strategy: it focused on the Lok Sabha elections as well as the Assembly elections slated for the following year. The campaign highlighted the 'achievements' of the Vajpayee government but also attacked the Lalu–Rabri regime for its 'failures', while projecting Nitish as the 'golden ray of hope'. The 'achievements' of the Vajpayee government on which the NDA campaign capitalized were: 8 per cent GDP growth, $110 billion of foreign exchange, prices of essential goods under control, 'connectivity revolution' (telecom, internet, highways and rural roads) and so on. The list was endless.

At the same time, the JD(U) campaign in its pamphlets prominently highlighted the numerous road, railway and agriculture projects and schemes that Nitish had got for Barh–Nalanda in particular and Bihar in general. Nitish released a special 'report card' listing what he had done for these two constituencies. The core strategy of the Nitish campaign was to sell the idea to the people that he had been able to get a much higher share of development for the state from the Central government as a minister in the Vajpayee cabinet and that proved that he would transform Bihar if the people decided to give him the mandate.

Lalu was rattled by the NDA's determined attempt to bring 'development' to the election centre stage. He also released a list of the RJD government's 'achievements' and introduced the issue of development in his speeches. However, he continued to essentially rely on political manipulation. The main thrust of Lalu's campaign was the scandals that had hit the NDA government (*Tehelka* exposé, Coffins Scam) and the pogrom of Muslims in the Gujarat riots that revealed the 'real' agenda of the BJP.

As elections drew nearer, the battle looked more difficult and the picture not so rosy (despite the general dissatisfaction with the Lalu–Rabri regime) for the NDA. Everyone, from Nitish to Fernandes to Sharad Yadav to the BJP leaders Sushil Modi and Shanawaz Hussain, was forced to concentrate their energies on their individual areas. More than 'India Shining', their campaign focused on the projects they had brought to their constituencies. The plan of the state NDA to market the idea of 'Bihar Shining'—based on the collective effort of Bihar ministers in the Vajpayee cabinet—had to be dropped in favour of constituency-level individual campaigns.

Results showed that poorer sections of people were not enamoured by the 'India Shining' story as the urban middle classes, and not they, were its beneficiaries. Voters were not even ready to back candidates who had done quite a lot for their constituencies. Only a month before elections, Nitish had managed to work through various departments of the Central government to get a special fund for the development of the Mokama tal—the first major issue he had taken up in his political career. The special fund of Rs 27 crore was for the revival of the traditional irrigation and flood-prevention systems and introduction of new schemes that would transform Mokama tal from a single-crop (pulses) to a multi-crop region. Still Nitish lost in Barh. He won convincingly in Nalanda, however.

It looked like a reversal of the 1999 verdict in the state, with 29 seats going to the RJD-led alliance and 11 to NDA. Lalu's social coalition of backward castes and Muslims had remained solid. Looking back, Nitish was to repent that he did not make any endeavour to break that coalition as he was to do before the next Assembly elections. Swayed by the BJP surveys and presentations that repeatedly said 'development will work', he ignored the social justice equations so vital to the Lalu vote.

In the Lok Sabha the Congress-led United Progressive Alliance (UPA) won 217 seats out of 539 and the NDA, 186. The UPA victory was, however, marred by a controversy over the candidature of Sonia Gandhi as prime minister triggered by the BJP on grounds of her foreign origin. Lalu openly backed Sonia, expressed disappointment when she decided not to be PM, but accepted Manmohan Singh as leader.

Lalu rode high with 22 seats from Bihar and began to swagger like a 'kingmaker' again, reminding many of 1996–97 when he had tried to play boss to Deve Gowda and I.K. Gujral. He demanded home portfolio for himself but the Congress did not agree. He showed some tantrums, but when the Congress would not relent, he insisted on railways. There, Paswan locked horns with him. In the tug of war for the railways ministry, Lalu beat Paswan—who was to bear the grudge that he suffered only because he was considered a minor player as the LJP had only 4 MPs.

Assembly elections were not too far away. Paswan decided not to have any alliance with Lalu. He wanted to show everyone he had the capability of becoming a big player in Bihar politics on his individual strength.

The trouncing of the NDA in the 2004 Lok Sabha polls, following a chain of victories in the three previous parliamentary elections, drove each of the three parties in the UPA alliance that had won seats—the RJD, the Congress and the LJP—to think the public mood was against the NDA in the state and it must make the most of it.

The Congress was upbeat after good results in the UP Assembly elections that the party leaders claimed as a process of revival after years of marginalization. Congress leaders were not happy with Lalu giving them only 4 seats in Bihar in the 2004 Lok Sabha elections. They wanted Lalu to leave them at least 100 seats in the Assembly elections of February 2005 but he was too puffed up with his success at the Lok Sabha polls and would not give them more than 30-odd.

Four rounds of meetings were held between the Congress and the RJD, the last one at the top level in Delhi between Sonia and Lalu, but no agreement could be reached. This was not unusual for the Congress that had allied with the RJD in the 1999 and 2004 Lok Sabha elections, and also participated in the Rabri government, but never had any poll alliance with the RJD in state Assembly elections.

According to the 'understanding' reached, the Congress would not set up candidates in the constituencies then held by its allies—the RJD, LJP, NCP (Nationalist Congress Party) and the left parties. Later when the Congress announced that it would set up candidates in 80 constituencies, Lalu tried to save himself from public embarrassment by saying that the RJD and the Congress would have 'friendly contests' and could consider withdrawing their candidate in favour of the other's. Lalu calculated that the Congress would set up mostly upper-caste candidates who would damage the upper-caste constituency of the NDA.

The Congress continued to woo Paswan, though. Paswan did not turn them down but showed no eagerness to reach any seat-sharing agreement with them. Paswan's endeavour since pulling out of the NDA in 2002, on the issue of Vajpayee's protection to Narendra Modi, had been to present himself as a champion of the Muslims. If Lalu had presented himself as a hero to the Muslims for having the guts to arrest Advani on his rath yatra, Paswan laid his claim to saviour status for taking on the 'Butcher of Gujarat'. And he had made 'sacrifices' which

Lalu never made: he had quit a ministerial position without any hope for immediate gains of a better position.

As the February 2005 Assembly elections drew closer, the NDA camp got jittery that Paswan might run away with a large number of Dalit and Muslim votes, spoiling the chances of a clear victory for them in Bihar. They were eager to avoid a repeat of 2000 when they fell short of the numbers. They must somehow get Paswan on their side. What could bring him in?

They told him he would be their chief ministerial candidate if the LJP became a part of the NDA. The NDA leaders publicly made the offer to him through the media. This offer directly threatened Nitish's position as the undisputed leader of the anti-Lalu front in Bihar. He had the option of walking out if Paswan joined the NDA and was actually chosen as its Bihar leader. But that option was worrying from the point of view of what he wanted to achieve in Bihar: it would divide the anti-Lalu vote and help Lalu perpetuate himself in power and lead to Nitish's political isolation. He chose his priorities: first, drive Lalu out of power and save Bihar from a collapse; then see how Paswan performs as chief minister and wait for an opportunity to take over.

When the NDA leaders started to claim publicly that they were ready to accept Paswan as leader, the media got curious about how Nitish would take it. They chased him wherever he went to gauge if he was indeed ready to accept NDA's decision. In order to convince them Nitish had to say, 'We [JD(U)] have extended the invitation to Paswan from the core of our heart to lead a grand alliance against the RJD in Bihar to rid the state of its corrupt and inefficient rule.'

On 8 November 2004, the media got a proof of this when Nitish attended Paswan's iftar party in Patna and photographed them hugging and smiling. The warmth between the two was reflected in Paswan's comment—'*Kabhi kabhi politics mein dil toot jaate hain aur iftar mein judte hain* (Sometimes broken ties in politics are restored at iftar)'; and in Nitish's remark—'Paswan is like my elder brother and I am prepared to make any sacrifice to bring about a regime change in Bihar.' Although both refused to answer queries whether an alliance was likely, Nitish said with a note of enthusiasm, 'Things are moving in the right direction.'

Nitish offered Paswan two choices: one, he ally with the NDA and become the chief ministerial candidate; two, the LJP reach a seat-sharing arrangement with the JD(U) and set up 'surrogate' candidates in constituencies contested by the BJP. The victorious surrogate candidates would formally join Paswan's party, so he would have a large number of MLAs on his side.

Although Nitish did not want to break up the JD(U)–BJP alliance, his meetings with Paswan and his indulgent comments about him in the media did create an impression that he was for severing ties with the BJP. Concerns grew within the BJP whose leaders felt Nitish was 'going out of the way' to court Paswan. In order to allay these concerns Nitish kept the BJP in the loop on his talks with Paswan, assuring them that he had no intention of leaving the alliance.

Eventually, Paswan did not accept either of Nitish's proposals. However, the silver lining for the NDA was that the LJP failed to partner with the Congress too. The RJD, the Congress and the LJP would fight separately. The split of the UPA vote was going to help the NDA.

However, there was still lack of clarity on the chief ministerial candidate in the NDA camp. The odds seemed to be in favour of Nitish: he had already been chosen chief minister in 2000 and the BJP was with him. But Fernandes was reluctant to back him. A week before the polling was to start Advani announced BJP endorsement of Nitish. Still, Fernandes did not confirm this. Fernandes's deliberate procrastination was to keep Nitish on tenterhooks so he could be more pliable on choice of candidates and conduct of the election campaign. 'The leadership issue will be decided after the election,' Fernandes told the media.

The elections were held in three phases. Votes were cast in the first phase without any clear NDA chief ministerial candidate. It was only in the middle of the second phase that Fernandes eventually endorsed Nitish. And the NDA paid a price for lack of clarity on chief ministerial candidate in the constituencies where polling took place in the first phase. The NDA share of seats, however, improved in the second phase and was the largest in the third phase.

The NDA failed to gain a majority a second time. It won 92 seats—JD(U) 55, BJP 37—in a house of 243. It had lost yet another opportunity. A large number of people disappointed with Lalu did not come out to vote because they did not see any credible leader as the alternative. The polling percentage at 46.5 per cent was the lowest in the state in the past four decades; the drop from 2000 was 16 per cent.

To the NDA's solace, Lalu did badly. He got only 75 seats, plunging RJD's vote by 3.27 per cent compared to 2000. A large section of Yadavs, Lalu's core constituency, moved away from him. The RJD won only 28 of the 77 Yadav-dominated seats, whereas the NDA won 29—JD(U) 19 and BJP 10. In 2000 the RJD had won 49 of the Yadav-dominated seats.

It was a hung Assembly again. The LJP got 29 seats, 23 of them against RJD candidates. Paswan held the key. He declared that he would neither support the 'communal' NDA nor the 'corrupt' RJD. When the Congress put pressure on him to support Lalu, he agreed, but on the condition that a Muslim from the RJD be elected chief minister. Lalu rejected the idea, insisting that Rabri and Rabri alone would be chief minister. The deadlock remained unbroken.

After none of the parties bought Paswan's idea of backing a Muslim chief minister, he began to replay his pre-poll idea about allying with the JD(U) if it broke away from the BJP. Nitish at first did not react to the proposal. He and other NDA leaders were talking to various parties and independents for support. Lalu's overtures to other parties received a cold response. The support for Nitish seemed to be growing, threatening a split in some parties.

Sonia was desperate to prevent the NDA from forming a government, to deny power to the BJP at any cost. The Manmohan Singh government directed the state Governor Buta Singh to place the Assembly in suspended animation.

Curiously, the man who was most hurt by the imposition of President's rule was Lalu. For it meant Rabri could not remain even as caretaker chief minister. All powers were transferred to the Governor. Lalu felt betrayed by the Congress that had not taken him into confidence before taking the decision. It came like a thunderbolt to someone who had enjoyed power for fifteen years.

To Lalu's discomfiture, the Congress saw in President's rule a good opportunity to shore up its own image in Bihar. The state Congress president Ram Jatan Sinha left no one in doubt when he said: 'The common people are heaving a sigh of relief. Everyone wanted to get rid of Lalu Prasad in Bihar and President's rule to be imposed. Even the judiciary said that Bihar was a fit case for the imposition of President's rule. Now that it has happened and things would improve and it could do the party [also] some good.'

The Lalu regime represented a culture of loot and larceny with open patronage to miscreants and roughnecks from the Yadav and other castes, whose premier symbols Sadhu and Subhash Yadav became. Lalu's rhetorical emphasis on political empowerment of the backward castes turned out to be, in reality, the political empowerment of crime syndicates. From the margins, crime had come to occupy the centre stage.

There was a mass reproduction of groups like those of Sadhu and Subhash, with ministers or MLAs of the RJD acting as their patrons, across the state. The towns and countryside of Bihar were infested with roughnecks who found extortion and robbery as the most profitable—and the safest—occupation. Officials at police stations would hesitate to register a complaint against delinquents who had the patronage of one or the other RJD leader.

Even when they were in prison owing to judicial intervention criminals enjoyed all facilities. A *Times of India* journalist, N.R. Mohanty, was dismayed when he was able to meet Shahabuddin in the Siwan jail after 9 p.m. without the required permission from the district judge or district magistrate. He was led into the jail superintendent's large chamber and was aghast to see the don sitting in the prison boss's chair, about a hundred of his supporters squatting before him. The jail superintendent, who had earlier refused Mohanty entry without an order from district authorities, was sitting undistinguished among the don's supporters on the floor! After the interview was over, Shahabuddin walked Mohanty to his car parked a short distance away from the jail.[14]

An NDTV reporter, Manuwant Choudhary, had a similar experience when he met the Vaishali don Munna Shukla without any permission in Hajipur jail. He found Shukla dressed in T-shirt and sneakers, sitting in the jail superintendent's office in a chair with his feet perched on the table, smoking as he spoke over a mobile phone. Another don, Rama Singh, in a kurta and a Nehru jacket stood close by. They were both fighting the 2000 Assembly elections and they both won campaigning from inside the jail.[15]

The crime for which the Lalu years became most infamous was kidnapping for ransom. Not that this crime was unknown in Bihar before Lalu took over. In 1987 the state witnessed fifty-seven kidnappings for ransom; in 1988, sixty, a rise of 13 per cent. In 1989 the figure rose by 48 per cent to 115. In the Lalu regime, according to official figures, it rose by 81 per cent to 209 in 1990—his first year in office. In 1991 it rose to 291, up by 39 per cent.

Businessmen, including traders, industrialists, auto fuel depot owners and goldsmiths, were the common targets of kidnappers. Among professionals, they went particularly after doctors with private clinics. Virtually nobody perceived to be possessing liquid assets was safe. And you could be picked up anywhere. On 6 December 1990 Ramanand Sahay, a retired IAS officer, was kidnapped from his agricultural fields in his native Simaria village in Rohtas district. On 24 August 1991 Ganga Prasad Kyal, a leading businessman of Hajipur was kidnapped in the early hours while bathing in the Ganga. In December 1993 Kishen Kumar Agarwal, a businessman in Bettiah in West Champaran district was kidnapped when he was about to close his grocery shop for the day.

Under Rabri crime registered a phenomenal growth. Kidnappings averaged about 400 a year during her tenure, double the average under Lalu. Even with this figure Bihar did not top the list of states in this category. Andhra Pradesh recorded nearly four times more kidnappings. The distinguishing feature of kidnappings in Bihar, however, was political patronage. It was not merely a criminal enterprise. The collaboration of local police in the lucrative crime was also apparent in several cases. The police usually did not succeed in rescuing the hostage and it was very common for the family of the hostage to be told by the police to pay up the ransom to secure his release. The number of abductions was several times more than shown on official records.

Business was crippled by the proliferation of kidnapping for ransom, robbery and extortion. According to a government estimate, about 10,000 terror-stricken businessmen moved out of Bihar during the Lalu–Rabri raj to relocate their businesses and families to Gujarat, West Bengal and other states. The feeling of insecurity among common people was so deep that shops, restaurants and movie houses attracted very few visitors in evenings. Women did not dare to venture out after dusk.

Everyone, businessmen or professionals, was extremely wary not to show any signs of 'affluence'. With thousands of criminals lurking around, affluence could mean capacity to cough up even a few thousand rupees. People dreaded even to put a fresh coat of paint on their house or car, lest it draw the attention of some extortionist. People at large had lost faith in the police.

The characteristic feature of the Lalu raj was the blurring of boundaries between white-collar and street crimes. While politicians made illicit earnings through fraud, cheating and deceit, they also shared the booty of kidnappers, robbers and extortionists to whom they provided patronage. While white-collar crime had been going on under other chief ministers in the past, Lalu would be remembered for opening up the avenue of an additional source of income to public servants through street crime.

After the imposition of President's rule, the Congress leaders pressured Governor Buta Singh to improve law and order. Buta Singh's police launched a statewide drive against the state-backed criminals. More than 20,000 hooligans who were declared 'absconding' and never found during the Lalu regime because of political protection were hauled up and dumped in jail. Police and court orders pending for years against Lalu's favourite dons Shahabuddin and Pappu Yadav were executed.

It was a tormenting period for Lalu. Buta's anti-crime campaign was sweeping away RJD hoodlums who had been 'managing' booths for Lalu. Voters who supported Opposition parties were scared away from polling booths in the past elections by these hoodlums. 'Booth management' had richly supplemented the vote of social rancour that had come voluntarily to the hypnotic ruler all these years.

When in power Lalu often bypassed top civil servants to speak directly on the phone to the members of the lower bureaucracy such as sub-inspectors heading police stations or block development officers (BDOs). Trained to take orders only from their superiors they would hesitate in the beginning to do anything in contravention of the norms, but gradually as Lalu

became immensely popular and most of the top bureaucrats succumbed
to his arbitrariness, junior officers in the districts had no reason to stand
on moral ground. The line of administrative command was subverted in
a very conscious manner in order to establish direct authority over the
heads of the field stations with whom the public had everyday dealing.

Scant regard for rules and procedures by the Lalu regime unnerved the
bureaucracy. There was a long shadow of cliques over the administration.
These would seize a residential or commercial property they set their
eyes on, evicting the owners with a ludicrously low payment as price or
no payment at all. The cliques got most of the government contracts
for supplies or construction; they took liquor sale outlet permits and
the booking agencies for buses across the state. Their leaders would call
officers or enter the bureaucrats' offices without appointment and ask
them to decide on a proposal in favour of a clique member. Dons like
Shahabuddin would sit in the district magistrate's chair when in the
latter's chamber and issue commands. The cliques would let loose their
hoodlums upon the uncompromising officers to terrorize or physically
assault them if they refused. It usually happened with officers who were
out in the field, in the districts, subdivisions and blocks.

In the clique–officer face-off, the officer was the loser. Top
bureaucrats such as chief secretary and director general of police, who
should have been backing their juniors out in the field, took the easier
route of averting any blow-up of the confrontation by transferring the
officer to another location. For lack of support, the officer, no matter
how upright and efficient he was, had to swallow his insult and hand
over his charge to a more flexible officer and move to a less prestigious
post. Integrity and administrative acumen, instead of being assets,
became liabilities in the Lalu administration.

A senior civil servant recalls: 'During Lalu's heyday, hotels in Patna
used to be full with *pairvikar*s, literally pleaders—small-time politicians,
professional touts and influence peddlers—from all parts of the state
who came to broker transfers and postings of officers or securing supply
and work contracts for businessmen.'

In an interview, Shivanand Tiwari, Rabri's excise minister, said
when one day he went to the CM's official residence to see Lalu, he
was summoned by Rabri. On going to the family room upstairs where

she usually sat, Tiwari was asked by her daughter Misa to withdraw the transfer of a Patna excise officer, against whom serious complaints had been lodged. Notwithstanding Tiwari's refusal, Misa kept repeating her 'order'; Tiwari walked out of the room fuming. When Tiwari met Lalu downstairs and complained about the 'girl's audacity', he 'in his typical clownish way, began to humour me, asking me to forget about it all'.

The influence of the cliques in the Lalu–Rabri raj represented a convergence of governmental authority and power of the outlaws.

Buta Singh told a media conference in Delhi on 26 April 2005: 'The [Rabri] administration was not run according to any system. It was not run as per the Constitution or rules. The government was being run according to whims and fancies.'

During the months of President's rule Lalu did not succeed in gaining support of any party. But a lot of activity was taking place in the Nitish and Paswan camps.

Paswan offered a new formula: a Congress-led government in partnership with the RJD and LJP headed by a Muslim MLA from the Congress as chief minister. Lalu rejected Paswan's new formula as *bakwaas*, utter nonsense. Paswan then wanted a Muslim from the NCP, another constituent of the UPA, to be chief minister. Both the RJD and the Congress pooh-poohed the idea.

Then Paswan turned to Nitish for an alliance. He would now make an effort to form a government without the RJD and the BJP. Nitish recalls: 'Paswan's posturings were turning obnoxious. I was very clear I was not going to form a government under the given circumstances. There was no mandate for any party or alliance. I knew a fresh election alone could decide who's going to rule. But I wanted . . . to isolate and expose him. I publicly announced that the JD(U) was ready to ally with the LJP. I took the BJP leaders into confidence and assured them our alliance was going to remain intact. By pretending to be open to his offer I also aimed to sow seeds of doubt in the Congress and weaken his position in the UPA. My other intention was to foster disaffection against Paswan among LJP MLAs. I knew no arrangements would eventually work out because the JD(U) and LJP together had only 84

MLAs and not all the parties we needed support from for a majority would ever come on board. But in the event of a failure it would be Paswan with his bag full of weird formulas who would be publicly seen as the stumbling block.'

Nitish's warm response to Paswan's offer really aroused concern among top Congress leaders that Paswan might switch over to the NDA. They sent out feelers to Ajit Singh, the leader of the Rashtriya Lok Dal which had 3 members in the Lok Sabha—as many as the LJP—to fill the gap created in the event of LJP's exit.

Nitish sat down with his JD(U) colleagues and drew up a common minimum programme (CMP). His party was ready, he said, to form an alliance with the parties and independents who agreed on the programme. He circulated copies of the CMP to six parties: LJP, SP (Samajwadi Party), BSP (Bahujan Samaj Party), NCP, CPI and CPI(ML), leaving out the Congress and CPI(M) that had already given their letters of support to the RJD.

Nitish then invited Paswan for a closed-door meeting on 1 April 2005 at the SP state president Dadan Pehalwan's residence in Patna. He did the arithmetic with him: JD(U) 55, LJP 29, SP 4, BSP 2, NCP 3, CPI 3, CPI(ML) 7 and independents 17, which added to 120. Once they got to that figure, they could always poach a couple of MLAs from some party to make the majority.

If this scenario fell through, Nitish had two formulas to offer Paswan. One, the JD(U) and the LJP form a government with outside support from the BJP: Paswan could tell the public he had made no compromise with communal forces as he was not sharing power with the BJP. According to the second formula, the JD(U) and the BJP would form a government with outside support of the LJP: Paswan could say he had maintained his stance of no truck with the RJD or the BJP.

Nitish knew very well that Paswan would not accept any of his formulas. But he continued to have talks with him to create an impression among the electorate that he was making a sincere effort to form a government and it was Paswan who was presenting the hurdles. Stalled negotiations were his ploy to subject Paswan to public denunciation. He planned to go into fresh elections with an appeal to the anti-Lalu voters to reject Paswan because he could prove to be a villain again and prevent the formation of a government that could replace Lalu's.

Discontentment began to build up in the LJP as many of its MLAs were eager to be ministers and held Paswan responsible for not agreeing to support the NDA. They said they had been elected with anti-Lalu votes and many of them, including the LJP general secretary Nagmani and the state party president Narendra Singh, started pressurizing Paswan to back the NDA and Nitish as chief minister. They approved of Nitish's formula of a JD(U)–LJP government with outside support from the BJP. Paswan would not agree, for it would antagonize the Congress and lead to the LJP's ouster from the UPA at the Centre and his loss of ministerial office.

In defiance, 16 of the 29 LJP MLAs opened negotiations with JD(U) leaders at a posh hotel in Jamshedpur in Jharkhand. Ruled by the BJP, Jharkhand was considered a safe territory for holding the rebel LJP MLAs in one place, with a strong police ring around the hotel to prevent entry of any Paswan emissary. The dissidents agreed to leave the LJP and back a Nitish-led NDA government. News of their secret parleys broke out on television, unnerving Paswan. He herded off all the remaining 13 party MLAs into a flight from Patna to Delhi where they were kept incommunicado.

Meanwhile, in addition to 16 rebel LJP MLAs, 17 independents declared their support for Nitish. That took him to a figure of 125, three more than he needed to prove a majority. 'Though the arithmetic sounded right,' says Nitish, 'I was still unwilling to form a government. This was not the public mandate, I was clear. A government formed with disparate fragments would not be credible in the public eye. And it was never going to last. I wanted to rule with a clear mandate. However, since we, technically speaking, had managed to cobble a majority I wanted to lay a claim, if not for anything, just to show the public that we were a stronger force than Lalu. I even announced to the media that I was going to present a list of MLAs supporting me to Buta Singh. I had made up my mind what I was going to do. I was going to prove my majority and immediately recommend dissolution of the Assembly for fresh elections.'

With the formation of a government led by Nitish nearly certain, Lalu was gripped by fear that some of his party MLAs would cross over to the

JD(U). Lalu sent an SOS to Sonia and Shivraj Patil. Buta Singh shot off two letters to Patil 'based on intelligence reports' raising an alarm over the 'horse trading' some parties were indulging in to form a government.

Acting on the report, the UPA government decided to dissolve the Assembly in order to prevent Nitish from submitting his list to the Governor.

The Congress earned opprobrium for dissolving an Assembly that was not even constituted and setting an unjustifiable precedent where no party or combination was allowed to seek confidence and test its strength. In a judgement some months later, the Supreme Court declared the presidential proclamation 'unconstitutional'. However, the brief order of the five-member bench came in early October 2005 by which time the Election Commission had already notified fresh elections. Keeping that in view the Supreme Court did not order *status quo ante*. The judgement created negative publicity for the UPA and boosted the mood in the NDA, which had been conducting a campaign against the dissolution since it was proclaimed.

A day after the dissolution the NDA called for a Bihar bandh and succeeded in enforcing shutdown of road and rail traffic and businesses in many parts for several hours of the day. Following the bandh, the NDA decided to organize a parade of the MLAs on its side before President Kalam in Delhi and Governor Buta in Patna. Quite a few of the MLAs on the NDA side were hoping that the pressure built by them on the UPA government, coupled with the 'expected result' of the litigation in the Supreme Court, would undo the dissolution, clearing the way for the formation of a government in which they would become ministers. But Nitish himself was seeking to use the protests to build up public support for the NDA in fresh elections.

'When the NDA decided to parade its MLAs before the President and the Governor,' says Nitish, 'I went along with it, but deep within my heart I knew we were doing it for relaying to the voters how prejudiced and unjust the decision to dissolve the Bihar House had been. The common man is a very rational being and always sides with the one against whom injustice has been done.'

Nitish led the protest march of 126 MLAs with Advani and Fernandes to the Rashtrapati Bhavan to meet President Kalam and convey to him that his proclamation amounted to 'murder of democracy'. The 16 rebel LJP MLAs joined the march. Nitish also carried letters of support from 4 more LJP MLAs who were in jail, taking the total to 130—quite a comfortable majority.

While these protests and media conferences to denounce the 'Congress–RJD–LJP conspiracy' behind the dissolution were going on, Nitish hit upon the idea of a Nyaya Yatra—March for Justice—across the state. None of the NDA leaders wanted their anti-dissolution campaign to lose steam, and Nitish thought the Nyaya Yatra, with a tour of districts, could very well be the start of their election campaign. The idea was approved by the NDA, and for several weeks beginning early July Nitish travelled through the districts addressing public meetings with Fernandes, Sharad Yadav, Arun Jaitley and Sushil Modi to rouse public sentiment against the 'injustice' meted out to the NDA.

The march provided an opportunity to the NDA, first of all, to clearly and undisputedly project Nitish as their chief ministerial candidate—something that could not happen before the February 2005 polls with Fernandes's stonewalling. All said and done, politics in Bihar had become personality-oriented. Nearly all the RJD vote was Lalu vote. In such a hero-centric polity, the alternative could only be another credible figure. Party organization did not matter. The RJD hardly had any organization or institutionalized structure and yet people voted for Lalu.

The JD(U) was no less deficient in organizational structure. And, much like the RJD, the JD(U) had men who had switched over to it from other parties—the most recent being the 20-odd MLAs from the LJP. There were no ideological criteria for recruitment to the party, no screening or training to be eligible for membership of the RJD or the JD(U).

Voters had accepted Lalu in spite of the farce his party was; so Nitish hoped they would accept him too without any real organization behind him. It seemed it was easier for ordinary people to judge a leader by his speech and performance than to study the literature of a party on its ideas and practice.

Nitish used the Nyaya Yatra to present himself as a potential 'redeemer' of the people. Much like in the previous elections, he talked about the collapse of systems under Lalu, but he would not make it merely a negative campaign. He devoted a significant part of his speeches to a positive campaign for development. He promised to end lawlessness and develop physical and human infrastructure. Vote for him would be vote for development.

Over the years Lalu had come to symbolize regression and Nitish, development. Lalu was identified more with politics than with governance, while the reverse was true for Nitish. His reputation as a performance-oriented minister at the Centre helped him a good deal, as also the projects and schemes he had brought to Bihar. Nitish fully capitalized on his image during his Nyaya Yatra. The advantage he enjoyed was that people—even those who idolized Lalu—desired development.

It was also during this yatra that Nitish for the first time tried to build a sense of Bihari identity among voters. He had come to realize that the Lalu phase of politics had further segregated the castes that were never one to begin with. Caste identity had become the identity of every individual, and people were driven to think in those terms owing to the naked play of caste in the Lalu regime. No one was ready to rise above caste, because that provided them security.

From his repeated failures to secure a clear majority in elections Nitish had come to understand that the secret of Lalu's strength lay in his ability to aggravate and accentuate caste polarization. Nitish too, like all politicians, based his electoral strategies and tactics on caste arithmetic. But Lalu dug his roots deep because he had beaten them all in that sport: he concentrated all his energies on working on the raw nerve, and with the kind of effrontery and bravado no other politician could. If one had to beat Lalu he had to hit at the source of his power: caste identity.

A state divided by castes would never develop, Nitish warned voters during the Nyaya Yatra. People must rise above caste. 'Bihar has a glorious past,' he told them. 'Biharis are talented and industrious. The state has sunk to the lowest bottom. Let us all pool our energies to bring the state at par with developed states.'

Above all, he told voters, 'Do not for god's sake send us to a hung

Assembly. You may vote for any party or alliance according to your choice ultimately. But vote with the idea of giving a clear majority to the party or alliance of your preference.'

Field reports on the election scenario indicated that Paswan was discredited in the public eye as a stumbling block to government formation and was likely to get a much smaller share of the anti-Lalu vote than he got in February. Nevertheless, he stuck to his election goal of ousting Lalu from power and getting a Muslim in the chief minister's office.

Congress struck up a seat-sharing alliance with the RJD, observing that 'we made the mistake of not making our position clear to the voters. We tried to carry everyone along, with the result that we were neither here nor there. We paid a heavy price for our ambiguity, which created confusion in the minds of voters'.[16]

Lalu put pressure on the Congress to ask Paswan to join the RJD–Congress–CPI(M) alliance or quit the UPA. The UPA set 23 September as the deadline for Paswan to agree or quit. Several rounds of negotiations failed to bring Paswan round. Even Sonia's appeal to him did not work. 'I will be politically finished if I support Lalu,' he told the Congress. To Lalu's discomfiture, the state unit of the CPI decided to part ways with Lalu because 'he has wasted no opportunity in trying to split or weaken us'. Lalu urged the Congress and the CPI(M) to get the CPI to join the RJD-led front or quit the UPA, but the CPI did not agree and went ahead to set up a Left Front with the CPI(ML). The Left Front tied up with Paswan.

Lalu went to elections on his old twin planks of social justice and secularism, speaking more of the latter than ever before. But he knew the winds were blowing against him. He knew people were not happy with his governance. Very often at his election meetings he would tender an apology to the audience for his mistakes and ask for their forgiveness: '*Humko maaf kar do. Humse jo bhi galti hui uske liye Lalu maafi mangta hai.*'

Apart from other factors, Lalu was greatly troubled by the Election Commission. In the past elections during his fifteen-year reign, Lalu had successfully done what he in his own jargon called 'booth management' despite the best efforts of the Election Commission. The core of his booth management team would comprise small-time rogues to dons like Shahabuddin, who had enough lethal power (men, firearms, lathis) to scare away voters from a booth. The polling officials at the booth were expected to provide support to the core group, either under intimidation or in accordance with a deal. With Rabri losing the caretaker CM's office in March, Lalu this time could not influence the postings of officials.

Lalu lost the election of November 2005. The NDA won an absolute majority with 140 seats, compared to 92 in February. The JD(U) got 86 (against 55 in February) and BJP 54 (against 37). The RJD's tally was reduced from 75 to 53 and the Congress's from 10 to 9.

Among the most important factors that gave the NDA a clear majority was Lalu's inability to add looted vote to his psychosocial vote with rigging. It was the first free and fair election held in the past fifteen years. No wonder the NDA supporters after election results shouted *Zindabad* (Long Live) slogans for both Nitish Kumar and the Election Commission adviser K.J. Rao.

The next key factor was the unambiguous projection of Nitish as the NDA chief ministerial candidate. It was for the first time that the NDA had fought elections with total clarity on who was going to lead the government. This worked wonders in attracting massive numbers of OBC and EBC voters who would see in Nitish the assurance that upper-caste primacy in politics and government was a thing of the past. The OBCs and EBCs were desperate to change only their leader, not the course of the social justice movement. This time, the swing of the EBCs in Nitish's favour was clearer. They were disillusioned with Lalu's partisanship towards Yadavs.

Nitish was acceptable to the upper castes too, because even though he had the same political roots and ideological grounding as Lalu, he was far from being rabid and hardcore anti-upper caste. While he favoured affirmative action in the form of job quotas and other privileges to the backwards he did not derive his strength from quota politics of the Lalu variety. He had advocated exclusion of the well-off sections of the OBCs from the benefit of reservations and backed a job quota for the economically poor among upper castes. He preferred to earn public goodwill in politics from his performance in tackling issues of development in a caste-neutral manner. Nitish's exhortation to voters to rise above caste and think about coming together to develop Bihar also assured the upper castes that unlike Lalu he was not for their complete exclusion from decision-making.

Lalu failed to prove his credentials as a development man despite trumpeting about the 'spectacular' improvement he had brought about in the railways during the year and a half of his tenure. Prime Minister Manmohan Singh in his election speech in Bihar endorsed Lalu's development credentials: 'The reforms brought about by [Laluji] in the railway ministry have no precedent . . . He is a leader of calibre and the state can make tremendous development under his stewardship.' Lalu's claims and the prime minister's endorsement fell flat on the people, who saw nothing but desolation all around.

People saw the Lalu–Rabri administration was in terrible shape. Its capacity for delivery was reduced to even lower levels than those in the pre-Lalu Congress regime. While the Central government, led by the Congress or the BJP, was trying to accelerate structural reforms of the economy, Bihar under the Lalu regime adopted a contrary stance. Lalu saw reforms as a 'great conspiracy' of the multinationals and the 'feudal forces' (Lalu's favourite term for the upper castes) to plunder and ruin the country (state) and leave the poor nowhere.

'You can't imagine what will happen when the multinationals take full control of the economy,' Lalu used to tell people. 'The poor will die. Even the middle-class people will have to fight for their survival. At present, everyone is vying for modern gadgets. But the time is not far off when they will be out of reach and redundant. Why not go back to our old traditions? We had so many good things—in science, healing, food from nature. We can only survive by reviving our traditions,' he would say in his public speeches. Whenever he was asked by the media why Bihar was not leveraging the IT revolution like the other states he would say: 'Computers render people useless. They destroy human skills acquired from centuries. What good is such technology?'

Lalu's positioning against 'modernity' drew from a curious mix of influences from his life experience, Lohia's swadeshi and Marxist anti-reform approach. His Luddite vision at the same time was quite evidently guided by his obsession with capitalizing on the fear of the unknown triggered by the reforms among the poor. He constantly tried to brainwash them with his precept that development was a pro-rich idea.

A social scientist recalls a Musahar (Dalit) landless labourer in a village in north Bihar narrating his encounter with Lalu during his election campaign in 2000. When the Musahar told Lalu he needed a road connection to his village, Lalu asked him: 'Do you have a *char-pahiya* [four-wheeler]?' The Musahar said no. 'Do you have a *du-pahiya* [a scooter or motorcycle]?' The Musahar shook his head. 'Do you at least have a bicycle?' The Musahar hung his head. 'Then why do you want a road?' Lalu said. 'If I construct a road only the upper castes and the well-off of your village will use it.'

Although he never openly said this, Lalu was reputed to hold the view that more government expenditure meant more illicit income for the upper castes who dominated the bureaucracy.[17] Stagnation served his objective of holding down the upper castes until the upper backward castes took over power fully. He blatantly patronized officers from the upper backward castes; they constituted a major segment of district magistrates who, together with SDOs (subdivisional officers) and BDOs (block development officers), made the government's public face. Wherever possible, SDOs and BDOs were picked up from the upper backward castes. Most of the state government officers, engineers or doctors who were promoted to IAS rank, were from the upper backward castes, nearly half of them Yadavs.

And with his messianic appeal drawing tens of thousands of poor people to his public meetings, his belief that success in politics had nothing to do with growth or retardation of development remained unchallenged. Politics of the kind he was pursuing was for political empowerment, not for economic empowerment. He saw his politics as a Great War of the Castes in which the backward classes were fighting for the sheer joy of gaining power, not for any material rewards. The bird of the Mandal revolution required spirit for its feed, not matter.

One of the favourite theories of Lalu critics about his unconcern for development has been that he did not want any improvement in the conditions of the poor because only if they were living in misery could he be sure of their continued support; his charisma could work with greater certainty with the naïve and gullible children of darkness. But this is too uncharitable. A truer picture of him would be of a messianic wonder whose bubble of euphoria took time to burst. He grew by capitalizing on the great accident of history in which Mandal collided head-on with Mandir in the early 1990s, and he thought he had amassed enough capital to last a lifetime. That is what convinced him that popularity created through the political route could be sustained only politically; economics had no role, except in a negative cast: to deny opportunities for aggrandizement to the upper castes in government, business and other vocations. In the process, he ended up denying opportunities even to the most oppressed classes and blocked the way for their economic betterment.

Apart from the alienation of the backwards, particularly the lower backwards, from Lalu, what favoured the NDA was the shift of a significant Muslim vote towards the JD(U). The NDA had very consciously kept Narendra Modi out of the October–November election campaign in order not to give Lalu any scope to whip up the Muslim phobia of the BJP. As in February, the BJP leaders kept their focus on development, avoiding sensitive issues such as Ayodhya.

An increasing number of Muslims, particularly younger ones, were disappointed with Lalu, for they felt all the benefits (jobs, contracts) in his regime had gone to Yadavs. Nitish during his election campaign tried to sharpen this cleavage by telling his audience: 'Although Laluji draws his political sustenance from M–Y combination, it is only Ys that have benefited, not Ms.' A section of Muslims was also unhappy with Lalu when he rejected Paswan's demand for a Muslim chief minister for his support to an RJD–Congress government after the February elections.

The poll outcome busted the great myth created by Lalu, co-promoted by the Congress and the CPI(M), that elections in Bihar are nothing but a polarization of two types of vote: secular and communal. In a blinkered analysis, CPI(M) leader Sitaram Yechury traced the defeat of the RJD-led front to a 'division in the secular vote' between Lalu's front and the LJP-led front.

It was a perception divorced from reality. The best illustration of this came from the plight of Paswan. He set out for the February 2005 elections with a claim to be a greater hero to Muslims than Lalu and made an effort to set up a Dalit–Muslim alliance. After the uncertain results he demanded a Muslim as chief minister. In the October–November elections he stuck to the idea saying 'it was his life's mission'.

What was the reality?

In the February elections Paswan did not give a single ticket to a Muslim. Many of his candidates were Hindus who had failed to get nominations from other parties; the rest included criminals and upper-caste men who were selected to lure their caste vote towards the LJP. It would be wrong to assume that the 29 seats Paswan got were entirely due to the secular vote. The proof of this came in the October–November elections when a large number of his supposedly 'secular' (read Hindu) voters did not vote for him just because he had committed himself to a Muslim as chief minister.

The inference to draw from the October–November elections was: There is a hardcore communal vote among Hindus as well as Muslims, but beyond that the vast section of people cannot be categorized as secular or communal. An overwhelming majority of Hindus might support the idea of having a Ram temple in Ayodhya but they may not necessarily vote the BJP. Likewise, an overwhelming majority of Muslims might support community-partisan issues but they may not necessarily vote the Congress, RJD or the left parties going about with a 'secularism' tag.

How does one explain Nitish and other JD(U) candidates getting the Muslim vote in spite of their alliance with the BJP? It shows that the average Muslim could think beyond the secular and communal categories that Lalu, the Congress and the CPI(M) had divided the people into. It showed that he was concerned with other issues.

The swing away from Paswan of the upper-caste and the OBC vote—because of his commitment to make a Muslim chief minister—showed that the same voters, who could be termed secular in February because they voted for the 'secular' party LJP, turned 'communal' in October–November! The LJP's shrinkage was therefore not because of the division in the secular vote, as Sitaram Yechury claimed, but because of the deep prejudices against Muslims in the minds of those considered to be secular voters.

The two facts—Nitish getting a section of the Muslim vote and Paswan losing the Hindu vote—went to prove that it is highly erroneous to see the secular and communal votes as watertight compartments. A secular voter can turn communal tomorrow and vice versa. People make rational decisions. The illusion of a permanent, unchanging secular vote lies only in the minds of politicians who have nothing but the sham of secularism to woo their electorate with, and can prove to be their unmaking, as it did in Lalu's case.

# II

## REINVENTING BIHAR

# government at the doorstep

The Bihar Nitish took over was a metaphor for the netherworld. When a daylight robbery or rape took place in Bengaluru, city residents would scream, 'This is not Karnataka. This is Bihar.' If the Opposition in Maharashtra wanted to hit out hard at the ruling party they lamented the 'Biharization' of the state.

As a member of the Bihari elite, Nitish, much like other Biharis working outside the state, had experienced the personal feeling of disgrace as an MP or Union minister with the contemptible image of Bihar. The collective pride of the Biharis was at the lowest ebb. Nitish made a resolve to restore Bihari pride. He was the first chief minister who would talk of Bihari *asmita*, identity, and work towards rebuilding it.

Rebuilding could not be done, however, merely with slogans: it had to be done with bricks of actual work. Nitish knew why Bihar had come to acquire the image of a pit of hopeless depression—thousands of illegal guns, ten murders a day, ransom kidnappings, robberies, abject poverty, high labour migration, collapse of education, miserable health care, unbridled public corruption and, above all, political patronage to criminals and to the corrupt. Where should he begin? What should be his priorities?

First of all, to steal some serene moments for his mental churnings to set his priorities, to hold meetings with his officers, to have discussions with his secretaries on proposals and to rest after the day's grind, he needed an office-cum-residence and had not got any. The department of building constructions—to which all the bungalows in the official district of western Patna belong—had allotted him 1 Anne Marg. And that was where Nitish encountered the first problem of his governance. Although the department had simultaneously allotted another bungalow to Rabri—10 Circular Road, which was located to the south of 1 Anne Marg across the street and had been occupied illegitimately with her blessings by Sadhu Yadav for several years—and asked them to move out, they refused to shift.

Lalu and Rabri wanted to retain the bungalow not only because they had stayed there for fifteen years but also because they considered it very blessed, bountiful and prolific for them. From a life of poverty, low social respect and anonymity, the couple had come to be raja and rani of Bihar: it was nothing short of a miracle. It could not have been possible without the creative energy and fecundity of the earth of 1 Anne Marg.

They went on delaying their departure. It was a stratagem to try out Nitish's patience: if they stayed on for long Nitish would be forced to give up 1 Anne Marg and move into another bungalow. Having known Nitish for many years, Lalu betted on his estranged chhota bhai's aversion to coarse methods and vulgar assaults, ruling out any forcible evacuation.

Lalu and Rabri had lived in the two adjacent government bungalows, 1 Anne Marg and 5 Deshratna Marg, arbitrarily joined by a pathway. In the twenty acres over which the two bungalows were spread they had created a *gwala* (pastoral) estate, with *khatal* (pens for cows and buffaloes), *murgi ghar* (enclosures for poultry), *bhusa ghar* (fodder store) and *gobar than* (cow dung yard). There was also a small pool for the devout Rabri to take an exclusive dip in before offering prayers to the Sun God during the festival of Chhath.

Nitish insisted he would have no other bungalow but 1 Anne Marg as his official residence. He did not ask officers to evacuate Lalu and Rabri, but he also did not give up his claim on the bungalow. The Lalu–Nitish patience game provided a ready topic to the media day after day. People lightened their after-work hours with jocular speculations on what Lalu or Nitish would do next.

The building constructions department served a notice to Lalu and Rabri to vacate the two bungalows by 21 December 2005. Media persons with cameras swarmed outside 1 Anne Marg from early on that day. For hours they found no trucks coming out of the bungalow. Lalu, they surmised, had decided not to comply with the notice. They expected an official squad, accompanied by the police, to arrive with trucks to haul up Lalu's things and unload them at 10 Circular Road. They were disappointed.

Nitish was faced with a dilemma. He had won with a promise to the people that he would restore rules, regulations and procedures in the government. Here was Lalu openly flouting the rules. What should he do? If it were someone else, he would have asked officers to evict him. But Lalu's was no ordinary case: Nitish had to weigh in several factors. Lalu would most likely gain from forced evacuation. Television media would focus on his plight, bringing back something of the public sympathy to him so soon after he had lost it, and project a negative image of Nitish. Secondly, Nitish had been friendly with Lalu for long and addressed Rabri as *bhabhi* (sister-in-law); he couldn't bring himself to use forcible ways against them.

At Nitish's instance, his building constructions minister Monazir Hasan told the media that the government was in no hurry to get 1 Anne Marg vacated. 'We will go by the rules and expect everyone to obey them,' Hasan said. When the media caught up with Nitish on the issue, he said: 'They can shift whenever they wish to. Please do not ask me about the house any more.' However, Nitish left no one in doubt, least of all Lalu and Rabri, that he would have no other bungalow but 1 Anne Marg as his official residence.

After he took oath, Nitish began to use the State Guest House, located north across the street from 1 Anne Marg, to conduct his official business. While being extremely careful about not hurting the couple's feelings, Nitish insisted on moving into 1 Anne Marg because he knew its tremendous symbolic significance. Lalu–Rabri's removal from there and his occupation of it would symbolize the departure of the bad and the arrival of the good, the jettisoning of the horrific past and the promise of a buoyant future.

One Anne Marg had been seen as the seat of power for fifteen years, as the 'palace' where the democratically elected 'shah' sat on the throne and passed orders. It had taken Nitish over a decade to realize his dream of becoming chief minister. He could have moved into any bungalow as chief minister, but 1 Anne Marg had a special place in his heart. That was where he had, before he broke away from Lalu, so often sat with him and Rabri upstairs in their private quarters, talking about political issues and personal affairs. When Lalu started showing indifference to serious issues, Nitish wondered at times why he should not be in his place, in that bungalow, to take the government on the course he had wanted his negligent, frivolous friend to do.

Actually, the tussle over 1 Anne Marg represented a conflict of two characters: one brazen, superstitious, acquisitive, intimidating and scheming, the other law-abiding, rationalist, well-mannered, shrewd and perseverant. Lalu went on giving one excuse after another to stay on: first, for several weeks it was because the building constructions department had 'not fully done up 10 Circular Road' allotted to them; then it was *kharmaas*—an inauspicious month according to the Hindu calendar—during which Biharis do not solemnize weddings or move into a new house.

The tug of war went on for nearly four months before Nitish won the patience game and Lalu and Rabri moved out. For nearly a week before they moved out no visitors were allowed into 1 Anne Marg. An apocryphal story had it that Lalu used the time to hide the piles of cash from the Fodder Scam somewhere on the premises. The reality became known only after Nitish moved in: Lalu and Rabri had dug up about one foot of earth from the fields where they used to grow vegetables and carted away the earth to spread it over the soil in their new bungalow. They believed that with the fecundity of the hallowed earth they would flourish again.

After Nitish moved in, his agricultural officers discovered to their horror that nothing could be grown in the fields in the compound as the stolen one foot of the topsoil contained all the natural nutrients. Truckloads of earth were brought to fill in the large pit. But, as the vehicles carted soil from many places, the fillings did not match the original character of the fields; the staff had to do vermiculture to generate nutrients in the soil.

As for the story of Lalu having hidden away his illicit crores somewhere, the staff was tipped by the grapevine that he was most likely to have concealed it in the swimming pool, underneath its floor tiles and behind its side walls. Pickaxes were brought and tiles were removed by labourers in many places below and on the sides, especially where they appeared to be not as immaculately fixed. After a good deal of digging they gave up, wondering where the lord of the poor had buried his treasure.

Nitish's aides who went round the premises after Lalu and Rabri left discovered things that could be seen as signs of occult practice, which they presumed to have been undertaken to harm Nitish. The walls in many rooms had palm impressions in red clay with traces of materials; the vermillion plant at the edge of a lawn had been cut away and it seemed to have been done so that Nitish's political life was cut short. There were also painted stones buried in the earth under some plants. 'It was quite an elaborate work of sorcery to cast an evil eye on Nitish, so that the couple were able to return to the bungalow soon, helped by the fecund soil they had carted away,' one of the aides observed.

'As young socialist youth activists, we all started out as anti-Brahmanists under Lohia's influence, totally contemptuous of the cultural regime of idolatory, customs and rituals the Brahmans had established to hold sway over society over the centuries,' said Nitish when asked about it. 'But somewhere in the middle of his reign Lalu began to feel extremely insecure about his continuance in power and perhaps gave in to age-old superstitions and started appeasing the gods by performing primitive rituals.'

The four months Nitish waited for Lalu and Rabri to vacate 1 Anne Marg were also the most problematic months for his government and the most expectant months for the public who wanted to see change. Although he had promised the people the moon during the elections he knew next to nothing of the problems in the state government and the intricacies of resolving them. The bureaucracy of Lalu's legacy was too timid, indolent, dilatory, divided and venal to fulfill even its routine duties, what to speak of displaying imagination and taking initiative. Was it possible to deliver promises to the people with the help of a body of shrunken, apprehensive and diffident civil servants?

Nitish weighed his options. He could, like the typical new chief minister, order a mass transfer of officers from the present posts and pick a new set on his secretariat's assessment. Or, he could go for hand-picked men in the key posts. Rejecting both the options in the initial stage, Nitish decided to work with the heads of department who were holding positions by order of the Rabri government.

Considering the public demand for speedy delivery, he had taken a big risk: some of the officers could be there largely by virtue of their loyalty, caste or otherwise, to Lalu, and they could sabotage his initiatives at Lalu's instance or be motivated by a devilry of their own, just to create a negative image of Nitish's regime. Some others could be thoroughly incompetent for their crucial stations, because in the previous regime, pliability and not executive ability was the prime test for officers' postings. And the reverse was equally true: the best officers might be frozen in lifeless, non-working chambers, isolated from the government mainstream.

Nitish had of course R.C.P. Singh, a 1975 batch UP cadre IAS officer, who joined him as his principal secretary during his first tenure as minister for railways, in the same position with him. Nitish had struck a bond with him as he had proved to be a highly intelligent and efficient officer, in addition to being from Nitish's native district and Awadhiya Kurmi caste. Next in line was his secretary Chanchal Kumar, a methodical, organized IAS officer of 1991 from Madhubani, who too had worked as his secretary in the ministry of railways.

Later Nitish brought S. Siddharth, an energetic, tech-savvy 1992 batch IAS officer from Tamil Nadu, as another secretary. But would these three capable and trustworthy secretaries be able to drive the administrative system to realize the goals of the new government by themselves? They could direct and monitor the bunch of departments Nitish allotted them, but for doing actual work, for implementing the plans of the government on the ground, good officers were crucial.

The course Nitish chose was this: generally, he would not look for a new officer until the present incumbent had proven to be entirely incompetent; but in the departments of his four principal priorities—home, roads and bridges, education and health—he would have new officers who could deliver results.

For the first three–four months of his tenure Nitish and his secretaries scouted for good IAS officers of Bihar cadre serving the state or Central government. They got Madan Mohan Jha for education, Deepak Kumar for health, R.K. Singh for roads and Pratyaya Amrit for bridges; all of them were serving in various capacities in Delhi.

Although the deformity and dysfunction of the administrative apparatus were not even touched by these few replacements, there was a strong undercurrent of reprieve in a large section of the bureaucracy—a sense of seeing some light at the end of the tunnel, a feeling of hope. No one in the high-caste-dominated IAS was sure how long it would last, because the new chief minister hadn't made his first real moves; and, what was more, they were aware that he too was a part of the Mandal league. Memories of the naked dance of Yadav/OBC power that they had witnessed still sent a chill down their spine. Would Nitish prove any better?

Nitish's reputation among senior civil servants from his conduct as a Union minister in various departments was good—and not only because he would not fling obscenities or files at officers as some chief ministers did. His insistence on norms was the most endearing part of his persona. In fact, Nitish was often taunted by critics for being more of a chief secretary than a chief minister. The truth was he was a bureaucrat among politicians and a politician among bureaucrats. He was unlike the typical minister who gave speeches and left all the work to the bureaucrats of his department. The typical minister was interested in work and files only if he had some private interest in it. Nitish spent a large part of his day with his officers, going over policies and programmes: he involved himself in the brainstorming and decision-making on all key issues.

Bureaucrats found it easier to work with him because he elicited their views, gave their ideas weight and respected their advice. Even though he strongly believed that in the democratic system the view of the elected executive must prevail over that of the permanent arm of the government, he held that the bureaucracy was a thinking, not a mechanical vehicle of governance.

Every day during the first weeks of his tenure Nitish—with his secretaries and the chief secretary sitting by his side at the State Guest House—conducted a review of the policies and programmes of all government departments. In a day he could review up to three or four departments. The secretary of the department would make a presentation, during which Nitish asked questions, suggested modifications and urged acceleration in implementation. As only four months of the financial year 2005–06 were left, his greatest emphasis was on assessing the work done so far and that remaining to be done.

He was astonished to find that despite the availability of funds, expenditure was low. The reason was traced to the indifference of the outgoing regime. Owing to a lack of interest in the progress of schemes, there was absence of data; very few officers bothered to collect it as they were never asked by the chief minister or ministers to provide it. It was not unusual for heads of department to fumble when Nitish asked for statistics or other information for arriving at some understanding.

He made it clear to the officers that governance was his top concern and, within that concern, crime prevention and improvements in education and health were his three topmost priorities. He also conveyed to them that he was not there as just another chief minister in office; he was there to work for a paradigm shift in the governance of the state.

The regimes before he took over—the Congress regimes as well as non-Congress ones—were what in bureaucratic parlance is known as *mai-baap sarkar*, literally, the government of mother and father. Governance in a mai-baap sarkar had two strong characteristics: one, it believed in framing and announcing some token schemes for the welfare of the poor; its 'concern' for the poor could also very often mean, as it did in the Lalu–Rabri regime, distribution of free saris, dhotis and blankets to large gatherings of the poor.

It seemed to be a carry-over from the past when kings used to gift provisions and clothes to the poor on their birthdays or festive/auspicious days. The sentiment was rooted in compassion and concern for the unfortunate, orphaned, helpless, handicapped or old. As the kings drew from the royal treasury for their philanthropy, so did the past chief ministers from the public treasury. Most of them never concentrated their energies on driving development that could not only reduce poverty but also provide enough resources in the hands of the state for public investment for accelerating growth.

The second strong characteristic of a mai-baap sarkar was the protection given to wrongdoers. Heads of government departments could not proceed against corrupt subordinates who had 'high connections'. Not that all corrupt officers had direct links with the chief minister; but they knew how to take the matter to his ears. In most cases proceedings against corrupt officials and criminals were stalled because a tacit message came from the chief minister's office. The corrupt men got their protection through intermediaries who could be the chief minister's cabinet colleagues, party men, financial backers or officials in the CMO, and the middle men were shrewd enough to persuade the top executive on the plea that the man was useful for mobilizing vote or providing money.

Nitish told top officers they were free to collect information and proceed against any officer without the slightest fear of him or some other minister stalling the process. He would not promote his family members nor allow any of them to exert influence in government affairs as Lalu's brothers-in-law did. Nitish's wife continued to work as a schoolteacher and lived with her brothers at their residence, not with Nitish at his official residence. His son Nishi, who could not complete his engineering course at BIT (Birla Institute of Technology), Mesra, owing to a serious illness, stayed with her. Nitish's elder brother Satish Kumar carried on with his humble practice as an Ayurveda physician. The private ladder the corrupt had used during the Lalu regime to get into the CMO was removed.

As a result, within a few months of his taking over, about two hundred doctors and engineers in government service who had managed to stall corruption proceedings against themselves during 2000–05 were awarded penalties. 'It was intended,' says a senior officer, 'to send a message down the line that *kisi ka koi mai-baap nahin hai* [wrongdoers no longer have a protector].'

Nitish seemed eager to work towards transforming governance from the mai-baap sarkar mould into a public-spirited, professional, impartial vehicle. With the same objective in view he would not follow the path of merely announcing some welfare schemes for the poor. In a state with about 40 per cent of the population below the minimum level of subsistence, poverty reduction had to be his uppermost concern; but he would take the institutional route for that, rather than resorting to occasional charity.

The task of bringing back the government machinery on track even in the five departments on his top priority absorbed so much of Nitish's energy, attention and time that he was delayed in honouring his foremost election pledge—to 'eliminate the criminals and gangs involved in violence, intimidation, kidnapping for ransom and extortion and make the state crime-free'.

It appeared a fanciful and extravagant guarantee in any case: the implausibility of making Bihar a sanctuary for peace where hoodlums would fear to tread in so short a time was apparent. No one had probably believed it: voters, desperate to get rid of the rogue raj, only hoped it would happen at some point. They were not hoping to be transported overnight out of hell into paradise. Yet the campaign promise that suggested the urgency Nitish gave the task of controlling crime did play a significant role in their voting for him.

The difficulties of fulfilling the vow became apparent to Nitish early on in his tenure. He realized that a *safaya*, literally extermination, of criminals and gangs could—if enforced through the existing police force without changing their mindset—result in hundreds of men, innocents unmarked from rogues, dead in fake encounters. This could tarnish his image, making him look like a butcher rather than a democrat, denting his credibility of being able to establish the rule of law.

His difficulty was he did not know how to fulfil his promise. He had given the assurance with absolutely no special plan in mind. The commitment was backed by nothing but sheer personal resolve. But he came to realize that even if the men in uniform were infected by his zeal the system could bring their efforts to naught. Despite the best intentions of policemen, cases against criminals made no progress or failed because people would not dare to depose as witnesses against them, or the courts were too burdened with backlog to deliver timely justice—the indefinite delay going to the advantage of the offenders out on bail.

Meanwhile, in the absence of any 'paradigm shift' in nabbing ruffians, crime was far from controlled. There was a drop in the number of serious offences such as murder, kidnapping, rape and robbery, but that owed more to the collapse of the political patronage networks than to any new stratagems and manoeuvres of the police or to efficient prosecution. There was in the home and police departments, as in others, an unusual enthusiasm among officers disappointed with the Lalu–Rabri regime; but there were no new ideas.

Nitish held several meetings with top police officers and the advocate general to find out ways to speed up trials for gaining convictions in order to stop armed criminals moving about freely. One of the ideas that came up was trial in fast-track courts. The other was to get the criminal courts to take up sensitive cases on priority.

A close cooperation between the judiciary and the police was needed. Nitish had consultations with the chief justice of the Patna High Court who shared his concerns and offered full support. It took some months of joint deliberations between the state government and the high court before they decided to discuss all the problems involved in speeding up trials in a joint two-day seminar-cum-workshop on 14–15 October 2006 in Patna in which Nitish, Deputy Chief Minister Sushil Modi, Chief Secretary A.K. Choudhary, Director General of Police A.R. Sinha, Chief Justice J.N. Bhatt, senior judge Aftab Alam and the advocate general participated. Public prosecutors and all the district magistrates and superintendents of police—those who were going to be the implementing instruments—also attended the seminar.

The state government wanted the high court to set up more fast-track courts and direct the trial courts to take up 'ripe' cases—cases which could be wound up in a few hearings—on a day-to-day basis. Chief Justice Bhatt welcomed the idea, for a number of accused had been awaiting trial for years, which was a violation of their right as citizens to speedy justice. Expeditious trial is an integral and essential part of the fundamental right to life and liberty enshrined in Article 21 of the Indian Constitution. The right was intended to ensure that defendants were not subjected to unduly long incarceration prior to a fair trial. In case the state failed to bring a case to trial within a reasonably short time after arrest, it could be cause for dismissal of the case. In *Hussainara Khatoon v. State of Bihar*, the Supreme Court had observed that 'speedy trial is of essence to criminal justice and there can be no doubt that the delay in trial by itself constitutes denial of justice'.

Although the judiciary's concern for speedy trial related to all citizens regardless of their social or economic status, the problem was most acute for defendants from a poor background. Even for minor offences they could be spending years and years in prison, waiting for their trial to conclude. While this was one of the basic reasons of setting up fast-track courts, the main reason was to secure conviction of criminals.

Nitish intended to create a negative climate for crime. The high court was enthusiastic about the state's intention as long as it brought all the witnesses and evidence to it expeditiously. In fact, the high court itself was worried about the anarchy in the state. On several occasions in the previous years, it had passed strictures or damning comments against the Lalu–Rabri government. Perhaps the strongest condemnation had come from the DGP R.R. Prasad who—when the judge asked him in a case in the high court about unauthorized constructions in Patna why no action had been taken—said that the officers were as powerless as 'the blind Dhritarashtra [in the Mahabharata] who cannot stop Draupadi's [here a metaphor for Bihar] *vastraharan* [disrobing]'.[1]

During the seminar an idea emerged that convictions could be faster if the provisions of the Arms Act, 1959, were invoked. Convictions could then be secured on three grounds: possession of illegal arms, use of licensed arms by a person not holding a gun licence and non-renewal of gun licence. Possession of illegal arms was punishable with imprisonment of three to seven years. Use of illegal firearms or illegal use of licensed firearms could invite a further imprisonment of three to seven years.

Apart from deterring criminals, a major consideration of the state government in using the Arms Act was to debar those among them who nursed political ambitions. The blurring of the boundaries between crime and politics in the Lalu–Rabri regime had emboldened a large number of small and big rogues to seek elections to local bodies, the Assembly and Parliament. Under the Election Commission rules, anyone convicted for two years was not eligible to file nominations, unless the high court suspended the conviction.

The advantage the prosecution enjoyed in arraignments under the Arms Act was that the key witnesses were policemen, as it was obvious that armed criminals could be nabbed only by the police. The ballistic expert, who was asked to examine the firearm in question, would testify that the victim had received injury or died from the ammunition fired by the gun used by the accused. The doctor, who treated the wounded or performed a post-mortem, confirmed that the wound/death was caused by the bullets fired by the criminal. The trio of government officials—policeman, ballistic expert and doctor—provided formidable, mutually corroborated evidence that the defendants' lawyers found hard to challenge.

Nitish jumped at the idea. However, the high court wanted the state government to first remove the bottlenecks in bringing a case to trial. One of the major bottlenecks was the lack of infrastructure and other provisions for the existing or proposed fast-track courts. Another big hurdle was the non-availability of the investigating officers (IOs) for examination and cross-examination in trial courts. The IOs, who were posted in police stations, would periodically get transferred from one place to another. As cases remained pending for trial for years, an IO could have served two or three tenures since he investigated the case.

With the bifurcation of the state in 2000, a number of IOs were transferred to Jharkhand. It was particularly difficult for the prosecution to locate the IO and bring him for deposition on a given date, as he had other duties and priorities. Every date thus lost would delay the trial by a few months.

For ensuring the presence of IOs two things were absolutely necessary: one, an updated chart with the police department showing which officer was posted where; and two, a dedicated cell in the department to instruct them to depose. Was it anywhere within the realm of possibility that the police department could carry out these responsibilities? With hundreds of IOs out in the field, and with each one having investigated several cases, they would be required to be present in courts on many occasions; and no matter how many men you put on the job it was not possible to keep every little bit of information updated and to act quickly on court summons; somewhere someone was sure to bungle or some file would be misplaced. Besides, where were so many men in the police department to spare for a large office-within-office for tracking down IOs?

The answer was eventually provided by technology. The state government requested the National Informatics Centre (NIC) to create a system to maintain updated information on the postings of police officers. For months NIC engineers worked with DIG Abhayanand and other police officers to develop a web portal, POINTS (police officers' information and tracking system), using which IOs could be quickly sought out and sent to courts to accelerate criminal justice.

Everyone was astonished by the results of the push for speedy trials, above all Nitish. During 2006, the state secured conviction of 6,839 offenders, which included death sentence for seventeen, life imprisonment for 1,389, sentence of more than ten years to 366 and less than ten years to 5,067. About 26 per cent of the accused were awarded a term of ten years and above, indicating the large volume of heinous crimes—murder, robbery and rape—committed in the state.

Of the 5,067 convictions of up to ten years, 1,609, or nearly 32 per cent, were secured under the Arms Act and the police still needed to arrest and prosecute thousands of others. In 2007 the number of convictions shot up by 44 per cent to 9,853, of which 2,887 (or over 29 per cent) were for more than ten years, reconfirming the high proportion of heinous crimes recorded in a year. Of the remaining 6,966 convictions up to ten years, 1,154 (or over 16 per cent) were under the Arms Act. There was a drop of over 28 per cent in convictions under the Arms Act compared to 2006.

The drop in Arms Act cases told a story. The number of convictions under the act fell from 1,609 in 2006 to 1,154 in 2007, 1,018 in 2008, 704 in 2009 and 495 in 2010. This decline was in sharp contrast to the rise in the total number of convictions from 6,839 in 2006 to 9,853, 12,007 and 13,146 in 2007, 2008 and 2009, respectively, the figure dropping to 10,498 in 2010 but still over 53 per cent higher than in 2006.

The primary reason behind the reduction in convictions under the Arms Act was the fall in the number of cases registered. The sight of criminals moving about openly with arms in the street in towns, or flaunting them out of the windows of their cars, or firing shots in the air at village weddings became rare. Many criminals fled the state to hide in Nepal; many others declared a 'farewell to arms', transforming themselves into good citizens to engage in farming or run a grocery store or operate local buses.

Speedy trial had frightened off hooligans. Although it was hard

Essential to Bihar's economic and infrastructural transformation has been the roads that the Nitish Kumar government has assiduously built and revived since 2005, boosting business and employment in the state. A state highway under construction is seen here.

This hi-tech flyover-cum-approach road, the Kankarbagh flyover in downtown Patna, was built with German technology and is proving to be the city's lifeline for traffic. Popularly known as the Chiraiyatand Bridge, it was inaugurated by Chief Minister Nitish Kumar on 11 June 2009.

Nitish Kumar's wedding with Manju Kumari on 22 February 1973 at Lajpat Rai Bhavan, Patna.

(From left to right:) Nitish Kumar, his wife Manju and his cousin on the occasion of the latter's wedding on 27 May 1985.

Nitish with his mother Parmeshwari Devi and elder brother Satish in their Bakhtiyarpur home, in 2003.

(From left to right:) Nitish's wife Manju, his mother, Nitish, his son Nishi and his brother Satish, in their Bakhtiyarpur house a day after Nitish's taking the oath of office, on 25 November 2005.

Nitish Kumar taking the solemn oath of office before Governor Buta Singh (extreme right) on 24 November 2005, after which he went on to serve his first full term as chief minister.

Nitish Kumar taking the oath of office before Governor Devanand Konwar (extreme right) on 25 November 2010, to enter his second term as chief minister of Bihar.

Nitish Kumar putting his signatures on the oath on 25 November 2010. The ceremony took place in Gandhi Maidan, Patna.

Janata ke Durbar mein Mukhya Mantri is a unique and significant public grievances redressal system, conducted every Monday, where the chief minister accepts petitions from the people directly. Nearly 1,500 people, including the disabled, come every Monday to this People's Court.

The CM launching the ambitious scheme Mukhya Mantri Balika Yojana intended to keep underprivileged girls interested in higher education. Every girl who takes admission to class nine is gifted a bicycle under this scheme.

Nitish Kumar visiting a supporter on one of his tours, a woman he affectionately calls 'Bengali maa' (mother), who stays next to his house in Kalyanbigha.

The chief minister receives Dr A.P.J. Abdul Kalam, former President of India, who visited Bihar in 2008 regarding the proposed Nalanda International University. This is a dream project of the Bihar government to rebuild the great international university at Nalanda that existed in ancient times and brought much glory to the subcontinent.

Nobel laureate Amartya Sen, head of the Nalanda (University) Mentor Group, speaking at a conference in Patna on 21 February 2009.

The Tibetan spiritual leader the Dalai Lama inaugurated the Buddha Smriti Park in Patna, where he planted a sapling of the Mahabodhi banyan tree brought from Sri Lanka, on 27 May 2010. The park was built by the Bihar government to commemorate the 2,550th anniversary of the *mahanirvana* (salvation) of the Buddha.

Bill and Melinda Gates discussing with the chief minister the possibility of expanding cooperation to the agricultural sector in Bihar through the Bill and Melinda Gates Foundation, in Patna on 23 March 2011. Impressed with Nitish Kumar's performance on rapid vaccination for children, the world's leading philanthropist said that 'people are hungry for visionary leaders'.

The chief minister with King of Bhutan Jigme Khesar Namgyel Wangchuck, during his Bhutan visit, 3–5 May 2011.

The chief minister with Prime Minister of Bhutan Jigmi Y. Thinley, during his Bhutan visit, 3–5 May 2011.

to accept the government's claim that speedy trial had completely re-established the writ of the state, there could be no dispute that the high rate of convictions had a direct bearing on the crime rate. The number of ransom kidnappings dropped from a peak of 411 in 2004 to 80 in 2009. During the same period, murders decreased from 3,861 to 3,152, dacoities from 1,297 to 654, robberies from 2,909 to 1,619 and road robberies from 1,875 to 962.

Speedy trial alone, however, could not work the magic. The state's extrajudicial engagements with criminals also played a significant role. Criminal gangs had acquired carbines, self-loading rifles, Kalashnikovs and other sophisticated guns from arms trafficking routes. The Bihar police stood little chance of being able to challenge them with their primitive arms. These arms worked if the policemen were facing an unarmed or stone-pelting mob, but proved worthless and fell dud in a confrontation with thugs. For the same reason the state police proved ineffective against radical communist groups. As both crime and peasant radicalism had got out of police control, the state needed to strengthen its law-enforcement organization with resources and training.

But the question that plagued Nitish and his zealous officers was: could the existing police personnel deliver, even if equipped with the best resources? Nitish was highly sceptical. He told his secretaries and police top brass that he did not believe the existing police force was capable of subduing criminal gangs and armed left groups. 'Thanks to their preoccupation with routine duties,' said Nitish to them, 'our police have ceased to be a fighting force.' He went on, 'Our police stations and policemen lack equipment. Even if we give them vehicles, arms, communications gadgets and everything, they can play a preventive role vis-à-vis crime but not a combative role.'

An exercise was undertaken in the CMO and police department on how to build a force to fight criminals and left extremists. It was during one of these brainstorming sessions with officers that DGP Prasad came up with the idea of setting up an altogether new force with ex-soldiers of the Indian Army. With their rugged training in warfare they would make the best combat force, he said; and besides, working on consolidated salaries under a contract, they would not make an unmanageable addition to the government staff salary bill. Based on this idea the State Auxiliary Police (SAP) was formed. Starting with a few thousand, the SAP became a force of 17,000 men by end 2009, equipped with sophisticated arms.

In various districts the SAP was involved in encounters with criminal gangs. The gangs suffered more casualties on their side than they ever had in their engagements with the state police. As in these encounters the rules of war apply, it is not known how many casualties occurred in exchange of fire and how many were killed point-blank on suspicion or recognition of being criminal.

Nitish's official stance to find a way to curb criminals 'within the framework of law' was sometimes side-stepped by the police that was loath to break with its brutal tradition of physically eliminating troublemakers. Annual reports of the state police listed such physical eliminations among their key achievements. 'Several notorious criminals were killed in encounters with police and large quantities of illegal firearms, ammunition and bombs were recovered from them,' says the police report of 2 March 2010. Their view was that higher casualties held back the criminal gangs from flagrantly violating the laws as before.

Nitish never officially or publicly sanctioned it, but suppression of criminals by force of arms went side by side along with the acceleration of their trials. In any case, armed suppression of left radical groups had his government's sanction. The SAP and other forces were given the authority to meet the challenges of the armed left groups as well. 'Between 2005 and 2009 there were 118 encounters between police and extremists in which 62 extremists were killed. A total of 835 illegal firearms, including 66 looted from police, 365 landmines/bombs, 116 hand grenades and 41,462 cartridges . . . were recovered from them,' says the same police report. The policemen working in areas where left groups were organized were given a number of incentives by the state government to suppress them.

Although fighting with criminal gangs and radical left groups was entrusted more and more to the SAP, Nitish provided financial and other resources to the police department on a scale no previous government had done. Police budget rose from Rs 1,153 crore in 2004–05 to Rs 2,650 crore in 2010–11, increasing by an incredible 130 per cent when in the normal course it should have risen by not more than 30 per cent. Every district was to have a model police station, *adarsh thana*, whose outer wall would be grenade/bullet-proof and which would have an armoury, barracks and a secured staircase to reach the roof, whose four corners would have fortification for armed encounters.

A combined effect of speedy trials and armed suppression did bring down the number of serious offences. However, the number of cases registered during the first Nitish regime was still very large. The success of his government lay more in detection than in prevention of crime.

In the past the number of offences was huge but the number of cases brought to trial was small. During the Lalu–Rabri regime wide gaps existed in crime control all along the line: between the commission of the crime and registration of the case, between the registration and the arrest of the offenders, between the arrest and investigation, between investigation and prosecution and between prosecution and judiciary. It would be highly unrealistic to expect a chief minister, no matter how honest and vigilant, to be able to bridge all these gaps in a few years. The police organization was the same as it was in the past: cocky, coercive, cruel, corrupt and clumsy. Traditions die hard.

One of the toughest challenges Nitish faced in implementing speedy trial related to the cases of the dozen or more mafia dons who were currently or former members of Parliament or Assembly. They were a terror in their constituencies and districts, as quick as they had been in eliminating anyone who raised a banner of revolt against them. Murder was routine for them. Some of them carried out mercenary killings for negotiated price (*supari*). Rare was the man who could summon up courage to give evidence against the criminal-politicians in court.

The dons had plenty of money, advanced firearms and hooligans to kill, assault, harass or intimidate anybody. So inebriated with illegitimate wealth and power were they that they gave officers of the government very little respect, expecting them, on the contrary, to show respect to them and obey their orders. The absolutism of the thugs reached its peak during the Lalu–Rabri regime, when appointments to key administrative posts in the districts began to be made with their consent. Officers who refused to do their bidding were made to pay the price: transfer, beating, even death.

Would they not make Nitish too pay a price if he insisted on bringing them to trial? Wasn't killing normal for them? Would they need any great planning to bump him off? He frequently went out on tours of districts where he directly interacted with people; the dons could hurt him any moment, at any place.

'All the security you see around me is just a show, illusory,' Nitish once told me. 'This cannot protect me if anyone wants to do something. It's only my sheer luck that nothing has happened to me so far.'

Pro-active legal action against dons not only posed a life risk but also political risk to him. Some of them were MLAs of his own party. A few of these MLAs had been with him since 2000, when they had worked hard to mobilize majority support for him after he was sworn in as chief minister. Speedy trial would alienate them; they would feel he had betrayed them despite their loyalty. As dons also enjoyed subterranean sympathy of their castes, other party MLAs from those communities could also resent aggressive judicial pursuit against them.Nitish thought: either he could avoid personal and political risks by contriving to exclude the cases against criminal-politicians from speedy trial, or he could, taking all the risks, push for their expeditious trial to promote a clean, bold, unsparing image of himself. The first option would give him short-term benefits, the second one, long-term advantage. Image mattered a lot in politics in a country where people voted more for personalities than parties. If he made compromises with the dons he would be as condemned as Lalu and fall in public esteem as a credible alternative.

The first don whose cases were brought to the court was Shahabuddin. The state government requested the Patna High Court to have a local sessions court hear the cases against him for their expeditious trial. Exercising the administrative powers conferred upon it under the Criminal Procedure Code (CrPC), the high court decided on 20 May 2006—four months after the speedy trial mechanism was first put in place—to set up a special court in the premises of the Siwan district jail, where he had been transferred from Bhagalpur Central Jail. Shahabuddin challenged the order, arguing natural justice was denied to him by shifting his trial from an open court to a special court in jail premises; but the high court dismissed his objections, noting that holding his trial in an open court might affect trials of other civil and criminal cases going on in the same building and no real prejudice was caused to him.

Shahabuddin then used political manoeuvres to stall the proceedings. Lalu and Congressmen projected his speedy trial as ruthless victimization; in an attempt to create sympathy for him they claimed that he was suffering from a serious spinal disorder and his health was deteriorating in the prison. Nitish responded by getting the high court to set up two special courts—a court of sessions judge and another of judicial magistrate—instead of one in the jail, so that all of the nearly fifty criminal cases in which Shahabuddin was accused were heard and decided in the quickest possible time to avoid any prolonged misery due to his ill health. That silenced Lalu and the Congressmen.

Cornered, Shahabuddin fell back on his own tricks. He ignored summons from sessions judge B.B. Gupta on three consecutive days. Gupta issued a production warrant for him, asking jail superintendent L.K. Sinha to produce the defendant before him. When Sinha approached Shahabuddin and read out the contents of the production warrant to him, he flew into a rage and hurled expletives at him. When Sinha protested that he was only performing his duty, Shahabuddin threatened to kill him.

As Sinha and the policemen accompanying him seemed determined to take him to the judge, Shahabuddin pretended his back pain was too severe to allow him to sit in the wheelchair they had brought. He said he could come with them if they arranged a stretcher. Some members of the jail staff were sent out to find a spare stretcher in some hospital in town, and when they brought that Shahabuddin refused to lie on it, complaining that it had a cloth strap which would aggravate his spinal pain. He demanded a stretcher with an iron sheet. That took the staff several hours more, so much so that by the time the iron stretcher arrived the court had risen for the day.

Shahabuddin had succeeded, but not without a price: the jail superintendent registered a complaint against him, saying that he had obstructed him in performing his duty and insulted him in everyone's presence and threatened to kill him. This complaint showed how far the bureaucracy had come from the dark days of demoralization in the

Lalu–Rabri raj when officers had to inveigle their way into the good books of the dons.

The emboldening of officers had a direct impact on Shahabuddin's trial. The unshackling was evident when police officers conducted a raid at his sprawling home at Pratappur village in Siwan district—the home the police had dared not go near during the Lalu–Rabri raj—in April 2006 and recovered a huge number of firearms and ammunition, many of them bearing marks of Pakistan Ordnance Factory.

Unobstructed investigations by and the free testimony of police officers resulted in Shahabuddin's conviction in several cases.

But Shahabuddin was relatively easier for Nitish to handle. He belonged to an Opposition party, which meant that he could do nothing to rock his government; also, police officers and prosecutors could go after him without a thought that they might receive a telephone call from the CMO to go slow or play some technical tricks to save him. This was not only true for Shahabuddin but for all the criminal-politicians in the Congress, the LJP or Bihar People's Party.

From their long experience, the bureaucracy had learnt to carefully distinguish between criminals in the ruling camp and criminals in the Opposition. Officers could clash head-on with criminals regardless of the ruler's patronage or its absence, but headstrong officers were more of an exception than the rule. The majority looked the other way when the criminal-politicians of the ruling camp violated the law.

It was a tradition, a habit that would not change seamlessly with the change of government. Although Nitish did not tire of conveying to the bureaucracy in his public speeches and at his meetings with officers that his objective was to establish the writ of the state without prejudice, down the line the officialdom believed it to be no more than the public face of political hypocrisy—the usual bluff and bluster of all chief ministers.

Narendra Kumar alias Sunil Pandey, the criminal-politician and JD(U) MLA from Piro in Bhojpur district checked into a five-star hotel in Patna on 25 June 2006 with his wife, son and armed bodyguards, ordered sumptuous meals and drinks, and refused to pay the bills. When the hotel staff persisted with the payment demand, the boozed-up bully scared them away by threatening to kill them.

Deciding to take bitter revenge, the hotel staff rang up TV newsrooms asking them to broadcast the 'real face' of Nitish's good governance (sushasan). Pandey was furious on seeing TV journalists barge into his suite. 'How dare you come here to spy on me? You will have to pay with your life,' he fumed, shouting out to one of his bodyguards, 'Vishwanath, shoot them!'

It became 'breaking news' on local TV channels, with a hurt media seeking bytes from Opposition leaders to ridicule Nitish's claims of curbing criminals. As if to emphasize the irony, the incident occurred soon after Nitish gave a speech in the city explaining how hard he had tried to re-establish the rule of law during his first seven months in office.

All administrators knew about the case as much as the man in the street did but they acted ignorant. When someone in the media asked Kundan Krishnan, the senior superintendent of police, Patna, what action he had taken, he said prosaically: 'No one has registered a complaint with the police. No victims or eyewitnesses have approached us so far.'

The matter would have rested there had the mood in the media, which had been very favourable to Nitish since he took over, not turned hostile. There was also a general reading among JD(U) party officials and the chief minister's office that the Pandey episode could severely dent the government's clean, rule-enforcing image. The Opposition would capitalize on it, using the incident as a burning example of Nitish's double standards.

Nitish saw the risk in not taking action against Pandey. But he also had to weigh in the risk of antagonizing him. How could he forget that Pandey had been his staunch supporter for several years? As a Samata MLA in 2000 he was among the leading party men engaged in getting the right numbers in the House for Nitish to be able to prove he enjoyed a majority.

True, Nitish had no great respect or special affection for Pandey; nor did he consider him good party material or a worthy colleague. He did not have any long-term view of his relationship with Pandey; with criminals like him looking for temporary shelter, he knew the connection could snap any moment. Yet it also remained true that Nitish had helped him earn social prestige by admitting him as a member of his party, first the Samata and then the JD(U), and then by giving him party ticket in Assembly elections in 2000 and 2005. He had nominated him despite being fully aware of his criminal antecedents and active association with the Ranvir Sena, because he was sure that with the support of his Bhumihar caste-men, who treated him like a hero, and by the power of arms Pandey would win the seat, which he did both times.

However, Nitish thought that his stakes as chief minister were far greater than his stakes in protecting one of his party MLAs. He could not allow his rule-of-law train to be derailed by a small rock on the track. On the contrary, if he removed it to keep the train moving at a steady speed he would gain strong public admiration and sympathy that would help him take the masses along in carrying out other tasks.

Nitish asked his principal secretary R.C.P. Singh to call the DGP to instruct the Patna SP to have a complaint registered against Pandey at Kotwali, the concerned police station. Accordingly, about twelve hours after the episode the police registered a case. As the police prepared to arrest him, Pandey went into hiding. 'Efforts to trace him are on,' the Patna SP Vikas Vaibhav told the media. Being in a foul mood the media took his statement with a pinch of salt, suspecting that it was all a stage-managed affair which, while boosting Nitish's image, brought no harm to Pandey.

Local dailies went to town the following morning with headlines and stories grossly critical of Nitish. One newspaper said there was no end to 'jungle raj'; another observed that the Lalu–Rabri raj was better than Nitish's, for never had such an incident happened during their fifteen-year reign.

On the other side, Pandey felt aggrieved by Nitish's instituting the case against him. To Pandey's advantage there was rancour among other criminal-politicians against the 'growing influence of bureaucracy' over the Nitish government. There were some party dissidents too who joined the malevolent chorus. As if to provide proof of the unbridled authority given to officers, SSP Kundan Krishnan used force to arrest another criminal-politician, Anand Mohan, in Patna. Pandey went on television to denounce Krishnan's 'high-handedness'; and he stunned everyone by adding that had Krishnan behaved with him in a similar manner, 'I would have shot him dead.'

Nitish had been receiving reports about Pandey's plot to mobilize a good number of party MLAs to demonstrate his strength to bully him: Pandey's daredevil statement on TV in denunciation of his government came as a confirmation of this. This was a direct challenge to Nitish, and he could have ignored it at his own peril. He spoke to the party president Sharad Yadav, who agreed that Pandey deserved disciplinary action. The party issued him a show cause notice, asking him why he should not be suspended for his statements. Pandey tried hard to get out of it with regrets and apologies like he had regarding the hotel episode, but in vain, as both Nitish and Sharad held that if his open defiance was condoned it could embolden others to make any statement they liked against the government or party leadership. Pandey was suspended from the primary membership of the party.

Nitish took a risk, and it paid off: Pandey dropped his plan of jolting Nitish and reconciled to the situation in which he had to fight his own legal battles. He missed no opportunity now to reaffirm his loyalty to the party and to Nitish, telling anyone who listened that the party or government had nothing to do with the cases filed against him; that the cases were regarding his acts, and it was he who would have to deal with them in the courts.

In September 2006 Pandey's petition for anticipatory bail was rejected by the court in a case of extortion for which he had been booked. As his arrest became inevitable, several of his supporters assembled outside 1 Anne Marg, demanding that Nitish allow Pandey to surrender before him and not before the magistrate or any official of the police station. Refusing to yield to the demand, Nitish conveyed to them that the appropriate place for Pandey to surrender was the court, not his office.

Although Nitish had taken in criminals just as other parties had done, he took enough care not to allow himself to be identified with them. Lalu never hid his intimacy with Shahabuddin; the don of Siwan was a regular visitor to 1 Anne Marg. Nitish, extremely conscious about guarding his clean public image, kept his party's criminal MLAs at a distance.

However, no sooner than Nitish had tackled Pandey, another thug in his party, Anant Singh, shot into public focus with his hooliganism. He began to terrorize shop owners in a market complex on Fraser Road in downtown Patna to eject them from their properties, claiming to be the bona fide owner of the plot on which the commercial building stood.

The plot originally belonged to a big landlord, Mehdi Hasan Imam, who had died issueless. Anant Singh claimed that Imam had given away the plot as gifts to his servants who had sold them to him. The shop owners refused to vacate their properties despite harassment by Anant Singh because they claimed to have legal titles. When the persecution by him crossed tolerable limits, they approached the local police station, but officials there declined to register any complaint. Anant Singh's intimidation continued. Here again, as in Sunil Pandey's case, the police was following double standards in dealing with criminals of the ruling party.

Anant Singh led the most powerful gang in Mokama, from where he was elected as MLA. In the election he received substantial support from his Bhumihar caste; the rest he made up with his terror. Mokama formed part of the Barh Lok Sabha constituency which Nitish had represented thrice. Nitish had used Anant Singh's mobilizing strength in his election campaigns in Barh. In that sense, Anant Singh had worked more closely with Nitish than Sunil Pandey or any other criminal in the JD(U).

So when unable to get the police to act against Anant Singh the harassed shop owners approached Nitish at his public interaction programme 'Janata ke Durbar mein Mukhya Mantri', Chief Minister in People's Court—that he held every Monday in an annexe at 1 Anne Marg—he faced a greater dilemma than he had in Sunil Pandey's case. But the quandary lasted not more than a moment, for his public image as a fair-minded ruler was at stake. He called the station house officer (SHO) of the Kotwali police station immediately to his office and asked him to register the shop owners' complaint against Anant Singh. He also called the inspector general of police (headquarters), Anil Sinha, and asked him to ensure that the complaint was registered and legal action taken against Anant Singh. To the media covering the programme he said: 'JD(U), RJD, Congress or BJP, it hardly matters which party, caste or religion one is from. All are equal in the eye of the law. We will act tough against anyone who tries to take the law in his hands.'

Anant Singh was far from subdued. A few weeks later a young Muslim woman shot off letters to Nitish, top cops and the media alleging that Anant Singh had raped her. Soon she was found murdered. Two TV journalists, who went to Anant Singh's residence to interview him on the rape-and-murder allegations, were battered by him and his bodyguards so mercilessly they had to be rushed to hospital. A group of journalists marched to Anant Singh's residence to protest the assault; they were assaulted too. The alleged rape and murder and the attack on journalists aroused public disgust and indignation against the brazen behaviour of a criminal who was seen as someone close to Nitish.

If there was anything Nitish feared above all it was the public developing a perception of his regime as being no different from the Lalu–Rabri regime in political patronage of criminals and lawlessness. He did not want any mud hurled on Singh to stick to him. He ordered the police to arrest Singh and his bodyguards. Under the chief judicial magistrate's order Singh was remanded to jail for nearly two weeks.

Speedy trial led to convictions of about a dozen criminal-politicians, regardless of their party affiliation. Shahabuddin was sentenced to life term for kidnapping a CPI(ML) worker Chhotelal Gupta, ten years for attempting to murder the Siwan SP S.K. Singhal on 3 May 1996 and to one-year rigorous imprisonment for threatening Sub-Inspector Harendra Rai in 2005 who was investigating cases against him; Anand Mohan was awarded death sentence and his wife Lovely Anand life term for the murder of the district magistrate of Gopalganj, G. Krishnaiah, on 5 December 1994. Krishnaiah was lynched by a mob when he tried to restrain the cortège of Chhotan Shukla—a local leader of the Bihar People's Party whose president was Anand Mohan—to prevent any revengeful attack by the angry mourners. Krishnaiah was mercilessly assaulted and then shot dead on the road. Vijay Kumar alias Munna Shukla, a JD(U) MLA and younger brother of Chhotan Shukla, who was also one of the accused, got life term.

Rajesh Ranjan alias Pappu Yadav, RJD MP, and Rajan Tiwary, former independent MLA from Govindganj, were sentenced to life term for the murder of Ajit Sarkar, CPI(M) MLA of Purnea on 14 June 1998. Suraj Bhan Singh, former LJP MP, Munna Shukla and Rajan Tiwary were awarded life term for the murder of Brij Behari Prasad, a minister in the Rabri cabinet on 13 June 1998. Anant Singh was sentenced to life term for kidnapping the renowned neurosurgeon of Patna Dr Ramesh Chandra in 2003.

Nearly all of the dozen thugs were convicted in multiple cases. As elections to the Lok Sabha were announced in 2009, they desperately tried to get their conviction suspended by the courts, which was necessary for them to be eligible for candidacy. When the courts rejected nearly all the petitions, some of them followed the Rabri model to gain party nominations for their wives. The proxies included Heena Saheb, Ranjeeta Ranjan, Lovely Anand and Veena Devi, wives of Shahabuddin, Pappu Yadav, Anand Mohan and Suraj Bhan Singh, respectively.

The dons got the greatest shock of their life when voters rejected their dummies. This clearly showed that much of the 'popular support' the dons claimed to enjoy in their constituencies was actually a result of coercion. Their long incarceration of around two years had prevented them from organizing their gangs to intimidate people into voting for them.

In the past, even when locked up in jail, several criminals had won elections. However, the reason why they could not succeed in 2009 lay in the unprecedented number of convictions. Key members of the incarcerated dons' gangs were either in prison like them, in hiding or lying low. With the might of the state sending the gangs on the run, people shed their fears and voted against the return of the dons.

Nitish had won the battle against criminal-politicians, which had seemed the toughest of all. There were two factors that had helped him: one, courage. 'I'm not afraid of getting killed. That would be liberation for me if it comes,' he said philosophically to his confidants who apprehended he might invite the wrath of the dons. Two, even-handedness. His endeavour to establish the rule of law through timely police action and speedy trials was directed against all criminals. The criminal-politicians saw that Nitish was not targeting any of them in particular: he was not selective and he was not 'going after' them. This became still clearer to them when Nitish showed no partiality towards the dons of his own party.

While Nitish allowed the law to take its course and distanced himself from the criminal-politicians in his party, he did not take a firm position on having no association with them. The JD(U) never framed a policy not to have men with criminal antecedents as its members or election nominees. Action by Nitish, whether as leader of government or of party, was taken only on occasions when they violated the law or party discipline.

The party did not expel Anant Singh, Sunil Pandey or other criminal-politicians in spite of the negative publicity they often brought to it. There was never a thug-cleansing launched by the party. The sole reason was that they had demonstrated their ability to win their constituencies: that assured a certain number of seats for the party. So, while the legal processes continued, the criminal-politicians were treated gently by Nitish and the party. After the media and public anger against Sunil Pandey had subsided, the suspension order against him was withdrawn by the party. And Anant Singh eventually managed to evict the shop owners and take possession of the commercial complex on Fraser Road, because he did have the valid papers and won the case.

Nitish had allowed Munna Shukla to be named by the Assembly Speaker as chairman of the Bihar Vidhan Sabha Awas Samiti (Assembly Housing Committee), a post that accorded him the status of a minister, with the privileges of an office in the legislature building, a secretary, allowances and a beacon on top of his car. Shukla was given the post before he was sentenced to life term in the Krishnaiah murder case: he was not removed from the post even after his conviction and imprisonment. The chamber allotted to him remained closed, and the housing committee non-functional in the absence of the chairman, but the Speaker did not take any step to replace him with another MLA.

The logic of realpolitik that worked here was that the housing committee was one among those seventeen committees of the Assembly that were not constitutional but only created to award decorative posts and ministerial ranks to MLAs of the Speaker's and chief minister's choice. Yet it was clear that Nitish did not press for Shukla's replacement because he did not want him to feel hurt. After all, despite his conviction, Shukla remained an MLA and with the proven ability to win the Lalganj constituency in Vaishali district. Nitish wouldn't like to lose a seat in the Assembly for being fanatically idealistic.

As long as the dons did not break party discipline, Nitish allowed them to be in the JD(U). In the Assembly elections of 2010, Nitish re-nominated all the criminal-politicians of the party for the constituencies they represented: Anant Singh, Sunil Pandey, Dhumal Singh and Neeraj Singh among them. In some places the party also nominated the wives of criminals who were in jail or dead, such as Annu Shukla, wife of Munna Shukla; Bima Bharti, wife of gangster Awadesh Mandal; Punam Devi, wife of criminal-politician Ranvir Yadav; and Lesi Singh, widow of gangster Butan Singh.

Nitish campaigned for many of them in their constituencies, sharing the dais with them, urging people to vote for them. Most of them won, too, and largely because people voted for Nitish regardless of who his candidate was. Yet, their victory also clearly suggested that the two factors that always helped criminals win elections—terror and caste—still remained crucial. A significant point to note was that their terror worked despite any open display or use of armed power by the gangsters owing to Nitish's campaign against crime and the Election Commission's constant vigilance against violence and rigging. Both terror and caste worked by word of mouth. However, the fact that the Nitish factor tilted the balance was clear from the success of most of the criminals or their wives nominated by the JD(U) and the failure of those nominated by the RJD and the LJP. It was not because of the power Nitish enjoyed but because of the popular support for him owing to his performance.

Nitish found it easier to restrain criminals than the Maoists who not only had arms but also the support of the rural poor in pockets of several districts. With the merger of three main radical groups, the Maoist Communist Centre (MCC), CPI(ML) Party Unity and CPI(ML) People's War, a strong organization had emerged in the form of

CPI (Maoist). The only major group out of it was CPI(ML) Liberation that had abandoned the line of armed struggle and taken to the parliamentary path: it did not pose any challenge to the state except as a radical party in the Opposition.

In contrast, the CPI (Maoist) had a guerrilla army, armed squads and secret committees for propaganda, communication and organization-building, apart from open fronts. Its leaders, cadres and activities in Bihar were a part of its national struggle for seizing political power. It also had strong links with the Communist Party of Nepal (Maoist) that had risen dramatically over the past decade and a half to become a leading political force in that Himalayan country.

A few days before Nitish took over as chief minister in November 2005, the Maoists carried out their biggest attack on the state forces ever to rescue their leaders and cadres incarcerated in the Jehanabad district jail. Half an hour before a Maoist force of about two hundred men mounted simultaneous assaults on the prison and the police barracks in the heart of the town (to prevent reinforcements from reaching the jail) at about nine o'clock in the evening, some party workers went round Jehanabad on motorcycles warning people to go indoors to avoid getting hurt in the action that was going to unfold.

Soon they cut off the electricity and started firing in several parts of the town to provide cover to their contingent assigned to take over the jail. The whole town was under their control for more than two hours. At the end of it, they escaped with about a hundred of their jailed comrades, including their party state secretary Ajay Kanu, after killing two of the key leaders of the Ranvir Sena, Bishveswar Rai and Bade Sharma, who were among inmates of the jail.

The episode brought home a chilling lesson to Nitish: the state seemed incapable of meeting the armed power of the Maoists. How could he re-establish the authority of the state in the areas of Maoist influence?

Maoism, like its earlier avatar Naxalism, could not be controlled in the same way as crime. It was rooted in deep anger against the state. The agricultural labourers and poor peasants who were active in CPI (Maoist) were disillusioned with the system owing to the state's collusion with their oppressors. They were constantly subjected to social discrimination, public humiliation and violence by the landed castes that included upper castes and upper backwards. Their women were frequent victims of molestation and rape. The local police, more often than not, lent its strength to the might of the oppressors, using laws and arms to repress the poor.

Development agencies of the government acted at the behest and in the interest of the rural rich. Democracy held no charm for the poor because the rich, in collusion with the police, rigged the elections, and the elected representatives in panchayats, the Assembly and in Parliament favoured their oppressors.

The room for Maoists (Naxalites) to step in was indeed created by the state. Maoism was a legitimate child of the hypocrisy of the 'egalitarian' state. The premise of the Maoist appeal was loss of confidence in the state's neutrality. The Maoists commonly identified the state in their propaganda and cadre indoctrination as 'the enemy'.

Nitish's predecessors, including Lalu, had followed a dual policy of repression and reform to contain armed communist groups. The reform part involved efforts to improve delivery of development and welfare programmes. However, the reforms had remained largely on paper: the actual emphasis was always on repression. In essence it came to mean that behind the smokescreen of sympathy for the poor, created to wean away the followers, the state carried on with its campaign to murder the leaders of Maoist groups.

This policy proved counter-productive, as it convinced the poor more than ever that the state was not interested in providing justice to them but in keeping them under primitive conditions of exploitation. The natural reaction to state repression was retaliation by armed Maoists on police forces. In the 1970s and 1980s this would mean attacks on police stations and outposts and ambushes of police patrol parties to kill policemen and loot their firearms. Later, attacks assumed more sophisticated and lethal forms with landmines, RDX and the Kalashnikovs.

Retaliation, resistance, self-defence: the Maoists were not only engaged in confrontation with the police and paramilitary forces but also with the *sena*s, the caste-based militias of landlords. And they were as brutal in their vengeance against the militias as they would be in their assaults on police forces. Their justification for barbarity was simple: it was a cumulative reaction to the centuries of savage treatment meted out to them. As for massacres, it was the landlord militias that had started them; the Maoists were only paying them back in the same coin.

When Nitish looked at his police force he realized the police was poorly equipped in every department: numbers, training, guns, mobility, communications, intelligence. To top it all, the average age of his policeman was thirty-eight.

Nitish could not win a military war against the Maoists. The Centre offered to help: Home Minister P. Chidambaram was ready to dispatch as many companies of paramilitary forces as Nitish required. Chidambaram offered to provide technical equipment too, even an Indian Air Force plane for logistics.

Nitish knew the growth of Maoism posed a serious threat to national security, and coordinated efforts of the Centre and states were needed to meet the challenge. Yet, after assessing the situation in the state he decided an all-out offensive against the Maoists might be counter-productive.

Nitish elaborates his stance on Maoism thus:

We have to understand that we are democrats. The Maoists are rebels. They can use any means. Their aim is to seize power with the power of guns. Are we going to be their followers? Do we do as they do? We have to understand that a vast number of people are deprived of education, health and other government services. We have failed to take development to them. Which of the quotations of Rajiv Gandhi is most famous? 'Only 15 paise of one rupee of development funds reaches the people.' What does that mean? That 85 paise is swallowed by the corrupt. Isn't it a pity that Rajiv just made that statement but did nothing to stop the leakage of 85 paise? What has his Congress party done to stop the leakage? Why are we elected by people, after all—to set things right, right? Who will stop that leakage? The basic task of an elected government is to ensure that the full one rupee reaches the people. The problem of Maoism is simple. The deprived have chosen the path of Maoism to get what elected governments have failed to give them. We have to adopt policies and implement programmes so development reaches them. Once that happens, the intellectual and military recruitments to the Maoist organization will automatically stop. The way to fight Maoism is to build as many schools and hospitals, provide employment to as many as possible, help people upgrade their skills.[2]

At the meetings Prime Minister Manmohan Singh had with chief ministers of the states under Maoist influence, Nitish, while endorsing police action and vigilance, argued that the problem could be tackled only by speeding up development. His strategy was to de-emphasize police action against Maoists not so much in actual practice as in public posturing. He would not talk about police strategy or police action to meet the armed might of the Maoists.

He told the Centre not to hold any high-profile meeting in Patna to discuss strategies to tackle the Maoist problem: should senior officials of the Union home ministry desire to have a meeting with senior state officials in Patna they could do so, but without letting the media get any whiff of it.

This approach was what was portrayed in the media as the Chidambaram–Nitish divide. Chidambaram was seen as pursuing a 'hard line' and Nitish a 'soft line'. The 'divide' became 'apparent' when Nitish failed to attend a meeting of chief ministers of Maoism-troubled states convened by Chidambaram in Kolkata. However, the reality was that Nitish had a prior appointment with the Dalai Lama at Dharamshala. Nitish wrote to Chidambaram explaining why he could not attend, assuring him that he would go by whatever decisions were taken at the meeting, which would be attended by his chief secretary and DGP. But somehow Chidambaram took it as an affront, and from his vague and insinuating remarks made to the national media about Nitish's approach, the impression of the hard line–soft line divide between the two got reinforced.

Nitish's government would not go after the Maoists; it would not conduct any campaign to burn the bushes to ashes. This meant that his government would not indiscriminately be a part of Operation Greenhunt, the Central government's campaign across the country for the purpose. His government preferred 'selective action' to a campaign: police forces would act only where they must to prevent Maoists from gathering with arms in a large number for launching an attack.

The underlying idea was that the police would not indulge in deliberate actions that would provoke the Maoists to launch retaliatory attacks on the state. Nitish's effort was to present himself before the Maoists as someone who believed in fair play and would not initiate brutalities or unscrupulous action: a man who saw Maoists not as 'enemies of the state' but as political rebels entitled to human rights.

The difference between Nitish's approach and Chidambaram's or Lalu's lay with respect to police brutality outside incidents of exchange of fire. One of the police's most gruesome ways of dealing with Maoists was to kill them in fake encounters. Once they caught a Maoist they would tie him to a tree and shoot him dead rather than taking the trouble of investigating his alleged crimes, submitting a charge sheet in court and prosecuting him. If the policemen were 'merciful' not to kill a Maoist they would subject him to torture at the police station during interrogation.

Fake encounters and third degree were also part of Indira's Emergency. The cold-blooded murder of a young 'Naxalite' Rajan, of Kerala, by the police during that time was one of the most popular examples of state brutality that had sensitized many a social democrat who also suffered during the 1975–77 repression to develop a commitment to human rights. Having experienced it in the formative stage of his political career, Nitish could not bring himself to allow his police to follow the horrific tradition. All through his fight with the Maoists, he would zealously safeguard his image of a human-rights-conscious politician.

Nitish's Maoist-containment policy would have three cardinal principles: one, the police would not kill anyone in fake encounters. Two, the police would not subject anyone to third degree. Three, no Maoist in jail would be shackled in *danda-beri* (iron bar and fetters).

Nitish's policy was outlined in his speech at the third meeting of chief ministers with the prime minister and Union home minister on internal security on 14 July 2010 in Delhi:

I share the concern of all of you about left-wing extremism in several states. My views on the framework of the solution to the problem may differ from that of some of those present here. Left-wing extremist elements are a part of our society misguidedly driven into violence. Enforcement action alone leads to wider alienation. A symptomatic treatment results in reappearance of the disease in a more virulent form. To prevent this, Bihar has adopted an integrated approach which can be the appropriate strategy for its effective and permanent solution . . . Only intensive, holistic development can be the final solution of left-wing extremism . . . The state government is committed to establish the rule of law by protecting human rights while protecting the interests of the citizens and ensuring security . . . I am happy to note that all our achievements [such as arrests of CPI(Maoist) area commanders and seizures of huge hauls of arms and ammunition] have been made without any complaints of violation of human rights.[3]

Although Nitish's Maoist policy eschewed an all-out offensive and human rights violations, it allowed the police to take action wherever necessary. Thus between 2006 and 2009, the police arrested 1,881 Maoists—350 of them hardcore and many of them 'area commanders' and 'zonal commanders' of the Maoist armed wing—compared to 1,160 during 2001–04. A total of 62,841 kg of explosives was seized from them during 2006–09 against only 94 kg during 2001–04.

Without making too much noise, Nitish took measures to strengthen his police. He approved the setting up of a Special Task Force (STF) on the model of Greyhounds that had successfully put down the armed Maoist challenge in Andhra Pradesh. The model police station he was building in every district would be fortified to fight off armed attackers. Police budget was nearly doubled in five years to recruit more policemen and to buy sophisticated firearms, transport vehicles and communication equipment for the police.

Between 2005 and 2009, twenty arms training camps of Maoists were destroyed and forty mini-gun factories were demolished. The police were engaged in 118 encounters in which sixty-two Maoists and eighty-six policemen were killed. Habits die hard: during their operations the policemen did not always exercise the highest level of restraint and respect for human rights as Nitish had instructed them to do. There were several cases of excesses during the police campaigns of encirclement and suppression and interrogation in police custody about which Nitish came to know from the media.

The second feature of Nitish's silent-but-stern police action against the Maoists was the use of the speedy trial mechanism. The cases of Maoists, like those of criminals, were brought to expeditious trial. Between 2006 and 2007, about two dozen Maoists were convicted in speedy trials. Between 2007 and 2009, convictions of 109 Maoists were obtained. This caused desperation in the Maoist ranks.

However, top Maoist leaders were not brought to speedy trial. Ajay Kanu, the second in command of the CPI (Maoist) in Bihar region, who was the mastermind of the Jehanabad jail break of 2005 and carried a reward of Rs 5 lakh on his head, was arrested in Patna in February 2007. A year earlier, the police had seized his property at his native village Chauhar in Arwal district. He was charged with serious crimes in several cases but the state home department did not put any of those on fast track. He was kept in the high-security Beur jail in Patna, but the government would not go for speedy trial of his cases despite the criticism of its 'soft approach' in the media.

Cases against another important Maoist leader Pramod Mishra were not put on speedy trial. These exceptions had Nitish's nod, for he did not want to burn all the bridges with the Maoists. The idea was in conformity with his strategy of stopping short of an all-out offensive against them, of creating an illusion that he was not marshalling all his powers to decimate them.

And in order to buttress his fair-minded image, he ordered speedy trials of members of landlord militias as well. Among the Maoists convicted in speedy trial, many had been involved in retaliatory massacres of the members of landlord militias and the men from higher castes who allegedly patronized them. Nitish was concerned when the Maoists started accusing his government of following double standards in pursuing the cases against them with vigour but not against the sena members. He realized that if the cases against the sena members were not taken up with similar zeal it would generate resentment among the lower castes and other sections of the rural poor and drive them into the camp of the Maoists.

The state government identified 369 cases in which upper-caste armies were involved in massacre, murder, rape and other forms of violence. It marked all these cases as 'sensitive' and recommended them to the Patna High Court for expeditious trial. Consequently, sixteen members of the Ranvir Sena were sentenced to death and ten to life for killing fifty-eight Dalits in Laxmanpur-Bathe. For the Bathani Tola massacre of twenty-one dalits, three were awarded death sentence and twenty, life term.

The police's relentless but low-profile pursuit of Maoists and the unprejudiced, even-handed speedy trial of Maoists and members of caste armies resulted in a break in the chain of massacres. Nitish had proven his critics wrong who had said he would not act against the Ranvir Sena as it enjoyed the protection of his partner in government, the BJP. Critics often pointed to the media-exposed observations of the Justice Amir Das Commission—set up by the Rabri regime to investigate massacres in central Bihar—about the close links of the BJP and Ranvir Sena leaders. The charge stuck also because the commission's term was not extended by Nitish after he assumed office on the grounds that the commission had been dragging on for six years and not submitted any report to the government.

By asking his police to arrest and prosecute the members of the landlord militias expeditiously through the speedy trial mechanism Nitish intended to convey a message to the rural poor that they need not seek the armed shelter of the Maoists, because unlike the Lalu–Rabri regime his government was taking action against feudal goons.

Nitish's approach impacted the Maoists in two ways. One, they resorted less frequently to violence. During 2006–09 there were only 338 Maoism-related incidents against 1,117 during 2001–04. The number of civilians killed by the Maoists during 2006–09 was 160, compared to 668 during 2001–04. Secondly, their main activity started to shift from central Bihar to districts in south-eastern Bihar bordering Jharkhand and districts in north Bihar bordering Nepal. The new zones provided the Maoists good catchment areas for recruits owing to higher prevalence of poverty than in other parts of the state. These areas also provided them cross-border mobility and, in many parts, security of the forested hills.

In the latter half of the 2000s the Maoists were in a fix. The militarist line they had followed in preference to mass movements had acted as a powerful deterrent, though not always effective, to feudal oppressors, but the revolution was far from winning areas and people's hearts. Emphasis on militarism meant dominance of the armed wing—grandiosely named People's Liberation Guerrilla Army, complete with uniform, hierarchy and training—over the members and supporters of the organization in mass movements.

Recruitments to the armed wing were made on the basis of the criteria of readiness for full-time occupation, quick shifting of camps, movement under harsh conditions, usually by night and at great risk, shooting and tactical ability: which criteria brought in elements that might be daredevils, lumpens or even criminals, rather than ordinary young men from peasant or labourer families whose family responsibilities did not permit full-time duty or life risks. Complaints of members of the armed wing collecting levies for private accumulation were not uncommon.

Despite the severe limitations of militarism, and the distortions that it brought to their movement, the CPI (Maoist) continued to pursue it. Reports from the Maoist camp suggested that they were in the process of setting up a People's Liberation Army, an upgradation of the People's Liberation Guerrilla Army. And the Maoists' militarist line did pose serious challenges to the state.

The greatest test of Nitish's Maoist policy came with a massive blunder committed by the SP of Lakhisarai, Ashok Singh, towards the end of August 2010. Acting on a vague intelligence input that thirty-odd Maoists had been seen moving around in the Lakhisarai forests, Singh assembled a force of forty-three men, twenty-three from the Bihar Military Police (BMP) and twenty from the State Auxiliary Police (SAP) to launch combat operations. A contingent of thirty-four men of the Central Reserve Police Force (CRPF) was put together to back the small BMP–SAP force, whose command Singh gave to Bhulan Yadav, the officer-in-charge of Kawaiya police outpost who had no training or experience in combat duty. Singh sent them into the forest without any preparations, detailed plan or strategy.

[Singh] did not follow the SOP (standard operating procedure) laid down after the Dantewada [Chhattisgarh] massacre [the deadliest-ever Maoist attack in which 76 CRPF men were killed in an ambush]. According to the SOP, once a force is assembled the commanders discuss the terrain, topography and intelligence. This is explained to the troops using sand models and Survey of India maps. A detailed strategy is formulated, GPS (ground positioning system) coordinates are set before the force begins its movement. But Ashok Singh did not make any plan . . . He knew that we were operating in undulating, hilly and forested terrain. He knew the topography. He should have been aware, after the recent ambushes in Chhattisgarh where [the Maoists] occupied higher ground and lured policemen into a trap . . . [4]

As feared, the police search party got into a trap at Sitlakodasi village in the forest, the advance group facing a rain of bullets from the top of the hills and the CRPF cover contingent straying away. The Maoists were about three hundred in number, not thirty-odd as the intelligence input had reported. Seven policemen were killed, including Commander Bhulan Yadav, and ten of them injured when the remaining members of the search party surrendered to the repeated calls of the Maoists over loudhailers.

After the policemen gave themselves up, the Maoists bandaged the wounds of the injured and gave them water to drink. They let everyone go except four of them—Abhay Yadav, SHO of Manikpur police station, trainee sub-inspector Rupesh Kumar Sinha, and BMP havaldar Mohammad Ehsan and jamadar Lukas Tete. They threatened to kill the four hostages if the state government did not release eight key Maoists in jail within two days.

In such situations in recent years other state governments had given in to Maoist demands. That would have been the easiest way for Nitish to resolve the crisis, which was heightened by media focus on the agonizing wives and mothers of the hostages assembled outside 1 Anne Marg. Instead, Nitish decided to build military and moral pressure on the Maoists to release the policemen. He ordered his top police officials to dispatch large contingents of troops to encircle the forest area where the hostages were held: this was to convey a message to the Maoists that 'you won't escape casualties if you kill our four men'.

On the other side, Nitish appealed to the Maoists not to harm the hostages, pleading that their eight colleagues whose release they demanded were being treated fairly and humanly in jail. He also used Track Two diplomacy: persuading some intellectuals who kept in touch with Maoist evangelists to open a channel of dialogue with CPI (Maoist) leaders. He also got a few of the Maoists working in open fronts, who used to meet him now and then, to put pressure on the hostage-takers.

However, with the expiry of the deadline, the Maoists killed one of the four hostages, Lukas Tete. That brought the state government's helplessness in full view: Nitish seemed incapable of dealing with the Maoists and protecting the policemen. The families of Tete and surviving hostages heaped all the blame on Nitish. Chidambaram seemed to be enjoying Nitish's plight: when the media asked him questions about the crisis he said Nitish Kumar was 'capable' of handling it. This was no time for a duel of political egos: Nitish needed more troops to seal the target area and two helicopters to fly over the forests for intelligence on the location of the Maoist forces. Chidambaram's ministry eventually provided these.

At the same time Nitish continued to build moral pressure on the Maoists through the media and civil society channels. He convened an all-party meeting at which a unanimous resolution was passed calling upon the Maoists to release the three policemen. He also announced that he was ready for face-to-face talks with Maoist representatives and assured them safe passage even if negotiations broke down. The offer set off discussions among the Maoists about whether they should accept it and who should represent them. No Maoists eventually came for talks, and they announced that they would voluntarily release the three hostages on humanitarian grounds.

Several factors worked to help Nitish come out of the crisis without a major damage to his and his government's image. There seemed to be division in the Maoist camp on the issue: one group was obviously for killing the four hostages to send a strong message to the government; it was evident from the killing of Tete, which was supposed to be the beginning. But there was another group that argued that killing Tete was not 'revolutionary conduct' and that killing the other policemen in captivity (prisoners of war) would create the image of Maoists as savages:

how different will the 'revolutionary forces' be if they indulged in similar brutalities as the feudal-bourgeois forces did? The latter view had the endorsement of the top Maoist leadership based in the Dandakaranya forests in Chhattisgarh, and that ultimately prevailed.

The Lakhisarai episode fully exposed the inadequacy of the state police forces to meet the Maoist challenge. The Maoists showed better planning, superior tactics and more sophisticated equipment. Policemen who survived Lakhisarai said publicly that they had no training in jungle warfare. From the word go, the Maoists dominated the engagement in Lakhisarai: they inflicted deaths and injuries upon the policemen, forced them to surrender and took four of them hostage. And it was because they showed mercy that the lives of the three hostages were saved.

The lesson the state learnt in Lakhisarai was that it could not win a military war over the Maoists. Nitish was convinced more than ever of the relevance of the reforms he had introduced in villages under Maoist influence in 2006 to reduce the scope of discontentment among the poorer sections.

The Maoists had built up their bases in the countryside not only by creating armed guerrilla squads to meet the aggression of the landlord militias and the police but also by fighting on social and political fronts. Because of the pressure of the mobilization by the Maoists, day wages had risen in the areas of their influence. Landless labourers and poor peasants had seized back plots of private and public lands occupied illegally by landlords. Although Maoists did not trust parliamentary democracy, their mobilization had helped the rural poor fight rigging of elections and cast their vote. Their mobilization had reduced the sexual oppression of the women from the low-caste peasant and labourer families by the landlords. The Maoist movement had instilled a sense of self-respect in the lower castes, as a result of which non-discrimination and equal treatment was becoming an accepted way of social intercourse.

The deep anger among the masses against exploitation and oppression created a ready base for recruitment to the armed squads, and these squads had indeed fought many bold and valiant battles against feudal and police forces during the past fifty years or more. However, the Maoists had failed to prove that armed struggle was the best way to seize political power.

Most radical factions of the original CPI(ML) had faded away. The main group of the movement, CPI(ML) Liberation, had realized the futility of continuing with armed struggle and decided to achieve revolution through parliamentary means. The CPI (Maoist) continued to believe in armed struggle despite the fact that its call for boycott of elections did not have much impact on the polling percentage. Emphasis on armed struggle in effect came to mean less emphasis on mass movements: the Maoist movement was characterized by high militarization and low politicization. Overdependence on arms led to internecine killings in the past between the MCC, CPI(ML) Party Unity and CPI(ML) Liberation. Armed power also created scope for criminalization of members of guerrilla squads, particularly with respect to amassing funds through private levies and embezzlement of organizational funds.

Yet, the alienation from the social and political systems was so profound that the Maoists were able to spread their areas of influence. Nitish had to do something concrete to control this trend. But how to do it? The issues of the poor required intervention of almost all government departments. How could all the limbs of the state be galvanized into action simultaneously? It seemed impossible.

Nitish decided to experiment his scheme in one village in the area of Maoist influence. 'We will try and see how it works,' he told his officials. After considering several names, the state government selected Sikaria village of Jehanabad.

For several years Sikaria had been an important centre of activity of the Mazdoor Kisan Sangharsh Samiti (MKSS)—Committee for the Struggle of Workers and Peasants—led by an independent radical, Vinayan, a young doctor from UP who was inspired by the JP movement to work among the rural poor. Vinayan was later joined by Jang Bahadur Singh, former *mukhiya*, chief of Sikaria panchayat, who had also been active in the JP movement. The mobilization of landless labourers and poor peasants by the MKSS in Sikaria and other villages of Jehanabad invited savage attacks by the Bhoomi Sena, the armed militia of Kurmi landlords. Between 1982 and 1985, as many as twenty-six MKSS supporters were killed by the Bhoomi Sena in Sikaria alone.

In order to meet the armed challenge, the MKSS joined forces with the CPI(ML) Party Unity, whose counter-attacks on the Bhoomi Sena eventually forced the militia to surrender to the MKSS and appeal for peace in 1985. Both sides agreed to withdraw the criminal cases they had filed against each other. The Kurmi landlords agreed to pay higher wages to labourers. A joint demand was made to withdraw the police camps in Sikaria and other villages of Jehanabad.

The reconciliation was followed by an increasing demand for development for the collective good: repair of the traditional *ahar–pyne* irrigation system, adequate power supply and agricultural inputs, health care and so on. The MKSS also used its organizational strength to deter government officials from demanding bribe for public services.

It was for these reasons that Nitish chose Sikaria for his experiment. Named 'Aapki Sarkar, Aapke Dwar', Government at Your Doorstep, the experiment was launched by Nitish at a public meeting in Sikaria on 21 January 2006, less than two months after taking over office. On the day of the launch itself Nitish inaugurated a number of development schemes in the village. The underlying idea of the programme was to 'fully saturate' Sikaria with developmental and welfare activities—roads, irrigation, housing, schools, health, human resource development, social security—so that 'all the eligible persons get the benefits of these activities at their doorsteps'.

According to the plans drawn, the Sikaria panchayat *sarkar bhavan*, panchayat administrative building, would have wings housing a computer training centre, public health centre, PDS (public distribution system) or ration shops, self-help group centres, warehouse and other services. Panchayat representatives and officials would be available in the administrative building for redressal of people's grievances. Officials of various departments would set up regular camps and sort out problems on the spot, including land mutation.

The experiment did not have the desired success, but it did accelerate growth in Sikaria. Rural connectivity and the delivery of public services improved. A number of economic activities that were started created jobs for men and women. After a visit to Sikaria in mid-December 2008, V. Bhaskar, a member of the thirteenth Finance Commission observed,

'To be frank enough, the Sikaria rural area development scheme can be a model for others to follow.'[5]

A Delhi journalist gave the following account:

Under an unforgiving sun, old-timers in the village of Sikaria, a half-hour drive from Jehanabad town, talk about a time when they were scared to sleep at night . . . But today, it's hard to believe those stories as you watch teenaged girls from neighbouring areas cycle in for sewing classes. The Bihar government's 'Aapki Sarkar, Aapke Dwar' programme has provided every possible facility in the village—from a public health centre to a Madhya Bihar Gramin Bank to a computer centre and facilities to provide subsidised farm inputs as well as purchase of farm produce, even a veterinary centre. It has even made Sikaria an attractive destination for private enterprise. Last month, Anil Kumar Singh, a schoolteacher, decided to sink all his savings and start an English medium private school here even though there's a government school not too far away. And in keeping with the new mood, the school has been named Ahimsa Vidyalaya by its proud owner. Indeed, Sikaria has become symbolic of the changes sweeping through what were once 'the killing fields of central Bihar'. The bloody clashes that left hundreds dead in the districts of Jehanabad, Gaya, Arwal, Nawada and Aurangabad now seem a thing of a distant past.[6]

Over the next four years, Aapki Sarkar, Aapke Dwar was extended to sixty-five other 'left-wing-extremism-affected' panchayats in the eight districts of the state, the plan being to cover all such panchayats in thirty-three of the thirty-eight districts. The development commissioner was made the nodal officer to coordinate and monitor the implementation of the programme in all the panchayats, and the chief secretary was asked to review the progress regularly.

A journalist who travelled with Nitish to Masaurhi, a village near Patna once considered a hotbed of Maoist activity, was told by him how Maoist influence was countered and virtually eliminated there: 'We struck at the root of the problem—poverty and underdevelopment. This was done primarily through the "Aapki Sarkar, Aapke Dwar" programme. Now nobody in the village wants to carry a gun or give shelter to the gun-carriers [armed Maoists]. This is the right approach and I would want the Centre to look at this.'[7]

There is no doubt Maoist violence has declined in the state, but all of it cannot be credited to the Government at Your Doorstep programme. The convictions of several Maoists under the speedy trial mechanism was also an important factor.

The main promise of the programme—delivery of the fruits of development to the grass-roots level with no leakages—remains far from fulfilled. If anything, corruption has increased at the lower levels with more public spending. Elected officials of the panchayati raj institutions have joined the lower bureaucrats and engineers in the loot of public money. Two citizen vigilantes discovered in 2008 that a junior engineer in charge of Sikaria had drawn and approved task estimates of construction of a new irrigation channel in the village under the MNREGA (Mahatma Gandhi National Rural Employment Guarantee Act) scheme without visiting the worksite for measurement and filling the measurement books.

> During our visit with the JE [junior engineer] to the construction of [the] irrigation channel, we were told that the work was being carried out on an already existing irrigation channel, which has been functional since the time of the British Raj. The JE admitted that he drew up the task estimates without visiting the worksite. The reason, he said, was that it would take two to three days to do that, and he did not have the time. As a JE of the entire block, he is at the moment monitoring 30 projects . . . There can be serious implications for not visiting the worksite before drawing task estimates, such as sanctioning far greater money than the project requires. This allows scope for corruption. However, it also raises micro and macro issues such as monitoring, budgeting and human resources on [M]NREGA worksites. Given the number of sites that one JE is in charge of—in the case of Bihar, at least 30 sites—it is impossible for a JE to visit every site on a regular basis.[8]

# green and not so green

One of the earliest ideas Nitish wanted to put into action on taking over office was the acceleration of land reforms. When he launched the *adarsh gram*, ideal village, model in Sikaria he also planned to initiate land reforms in his development programmes there. Not only would land reform make an important component of development but it would also prove to be an effective check on Maoist influence. Better implementation of development and welfare measures under the Aapki Sarkar, Aapke Dwar programme could still be no more than firefighting. An assault on the sustaining power of the Maoists could only be made with a transformation in the economic equations, and hence social and political equations, in the villages.

The idea of neutralizing the appeal of left-wing extremism with land reforms was not new. Congress regimes in the state since Independence had framed several laws relating to land reforms, but, except for the abolition of zamindari, did not enforce them for the fear of losing the patronage of the upper castes who were big landholders. Over the years they passed several amendments purportedly to make the laws more specific, stringent and effective, but these were not implemented with any zeal.

In the mid-1960s the political coalitions with strong socialist and communist presence that removed the Congress from power in the state tried to put some life into the dormant land reform laws, but their tenures were too short to make any difference. A second attempt by a non-Congress regime was made in 1977–78 when Chief Minister Karpoori Thakur drew up a plan called Kosi Kranti to implement land reform laws in the command area of a branch canal in the Kosi River irrigation system in five blocks of Purnea district. Although his cabinet colleagues were hostile or indifferent to the project, Karpoori, driven by his socialist commitment, was keen to go ahead with the support of two zealous and reformist top officers, P.S. Appu and K.B. Saxena.

Karpoori's dream was that once Kosi Kranti became successful it could be replicated throughout the state. The main focus of the project would be to prepare an accurate, up-to-date record of land titles and tenures in order to provide security of tenure to sharecroppers. As Purnea had some of the largest landholdings in the state, the number of sharecroppers in the district was huge.

And Kosi Kranti was going to be no ordinary recording of rights with revenue officials and clerks camping in villages and hearing claims and counter-claims. Much like what Operation Barga in West Bengal became famous for later, Kosi Kranti intended to rely on mobilization of the peasantry, peasant organizations and NGOs on the one hand and the motivation of civil servants on the other. In actual practice, however, hardly had the mobilization begun in a few villages when upper-caste ministers and MLAs of the Janata Party warned Karpoori that the programme may trigger violent clashes between landlords and sharecroppers. 'Kosi Kranti is going to turn into a *khooni kranti*, bloody war,' they said. Dependent on upper-caste MLAs' support as he was, to survive in office, Karpoori thought it better to wind up the Kosi Kranti project.

Yet, despite political parties not wanting to implement them, land reforms were taking place in the state in unique ways. The first changes were brought by the legal enactments and their sporadic implementation, which forced big landowners to divide their holdings into ceiling-compliant sizes, and in some cases sell off pieces to their tenants or attached labourers to avoid losing them to the government. The laws, even though no more fearsome than scarecrows—as they were hardly ever implemented—created a climate of uncertainty among landowners about not being able to hold on to their estates for long; and this climate contributed to the growth of the land market in the countryside.

Division of land among male members of joint families—their numbers being large with no family planning in the past—parcelled out the landholdings, leaving every descendant free to do whatever he wanted with his land, which further increased the scope of the land market. Former zamindars and big landholders also sold plots of land to meet sudden demands of high expenditure. It was not uncommon for middle and poor peasants to sell off parcels of their land to pay dowry for their daughters. Poor peasants were also forced to sell their lands due to their sheer inability to meet the high costs of agricultural labour and production. All these factors combined to bring in transformation in the rural landownership pattern in the state.

Urban employment and seasonal migration to the green revolution states, Punjab and Haryana, put cash into the hands of landless labourers and poor peasants which boosted the demand for land. In several areas, absentee landlords leased out their plots to these new industrious marginal farmers. Spread of irrigation ushered in dramatic changes in tenurial relations, with big farmers leasing in plots of small and marginal farmers deterred by costs—the phenomenon of 'reverse tenancy' characteristic of Punjab.

Mobilization of landless labourers and poor peasants proved to be a far bigger factor than those mentioned above in bringing about changes in agrarian relations. Militant but non-violent campaigns conducted by JP-inspired youth, socialists and communists for security to sharecroppers and distribution of ceiling-surplus land held by former zamindars and religious trusts, as well as armed campaigns by radical communist organizations before these created a much more hostile climate for the feudal forces than the land laws and their sporadic implementation had ever done. These campaigns did not stop at setting up confrontations with landlords or attempting to goad the government into action; in several cases they decided to seize the lands they knew for certain were being held in violation of laws.

Almost in every village, landlords had appropriated by force large portions of village common lands (*gair mazarua aam*), government land (*gair mazarua khas*), public ponds and other government and community properties. They were cultivating and fishing and deriving personal income out of them. Labourers and peasants organized by radical communist groups fought for eviction of the landlords from these properties and were able to take over the gair mazarua plots and ponds in several villages. To some extent the mobilization also had a positive effect on terms of crop tenancy and wage rates for the sharecroppers and labourers.

Structural changes in land relations in Bihar were thus following their own dynamics. These changes were taking place in spite of the deep collusion between politicians and landlords. Contributing to these changes were the legislations the political class had to pass to sustain its populist illusion, new avenues of income that had opened to various rural classes outside the village by the market and the campaign of the peasant organizations. It could be said that the laws nudged the horse of land reforms, the market forces tempted it and the peasant organizations got it trotting.

The cumulative impact of the land reforms brought about by the state and non-state forces had a strong bearing on social relations as well. A majority of those who benefited through land reform were backward castes and Dalits; the largest benefit accrued to the upper backwards—the Yadavs, Kurmis and Koeries. Land transfers to the backward castes and Dalits infused them with a sense of self-worth, and this feeling led them to challenge the age-old domination of the upper castes in social, cultural and political spheres. Much of the Lalu phenomenon was rooted in the celebration of the shift in the landownership pattern.

Land reforms triggered by laws, market dynamics and peasant militancy did not transform the agrarian scene in Bihar in a uniform manner. Changes were taking place in a localized, random, haphazard way: there was no one method working, no measurable pace or sense of direction. The changes seemed to be more like trade-offs, adjustments and compromises, rather than copybook land reforms. Old and new forms of land relations could be found coexisting in the same village.

Despite the complexities, and despite a tell-tale record of failures of past governments, Nitish wanted to go ahead with land reforms. He was confident he would be able to do it. But he wasn't sure how. The JD(U) manifesto, both in the February 2005 and the October–November 2005 Assembly elections, promised land reforms because, it said, 'to a large extent, land inequity is the cause of low agricultural growth'.

Land reform was also promised in the common manifesto of the NDA.

But Nitish did not want to tread the conventional path to enforce the reforms. The party manifesto had listed three priorities: distribution of ceiling-surplus land among the landless, preparation of up-to-date land records and issue of passbooks to title holders. Although the JD(U) February 2005 manifesto made no mention of this, the October–November 2005 one promised to establish a land reforms commission 'in consultation with representatives of political parties and social scientists'.

The question was: did Nitish have to set up a commission to start implementing land reforms? Weren't the concepts, laws, evaluations, loopholes and processes already known to the revenue and rural development departments? No survey and settlement of land records had been done in the state since 1959. Survey and settlement was a purely administrative process: why couldn't the state government do it right away?

Study after study had presented an identical diagnosis of the malady: political ambivalence. According to an official study, about eighty landlords in the state owned 500 acres and above, their total holding estimated at 54,000 acres, a major portion of which could be acquired under the ceiling law. In Purnea district alone redistribution of 86,000 acres of ceiling-surplus land held by just seven landlords had been pending since 1998. Another official report said more than 700 landlords held 200 acres and above, together more than 1 lakh acres in excess of ceiling. About 6 lakh acres of Bhoodan land was still undistributed. In addition, there was gair mazarua land in almost every village that was in illegal occupation of the bullies among landowners.

All these problems could be dealt with by making the administrative system pro-actively reformist, efficient and fast-paced. For instance, the revenue department had not yet identified the ceiling-surplus lands of all the eighty-odd landlords who held 500–1,000 acres. This only required galvanizing revenue officials into action. A task force could be devoted exclusively to identify all gair mazarua lands in the state, so the government could start the process of eviction of illegal occupants simultaneously with allotment of its plots to the landless.

There were about 4.5 lakh acres of ceiling-surplus land whose acquisition by the government was disputed by the landowners. Their cases were pending in various courts—circle officers, revenue courts, district magistrates, lower courts, high court and Supreme Court. Of the 4.5 lakh acres, litigation over 4 lakh acres was in the administrative courts from circle officers to district magistrates. All that Nitish needed to do was to follow the formula of speedy trial he had used in criminal cases to gain quick verdicts in the ceiling cases.

After all, independent of the Land Reforms Commission he had set up, which was headed by the retired IAS officer D. Bandyopadhyaya (a key architect of Operation Barga in West Bengal), Nitish had got a law passed, providing for establishment of a Land Tribunal to hear disputes relating to the implementation of land reform legislations.

Nine out of ten Dalit households had no land to cultivate. There were about 22.5 lakh landless families among Dalits in the state in 2001. The state government could have easily found one acre to distribute to each one of them from the ceiling-surplus acquisitions, gair mazarua evictions and Bhoodan donations. However, the Nitish regime could manage to distribute ceiling-surplus land only to about 1,200 landless persons in 2005–06, about 2,200 in 2006–07 and about 1,800 in 2007–08. Gair mazarua land too was allotted to only about 1,200 landless persons in 2005–06, about 2,700 in 2006–07 and about 1,400 in 2007–08. All the beneficiaries taken together came to 10,500, or 0.0046 per cent of the total landless Dalit families. If the landless of other communities are included, the redistribution would literally amount to a drop in the ocean.

Bandyopadhyaya was a liberal, professional bureaucrat endowed with the administrative skill, broad perspective and a flair for writing that some of the British officers became famous for in colonial India. Nitish had a preliminary meeting with him in May 2006 and decided to make him the chairman of a three-member Land Reforms Commission (the other two being member, Board of Revenue, and principal secretary, revenue, both of the state government) for two principal reasons. One, with the success of land reforms in the neighbouring state to his credit, Bandyopadhyaya was the best person to prescribe the right mantra for breaking the agrarian reform jinx in Bihar. Bihar had been under the same zamindari system as West Bengal. Besides, due to land reforms and incentives West Bengal had achieved the highest growth rate in agriculture and productivity among the states of eastern India. Secondly, Nitish hoped to consolidate his rule with land reforms. Jyoti Basu and the Left Front had enjoyed an unbroken reign for over twenty-five years owing to the popular support generated by land reforms.

The setting up of the Land Reforms Commission or the choice of Bandyopadhyaya as its chairman did not stir up immediate trouble, but as the commission travelled from district to district meeting officials and holding public hearings (*jan sunwai*), murmurings started in political parties, including the BJP and Nitish's own JD(U), reflecting the apprehensions of landlords about the Nitish government planning to bring about radical land reforms based on the West Bengal model.

About two years after it was set up, the commission submitted its report to the government. Bandyopadhyaya did not make any formal presentation of the report to the chief minister: he handed it to a deputy secretary in the CMO and left. Nitish had no clue about the commission's findings. The principal secretary, revenue, Ashok Vardhan, offered to explain the contents to Nitish. 'It won't take more than an hour,' he told him. The presentation that he made stretched to two days. The revenue and land reforms minister and several officials were also present. Nitish heard Vardhan's presentation patiently and asked him a number of questions.

In the coming days, while Nitish was still mulling over the commission's recommendations to decide what he could or could not do, rumours started floating that his government was going to pass a law to grant perpetual security of tenure to *bataidar*s, sharecroppers. Some of the officials who attended Vardhan's presentation had obviously leaked out the key recommendations of the commission.

The rumours meant great political trouble for Nitish. Security of tenure had been a highly explosive issue since even before Independence. In the following decades a great deal of bloodshed had taken place on the issue.

*Bataidari*, sharecropping, was a tenure based on spoken understanding, with the landowner enjoying half the share of the harvest without sharing the costs of production with the tenant. Whenever landowners got the slightest whiff of any government move to provide security of tenure to bataidars they evicted them to deny them any opportunity of proving their 'actual under-tenancy' on site to any official team. The bataidars who took the initiative to claim entitlement to permanent security of tenure—as they had tilled the plot for twelve years continuously as required by the law—could produce no proof of it in the revenue court and ended up losing the land in punitive ejection by the landlord. Government initiatives to provide protection to bataidars actually ended up increasing their insecurity.

For fear of eviction, the bataidars stopped bringing up claims. Owing to a conspiracy of silence between the landowner and the bataidar, under-tenancy covertly enjoyed a cosy existence. It did help the landowner and the tiller to get some produce out of the plots, but it did not help capitalist growth in agriculture. Official and unofficial estimates of land under bataidari in the state varied from 15 to 40 per cent of the total cultivated land. Even taking a mean of it would leave about one-fourth of the total cultivated land in the state in the hands of tillers who had no papers to show to a bank to get credit, or to the block and panchayat officials to get subsidy or any other government assistance.

One of the main inspirations Nitish had drawn from Operation Barga was grant of *parcha*, tenancy entitlement, to *bargadars*, sharecroppers, which made their tenure secure for life and also heritable. With this entitlement the bargadars became eligible for credit and subsidy. However, the entitlement alone would not induce the sharecropper to make investments to improve the quality and quantity of production, for while the landlord would take away half the produce without spending a single rupee, his share would come to far less after deducting the costs of production. In order to motivate the sharecroppers, the renting terms had to be in the sharecroppers' favour. In Operation Barga the landowner was allowed 50 per cent of the harvest if he provided the non-labour inputs and 25 per cent if he did not.

Bandyopadhyaya recommended a softer model for tenancy than Operation Barga for Bihar. He did not recommend permanent and heritable security of tenure to sharecroppers. He suggested a five-year written contract between the landowner and the sharecropper, which contract could be the proof of land possession for the tiller to qualify for credit, subsidy and incentives. But he made his recommendation on harvest-sharing more radical than Operation Barga. He suggested 40 per cent share to the landowner on the condition that he bore the costs of non-labour inputs and 25 per cent if he did not.

Even more radical was his recommendation to fix a ceiling of fifteen acres for all categories of landowners—individuals, religious trusts, sugar mills—which Nitish was not inclined to accept. But Nitish wanted to implement the recommendations about the bataidars—if politicians within his party and outside, who were dependent on upper-caste support in their constituencies, allowed him.

Their statements appeared in the media warning Nitish a new law to launch an Operation Batai on the model of Operation Barga would unleash a bloody conflict in the state. There were rumours of landowners evicting bataidars. The atmosphere was so charged Nitish decided to put the commission report on the back burner. On the insistence of the Opposition members in April 2009, the state government provided each MLA a compact disc of the commission report but refused to table it in the House, saying that it was not obliged by rules to do so. The truth was Nitish did not want the government to get into any discussion on the report. To calm things further he announced that a committee headed by Ashok Vardhan had been set up to study the commission report and send its suggestions to the government within three months.

Lalu and Paswan tried to make the most of Nitish's plight by declaring from every forum that he was bent upon bringing a bataidari law. Initially when the media confronted Nitish his response was evasive: 'A committee is studying the commission report,' 'Nothing has been decided yet.' But as the political aggression became more virulent his replies were conclusive: 'The state government has drawn no proposal for a bataidari law,' 'The Opposition is making an issue out of nothing.'

If his stance sounded unfavourable to bataidars, he could not help it, for he was in danger of losing upper-caste support owing to the Opposition's malevolent campaign. The backing of the upper castes alienated from Lalu had been extremely crucial to Nitish's political ascendance since he formed the Samata Party in 1994. Their continued support was essential not only for his sustenance in power but also for pursuing his agenda for all-round development of Bihar.

Something of a final warning came to him from the results of the by-elections to 18 Assembly seats in October 2009. The dissidents within his party—some peeved with him for rejecting dynastic nominations of their family members for the seats—in collusion with the Opposition were able to stir up wide-scale concern among the upper castes over the 'proposed' bataidari bill. Fighting as an alliance, Lalu's RJD and Paswan's LJP won 12 of the 18 seats, giving substance to their boast that this was the 'rehearsal' of the general Assembly elections expected a year thence. Nitish would not know exactly how much of the vote away from the NDA was attributable to the fear of a bataidari bill; but he was certain his political rivals and dissidents had used it to incite sections of the upper castes to 'teach Nitish a lesson for betraying our trust'. After the by-elections, therefore, Nitish gave the commission report a quiet burial.

Despite his denials, Lalu and Paswan continued to whip up the issue, only to be very actively helped by JD(U) dissidents who organized a huge kisan rally in Patna to voice protest on behalf of 'small and medium farmers' to the 'proposed' bataidari bill. Prominent among collaborators of Lalu and Paswan was Lallan Singh, Nitish's closest political comrade since Samata days. Faced with Nitish's strong disapproval of his influence peddling as 'de facto CM' with ministers and officers for undeserved favours to his clients, Lallan resigned as JD(U) state president. He blamed Nitish's 'dictatorial attitude' for the ills of the party whose 'senior leaders are never allowed any say or consulted by him in decision-making'.

Lallan, while continuing as an MP of the JD(U), shared the platform with Congress campaigners in the Assembly elections 2010 to stir up upper-caste animosity against Nitish. Lallan's hostile propaganda was expected to work most effectively among men of his Bhumihar caste. Lalu and Paswan were expecting to alienate the other major landed caste, the Rajputs, from Nitish. Before the elections it seemed quite likely that the ghost of the bataidari bill would frighten the upper castes away from Nitish. But that did not happen. The upper castes believed in Nitish's assurance that his government was not contemplating to introduce any such bill. That was not a good thing for an economic reformer, but Nitish knew he could push land reforms only at the peril of derailing his development train.

The Bandyopadhyaya commission report is gathering dust. But could Nitish have been able to replicate Operation Barga in Bihar as he wanted to? Were the instruments that contributed to the success of Operation Barga available to him?

Behind the success of Operation Barga the strongest force was the Left Front government which was driven by a commitment. Nitish's NDA government lacked such a consensus and passion. The second instrument was the bureaucracy. In West Bengal, a majority of civil servants had no landed interests, so they could act with a sense of neutrality and motivation in Operation Barga. In Bihar, top officers were largely from the upper castes, several from a feudal background. They would have conspired to sabotage Operation Batai had Nitish been able to launch it.

The third instrument was peasant organizations of the parties of the Left Front, predominantly of the CPI(M). They were the ones who mobilized the bargadars, worked with the government officials to hold awareness-raising programmes to motivate the bargadars to register their names in the land records. Here, Nitish had a party that revolved around him and hardly had any organization in the real sense. The party had offices and office bearers in most places in the state but they were mostly active during Nitish's public meetings or elections. The party even had a peasant front but that was only in name: to expect it to mobilize and motivate bataidars across the state was like dreaming of a hand fan causing a windstorm.

In all probability, Nitish would have had to depend on the administrative machinery to implement the land reform measures recommended by the Bandyopadhyaya commission. And that would have meant no more than a re-enactment of the farce that had been going on in the name of agrarian reforms in the state. With political ambivalence constraining Nitish, the farce continues. Land reforms in Bihar are destined to be largely driven by market forces and militant peasant movements.


How to accelerate agricultural development without accelerating land reforms? This was the challenge Nitish now faced. It was absurd to talk about development of Bihar without development of its agriculture. About 80 per cent of its working population was engaged in it as cultivators or labourers.

In its initial triumphant march the green revolution had virtually bypassed Bihar. Between 1962–65 and 1971–74 foodgrain production grew at 1.67 per cent annually in Bihar, compared to 8.35 per cent in Punjab, 6.66 per cent in Haryana and 3.14 per cent in West Bengal. Taken over a longer period, 1961–62 to 1978–79, Bihar's annual growth rate in foodgrains production was 1.8 per cent against 6.4 per cent of Punjab, 5.1 per cent of Haryana and 2.5 per cent of West Bengal.

The reason for the increasing disparity between Punjab and Haryana and Bihar was the non-availability of new technologies to the state's farmers. Even the neighbouring West Bengal, which had natural endowments, farming skills and agrarian constraints similar to Bihar, had moved faster in adopting the latest technologies.

Even in 1977–78, more than a decade after the coming of the green revolution, Bihar was using only 17.2 kg of fertilizers per hectare, compared to 94.6 kg in Punjab, 37.4 kg in Haryana and 30.6 kg in West Bengal. Among states in eastern India, West Bengal had already taken a big lead. In several respects, even Assam was making faster advances in agriculture than Bihar.

What to speak of producing a marketable surplus, Bihar was not able to produce enough food for its population till the early 1990s. In a normal year, it would need to import about two million tonnes of wheat, maize and other cereals to meet its requirements. In a year of natural calamity it would be on the nation's street with a begging bowl. The world pitied Bihar as the 'poor man of India' since a great famine hit it in 1966–67, quite paradoxically the nascent year of the green revolution.

With increased coverage under high-yielding varieties of seeds, fertilizers and irrigation, the growth rate in the state's foodgrains output caught up with the national growth rate in the second half of the 1980s. Because of the government-assured market for wheat and rice Bihar's agriculture started following the Punjab–Haryana way of shifting to a rice–wheat cropping system at the cost of pulses, oilseeds and coarse cereals.

Between 1960–61 and 1980–81 the area under pulses declined

from 23.22 lakh hectares to 13.68 lakh hectares. The decline has been unremitting since then, the acreage plunging to 5.64 lakh hectares in 2005–06. In other words, in the mid-2000s the state was sowing pulses in less than 25 per cent of the area it was using in 1960–61 and producing only 35 per cent of the yield it did in 1960–61.

It was one of the saddest footnotes to the history of the extension of the green revolution to Bihar. Dal, the collective term for pulses, is a very important component of Biharis' traditional diet, rich or poor, as it provides protein. Earlier, they could get it from the fields—all classes of farmers from their harvest and the labourers as wages in kind. Now they had to buy it at market price. As the average rural family spent the major part of its small income on food, dal got de-emphasized in preference to the main cereals like rice or wheat for quantitative reasons. The tendency grew to find protein from other foods such as milk, eggs and meat if one could afford it.

But did the Bihari farmers riding the horse of the green revolution get any closer to the farmers of the agriculturally developed states? The state's production of rice rose from 42.63 lakh tonnes in 1965–66 to 58.12 lakh tonnes in 1996–67 and that of wheat from 4.78 lakh tonnes to 44.70 lakh tonnes during the period. The green revolution was more dramatic for wheat in Bihar than for rice. The area under wheat increased from 6.75 lakh hectares in 1965–66 to 20.33 lakh hectares in 1996–97.

However, productivity in the state lagged behind the national average. Bihar produced 1,523 kg per hectare of rice against the national average of 2,051 kg/ha, and 1,761 kg/ha of wheat against the national average of 2,707 kg/ha in 2003–04. In 2000–01 Bihar's wheat yield was 2,173 kg/ha, compared to 4,531 kg/ha in Punjab, 4,066 in Haryana and 2,321 in West Bengal.

Seeing the consistent rise in the productivity of rice and wheat in the state since the new technologies were introduced, it would be wrong to describe Bihar's agriculture as stagnant. Even though there was inadequate state and market support, with their wisdom and skills the farmers in Bihar were able to maintain a much higher yield in pulses and maize than the national average. And in oilseeds they were very close to the national average.

It is not that Bihari farmers failed in maximizing farm returns. The productivity of the principal crops is higher than the national average in some districts of the state. In 2006–07 Rohtas produced 3,112 kg/ha, Bhojpur 2,633 kg/ha, Lakhisarai 2,641 kg/ha, Buxar 2,559 kg/ha, Aurangabad 2,511 kg/ha and Kaimur 2,149 kg/ha of rice against the national average of 2,127 kg/ha.

Wheat productivity in the same year was 2,789 kg/ha in Samastipur, more than the national average of 2,675 kg/ha; and Bhojpur with 2,527 kg/ha and Gopalganj with 2,502 kg/ha were quite close to the national average. At the same time, thirteen of the thirty-eight districts gave a yield of less than 1,000 kg of rice and eighteen districts produced less than 2,000 kg of wheat per hectare. The laggard districts pulled down the state average to below the national average.

Bihar had fertile soil, abundant water, sufficient rainfall, excellent climate and a rich peasant tradition. Why should the state be lagging behind others in agricultural production and productivity? The problem lay in the landownership pattern. There were a total of about 1.04 crore landholdings in the state, 83 per cent of which were below one hectare (marginal), 9.6 per cent between one and two hectares (small), 5.7 per cent between two and four hectares (semi-medium), 1.7 per cent between four and ten hectares (medium) and 0.1 per cent above ten hectares (large).

As the minimal size of landholding generally considered viable was two hectares, about 92.5 per cent of holdings lay beyond the outer margins of the green revolution. These holdings were worked largely for subsistence than for producing a marketable surplus. The beneficiaries of the distribution of ceiling-surplus, gair mazarua and Bhoodan lands by the government only added to the multitude of farmers producing food for family consumption alone. In essence, the small and marginal holdings (two hectares tapering down to less than one hectare), which together operated 60 per cent of the total agricultural land, were not active participants in the growth story.

Agricultural growth had to bet on the semi-medium, medium and large holdings, which together constituted 7.5 per cent of the total and operated 40 per cent of agricultural land. These holdings formed the core and the small and marginal ones the periphery of the circle of the green revolution.

However, the core faced two major impediments. One was fragmentation. Consolidation of holdings had been one of the principal contributory factors for the success of the green revolution in Punjab and Haryana. In Bihar, consolidation did not make much headway and has now been virtually abandoned. Consolidation presumed agreement between two or more landholders for mutual benefit, which was often made impossible by those more powerful and shrewd trying to cheat the small and weak landholders out of better lands in exchange for less fertile lands. Past governments could make little progress on motivating landholders on consolidation, leaving it to the farmers to reach an agreement where possible. Nitish followed the same laissez faire policy on consolidation.

The second constraint was concealed under-tenancy that left the tiller ineligible for institutional credit, subsidy and incentives. And Nitish had left the problem untouched.

Regardless of the impediments to growth inherent in the agrarian structure, Nitish had prepared a road map for agricultural growth that relied on infrastructure and incentives. In order to engage farmers, Nitish had the draft road map presented to more than 2,000 of them drawn from various districts to elicit their views on its goals on 17 February 2008 in Patna. The conference, called Kisan Panchayat, was attended by agricultural scientists and experts who also made their comments. The final road map incorporated the suggestions of the scientists, experts and farmers.

The core objective was to increase productivity by increasing quality seed coverage, irrigation, power supply, fertilizer use and credit. Cultivators in Bihar traditionally used farm-saved seeds which were genetically poor and gave diminishing yield if not replaced periodically. The seed replacement rate (SRR)—that is, the percentage of area sown with certified/quality seeds out of the total area under a crop in a season—was low during the Lalu–Rabri regime. In 2003–04 the seed replacement rate for paddy was 6.8 per cent, for wheat 8.1 per cent and for maize 30 per cent. The infrastructure for producing, certifying and distributing quality seeds was wretched. The state undertaking, Bihar

State Seed Corporation, was virtually dead; the state seed multiplication farms were poorly managed, and so was the state seed certification agency.

Nitish took initiatives to revive and strengthen them, adding some innovative programmes, including Mukhya Mantri Teevr Beej Yojana, Chief Minister's Crash Seed Programme, to increase the production and certification of quality seeds. The seed replacement rate under Nitish years was higher than that under the Lalu–Rabri years, but it fell short of the targets and was still way behind the rate in developed states. Also, although the SRR in rice increased from 11 per cent in 2005–06 to 26 per cent in 2009–10—a 150 per cent rise—rice yield reflected very little of it.

The HYV (high yielding variety) technology depended for its success on fertilizer use and water. In 1992–93 fertilizer consumption in the state was only 57.2 kg/ha against 162.2 kg/ha in Punjab, 107 kg/ha in Haryana and 86 kg/ha in UP. The consumption was not low throughout the state: in some districts such as Patna (133.86 kg/ha), Nalanda (116.74 kg/ha), Begusarai (103.62 kg/ha), Nawada (92.71 kg/ha) and Bhojpur (92.71 kg/ha) it was comparable to that in developed states and much higher than the national average of 67.1 kg/ha. Higher consumption of chemical nutrients was recorded in areas of assured irrigation.

Fertilizer use, which rose from 57.2 kg/ha in 1992–93 to 94 kg/ha in 2001–02, increased to 110 kg/ha in 2005–06 and 170 kg/ha in 2008–09. Thus the growth rate in fertilizer consumption rate improved from about 8 per cent per annum in the Lalu–Rabri years to 13 per cent in the Nitish years. However, as a whole, use of chemical nutrients still remained far below the national average.

Low fertilizer consumption in the state was due to a number of factors: uneven irrigation, lack of farmer access to credit, supply bottlenecks and poor extension services. Extension services continued to be the weakest link in the agricultural growth chain during Nitish's first term. Under the previous regime, the village-level extension services had collapsed, with employees designated for these services being deployed in rural construction works, panchayats and elsewhere.

Extension services are crucial not only for increasing fertilizer use but also for guiding farmers to use a balanced NPK (nitrogen, phosphorous and potassium) mix (4:2:1). With some effort, Nitish's agriculture officials managed to reduce the NPK ratio from 10.5:2.3:1 in 2006–07 to 8:2:1 in 2009–10, but it needs a far greater and more sincere effort to enhance use of fertilizers and ensure their optimal mix. Farmers are in need of information in every region, every season and at every stage. The institutional support for information, advice and SOS closer to their villages and fields is still very weak.

The Nitish government introduced a number of programmes such as Kisan Vikas Shivir (Farmers' Development Camp) for farmer–scientist interface and Kisan Pathshala (Farmers' Field School) for imparting knowledge to farmers about seed management, new varieties and crop diversification. The government decided to appoint a kisan salahkar (farmers' counsellor) in every panchayat and one subject matter specialist for every two panchayats to improve the extension services. However, these initiatives have failed to take shape and make any substantive impact on agricultural production and productivity so far.

Much like land reforms, irrigation in Bihar is driven more by the market and the people than by the state. Despite a luxuriant endowment of rivers, canal irrigation remains highly underdeveloped. Farmers in north Bihar plains, which are criss-crossed by a number of Himalayan rivers, had seen their dream of canal irrigation shattered long ago and come to depend increasingly on tube wells. In 2005–06 more than 80 per cent of the cultivated area in north Bihar plains was being irrigated by tube wells, river canals providing water only to 14 per cent of the land—just 4 per cent more than miscellaneous minor sources such as wells, tanks and barge lifts.

The state's failure to exploit the bounties of rivers is best symbolized by the collapse of the Gandak canal system. One of the first river irrigation projects of the state government, started in 1960, Gandak guzzled hundreds of crores without making the desired progress in plan after plan, driving the Planning Commission to shut it down in 1985. In 2003 the Planning Commission, on the recommendation of the Central Water Commission and the state government, agreed to make fund allocations for the revival of an irrigation capacity of 3.96 lakh hectares of the Gandak project, out of the capacity of 8.96 lakh hectares created when it was shut down. This revival would double the canal irrigation capacity in the north Bihar plains.

There are a number of river irrigation projects in various stages of planning or execution that are expected to add to canal-watered area in the north Bihar plains. But the signs are clear: farmers of this agro-climatic region have adopted tube wells in a big way and the trend is going to grow.

South Bihar, which has the oldest canal irrigation system in the state developed by the British on the river Sone, has maintained an even balance between canal irrigation (43 per cent) and tube wells (45 per cent). This agro-climatic region receives the least rainfall and when that is insufficient or delayed, the existing irrigation capacity, whether of canals or tube wells, drops to cause losses in agricultural production. This region had a very good traditional irrigation system managed by the community in every village called ahar–pyne in which water used to be collected in a reservoir (ahar) to be distributed to the fields through a grid of channels (pyne). People of all castes contributed labour to build and manage this system.

During the Congress regimes since Independence the ahars and pynes were allowed to fall into disrepair. During the Lalu–Rabri regime this system, like most others, collapsed.

Nitish's irrigation officials identified about 20,000 ahar–pynes in the south Bihar Gangetic plains that could contribute substantially to irrigation in the region if revived. The irrigation department drew up a plan for the revival and modernization of the ahar–pynes. By 2008–09, the year which was declared the Year of Agriculture by the Nitish government, financial provisions were also made in the state plan for the revival of about 300 ahar–pynes. However, the grass-roots problems the revival faces are far from resolved. The progress is very slow and unsatisfactory.

The process of revival could pick up only after understanding the reasons that had led to the system's collapse. It has to be determined whether a community still exists in every village willing to provide collective management to the system, or whether individual farmers are more interested in private irrigation with their own tube wells. The irrigation department cannot afford to add to its already high overheads to manage the systems on its own. An ideal solution could be that the irrigation department completes the revival and modernization of the ahar–pynes and then hands them over to users' cooperatives. These cooperatives would be responsible for collecting the irrigation tax and managing the maintenance of the system on payment of a share of the collections to the irrigation department. This type of arrangement is already being favoured in the canal system by the irrigation department.

Predominance of tube wells in irrigation has been both a boon and a bane for Bihar's agricultural growth. Tube wells are economically efficient when run on electricity. But the power situation in Bihar was bad during the Lalu–Rabri regime and has not much improved in the Nitish years. Although 70 per cent of the state's villages are electrified on paper, the quantum and quality of power available to them have both been deficient. Farmers are compelled to use diesel to operate their tube wells which proves costlier, adversely affecting their return from agriculture.

Electricity is not only crucial for irrigation to assure a consistently good harvest to the farmers, but also to provide them with the post-harvest technologies, the entire farm-to-market infrastructure. Operating a cold storage on diesel is very expensive. Use of biomass for power generation could be cheaper but is not universalized.

The Nitish government's Road Map for Agriculture and Allied Sectors 2008–13 provided for the setting up of 5,000 on-farm primary processing centres (OFPPCs) in the first year of its implementation in 2008–09. The OFPPCs were to be an important link in the farm-to-market chain. Processing of farm harvest includes facilities of handling, sorting, grading, washing and weighing of the produce. All these would be possible with equipment that could not run without electricity. Should there be the need to develop well-equipped packing houses in the villages, the power requirement would be much more than could be presently met. Without power, the state could not develop its post-harvest technologies and scientific warehousing.

Bihar has a huge untapped potential for horticulture, livestock and fisheries. Among states in the mid-2000s, when Nitish took over, the state was the largest producer of okra, guava, litchi and fox nuts; the third largest producer of potato, onion, brinjal, cauliflower and pineapple; the fourth largest producer of banana; and the seventh largest producer of milk. Somewhere in the middle of his first term, Nitish coined a unique 'mission statement' to boost horticultural development: 'At least one farm produce of Bihar on every Indian's platter'. One of the things that inspired him was the expanding domestic market for fox nuts (*makhana*), the spherical nut with a crunchy top and soft core ideal for a snack.

Grown earlier by farmers of north-eastern Bihar in small quantities, fox nuts not only lacked a market but also the support of a trade chain to reach the consumer. Even Biharis working in other parts of India could not get to eat fox nuts because the commercial network was not interested. With the opening up of the economy and improving incomes, the tendency to try food from different parts has grown in the middle classes across the country. This is fuelling the growth of the fox nut market, which in turn is spurring the growth of its cultivation in Bihar.

There has been a significant growth in the area and production of all fruits and vegetables in the state. This did not happen with Nitish's coming: following the policy directions of the Central government the state had encouraged farmers to diversify from cereals to high-value crops such as fruits and vegetables during the second half of the Lalu–Rabri regime. Farmers' private initiatives, triggered by the opening up of markets post-reforms in the 1990s, worked in favour of the state effort. As a result, the area under cereals dropped from 94.31 lakh hectares in 1990–91 to 58.38 lakh hectares in 2004–05. In 2009–10 about 15 per cent of the total cultivated area was under fruits and vegetables.

During the first four years of Nitish's rule, from 2005–06 to 2008–09, the area under vegetables increased by 66 per cent from 4.96 lakh hectares to 8.26 lakh hectares and total production by 84 per cent from 72.62 lakh tonnes to 133.85 lakh tonnes.

Vegetable cultivation is done throughout the state but a major part of its production is concentrated in a few districts—Patna, Nalanda and Gaya in the south Bihar plains and Saran, Gopalganj, Vaishali, Muzaffarpur, Samastipur, East Champaran and West Champaran in the north-west plains. In horticulture the north-west plains are destined to lead the state as this zone is also the largest producer of fruits.

Nitish's dream of seeing at least one produce of Bihar in every Indian's *thali* seems far from being realized because of the long list of farmers' issues yet to be tackled. Loss due to the lack of proper handling and storage facilities for onward transport continues to be a major problem. Lack of knowledge about the prevailing trends of prices in the domestic and international markets makes them easy victims to well-informed primary traders and wholesalers who maximize their margins.

Then there are a host of problems relating to inputs costs and credit that often act as disincentives to growth. Every few years, nature turns unkind to the state, unleashing floods in north Bihar or drought in south Bihar, damaging crops. The risk factors are still too many for farmers to turn to horticulture (and livestock) in a big way. The key to the prosperity of Biharis lies in the development of horticulture and animal husbandry. These two sectors can cause an explosion of employment and self-employment opportunities throughout the state. There are skills, there is interest and there are resources in every district to grow these sectors. Only the public and private infrastructures are missing.

Public warehousing is grossly inadequate; even the existing godowns are not properly maintained. A few primary agricultural cooperative societies (PACS) have raised credit and set up warehouses, but many more need to do that and make their operation efficient. Private investments in storage and processing did not flow owing to power shortage and the fear of Lalu returning to power in 2010. With Nitish getting a second mandate, investment proposals are beginning to flow. However, much would depend on the pace of development of the infrastructure. Power is an important issue of concern, of course, but then roads connecting villages do not exist in many parts of the state.

One of the showcase accomplishments of Nitish's first term was rehabilitation/construction of roads. This was a key factor that swung the election in 2010 in his favour. But the scale of achievements in rural roads was much lower than required.

Much like horticulture, livestock potential is waiting to be fully exploited in Bihar. The state's per capita per day milk consumption in 2009–10 was 154 grams against the national average of 241 grams. The average annual intake of meat was 2.58 kg against the national average of 4.74 kg and of eggs sixteen per year against the national average of forty-five.

Livestock development will not only mean development of the state's economy but also more income, food and nutrition to the rural poor. For agricultural labourers, who make 40 per cent of the state's rural population—15 per cent owning less than one hectare and 25 per cent landless—livestock is an important supplementary source of livelihood. Small farmers (owning one to two hectares) also rear different species of livestock. For reasons of fodder and other costs, the landless usually keep small ruminants like goat, poultry and sheep, while the small and marginal farmers keep cows and buffaloes.

The supplementary income from livestock products helps the poor rural families ward off extreme penury and starvation, which could be the reason why despite low wages, unstable harvest, high expenditure on social occasions such as weddings, indebtedness and frequent crises, farmers in Bihar do not commit suicide.

On the contrary, they have shown they can do more than survive—they can even develop with livestock. The greatest proof that the rural poor can break out of the subsistence fix and participate in growth is available in the incredible success of the Bihar Cooperative Milk Federation (COMFED). The COMFED with its brand Sudha is fast becoming the next great story in white revolution after the Gujarat Cooperative Milk Marketing Federation with its Amul brand. Sudha supplies milk and milk products to more than a hundred cities in Bihar, Jharkhand, UP, West Bengal, Orissa, Assam, Delhi and Nepal. In 2007 the COMFED collected milk from about 7,750 villages (about 20 per cent of inhabited villages in the state) distributing 65 per cent of its income to the members of the dairy cooperatives.

It is hard to believe that Sudha achieved exponential growth even during the Lalu–Rabri raj. Although ruling largely with the support of his pastoral caste, the Yadavs, Lalu did little to promote them in milk production, the area of their traditional excellence. Sudha grew in spite of the grossly adverse climate Lalu created for dairy development. Work in the animal husbandry department virtually came to a standstill after the exposé of the Fodder Scam. There was no expansion of the support services of the department and the extent and quality of the services declined. The COMFED developed its independent support system for artificial insemination, vaccination, knowledge dissemination, fodder and other services. In the Nitish years the animal husbandry department has resumed its services, but progress has been slow.

There is a long way to go. In 2009–10 the COMFED procured 12 lakh kg of milk per day, only about 8 per cent of the state's total milk production. The challenge is to bring a lot more of the unorganized milk production (92 per cent of total production) under COMFED coverage. Milk production needs to double to meet the state's demand. This cannot happen without an increase in productivity by replacing the indigenous milch animals with crossbred ones. The crossbreds today make about 10 per cent of the state's bovine population.

Nitish's Road Map for Agriculture and Allied Sectors envisages expanding the artificial insemination programme in a big way and taking it to the farmer's doorstep to genetically improve the breed of milch animals. The rate at which it will actually grow is bound to be low with the poor support system provided by the government.

# 12

## fast and slow lanes

Road connectivity was essential to transform the state's subsistence-oriented agriculture with faster access to inputs and market. Only 57 per cent of the villages in Bihar were connected through roads against the national average of 62 per cent. How much of the village road length was actually in service by the end of the Lalu–Rabri rule when national highways, state highways and major district roads lay in total disrepair is anybody's guess.

Poor village connectivity was hard to explain in a state whose rural population formed 90 per cent of the total population. In 2004–05 village roads made 77.5 per cent of the total road length of 81,655 km in Bihar, which showed how crucial they were to the economic growth of the state. But of the 63,262 km of village roads, 35,862 km, or 57 per cent, was unpaved. Not all the road length for village connectivity was good in all seasons. In north Bihar, stretches of village roads could be lost in floods or ruined by heavy rains. And some lengths proved useless in the absence of missing links, culverts and bridges to connect them to major roadways.

The scheme for rural connectivity, Pradhan Mantri Gram Sadak Yojana (PMGSY), or the Prime Minister's Rural Roads Programme, started by the Vajpayee government in 2000 envisaged connection of all unconnected habitations—inhabited parts of villages spaced from each other—by all-weather roads entirely with Central funding. It entrusted the planning and execution of the programme to state governments. All habitations with a population of 1,000 and more were to be connected by 2003 and those with a population of 500–999 by 2007.

Under the programme, Bihar was to be allocated Rs 150 crore per annum by the Centre. The Rabri government identified a total of 25,259 unconnected habitations in the state, 10,120 with a population of 1,000 and more, 6,144 of 500–999 and the rest of less than 500. But the execution of the programme by the state was extremely slow. In 2002–03 the Union rural development ministry, which looked after the programme, did not allot any fund for PMGSY to the state 'due to poor pace of expenditure by the state government'. By 2003, the state could provide connectivity only to 636 or just 6 per cent of all unconnected habitations with 1,000 and more population and to 2 per cent of those with 500–999 population.

The Centre expected states to make detailed project reports based on sound field studies and considered views of the panchayats and MLAs and MPs who represented the area. States were also expected to create an agency with high capacity for execution. Characterized by slow decision-making, the Rabri government failed to meet these expectations. If a proposal for a PMGSY project got stuck at any level, there was no system in place to find the reasons and get it moving again. If the Union rural development ministry asked the state for any missing details before project clearance or fund release, responses took months to come. The state's PMGSY performance touched rock bottom when it failed to provide connectivity to a single unconnected habitation in 2003–04.

After the Lok Sabha elections of 2004 the UPA replaced NDA at the Centre, with Lalu getting the railway ministry and his party colleague Raghuvansh Prasad Singh the rural development ministry. The NDA government had kept the Rabri government under pressure on implementation of PMGSY and missed no opportunity in censuring it for its poor performance. Soon after taking office, Lalu made a bailout plan for Rabri in concert with Raghuvansh: the Centre would take over the responsibility of implementing PMGSY projects from the government of Bihar. This was an exception to the rule, but Raghuvansh was only too willing to oblige his 'sahib'. And the Congress was too indulgent towards Lalu to stop Raghuvansh breaking the rule for Bihar.

Lalu and Raghuvansh used their influence to get five Central agencies—National Building Construction Corporation (NBCC),

National Hydel Power Corporation (NHPC), National Projects Construction Corporation (NPCC), Indian Railways Construction International (IRCON) and Central Public Works Department (CPWD)—to share the responsibility of constructing 18,900 km of the total proposed length under PMGSY in Bihar. After a series of meetings, each of the agencies signed tripartite agreements with the Union rural development ministry and Bihar's rural works department for the purpose.

It soon became clear that building rural roads in Bihar was not among the priorities of any of these agencies. In the four years since they took over the responsibility in August 2004, they completed only 27 per cent of the total road length of 18,900 km assigned to them.

Rather than taking the agencies to task, the UPA government blamed the Nitish government for the poor performance in PMGSY. Having no powers over the agencies, Nitish did not know how to drive them faster, until he decided to take back the projects. The state government had also to revise its schedule: connectivity to all habitations with 1,000 and more population would be provided by 2009 and those with 500–999 population by 2010.

One of the reasons for the poor performance of the Central agencies was also lower cost estimates of the projects. The guidelines framed for PMGSY provided for no revision in estimates and adjustment of rise in prices of inputs. This had adverse consequences on PMGSY in Bihar. As the projects were delayed and the input prices rose, contractors were not willing to bid for tenders floated by the Central agencies. The contractors who took up projects saved their profit margins by executing substandard work. Quality assurance by the Central agencies was unsatisfactory.

The guidelines clearly stipulated that should a PMGSY project be delayed beyond its time frame of fifteen months, any escalation in cost would have to be borne by the state government. While assigning the PMGSY projects to the Central agencies, Lalu and Raghuvansh made no provision for meeting cost escalation. Low execution by the Rabri government had already delayed most projects leading to escalation. In the tripartite agreements there should have been commitment from the state government to make special allocations to meet this additional expenditure. The financial management of the Rabri government was too poor to make budgetary provisions in such cases. In the absence of state support, the Central agencies offered old estimates to contractors, failing to interest them.

It was only after the Nitish government started taking back PMGSY projects from the Central agencies and made a special allocation of Rs 663 crore to meet the cost escalations in 2009–10 that contractors started bidding for the projects. Nitish also started the state's own scheme, Mukhya Mantri Gram Sadak Yojana (MMGSY), or the Chief Minister's Rural Roads Programme, to construct all-weather roads to link habitations with a population of 500–999 in the shortest possible time.

However, the performance in both PMGSY and MMGSY during Nitish's first tenure was poor and inconsistent. In 2006–07, against a target of 600 km in PMGSY only 131 km or 22 per cent was completed. The achievement in MMGSY in 2006–07, its first year, was virtually nil, with only 8 km constructed out of a target of 2,637 km. The next year MMGSY performance relatively improved but still remained unsatisfactory: 423 km constructed out of a target of 1,635 km. The following two years were virtually used to complete the backlog. The achievement in PMGSY in 2007–08, 2008–09 and 2009–10 (up to October) was 19 per cent, 5 per cent and 2 per cent, respectively.

Both the rural works department (RWD) and the Bihar Rural Roads Development Agency (BRRDA), the state-level implementing agency, which were supposed to be looking after all the schemes related to village roads, failed to deliver results. Nitish's fame for building roads during his first tenure—one of the key factors behind his second mandate—was largely about national and state highways and major district roads rather than rural roads.

What redeemed his RWD's performance was the much higher number of village roads it constructed than Rabri's RWD did. But that could barely hide the miserable performance of Nitish's RWD against the marvellous achievements of his RCD (road construction department). It proved that a chief minister, no matter how zealous and passionate about development, cannot do much in an area being looked after by officers who do not share his fervour. Managerial ability and integrity in key bureaucrats are the other two crucial factors that determine the pace of development.

Considering the importance of rural connectivity to the growth of agriculture and agro-based industry Nitish could have paid closer attention to the performance of the RWD. The chief task at hand here was capacity building to distinguish his regime from Rabri's, which had to hand over PMGSY projects to Central agencies owing to its low execution capacity. The RWD and BRRDA were expected to have the capability to handle village road projects from the proposal-making to construction to the quality-certification stages—both technical as well as administrative capability. Fluctuating year-to-year achievement rates in PMGSY and MMGSY showed the institutional structure was not yet strong enough to enable consistent performance.

When he began, Nitish seemed to have no immediate solution even for accelerating the growth of national and state highways and major and other district roads. 'I have a dream,' he said to his officials, 'to make sure that journey from any corner of the state to Patna does not take more than five hours.' Later, after a closer technical assessment, he raised the maximum time of the journey to six hours, but he would never miss out mentioning his dream in any of his public speeches.

This favourite chant was meant to convey to everybody—voters, administrators, engineers, investors, financial institutions and the Central government—that development of a good road infrastructure was his top priority. In order to reaffirm this, his government adopted a mission statement in respect of roads that promised 'provision of road infrastructure equal to the best in the country by 2015'.

One of the first realities that hit Nitish in the face was the pathetic condition of nearly the entire 3,600-odd km length of the twenty-seven national highways criss-crossing the state. The national highways had remained in disrepair for long even in the past but in short, scattered stretches. During the Rabri years their condition worsened throughout the state. A master of political histrionics that he was, Lalu would order signboards to be put up by the edge of the non-motorable national highway stretches, saying 'The repair of this road is the responsibility of the Government of India' just to make the NDA government the scapegoat.

'I wanted to improve road connectivity quickly,' Nitish told me in an interview. 'I did not have time to waste on political posturings on vital issues of economic development as Lalu did.' He asked the Centre to sanction funds for the repair and upgradation of the national highways. Of the 3,600-odd kilometres of national highways in the state, about 80 per cent were single- to double-lane which Nitish proposed to upgrade to four-lane. The Union ministries of surface transport and finance did not quickly respond to the state government's proposal despite several reminders. There seemed to be indefinite delay in the decision-making of the Central government on the issue. 'For Bihar, time was running out,' Nitish recalls.

Not just in repair of the existing national highways, the Nitish government also had problems with the Central government on new national highway constructions. As many as sixteen national highway projects in the state were delayed for years without any effective initiatives from the National Highway Authority of India (NHAI) and the state government. The work on the NH-31 stretch between Purnea and Gayakota started in 1999 and was scheduled for completion in 2002 but it remained incomplete till 2008. The nineteen-kilometre rail-cum-road bridge project over the Ganga in Patna, approved in 2001, remained incomplete because the NHAI, which was to construct fourteen kilometres of road approaches to the bridge, had failed to provide a cost estimate.

The upgradation of over 1,000 km of national highways, including the stretch connecting Patna to Muzaffarpur, was held up because the NHAI could not find any bidders for its tenders. Progress on the East–West Corridor to provide four-lane connectivity between Gopalganj on the UP border and Purnea near Nepal was also very slow. Pleading not guilty, the NHAI put the entire blame on the state—in effect, the Lalu–Rabri regime. The NHAI said it faced problems in acquiring land for the projects and removing houses, trees and electric poles that came in the way. The previous state government had provided it little assistance in overcoming these obstacles.

Then the prevalent culture of robbery and extortion posed its own problem in that contractors of national repute were not willing to put their men, equipment and investments at risk. Maoists in their areas of influence also demanded cuts from contractors. A few cases of murder of contractors' employees and arson at their worksites by criminal gangs and Maoists had also taken place when their demands for extortion were not met. Worse, crime and politics had inter-penetrated each other, creating a new breed of elected representatives from among criminals who continued to indulge in extortions. Apart from them, there were politicians of the old breed who provided patronage to criminals.

It was for the fear of this strong politician–criminal nexus in Bihar during the Lalu–Rabri raj that road construction companies refused to do NHAI projects on a toll-based contract. According to the Central government policy, all NH projects must be executed on the BOT (build-operate-transfer) toll model. The tenders issued by the NHAI would not attract bidders because they thought the loss owing to extortions was quite high in the toll model. They were willing to execute projects on a BOT annuity basis in which they would meet the costs of construction up front, to be paid in pre-decided annuities by the NHAI.

However, the long list of constraints cited by the NHAI could barely hide the inefficiency of the NHAI and the various Union ministries that was responsible for the lag in national highway development in the state. A proposal for the upgradation of 890 km of national highways to four-lane in the state in 2006 was not approved by the Union cabinet and sent back to the committee of secretaries (CoS) with several queries. The cabinet primarily wanted to know whether traffic density was enough to justify the four-laning of the 890-km length. It took months of arguing by the Nitish government before the cabinet cleared the proposal, after a year's delay, in May 2007. In the rail-cum-road bridge project over the Ganga in Patna, the years of delay and cost escalation had resulted from the NHAI's slothfulness in making a cost estimate and coordinating with the railways.

The NHAI and concerned Union ministries allowed the stalemate in national highway development in Bihar to continue for several years over the contractors' issue with the toll model. A decision could have been taken on a case-to-case basis to allow development under the annuity model. But it was only in 2008, the third year of Nitish's rule, that the Cabinet Committee on Economic Affairs granted approval to the NHAI proposal of award of two national highway projects for a 60-km stretch between Patna and Muzaffarpur under the annuity mode.

To inspire road construction companies the Nitish government did its bit by controlling crime. Extortion by politicians and criminals was no more a common feature of the businessman's life in the state. However, the same could not be said of the Maoists who were still able to attack worksites of contractors and set earth-moving and other equipment on fire if they did not pay up.

Many of the problems—such as land acquisition and removal of houses, trees and electric poles—could be resolved through good coordination with the state government, but they were left lingering in the past because the Lalu–Rabri regime was unable to resolve them. The Lalu–Rabri regime had incapacitated itself so much that resolution of even a minor problem looked impossible. For example, if the NHAI wanted electric poles to be removed the Lalu–Rabri government had no capacity to quickly make the Bihar State Electricity Board (BSEB) draw up a proposal for shifting them, to fund the shifting and to execute it.

Not that the NHAI–state coordination became excellent in the Nitish years. Decision-making was still slow in many areas. However, it was much faster than before. If trees needed to be cut, clearance from the forest department came quicker; if electric poles came in the way, the BSEB chairman activated his system; if houses needed to be demolished, the district magistrates and subdivisional officers extended help. The responses were of course not always prompt.

To resolve the biggest problem, land acquisition, the Nitish government formulated a land acquisition policy. Earlier the state government used to pay for land the rate at which it was registered, adding a 'solatium'—a term the Bihar government uses to imply monetary compensation given as solace for loss or injured feelings. Under the new policy the government still paid at the rate for which the land was registered but also added 50 per cent of the market rate to it. If the owner sold the land willingly he got a solatium of 60 per cent. If, for example, Rs 100 per unit was the registered price of the land he thus got Rs 240 per unit.

Government expenditure on road construction rose from Rs 133 crore in 2004–05 to Rs 2,489 crore in 2008–09, almost a twenty-times jump, the average annual growth working out to 465 per cent. In 2009–10 Bihar was among the top ten states spending more than the national average on maintenance of national highways. In terms of achievement, against 384 km constructed in 2004–05, about 3,474 km was built in 2009–10, a nine-fold increase in RCD road development capacity in five years.

Increased spending on roads resulted from three factors: one, the top priority for road development given by the Nitish government; the plan outlay on roads, which used to be about 5 per cent of the total state plan size, increased to 25–30 per cent during Nitish's first term; two, the support of the Rashtriya Sam Vikas Yojana (RSVY), the Backward Region Grant Fund, a Centrally sponsored programme[9] which provided for the development of roads, irrigation and horticulture; and three, availability of extra funds with the state government. The state government now had extra funds due to three reasons: first, carryover of funds unspent over financial years 2003–04 and 2004–05, both of which were election years; secondly, based on good expenditure performance in 2006–07 owing to accruals of unspent money of previous two years, the thirteenth Finance Commission allocated a much higher share from the divisible tax pool than the state expected; and thirdly, there was a remarkable growth in internal resource mobilization by the new government.

Beginning with an allocation of Rs 247 crore in 2006–07, the state decided to spend about Rs 1,100 crore on the rehabilitation and upgradation of over 2,400 km of national highways from its own funds pending Central government sanction. The state wanted the Centre to reimburse the expenditure. Several letters were sent by the state road construction department to the Centre, pleading for reimbursement. However, the Central government refused it on the grounds that the state had not obtained their sanction before spending the money—whereas the truth was that the Central government had not responded to the state government's repeated requests for grant of funds. The state was being punished for its initiative. Even Nitish's letters to Prime Minister Manmohan Singh urging him for reimbursement elicited no response.

However, this did not stop Nitish from enhancing the state's own spending on roads. The state highways, next in importance to national highways, were in bad shape for lack of maintenance. Over 70 per cent of the total 3,128 km of state highways was single lane, only 2 per cent two or more lanes, the rest of intermediate width between single- and double-lane. The state government decided to rehabilitate and upgrade the entire length of state highways to two-lane. The RCD outsourced the works for development of the existing state highways to Central agencies such as IRCON and CPWD using RSVY funds.

In addition the state declared 4,880 km of major district roads as new state highways. For converting 820 km of the new state highways into two-lane roads, the state secured a Rs 1,825-crore credit from the Asian Development Bank (ADB): the ADB was already engaged in the state's road construction as a lender for national highways and PMGSY.

For the ADB loan project the executing agencies were to be the state road construction department and its newly formed PSU, Bihar State Road Development Corporation (BSRDC). Nitish placed one of the whiz kids of civil service, Pratyaya Amrit—who had pulled the Bihar Rajya Pul Nirman Nigam (BRPNN), or the Bihar State Bridge Construction Corporation, out of its coffin and turned it into a miracle worker—as both the secretary of the RCD and managing director of BSRDC.

Amrit shared Nitish's dream of developing the capacity of state agencies to national and international standards. When Nitish gave him the charge of BRPNN, he told Amrit: 'The UP Bridge Construction Corporation is so well developed, it bids for and gets major bridge contracts across the country. Why can't we make our corporation capable of doing the same?' The turnaround of BRPNN had won national and international recognition and put it in line with the competition for bidding for projects outside the state.

So when the ADB offered, along with the loan, technical assistance for capacity development of the RCD and BSRDC Nitish wholeheartedly welcomed it. The ADB would provide training for the restructuring and modernization of the RCD and BSRDC to transform them into state-of-the-art agencies capable of implementing new business procedures in planning, contracting, engineering, human resource management and quality assurance. That alone could help Nitish realize his mission of providing 'road infrastructure equal to the best in the country by 2015'.

Soon after he took over, Nitish initiated reforms in the RCD. He was enthusiastically assisted in implementing them by the RCD principal secretary R.K. Singh. One of the primary reforms related to capacity building. Usually, the RCD would take several months to make estimates of a road proposal. There was no timeline and no accountability for delay. The new government set up mechanisms to make speedy estimates. The decision-making for project clearance and beginning of execution were also made quicker.

During the Lalu–Rabri regime, quality private investments in road development were absent. To some extent it was due to the open favouritism towards Yadav contractors. But it was also due to very low cost estimates the state offered them. The RCD's estimates were much lower than those offered by Central agencies such as NHAI. The Nitish government brought about a substantial increase in project estimates by calculating the costs of inputs according to prevalent market rates. As a result of this rationalization, RCD projects started attracting financially sound and fully equipped contractors from outside the state.

By 2009 there was hardly any reputed national construction company that was not doing civil works in the state. Civil works, which included construction of roads, bridges and culverts, suddenly turned from a market of a few hundred crore to several thousand crore. Every part of the state was abuzz with activities of earth movers, cranes, hot mixers and trucks. The preponderance of the big players, however, carried the risk of suppression of local enterprise in road development. Nitish got the RCD to follow a policy of building and strengthening the capacity of local contractors by enabling them to acquire experience through execution of works of assured quality.

In the Lalu–Rabri raj the tendering process had lost its credibility due to the lack of adherence to rules and norms. Documents from papers submitted by bidders could go missing so the decision-makers could exclude the deserving ones and favour the undeserving. Midway, technical specifications of requirements could be changed with the intention of favouring a bidder. The Nitish government made the tendering process transparent and allowed no changes in bidding terms once they were publicized in tender notices.

In the past, road contractors would cheat on quality of construction. There were three reasons. One, there was corruption in the RCD; the contractor bribed engineers and got away with shoddy work. Two, the RCD's quality control was poor. Three, the contractor was engaged only for construction of a road, not for its maintenance.

Nitish or his RCD principal secretary R.K. Singh could not turn RCD engineers into saints by any order or instruction or anti-graft vigilance. Corruption, in as much as it meant passing of money from one hand to another, was hard to stop. Where checks could be placed was quality assurance. The RCD, in addition to improving its own quality control instrument, introduced third-party quality assurance. National and international firms were hired for the purpose. The government hoped that with strict adherence to quality, the scope of corruption would reduce.

For further assurance of quality the new government introduced three-year, performance-based maintenance contracts post-construction. The RCD held back 10 per cent of the contractor's security deposit until he had carried out satisfactory maintenance for the third year of the road he had constructed. Despite the contract, the RCD experience was not good with all contractors. Several of them did not spend any money on maintenance in the third year, deciding it was cheaper to lose 10 per cent of the security money; this caused deterioration in roads. That made the Nitish government work further on a road-maintenance policy and introduce a five-year maintenance contract.

Quality assurance continues to be very inadequate despite government quality control, mobile quality assurance labs, third-party checks and performance-based maintenance contracts. The scale of civil works is too gigantic and the reach of the quality assurance instruments too small. The government quality control unit is based in Patna, and not under the charge of the RCD. It was only at the beginning of his second term that Nitish could have a proposal moved for transfer of the state quality control unit to the RCD. After that happens, the RCD will have to open quality control units in the field—in the divisional headquarters, to begin with—in order to expand coverage.

Bihar is drained by several small and large rivers, which have been traditionally negotiated by steamers or boats. The British built a bridge over a river largely where the railways needed one. After Independence, bridges were built as a part of roadways, but the focus, owing to budget constraints, was on linking one or two key points of the large rivers.

Twenty-eight of the thirty-eight districts of the state were flood prone. The rainy season meant hell as un-bridged rivers in spate made navigation difficult, risky or impossible. People, if left with no option but to travel, had to take long, tiring and expensive detours to reach destinations they could have managed in a few hours. Agriculture, trade and industry suffered. Dispatch of relief to affected areas was hampered.

The BRPNN was established as a state government corporation in 1975 to be its implementing agency to build bridges in flood-prone areas. Like most other state government undertakings, the BRPNN ended up being a liability. The size of the workforce increased, while the number of projects it handled decreased owing to smaller allocations for bridges in the state plan and low Central and institutional (such as NABARD) allocations under the head in the pre-reform years. Absence of professional management of human resources and projects by the top ranks of technical and administrative executives in the BRPNN and its parent department RCD resulted in tardy and shoddy execution, leaving the entity very little self-pride to be able to demand works from the government. No one applied his mind to find ways of making the corporation earn profits on its own through projects.

Politicians (the chairman of BRPNN was always a politician) and senior officers recruited less-deserving candidates, so the quality of the human resource was poor. A stage came when the corporation would not have enough money to pay salaries to the staff. Already spending 90 per cent of its earnings on staff salaries and pensions annually, the state government could not always find resources to pay the staff of its loss-making PSUs, BRPNN included. BRPNN employees were not paid salaries for months. In the absence of any salary or work, they began to look like pariahs, and their collective pride was very low.

Pratyaya Amrit's initial impression of the state of BRPNN when he took over as its first officer chairman in April 2006 was so awful he never forgets to mention it to anyone who asks how he turned the bankrupt public company around. His office and the passage to it were nauseating with the stench of urine, broken chairs, cracked floor, shabby curtains and heaps of files in disorder all around the room.

Amrit recalls: 'One part of my heart said, "run away!" The other part said, "You get but one opportunity in life. It has come to you. It's here. Grab it and show the world what you can do."'

When Nitish was advised to get Amrit from his job as a secretary in the ministry of civil aviation to Bihar he was only told the officer was young, intelligent, honest and hard-working. Nitish did not know his real capability, and he could not be sure how well he would perform in the BRPNN. But Nitish decided to give him independence and test his mettle. Instead of making him managing director of BRPNN, as IAS officers were in the past, he made him its chairman.

In a corporation the real powers lie with the managing director, but Nitish made him chairman so he could give the entity a perspective and direction without interference by a politician-chairman. Enjoying full backing of the chief minister, Amrit actually ended up usurping all the powers and taking over the responsibilities of the managing director too.

The challenges were unnerving: no funds, low employee morale, stalled projects, no system in place for tendering, monitoring, quality assurance and accountability. As far as funds were concerned, Nitish assured him a huge allocation under a new scheme started with the state's own resources called Mukhya Mantri Setu Nirman Yojana (MMSNY), the Chief Minister's Bridge Construction Programme. But how would Amrit deal with the general despondency? How would he fight the lack of self-belief among employees? How could he make them start believing that even the dodo could be brought back to life?

Amrit is one of those civil servants of the new breed who believe the basic principles of management in a government agency are the same as in the private business organization. He loves to read management books, to learn about and be inspired by turnaround stories, particularly the one about IBM, *Who Says Elephants Can't Dance* by Louis V. Gerstner Jr. Yet, one man doesn't make an organization. The 500 employees of BRPNN had known only one management system: a file moves for

everything from desk to desk and often gets stuck at some desks for
indefinite periods. Questions that are asked in private organizations
were never asked in BRPNN. The boss was not eager to show results,
to prove his worth to his employer. The employer himself, in this case
the government represented by the minister or chief minister, never
asked any questions.

But in the current case, the employer was keenly engaged. Bridges
were complementary to the road infrastructure which was Nitish's
top priority. He was ready to give Amrit all support and would keep a
vigilant eye on the results. When Amrit told his boss R.K. Singh about
the nauseating scene at the BRPNN office, Singh told him the chief
minister had chosen him for the assignment and he must execute it
following the best practices and not come back complaining to him.

'I decided to take up the challenge,' Amrit said in an interview to
me. 'I thought CM has given me a free hand. He wants results and I
must give him results. In later months I had direct experience of CM's
zeal. He was always willing to give time for any presentations I wanted
to make to him.'

Prem Kumar, RCD minister from the BJP quota, and R.K. Singh
also extended Amrit full support. 'Prem Kumar is an unsung hero in the
BRPNN turnaround story,' says Amrit. 'He is a rare politician who never
interfered in my work and always supported me at critical junctures.
Without his and R.K. Singh's backing I would not have been able to
transform the corporation despite CM's best intentions.'

Nitish infused new life into the corporation by allocating Rs 1,132
crore to it under MMSNY to build 520 bridges. In addition, he decided
to award all road and bridge works of cost estimates up to Rs 50 crore to
the BRPNN. The corporation was also made the implementing agency
for more than a hundred bridges under various funds—the state plan
and non-plan, Additional Central Assistance (ACA), Central Road Fund
(CRF) and Rural Infrastructure Development Fund (RIDF).

Amrit recalls how the corporation employees were stupefied and
confounded by the sudden avalanche of projects:

I recall a meeting with the BRPNN engineers in my office in May
2006, a few months after I had taken over. When I told them that we

would build 500 bridges in two years under the recently introduced MMSNY, they were flabbergasted. They thought I was crazy (of course, they did not say so). 'Sir, this is impossible; we would have worked wonders if we are able to build 15 bridges,' they said almost in unison. Their disbelief was symptomatic of the diffidence that had set in over the years of neglect, sloth and lack of direction in the corporation. The meeting had begun early in the morning and ended late at night. I took on all their doubts and misgivings one by one and tried to reassure them that the target was very much achievable.

This meeting, along with the feedback that I received during my field trips, made me realize that the corporation's staff had to be yanked out of their collective slumber and hopelessness. I am an eternal optimist and I strongly believe that any target is achievable if the human resource is managed well. Therefore, the first step was to instil a sense of faith in [one's own ability] in the workforce.[10]

Amrit had the money. He now had to try and prove that the corporation could work like a professionally managed organization and deliver results. He decided to start by example. He selected the Kataunjha high-level bridge project for that. This project over the river Bagmati on NH-77 between Muzaffarpur and Sitamarhi was assigned to BRPNN eighteen years ago. It had started work but then stopped. A high-level bridge had been approved for Kataunjha because in the past a bridge had been made but declared unfit for public use. After a few years, another bridge was built parallel to the old one which got inundated almost every year during the rains. People living in the small towns and villages on either side of the river had to undergo a lot of suffering during those months.

Owing to damages by floods the bridge was declared unsafe by the government for plying of heavy vehicles towards the end of the 1990s. The government, however, did not do anything to stop heavy vehicles passing through the bridge other than putting up a signboard, and trucks and buses passed unrestricted. In order to keep the bridge from giving way, the government spent money on 'repairs' which did not much help.

In 2002 the local people set up an agitation that culminated in a five-day fast and threat of self-immolation by a group of youths to demand beginning of the construction of the proposed bridge by the government (BRPNN). The public agitation was quite justified because the new bridge project had been approved by the Union ministry of road transport and highways, which had also sanctioned Rs 11 crore for it under the Central Road Fund. The cause of the agitation was so legitimate that local leaders of all parties including the ruling RJD supported it. The agitation, however, failed to compel the Rabri government to take steps to make the BRPNN resume construction. On the contrary, the government decided to liquidate the BRPNN.

There were ten major bridge projects assigned to the BRPNN that had been under construction for the past fifteen to eighteen years. A decision was taken in June 2006 to complete all of them by May 2008. In consultation with his engineers, Amrit chose Kataunjha from among them as his first project, not only because of its importance to the connectivity between Muzaffarpur—the business hub of north Bihar—and Sitamarhi on the Nepal border, but also because of the history of public agitation around it. The deadline set for Kataunjha was April 2007.

One of the first things Amrit did was to replace the non-performing executive engineer of BRPNN in charge of the Kataunjha bridge with a younger engineer, Sunil Kumar. He had identified Kumar in consultation with senior engineers in the corporation who thought he was systematic, hard-working and a good team leader. The second step: he created a new division closer to the worksite for tighter supervision, where in the past the omnibus Muzaffarpur division had looked after it without being able to give it particular attention.

Third, Sunil Kumar and other BRPNN staff engaged in the project were told that they would be punished if they failed to construct the bridge by the deadline and rewarded if they did. Fourth, contractors for the project were selected strictly on professional criteria: experience, track record, capability and financial viability. Fifth, third-party quality check was introduced. Sixth, Sunil Kumar and his team as well as the contractors were kept on their toes with constant inspections by flying squads, the chairman and senior engineers of the BRPNN.

Sunil Kumar and his team sensed early on that this government and the new corporation leadership were unlike the previous ones: they were full of determination and zeal to build bridges to develop infrastructure. They saw Kataunjha as an opportunity to demonstrate to the leadership that the corporation was in a bad state not because of any lack of capability but because of the indifference to infrastructure development of past governments. Sunil Kumar turned out to be a good leader. The project was completed by April 2007. Amrit rewarded him with a cash incentive and a trip to Singapore and Nitish came to the function held to appreciate Kumar's work and honour him. In later years, six other engineers were rewarded with foreign holidays and cash incentives.

Kataunjha was the turning point for the BRPNN. The completion on schedule with full quality assurance filled the staff with self-belief. The cash rewards and foreign holidays sent out a message that the organization valued professional efficiency.

In the months to come, the organization took a number of other measures to increase employee satisfaction and self-worth. Amrit moved a proposal for allowing the BRPNN to charge a 9 per cent centage (commission) on each project. This was based on the model of the UP State Bridge Corporation. Nitish promptly endorsed the proposal, which then received cabinet approval. The earnings from the centage filled the once-bankrupt corporation's coffers, making it possible for it to disburse salaries to the staff regularly, and also meet additional staff and administrative costs. The BRPNN office was redesigned to look like a corporate office, with air-conditioned rooms, Wi-Fi connectivity and a gymnasium.

Amrit had inherited a corporation which had a surplus of desk assistants and peons (thanks to illegitimate recruitments by politicians and officers) and a shortage of engineers. In a typical corporate-style overhaul, a good number of lower-rank staff would have been laid off and more engineers recruited. It made good economic sense, but Nitish would never have approved of retrenchment for political reasons.

It was impossible in any case for the staff to handle the deluge of projects under MMSNY. With their newfound zeal and motivation they could complete all the pending projects by May 2008, but managing all the processes and executing 520 MMSNY projects on their own was beyond their capacity. Amrit had no option but to outsource all works of these projects as Nitish insisted on the fastest execution possible. 'You can't be not keen on schedule when you have a CM who can call you on a Sunday afternoon to ask about the progress of a bridge project,' says Amrit.

A number of consultants and contractors were hired by the BRPNN for preparation of detailed project reports (DPRs) and supply of building materials, equipment, engineers and manpower. They were selected through a reformed tendering process that was electronic, transparent and free from manipulation. Even quality assurance was outsourced.

Monitoring of so many projects during execution was a gigantic task. An online monitoring system was set up at the corporation head office. The corporation introduced a software called 'mobile inspector' developed by two young engineers from Bihar. All executive engineers were given mobile phones with a GPRS-enabled SIM card, using which they could send a photograph of a bridge under construction with their comment on its progress after site visits to the head office. The software did three things at a time: it forced the executive engineers to make site visits; the organization centre had an update on the status of projects under way; and Amrit always went to the review meetings Nitish periodically called with an updated study on every ongoing project.

So far, the BRPNN has not started bidding for bridge projects outside Bihar. But it has developed its capacity and proven its competence to be among the bidders. In a way, the turnaround of the BRPNN is iconic for the turnaround of Bihar.

Could roads and bridges alone lead to development? The story of economic growth in Nitish's first term was a mixed bag. The average annual growth of Bihar's GDP between 2005 and 2009 was 10.74 per cent, more than three times that between 2001 and 2005 (3.53 per cent). Although the state's GDP grew by 11.82 per cent and 12.17 per cent in 2002–03 and 2004–05, respectively, more than the 2005–2009 average of 10.74 per cent, the 2001–2005 average was very low owing to negative growth in 2001–02 (–4.73 per cent) and 2003–04 (–5.14 per cent).

Nitish's first four years witnessed GDP growth by 1.49 per cent in 2005–06, 22 per cent in 2006–07, 8.04 per cent in 2007–08 and

11.44 per cent in 2008–09. Except for one year, 2006–07, GDP growth rate in Nitish years was less than the highs of 2002–03 and 2004–05 of the Rabri years.

Yet, the change that was apparent in the Nitish years was absence of negative growth. Year-on-year fluctuations in the growth rate were still quite wide, but a new high had been achieved (22 per cent in 2006–07) and it appeared to be somewhat steadying. Bihar had broken out of the old growth pattern as a result of better management of the economy. The highs in the post-Jharkhand Rabri years had been mostly accidental—achieved despite the lack of government initiatives and efforts and attributable largely to market dynamics. With government adopting proactive approach in the Nitish years, the market and bureaucracy worked with greater freedom and speed. And the result was lower volatility in growth.

Even so, growth in Nitish's Bihar was very skewed and uneven. Higher growth rate was powered largely by three sectors: trade, hotels and restaurants; construction; and communication. These sectors had achieved a high growth rate in certain Rabri years, but then there would be dips. Trade, hotels and restaurants had grown by 19.18 per cent in 2002–03 and 21.51 per cent in 2004–05, but the 2001–2005 average was 12.69 per cent. During 2005–2009 the average annual growth rose to 17.41 per cent.

In construction the average annual growth was 37.10 per cent during 2005–09, against 17.45 per cent during 2001–05. Communication, largely owing to the spread of mobile connectivity, grew from the 2001–05 annual average of 12.59 per cent to 18.41 per cent during 2005–09. Between 2005–06 and 2008–09, the number of mobile connections in the state increased from 23.55 lakh to 151.78 lakh. Tele density—the number of phones per 100 individuals—rose from 5.34 in 2006 to 22.18 in 2009. Tele density in rural Bihar grew faster than that in urban Bihar, registering a jump from 0.66 to 9.17 (1,300 times) during the period, largely owing to migrant labour remittances.

Exponential growth in trade, hotels and restaurants and construction was the consequence of two major Nitish initiatives: high public expenditure and improvement in law and order. High public expenditure resulted from good resource mobilization, fund utilization and deficit and debt management. The own tax revenue of the state government rose annually by 29 per cent from Rs 3,342 crore to Rs 8,139 crore between 2004–05 and 2009–10. The total revenue of the state government—the sum of its own tax revenue, tax share from the Central government and Central grants—increased from Rs 15,174 crore to Rs 37,870 crore during the period. Plan expenditure rose from Rs 3,476 crore to Rs 14,184 crore during the period. The state government introduced and was implementing about forty schemes entirely with its own funds.

Higher growth of the state's economy increased collection of taxes on commodities and services such as sales tax and taxes on vehicles and goods for entry into local areas for consumption in the normal course. Where the Nitish government had to be innovative was in raising the revenue from excise duty, particularly in liquor where there was wide-scale evasion. The liquor business was in the control of a few hands. The state government had no idea how many bottles were imported into the state by wholesalers and how many were sold by retailers. As many of the wholesalers also had retail outlets of their own, it was easy for them to fudge the books.

In order to prevent evasion, the Nitish government followed the Tamil Nadu model to set up a company of its own, called Bihar State Beverages Corporation, in 2006 that would be the sole wholesaler for all kinds of liquor—Indian Made Foreign Liquor (IMFL), Foreign Made Foreign Liquor (FMFL), beer, wine, country-made liquor and spicy liquor. All liquor manufacturers desirous of selling their brands in the state had to send their consignments to the corporation at its designated warehouses before these could be distributed through retail outlets to the buyers. The corporation charged the manufacturers a margin of 5 per cent of the minimum retail price of the brand, which was later raised to 10 per cent. By becoming the sole gateway to the Bihar market for liquor, the corporation was able to account for all the legal sales of liquor. This led to a dramatic increase in excise revenue from Rs 272 crore in 2004–05 to Rs 679 crore in 2008–09.

Taxes on goods and passengers increased from Rs 473 crore in 2004–05 to Rs 1,279 crore in 2008–09. Taxes on sales, trade, etc., increased from Rs 1,819 crore to Rs 3,016 crore during the period. While the rise in excise revenue was substantially a result of government intervention in enforcing tax compliance, and not because of any remarkable increase in the size of the market, the rise in these taxes was directly related to the jump in the volume of business owing to improved road connectivity and law and order.

Two grass-roots reports suggest how the change in social climate was pushing trade.

Those dark days [of Lalu–Rabri years] have made way for some sense of optimism and the first thing that people mention while listing the changes that have taken place [under Nitish raj] in the state is their ability to stay out with their families till late evening. Earlier, 7 pm was a deadline of sorts. 'That clearly is the biggest change impacting ordinary life and businesses; people are not scared to roam in big cars or to invest,' says Gaurav Singh, a young management professional who left his job at a multinational firm in Mumbai to return to Patna a few years ago. With the bustle in the market, a return to the cinemas and restaurants, girls driving back from coaching classes in the night, even lovers chatting on parked motorbikes on the road to the Gandhi Setu—law and order has improved in the capital [Patna] and also in other parts of the state. 'Fear has receded,' says the owner of a cloth shop in Chhapra's Hathua Market, which has been a prominent bazaar in the area since the late 18th century . . .

'There was a time when Dabang-neta [bully] types would enter the shop and you would feel nervous. Now it is not so. A few years ago wholesalers from other states would hardly send their agents with samples of saris; [nor] would they give us goods on credit,' adds a businessman whose family has been in the cloth trade over two generations. 'Now not less than 15, 20 agents come in a month and getting credit is no longer a problem.'[11]

After the bridge at Kataunjha over the Bagmati was opened to the public, a journalist met a couple of local businessmen:

Mohammad Murtaza who owns a sweet shop at Sairpur chowk on the Sitamarhi side, recalling those flood-hit days, said he along with other shop-owners had a tough time earning their daily bread. 'Our shops were inundated and we went out of business the entire monsoon season,' he said.

Babban Kumar, who lives in Muzaffarpur and has a clothes shop in Sitamarhi across the river agreed. 'Since it was a must for me to cross the river to reach my shop, I risked my life every day crossing the flooded bridge delicately balancing my feet on it,' he said.

Like Babban and Murtaza, there were a thousand others who were stranded on both ends of the bridge during the monsoon. Following the construction of the bridge, Babban's and Murtaza's customers have increased in number. 'While earlier people came to us only from one end of the bridge, today they come from both the districts,' Babban said.

Rajendra Prasad, who owns a saree shop at Janak Chowk, some 500 metres from the bridge on Muzaffarpur side, said the livelihood of 20 villages today hinges on the Kataunjha bridge. 'You would not be able to appreciate the importance unless you belong here,' he said.[12]

Evenings are peak business time for stores, restaurants, cinemas, theatres and events. In the Lalu–Rabri years, evenings were very dull for these businesses as people wanted to return home as soon as they could after work. Women and children, who motivate spending by men, stayed at home in the evenings. With the convictions of criminals in speedy trial in Nitish years, the major crimes, particularly kidnapping for ransom, murders and robberies, were reduced, generating a feeling of security.

Consumption was muted in the state earlier. People avoided buying and flaunting things, fearing that it could attract the attention of extortionists. An extortionist was lurking in every street corner. The Nitish years saw a burst of expenditure by people for the fulfilment of their suppressed desires.

Consumption also increased because of regular payment of salaries to government staff, including college and school teachers as also because of a cut-down in delay in payment by government to contractors and suppliers.

Trade, hotels and restaurants witnessed a boost as a result of the increase in the number of visitors to Bihar for business and tourism. The number of domestic passengers at the Patna airport increased from

1.67 lakh to 1.76 lakh between 2001–02 and 2004–05, or by 5 per cent. Between 2004–05 and 2008–09 it rose by 110 per cent to 3.69 lakh. The number of domestic tourists to Bihar increased from 68.80 lakh in 2005 to 1.55 crore in 2009, and of foreign tourists from 63,000 to 4.23 lakh during the period.

A major concern was that the state of high growth in the Nitish years was a consequence of a quantum jump in growth only in trade, hotels and restaurants, and construction and communication. This cast a shadow of doubt on the sustainability of the growth and made the state GDP vault look like a bubble. Helping the scepticism was the sluggish growth of industry and the volatility of agriculture owing to natural calamities.

Most of the major private and public industries—coal, mica, basic metals, steel, heavy engineering and their ancillaries—went to Jharkhand, leaving Bihar predominantly with small, tiny and artisan-based units after bifurcation. Of the 1,528 registered industrial units in divided Bihar, nearly 85 per cent were small and micro. The 236 medium and large units were largely agro-based, turning out food, tobacco and leather products.

Nitish made his first serious attempt to industrialize the state by doing the groundwork for making Bihar an ethanol hub. It was an overambitious idea considering that other states had already taken a huge lead in establishing ethanol plants: Maharashtra (seventy-one units), UP (fourteen) and Gujarat (twelve). But the market for ethanol was huge and fully assured with the Central government. To fulfil its international commitment to reduce environmental pollution, it had made 5 per cent blending of petrol with ethanol mandatory for oil companies. It could not have used MTBE for the same purpose as it was banned globally due to the carcinogenic factor. The Central government had written to Bihar, as it had done to other state governments, to encourage ethanol production to meet the requirement of the oil companies.

Nitish saw a great opportunity in ethanol: it could put the state on the fast track in industrial development, provide a great boost to agriculture with expansion in sugar cane farming and create a large number of jobs. He framed an incentive policy for encouraging investment in ethanol production in 2007. He bet on the strong base of sugar industry the state had. The north Bihar plains had an extremely suitable climate for sugar cane. Five lakh farmers and 50,000 technically skilled hands were engaged in the industry. Bihar had a thriving sugar industry in the earlier decades of Independence, constituting 25 per cent of the national sugar production.

When Nitish took over, nineteen of the twenty-eight sugar factories were out of operation. Of the nineteen, fifteen were owned by the state government through Bihar State Sugar Corporation, which like other state companies had turned bankrupt in the Lalu–Rabri years. In order to revive the state-owned mills, to produce ethanol along with sugar and electricity, the state government decided to auction them for a sixty-year lease. Five mills were taken by major private and public sector players, three mills did not receive any bids and for the remaining seven, bids fell below the reserve price. The state government had to put the ten mills to fresh auction.

The revival of the ten mills was too delayed for Nitish to start seeing ethanol flow out of them. Of the five mills auctioned the formal transfer could be completed for only two by 2009. Thus a combination of factors—the bureaucracy's unrealistic price estimates for most mills and lethargy in completion of the transfer of assets to the successful bidders, and the overcapacity of existing sugar factories—stymied the Nitish government's effort to capitalize on the existing infrastructure to launch Bihar on to the ethanol-driven industrial pathway quickly.

By 2008 the State Investment Promotion Board (SIPB) approved twenty-five investment proposals for sugar mills with distilleries to produce ethanol. However, twenty-one of them are still not set up as investors think it imprudent to start off when production capacity has pulled down sugar prices. The progress on the remaining four is slow. As the main product of these projects is sugar, they would not start until sugar prices increase. That holds up production of ethanol in them.

The SIPB also approved thirteen proposals for standalone ethanol plants, ten to produce it from sugar cane, three from maize. The plants were also to generate 2,000 MW of power, 70 per cent of which was to be purchased by the state government. Misfortune hit these projects too. This time it was not the market or state bureaucracy but the Central government. In 2008 the Union ministry of agriculture amended the 1966 Sugarcane Control Order, restricting production of ethanol from sugar cane juice only to sugar factories. This threatened to shatter Nitish's dream of making Bihar an ethanol hub. Sharad Pawar, who headed the Union agriculture ministry, argued that ethanol-only plants were economically unviable, giving the example of his own Maharashtra state where eleven such plants were closed down within a few years of their launch.

Nitish shot off a letter to Pawar, pleading that his concerns on standalone ethanol plants were highly misplaced. He argued that the primary reason for the non-viability was the low price (Rs 22.50 per litre) of ethanol offered by the oil companies. This price had been set in 2003 when the crude price was nearly half of that in 2008, and must be revised according to the prevailing market rates by the oil companies; once that was done, it would make standalone ethanol plants economically viable.

However, the thirteen exclusive plants approved by his government were not concerned with domestic prices of ethanol as they were to produce ethanol 100 per cent for export. 'The experience of Maharashtra in ethanol production,' Nitish went on in his letter to Pawar, 'may not have much relevance for Bihar in view of the fact that the production of ethanol is not targeted to meet the domestic supply.'

One of Pawar's reservations on exclusive ethanol plants was also that they would eat into the existing sugar cane supply, reducing the input to sugar factories. Nitish assured Pawar that the projects in his state would depend on incremental production of sugar cane and 'not have any adverse impact on the existing sugar cane supply'. Pawar made a statement in Parliament that he was prepared to relax the Sugarcane Control Order for three years for Bihar in case the state government gave a commitment that it would bear the costs of closure of exclusive ethanol factories in the future on its own. The state government was willing to give such an undertaking. But Pawar did not follow up on his statement. And the matter got stuck there, with the Centre not relenting and Bihar's wait for industrialization through the ethanol route becoming protracted.

Not all the blame for Bihar's failure to rapidly emerge as an ethanol hub could be apportioned to the Centre, however. The inertia of the state bureaucracy and adverse market trends were equally responsible.

The Sugarcane Control Order allowed production of ethanol from sugar juice or molasses as an 'option' to producers of sugar. The Central government also increased ethanol blending percentage in petrol from 5 to 10. This amounted to doubling of the size of the domestic market in ethanol. The Central government was expected to announce ethanol blending with high-speed diesel too.

It offered a huge opportunity to the existing and newly approved sugar factories in the state. Production of ethanol could have been started and speeded up in these factories had standalone ethanol proposals not been constrained by the Central government restriction.

The share of the manufacturing sector in state GDP was dropping. Both registered and unregistered units, which included small and micro (artisan-based) units, contributed to the decline.

During the first four years of Nitish's reign, the SIPB approved 342 proposals with a potential investment of Rs 1,67,319 crore. Only forty-seven of the projects (about 14 per cent of the total approved) fructified with an investment of 1,171 crore (0.7 per cent of the total projected). The government's explanation for poor realization of investment projects was the lack of assurance that the favourable business climate would continue: investors had decided to wait until the results of the 2010 elections to stake their capital in Bihar.

That could, however, be only part of the story. Growth of enterprises was also impeded by inadequate road connectivity, acute shortage of power, problems in sourcing raw materials and credit constraints.

The road network had vastly improved from the Rabri years, but many parts were yet to be connected. As for power, Bihar after bifurcation was left with only 584 MW of the total generation capacity of 1,974 MW. Even the reduced capacity of 584 MW was notional as 540 MW of it came from two thermal power stations, one at Barauni (Begusarai district) and another at Kanti (Muzaffarpur district) whose outputs were much lower than the installed capacity due to obsolete technology and poor management. The loss of power in transmission and distribution was 40 per cent, the years of Nitish's first term witnessing no reduction in the losses.

Peak demand remained unmet. From 4.6 per cent in 2002–03, the peak deficit rose to 16.9 per cent in 2006–07 and 32 per cent in 2012–13. During Nitish's first term, nineteen power-plant proposals were approved, thirteen of which were from private companies. Of the remaining six, three projects with a capacity of 1,320 MW each were to be set up in a public–private partnership at Kajra, Chausa and Pirpainti; two as NTPC (National Thermal Power Corporation)–Bihar government joint ventures at Nabinagar (1,980 MW) and Kanti (500 MW); and one (500 MW) at the state government's Barauni thermal plant.

None of these projects fructified during Nitish's first and second terms, owing to private partners backing out or showing little interest, protests by local people and the delay by the Central government in granting coal block linkages. Even in his third term, the Kajra project had not taken off; Chausa and Pirpainti were still in progress; Barauni and Kanti were completed only in 2018 and Nabinagar in 2019.

Bihar lost almost its entire mineral and industrial wealth to Jharkhand in the bifurcation and was largely reduced to an agricultural state. As industry, all it was left with was 250-odd large and medium enterprises, the biggest of which in terms of output value and employment were the government of India's undertakings, Indian Oil (oil refinery at Barauni) and the Hindustan Fertilizer Corporation (fertilizer plant at Barauni). Even these few enterprises were unevenly distributed over the state. Ten of the 38 districts of the state had none of them, eleven districts had less than five of them, while areas around Patna, the business nucleus of south Bihar, and around Muzaffarpur, the business centre of north Bihar, got most of the lean industrial meat. No big investors came to Bihar for ten years after the bifurcation.

If you moved around Bihar, though, you would find industries everywhere, like spots on a leopard. They were in homes, sheds, workshops and tiny factories, owned and managed by traditional artisans or small entrepreneurs. According to official statistics, there were 1.81 lakh of them in 2009–10, with an average investment of Rs 6 lakh and an average employment of three persons. By the end of Nitish's second term in 2014–15, their number rose to 1.99 lakh, but they were still providing bread to no more than three persons each.

These small and micro industries, which made up 95 per cent of the medium, small and micro enterprises (MSME) category carried within themselves an unlimited potential to generate non-farm employment—their per unit average employment, according to industry sources, could be increased to ten—but they remained prone to sickness owing to poor skills in business management and the absence of committed hand-holding by the government. No wonder, the migration of surplus agricultural labour from Bihar to other states increased year after year with the MSMEs not providing enough employment.

These enterprises were expected to serve as a nursery of business skills from which Bihar's own big entrepreneurs would emerge to make up for the absence of big investors from outside. How long the state had cherished this dream! Yet, if you wanted to realize your dream, you had to work with a focus, which the state government was not doing. As a consequence, the enterprises, instead of generating more employment, were pushing more workers towards the migration train.

Pieces of the state's shattered dream could be seen in the handloom industry. About 70,000 weavers owned 30,000 handlooms and operated them with two hired hands per handloom. The worker-weavers had to do other jobs, even migrate to other states, in order to keep the pot boiling at home. Most owner-weavers too were forced to seek a supplementary income. This was happening even in Bhagalpur, the city that was historically famous for its silk saris, *chadar*s and furnishing cloth. The condition of the weavers producing tussar silk cloth in Banka and Nawada, and woollen carpets in Aurangabad, Rohtas and Kaimur, were no better. It was really a huge pity: there was a domestic and international market for Bihar's handloom products, there were centuries of skill making them, but there were no good bridges between producers and consumers, no good ambassadors to inform the producers of consumer tastes, no good designers to guide them on how to cater to their tastes. The Nitish government had introduced schemes to help weavers in product development and marketing, but it needed to do much more to make handlooms a significant sector of Bihar's economy.

If poverty and migration were not to protrude as the defining features of Bihar's face, the small and micro enterprises like handlooms had to establish strong linkages with agriculture too. The silk and wool industries would not grow without growing silk and sheep farming, but these two sectors did not even figure in the state government's 2008–12 agricultural map. Nearly half of the 250-odd large and medium enterprises Bihar retained after bifurcation were agro-based. That was the industrial base Bihar needed to build upon. However, while the state's yield of vegetables and fruits was one-tenth of the national yield, it barely processed 1 per cent of it. The state produced about 50 varieties of scented rice—katarni, tulsi manjari, badshah bhog, Champaran basmati, to name a few—that had fine, short grains and a rich, soft taste. But they were getting extinct and not being processed and marketed in India and abroad.

# restoring bihari pride

The secret of Nitish's landslide victory in the 2010 Assembly elections was as much due to the visibility of the development works he had undertaken—roads, girls riding on bicycles in groups to school, functioning primary health centres and deterrence to lawlessness—as to the direct connection he tried to establish with the people in various ways. Normally politicians only speak to the people: he also listened. That was his way of knowing how much development was actually translating on the ground. That alone could keep the bureaucracy on its toes.

Whenever he visited a town or village for a day or more he set aside a few hours, apart from his official duties—such as meetings, inaugurations or laying the foundation for a project—for listening to local people and receiving their petitions.

He accepted pleas even at his public meetings. I once flew with him in a helicopter to a public meeting at a village in Jehanabad district where I saw him collect memoranda from people's outstretched hands as he walked towards the dais. I pitied the district magistrate and the SP of Jehanabad who were pushed around and squeezed into insignificance by the eager, rustic surge of petitioners. Nitish collected appeals until he got on to the steps to the rostrum, but the flow of memoranda did not stop even after he had settled down in his seat. Unsuccessful supplicants passed on their requests to him through security men and organizers.

While preliminary announcements and speeches were being made, Nitish, putting on his glasses, glanced through each petition, picking up the ones requiring immediate attention and asking the district magistrate or other concerned officers, who would be sitting or standing within his hearing distance, to act in earnest on them. The pleas that required government initiatives at a higher level were handed to his principal secretary R.C.P. Singh who sat in the row behind him.

Sometimes Nitish himself responded to a request on the spot. At another public meeting on another day at a village in Buxar district, he was handed a memorandum by the local residents for a bridge over a small stream a little way to the north of the village to facilitate movement of people and goods. The village was known for a high production of tomatoes and farmers were looking for a faster way to reach marketing outlets.

The first thing Nitish announced in his speech was immediately starting work on the construction of a bridge. 'You placed your demand which I found long-awaited and just,' he said. 'From here only a few minutes ago I spoke to the concerned officials in Patna and instructed them to begin work right away. Engineers will arrive here within a week to take measurements and do other preliminaries. You will have a bridge ready very soon. And that will help fulfil not only your dream but also my dream. I want at least one food produce of Bihar on every Indian's meal plate. With this bridge your tomatoes can travel faster to the world.' The work for the bridge started within a few months.

Nitish's passion for listening was not satiated by the interaction he had with people during his occasional visits out of Patna. He wanted to do it in a regular and structured way. Amusingly, it was a rumour that many believed was fuelled by the Lalu camp that pushed Nitish into setting up a unique listening mechanism no chief minister ever had. The rumour, which said financial assistance was being offered to poor parents for the marriage of their daughters by the chief minister, brought in an increasing number of supplicants from all parts of the state to 1 Anne Marg.

Actually, Nitish had been toying with the idea of giving a grant for daughters' weddings to poor parents. Though the idea was still in a nebulous stage he had once talked about it to some journalists. One of them picked it up, and the Opposition camp did the rest to draw crowds

of people especially from villages. The office and security staff at 1 Anne
Marg found it difficult to stem the flow of supplicants. Nitish decided
to announce the scheme for financial assistance that would be available
to parents from a designated government official in their native areas.

The crowds that came for assistance nevertheless gave Nitish a good
idea of connecting with the people. He saw it as a positive sign that
ordinary people from villages and towns felt little fear or hesitation in
coming over to the chief minister's residence to put up their pleas. He
wanted to encourage them.

'In a democracy people hold the sovereign power,' he told me. 'The
core objective of the 1974 Bihar Movement was real empowerment of the
people. JP had a dream of making *rajsatta* [state power] subservient to
*loksatta* [people's power]. I was always thinking of ways to make people
bolder in making their representatives do what they had been elected for.'

That's how the Janata ke Durbar mein Mukhya Mantri was
conceived where people from all parts of the state were invited every
Monday to express their grievances on matters relating to a particular
department. One Monday it could be police and revenue, another
Monday, education and health and so on. People sometimes gathered
from Sunday night to be ahead in the queue to be heard. Every petition
was registered and given a number, using which the status of the action
taken on the case could be tracked.

Nitish sat from 9 a.m. to 5 p.m. hearing people's grievances in a
large hall that Lalu and Rabri had used as fodder store for their cattle
and poultry. The ministers of the departments concerned would also sit
along with him, and so would the principal secretaries, secretaries and
other senior officers. After glancing through a petition and throwing
a query or two to the petitioner, Nitish referred him to the minister
or concerned officer. In cases in which he noticed a serious lapse or
deliberate act of an officer at the district or lower level, he would ask
the top bureaucrats present to immediately telephone the concerned
field official to remedy the grievance.

Nitish has attended the janata durbar every Monday without
fail, except on a very few occasions such as during Assembly sessions.
He listened to people's grievances in the janata durbar even on
2 January 2011, less than twenty-four hours after the death of his mother,

saying, 'I cannot fail to do my *raj dharma*, duties as a ruler.'

Not all the grievances Nitish hears every Monday get immediate redressal. There may be a large number of cases that do not get settled at all. The volume of cases under process has been growing without any stringent monitoring apparatus. The officers of the CMO are too overburdened to follow up. The implementation is eventually left to the district officers who have been given separate IDs and passwords to access the cases pertaining to their districts brought before the CM at the janata durbar.

There is no quick fix in government. Every proposal has to pass through a number of officers and clerks who examine its pros and cons in detail according to the provisions in the rules or according to norms and conventions. In many cases the lower bureaucrats are familiar with the grievances referred from the janata durbar to them since the petitioners first tried to get them remedied at their level. The field officers may already have an opinion on the case. So, if a plea was not accepted because it did not meet the requirements of rules and regulations it would not be processed just because the petitioner went to the CM's people's court.

Nitish is a chief minister who goes by the rule of law. The lower bureaucracy was assured that as long as they stood on the right side of the law they were safe. But there was a sense of fear and insecurity among officers who were denying anyone what was due to him according to law or administrative stipulations, or delaying its delivery in expectation of a bribe, out of prejudice or because of their inefficiency.

If there was a positive impact of the janata durbar on governance, it was qualitative rather than quantitative. The number of unresolved cases would be huge. But the few cases that did get resolved sent a message through the administration that any day, anyone could approach the CM in the janata durbar and an officer could be pulled up for his omission or commission. And it sent out a message to the people that things could get resolved if you take it to the chief minister. No wonder the queues every Monday at the janata durbar keep growing. The janata durbar would not be restricted to the chief minister. Deputy Chief Minister Sushil Modi also had his janata durbar. Even district magistrates and other field officers had to hold janata durbars.

Janata durbar owed its origin to the Indian tradition of *darshan* in which devotees came to a temple to worship a deity, to a hermitage to pay respect to a saint or, in medieval times, to the Mughal king's court to pay obeisance. Gandhi's charisma drew huge crowds to wherever he stayed for a darshan of him. With ministers seen as embodiments of power in postcolonial India, people started coming to them for a darshan, especially to the prime minister and chief ministers.

Darshan seldom meant an audience: there was no formal hearing by or interview with the prime minister or chief minister. Usually the *darshanarthi*s, audience seekers, who gathered outside the PM's or CM's residence were herded away to, or barricaded at, a safe distance from the minister; unmindful of how long they had waited, the minister would come out at his convenience and, standing quite far from them, wave smilingly and that was all. Darshan meant a glimpse of the leader as during monarchical times.

Nitish changed the pattern; he transformed darshan from view of the leader to interview with him. It was not that he was condescending to grant the visitor an interview; it was a recognition of the right of the people to demand service from their elected representatives. And it was one of the best ways to connect to people and develop popular support for a second mandate.

Another Indian tradition Nitish exploited to his fullest advantage was that of yatra. In ancient India founders of religions had undertaken yatras—journeys in search of truth. The places where they meditated or preached became shrines to their followers who went on a pilgrimage, *teerth yatra*, to them. Gandhi was the first Indian leader to make political use of the yatra tradition. The Dandi Yatra led by him to defy the British government's ban on people's right to make salt from sea water mobilized millions of people.

In independent India, political leaders and civil society organizations often undertook yatras to build up public opinion in support of their causes. One of the most well known was the BJP leader L.K. Advani's Ram rath yatra.

Although Nitish had seen many political yatras, he would not have understood the importance of it had he not undertaken the Nyaya Yatra in the summer of 2005. He struck upon the idea of a Nyaya Yatra to make people aware of the *anyaya*, injustice, done by the Congress-led Central government in dissolving the Assembly and to motivate them to give a clear mandate to the NDA so as to prevent horse-trading. Nitish attributes the NDA success in Bihar in the November 2005 elections significantly to his Nyaya Yatra.

Nitish confesses to his infatuation (*sammohan*) with yatra. 'Yatra is a wonderful medium of communicating with the people,' he says. 'You can feel the pulse of the people as you travel from place to place.' He was so enthused by the popular response to his Nyaya Yatra that he pledged to public gatherings to continue his yatra if they elected him with a majority.

His first yatra as chief minister was Vikas Yatra, Development Journey (January–February 2009). He had decided to go on a Vikas Yatra in 2007, after two years in office, but that year the floods and the illness and demise of his wife Manju prevented him. Although Manju had never lived with him except during his tenure as an MLA between 1985 and 1989 in Patna, and then when he was minister of state for agriculture in 1989–90 in Delhi, he often visited her and they continued to be in constant touch. She came to witness his swearing in at Gandhi Maidan in Patna, but she preferred to stay at her father's house in Kankarbagh as she found it convenient to travel to and from her school. 'I was hoping,' laments Nitish, 'that she would start living with me at 1 Anne Marg once she retired in a few years. But the Almighty had other plans.'

The year 2007 was a year of mourning for him. In 2008 the Kosi floods devastated several parts in north-eastern Bihar. So he could undertake the Vikas Yatra only in 2009.

Nitish had two objectives in mind when he undertook that yatra: one, to see how the plans and schemes launched by his government were being implemented at the grass-roots level; and two, to know what ideas people had for improvement in the programmes or the methods of their execution. He took the principal secretaries of all departments along with him who stayed with him in tents in appointed villages.

One of the most important programmes of the Vikas Yatra was *samvad*, dialogue with the people, which was held in the evenings in the villages where Nitish camped. After speaking for five-odd minutes, Nitish would invite members of the audience to the rostrum to voice their grievances. 'Those who are satisfied with my work can go home and take rest,' he would say. 'I want those who have a complaint about anything to come up on the stage and give vent to it. Because I believe all praise must be done behind your back and all criticism to your face. Anyone is welcome. Only, he should not be a political worker. I want common people. And no one should take the mike to air his personal grievance. For that we will have a janata durbar tomorrow morning. Those who come up here must bring up only public interest complaints.'

Nitish told me:

Usually a few minutes passed before someone stood up hesitatingly in the crowd in response to my invitation. It required a phenomenal amount of courage to voice complaints against local officers, which is what complaints about non-delivery, irregularities and corruption actually amount to. There was a very real danger of vengeance being wreaked on the complainant. And the thought of voicing a complaint from a rostrum standing close to the chief minister could make anyone's legs tremble and scare the bravest of hearts. More so, because bringing to light any disorder would mean an indictment of the chief minister's governance. My idea was to make them open up, to embolden them. I wanted those ordinary people to speak and then go back and think that if they can speak out boldly before the chief minister they could speak before anyone. Such boldness, if inculcated, could change the equation common people today have with the politicians and government officers. Loksatta would be on top of rajsatta. Voters would become rulers in the real sense. That was the main aim of the Bihar Movement. That was the goal closest to JP's heart . . . At samvad, slowly all sorts of people came up on the stage, each expressing his grievances in his own unique way. They were nervous, short of words, some excited and angry. Someone complained about the attendance and quality of primary schoolteachers, another about bribes being demanded by block officials for release of grant in some scheme, yet another about poor irrigation. I would know the gravity of the issue from the quality of response a grievance evoked in the gathering. I would instruct officers to take immediate action on the complaints that aroused biggest applause.

The following morning Nitish would visit a village in the vicinity of the camp village for an inspection of development works. The visit also provided him an opportunity to listen to the residents' views on them. Returning to the camp village he would attend a janata durbar.

Nitish was to undertake four more yatras during his first term, each with a unique structure and mission—Dhanyawad Yatra, Thanksgiving Journey (June 2009), to express gratitude to the voters who gave the NDA the maximum number of seats in Bihar in the Lok Sabha elections that year; Pravas Yatra, Itinerant Journey (December 2009–January 2010), to visit Bihar's famous archaeological sites to raise public awareness about them; Vishwas Yatra, Confidence Journey (April–June 2010), to judge people's confidence in his governance; and Janadesh Yatra, Mandate Journey (August–October 2010), to seek people's blessings before beginning his second term in office.

Much like the Vikas Yatra, the Vishwas Yatra also focused on knowing the realities of the government performance on the ground. But the Vishwas Yatra had a strong element of surprise. The CMO shortlisted ten or twelve villages in every district to select one that Nitish would visit. They asked the district authorities to speedily complete the development schemes under way in all the villages as the chief minister would decide which village to visit only two days in advance. Many of the villages shortlisted were where the Aapki Sarkar, Aapke Dwar scheme was implemented to contain Maoism, and even the villages that Nitish did not visit witnessed acceleration in the progress of development works.

During the Vishwas Yatra, Nitish paid surprise visits to *anganwadi* centres and primary schools, seeing their conditions, quizzing children; to primary health centres, asking patients whether they were satisfied with the service; to PDS shops, checking the books and the quality of food items being distributed; and to the block offices for an inspection of their functioning. During the visits, the chief secretary or development commissioner, the principal secretaries and secretaries of all departments and district officials would accompany Nitish, who told them to take corrective action immediately wherever he found lapses.

These visits were followed up by a review of the progress of development works in the district in which all the visiting top state officials and district officials would be present. For the first time, a chief minister did reviews at the district level in the state.

Did Nitish find the desired progress during his review? He says:

> As one conceptualizes and launches programmes at the apex level it is
> equally necessary that one scrutinizes what is happening on the ground.
> Without an inspection you would not know what are the problems
> facing the implementation, what is the capacity of your men and
> mechanisms to execute what you want or whether your field officers
> have understood the policy or programme directives correctly or are
> doing something totally different and unwarranted.

With Nitish's inspection of a few of the thousands of villages of
the state the bureaucracy could not be expected to become efficient
or virtuous overnight. Bureaucrats are very good at dressing up things
before a VIP visit. Trained local residents could be set up to present a
rosy picture to the VIP.

In the middle of January 2011, I visited Sikaria village in
Jehanabad district, which was presented as a development model for
Maoism-influenced villages throughout the country. We found the
whole panchayat complex lifeless that had been mentioned in official
propaganda as throbbing with activity.

The computer training centre that was believed by top officials in
Patna to be sending out boys and girls to the Bengaluru IT industry
was locked up. It had remained closed for more than a year. Inside,
three computers lay covered in a dark grey plastic sheet like corpses
in a morgue. An employee who opened the centre for us to see said it
was shut down after the computer teacher left complaining of very low
salary. The local administration never found a replacement. Neither the
district magistrate nor any other official has bothered to visit the centre
or the panchayat complex to see what was happening there.

At the sub-primary health centre in the complex, the doctor was
absent in the morning hours when most patients come. The marketing
yard where local farmers were supposed to bring their agricultural
produce and meet wholesalers to negotiate their sales never saw a single
peasant or trader. The warehouse where farmers were supposed to store
their produce for good market returns in lean seasons was being used

by the contractors of a road under construction to keep cement bags.

At a meeting with Nitish at 1 Anne Marg I brought the closure of the computer centre at Sikaria to his notice. He looked upset and immediately asked his secretary Chanchal Kumar to make an inquiry. Chanchal Kumar went to his chamber, spoke to the district magistrate of Jehanabad and came back to explain to Nitish that it had been closed due to a criteria hitch (about who can qualify for admission to the centre for training) between the Central government (which supported the computer training scheme) and the state government—a knot the state finance department had taken too long to untie. 'The finance department should have taken it up in earnest and resolved it,' Nitish said after hearing Chanchal Kumar. 'The district magistrate says the matter is resolved and the centre would be reopened very soon,' Chanchal Kumar said.

What was the truth? Was the computer centre closed because the district administration did not bother to find teachers and pay them a respectable salary as the lowest-rung employee at the computer centre had said? Or was it because of the bureaucratic volleyball between the Centre and the state on whether candidates only from BPL (below poverty line) families were eligible for training at the centre? No one in Patna can know the truth. This is the kind of bureaucratic labyrinth any chief minister would find impossible to negotiate on his own. Follow-up and chasing should have been the duty of the top civil servants but they have not been doing it. Poor monitoring has been the cause of less than satisfactory results in most government programmes.

Nitish started taking measures to tackle this problem early on in his second tenure whose efficacy we will be able to judge only after a few years.

Even though Nitish's janata durbar and yatras did not solve all problems, people did appreciate that he was at least willing to solve them. Combined with his clean image, his persistent striving to remedy people's grievances created an impression of him that was better and greater than Lalu's had ever been. Lalu's forte was hypnotism. Nitish's strong point would be diligence.

The rejection of Lalu had shown that voters had come a long mile from deifying political leaders. They were not going to deify Nitish either. They saw him as an imperfect leader and his governance as imperfect governance—after all, he had criminals in his party, had poached shady politicians from other parties, had corrupt ministers in his cabinet and had failed to bridle corruption. But they also knew no one can be perfect. They gave Nitish a second mandate because they saw him trying earnestly to take on the powerful and corrupt system. They wanted to back him.

The other thing that sustained the Nitish bubble was his conscious effort to promote inclusive politics. That was distinctly different from Lalu who thrived on divisive politics. From every platform he could find, Nitish projected himself as a politician for everyone. Very often he said, '*Ham tanav ki kheti nahin karte* (I do not live on harvest from conflict).' Lalu emphasized caste and religious antagonisms; Nitish de-emphasized them. His emphasis was on *samarasta*, social reconciliation and harmony, on collective Bihari identity. His call to the people was: 'Sink the differences of caste and religion. Come, let us think of ourselves as Biharis and develop our state which has been left behind in the race for prosperity.'

What Nitish's samarasta campaign did was not end caste discrimination or religious antagonisms, or even paper them over; the conditions and factors that were at the root of these conflicts and caused violent eruptions in extreme cases were far from removed; but it did succeed in building a popular consensus in favour of development. A number of Muslims voted for the BJP for the first time in 2010 because that would keep Nitish in power. 'My heart was pounding, my hands trembling, but I drew a sigh and pressed the button against the lotus [election symbol of the BJP], which I had never done in my life,' a Muslim voter from south-eastern Bihar said.

A combination of circumstances led Nitish to discover the appeal of Bihari pride. Biharis are not touched by parochialism the way some other regional communities in India are. Biharis have never attacked non-Biharis in their land, nor poured venom on them in public speeches nor insulted them in private gatherings. Biharis see themselves among custodians of Indian nationalism, as a part of the 'centre': the attitude of a separate identity away from the mainstream is absent in them.

Deep in their hearts (though they do not blow any trumpets about it) they have a fierce pride in their history. Their motherland was a cradle of civilizations in ancient times, fostering religious philosophies and engendering territorial expansions that were to make much of the cultural and political identity of India. Their sense of pride in this was strengthened in recent history when Gandhi launched his first satyagraha in Champaran, and when Bihar became the theatre of the JP movement that changed the course of Indian politics.

However, post-Independence Bihar had fallen behind other states in development indices and law and order due to the governance deficit of Congress regimes. This caused desperation among various sections of society for acquiring or retaining resources for their survival or progress such as cultivable land, urban land and money. A culture of violence set in, leading to proliferation of illegal arms, extortion and looting and massacres. During the fifteen years of the Lalu–Rabri rule even more horrendous and bizarre incidents took place. Bihar in the rest of India's perception became a land of horrors, a metaphor for the inferno.

The degradation hurt Bihari pride. Bihari professionals, artisans and workers working in other states felt so ashamed that they began to avoid disclosing their Bihari identity. Biharis were forced by circumstances to migrate, and they met with insult and scorn wherever they went. The 'makers of India' were being mocked, reviled and abused in the country they had made.

The Delhi chief minister Sheila Dikshit blamed them for several ills in the nation's capital. The Maharashtra Navnirman Sena (MNS) ruffians physically assaulted Biharis and 'banned' them from celebrating Chhath—their most sacred festival in which they worship the sun—on the beaches of the Arabian Sea in Mumbai. When a highly agitated Bihari youth, armed with a country pistol, 'hijacked' a Mumbai bus to protest the MNS hate campaign against Biharis, the Mumbai police, without making any effort to overpower him, shot him dead.

During his years in Parliament as an MP, and as minister for fifteen years, Nitish had often met migrant Biharis who nursed a wounded pride owing to the widespread lawlessness, penury and stagnation in the state and the indignities they were subjected to elsewhere. People back in Bihar knew about the sneering, discrimination and violence against Biharis from their migrant acquaintances and from their own experiences when they travelled to other parts of the country. There was a wide base of hurt pride Nitish thought he could work on. It occurred to him first in mid-2005 when the UPA government at the Centre dissolved the Assembly.

Nitish said to me in an interview:

From the time I stepped into politics I have not got over the pain of seeing Bihar in neglect. The British neglected it. The governments at the Centre and in the state neglected it. It seemed incredible that the nation had abandoned and forsaken its ancient seat of learning and seat of power. And then a time came when Bihar was pushed so far back that everybody gave up hope and decided that Bihar was incapable of playing any role in the progress of the nation. The fall from historical grandeur to the margins in free India pierced Bihari pride to the core. Biharis wanted Bihar to make progress so that their pride was restored. But no political party or leader took initiatives in this regard. I decided to work to re-awaken the sense of historical glory in the Biharis.

Nitish started championing the cause of restoring Bihari pride during his Nyaya Yatra. Although with the LJP split and independents coming over he had got a majority, Nitish was aware that he (NDA) had not got a majority on its own. He wanted a clear mandate. And he thought he could be surer of a clear mandate if he went for a broader mass base. And he could get that only by exhorting people to join him in his endeavour to salvage Bihari pride, to reclaim the land's lost glory. By arousing Bihari identity, Nitish hoped to maximize the support he was getting from the Lalu-alienated upper castes from which came most of the middle-class migrants who nursed the deepest angst.

Nitish was from the same political stream as Lalu; his support base was carved out of the Lalu base among the backward classes. While Nitish took more and more electoral territories away from Lalu and created new support among the backward classes, he still fell short until he marshalled upper-caste support. He had to strike a fine balance in order to get support both from the upper and the backward castes. Bihari identity proved to be a good glue to bind all castes.

Nitish says:

> Bihari pride could not be revived without bringing about development in the state. And development could not be brought about without arousing that sense, because people were moving about with banners of caste identity. A larger identity had to be created in order to subsume the fragmentary identity of caste that Lalu's politics had banked upon. I carried the message of goodwill (*sadbhav*) and brotherhood (*bhaichara*) from village to village during my tours after elections and especially during my Vikas Yatra. I wanted to awaken the Bihari identity, to revive pride in Bihar's glory, to urge people to take a pledge to take the state to great heights striving together as Biharis. 'I have a dream,' I told them, 'to see Bihar achieve similar glory that it had attained in the past. I want to make Bihar so glorious that Bihari identity is associated not with shame but with pride [*Bihari kehlana apmaan ka nahin shaan ka vishay ho jaye*].'

In order to give impetus to his plan, Nitish undertook the Pravas Yatra during which he travelled to Bihar's heritage sites, from the most famous to the lesser known. Accompanied by archaeologists and historians, he visited the hills and caves of Rajgir, the old capital of Magadh, where the first Buddhist council was held and where Buddha had stayed. He wanted to learn from experts at first hand the importance of the sites to those times. He visited Chechar, Chirand and Manjhi in Vaishali where objects such as pottery and tools related to Neolithic, Chalcolithic and neo-Chalcolithic civilizations dating back between 8000 and 600 BC had been found. Nitish says:

> My objective of travelling to those sites was to arouse people's awareness about their glorious ancient past. . . . When the chief minister goes to those sites with archaeologists and historians, the media gives it wide coverage, triggering conversations among both the educated and the illiterate Biharis alike about the greatness of their ancestry. I wanted them to connect to those treasures. And I must admit I was highly amazed myself at the evidence of the robust civilizations I saw. I told

myself there must be something unique in this land . . . We had to
do everything we could to reanimate this land.

The initiative to revive the ancient Nalanda University as a world
university with global cooperation is a part of Nitish's campaign for
reawakening Bihari pride. He took a number of other initiatives too:
for the first time, on 22 March 2010, Bihar Diwas, or Bihar Day, was
celebrated throughout the state to commemorate the formation of Bihar
as a separate province on that day in 1912. The state government declared
it as a holiday for government offices, banks, schools and colleges and
invited people to join the main celebration at Patna's Gandhi Maidan
where a twelve-foot statue of the Buddha, a thirty-foot-high Ashoka
pillar and replicas of important monuments were displayed. The day
was also to be celebrated in the five metropolises—New Delhi, Mumbai,
Chennai, Kolkata and Bengaluru—where large numbers of Biharis
reside, with a showcase of the state's art, culture and cuisines.

At every village he camped during his Vikas Yatra, Nitish would have
a troupe accompanying him that sang the Bihar *Gaurav Gaan*, the Song
of Bihar's Glory, to the audience. At the beginning of his second term,
he decided to take his pride-instilling campaign further with a *Bihar
Geet*, an anthem of Bihari sub-nationalism. He had announced during
his address at the first Bihar Diwas gathering at the Gandhi Maidan in
2010 that the state would have a song to reflect the pride Biharis have
for their motherland.

Nitish's master stroke lay in making the revival of Bihari pride appear
synonymous with his government's objective of 'development with
justice'. In his public speeches he would say: 'Nothing can stop Bihar
from forging ahead if all of us add our might to the effort. People of
the state are intelligent. They are hard-working. Be they Hindu or
Muslim, forward or backward, male or female, extremely backward,
Dalit or Maha Dalit, when the strengths of all are pooled, a powerful
Bihar can be created.'

Nitish's call for a collective effort to develop Bihar was partly meant
to motivate the upper castes to accept the schemes and measures for

the empowerment of the extremely backward castes, the Maha Dalits and the Muslims; the sense of Bihari identity was more ingrained in the upper castes than the lower castes.

It may be naïve to expect the upper castes to transcend their prejudices, especially when 20 per cent reservation for extremely backward classes in rural and urban bodies had shrunk the number of offices the upper castes could get themselves elected to. However, even though not supportive of Nitish's 'justice' component of development, the upper castes backed him for better governance.

> N.K. Rai of Bettiah, the headquarters of West Champaran district in Bihar, is in a dilemma. A Bhumihar with over 100 acres of land, Rai feels Nitish Kumar is out there to ruin them [Bhumihars]. 'If he [Nitish] returns to power, he will again try to bring the Bataidari scheme. He has given reservation to extremely backward castes in panchayats, further sidelining us politically,' he argues. However, he agrees Nitish Kumar has helped them to live in peace during the past five years by improving the law and order situation.[13]

Nitish was able to sell 'development' as the principal cause to the electorate also because it was doing wonders for Bihari identity. With the stories of convictions of thousands of criminals, building of roads and bridges and out-of-school girls and boys going to school on government-given bicycles appearing in the media, the image of Bihar had undergone a change from a dead state to a thriving state. Where only bad things happened, good things were finally happening.

'See, the Biharis are not damned worthless fellows after all. They have the intelligence and spirit to do things, provided they have a good leader,' the Bihari migrant seemed to be telling others.

The identification of Bihar's development with their collective self-pride led the Biharis in general, and the migrant Biharis in particular, to acquire a sense of gratitude towards the man who had made it possible. A comment posted by an Amiet on Nitish's blog[14] said:

> Dear Sir, I would like to thanx [thank] you [for whatever] u [you] have done for bihar. Today we can say i belong to Magadh/Bihar,

Pataliputra/Patna. See our GDP growth rate, etc. . . . we people were very happy when you got best CM award as well as best business performer award etc. We were feeling that we were getting [the] award[s].

A Bhavesh commented thus:

Dear Nitish babu, I have been out of the state since you became the chief minister in 2005. But I do occasionally visit my home in Bhagalpur district and keep an eye on the latest happening in my home state. The announcement of [you getting] the best chief minister award [from] a media house made me proud . . . The development in our state and the honour you received across the country has [been] chang[ing] the image of Bihar and Biharis.

A Priyesh Pritam posted the following comment:

*Apne bihar ki kaya palat ke rakh di . . . jati-pati ke daldal se bihar ko na sirf bahar nikala apitu vikas ki ek nai roshni bhi dikhai. bihariyon ko bahar jake ab khud ko bihari kahne mein garv mahsus hone laga hai . . . ye bhav bhi aapke karan hi aaya . . . apki sarkar zarur poore bahumat se aaegi . . . ye bihariyon ki zarurat hai . . . Jai Bihar!*
[You have transformed Bihar . . . you have pulled it out of the morass of casteism and put it on the road to development. Biharis now feel proud to identify themselves as Biharis outside Bihar . . . We owe it to you. You will surely win with an absolute majority. This is the need of the Biharis . . . Victory to Bihar!]

If the engine of Lalu's political train was social justice with no coaches of development, the engine of Nitish's political train was development with coaches of social justice. Nitish kept development at the forefront, without talking of social justice in an aggressive manner. That kept the upper castes on his side and helped him frame laws, policies and programmes to provide special opportunities for the lower castes without inviting high-caste anger.

Nitish took but a few measures by way of social justice. Many of them—such as reservations in government employment and educational institutions and special schemes for housing, student scholarships, subsidies and loans for the SCs, STs and OBCs—were already in operation.

Nitish went for a finer cut in affirmative action: he focused on the most deprived among the OBCs and SCs and on women who were the most deprived in all castes. The political objective was to gain support of the marginalized castes and sections of society that felt that the lion's share of the benefits of affirmative action was being appropriated by a few 'advanced' communities within the OBC or SC category—and across the board by men of all castes.

Since falling out with Lalu, Nitish had capitalized on the grievances of EBCs about Yadavs cornering most of the benefits under Lalu. The swing of the EBC vote from Lalu to him had brought him victory in 2005. Now was the time to consolidate their support with strong affirmative action for their empowerment. That action came by way of a government decision to reserve 20 per cent of seats in the panchayati raj institutions (PRIs) for the EBCs in 2006. As a result of this decision, a number of men and women from the EBCs were elected as heads and members of PRIs.

For identifying the most deprived among SCs, the Nitish government appointed a Maha Dalit Commission which revealed that out of the twenty-two Scheduled Castes in the state, twenty-one are 'acutely deprived' in terms of educational, economic, socio-cultural and political status; and the population belonging to these castes had not benefited from affirmative action meant exclusively for Scheduled Castes. Although constitutional provisions and Central government directives did not provide for a sub-classification among Scheduled Castes, the Nitish government placed these 'acutely deprived' Scheduled Castes under a special category—Maha Dalit.

An important political purpose this sub-categorization served was the marginalization of Ram Vilas Paswan as a leader of Dalits in the state. He belonged to the Dusadh caste, the one caste that had been left out of the Maha Dalit category as the commission had found their status better than the rest. The implication was that the Dusadhs by virtue of being economically and educationally most advanced—a conclusion the Maha Dalits agreed with—grabbed the major share of the benefits meant for the Scheduled Castes.

The sub-categorization caused a divide between the Dusadhs and the Maha Dalits. And Nitish worked to widen the divide by introducing a spate of special schemes to improve the educational and economic status of the Maha Dalits: land for housing to each homeless family, promotion of female self-help groups for household business, centres to teach out-of-school children, a Maha Dalit Development Mission to implement welfare schemes and so on.

For women, the Nitish government introduced some schemes that achieved success beyond his expectations. One of them provided a bicycle to every schoolgirl of class nine. The scheme came to Nitish's mind while he was distributing bicycles to Dalit girls and boys at a Patna district official function. He thought the bicycle could be used as an incentive to encourage female school education.

The idea worked wonders. The bicycles not only helped stem the dropout rate and increase female enrolment but actually became a symbol of self-respect for girls. Groups of girls rode bicycles from home to school and back without any fear of being teased. Girls also rode to stores to run errands.

Two other schemes were introduced by the Nitish government to enhance girls' self-respect. Under one scheme, the government would issue a bond of Rs 2,000 in the name of every girl child immediately after her birth. The maturity value of the bond would be paid to the girl at the attainment of eighteen years of age for helping the family meet expenses for her wedding. Under another scheme, for each girl child of a BPL family the government, through the State Women Development Corporation, would invest Rs 2,000 in the UTI–Children's Career Balanced Plan-Growth Option. If a family's second issue was also a girl child, the government would also include her in the scheme. On completion of eighteen years the girl would be paid the maturity value (Rs 18,000), which she could use for pursuing higher education or starting a small business.

For the first time in 2008–09, the government presented a gender-sensitive budget in the Assembly, with special focus on the socio-economic development of women. In 2008–09 about 15 per cent of the total budgetary allocations for ten relevant departments were earmarked for women empowerment. In 2009–10 the share increased to 26 per cent.

More than 20,000 self-help groups (SHGs) with two lakh women from deprived sections had been created in the state during Nitish's first tenure. These SHGs were producing a variety of goods for the market, some of them in unconventional areas. Some SHGs at Bidupur (Vaishali) and Phulwarisharif (Patna) were producing a brand of sanitary napkins called Bharti and making reasonable profits.

Employment for women had also been generated in other ways. A number of women were recruited for motivating and helping pregnant women have institutional deliveries—deliveries done through the state health-care system. Of the two lakh primary teachers appointed in Nitish's first five years, 50 per cent were women.

The most significant decision of the Nitish government to empower women was reservation of seats for them in rural and urban local bodies in 2006. Of the 50 per cent of seats reserved in these bodies for backward classes, Scheduled Castes and Scheduled Tribes, half would go to the women from these classes. Of the 50 per cent unreserved seats too, half would be designated for women. Apart from these quotas, women were free to fight from other seats as well. The result was that rural and urban local bodies came to be dominated by women—women of all castes, upper, backward and Dalit, as well as from Muslim and tribal communities.

It was the first time for a majority of them and the inexperience did leave scope for their menfolk or government officials to be able to influence their decisions or viewpoints. But as a whole it caused a social revolution by drawing women from households and placing them in public offices. A fierce debate was triggered over the worthiness of women for public service in every home, in teashops and in social gatherings. The reality of female-majority panchayats has not led to end of 'remote control' by husbands or elimination of male prejudices, but there was no real opposition put up by men to the 50 per cent women quota for both reserved and unreserved seats. A major reason was that it had not yet upset the balance of social power: upper castes could still retain a majority of the 50 per cent general seats with them through their women.

It was due to Nitish's fear of this balance of social power getting disturbed that he disapproved of Sharad Yadav's opposition to the Women's Reservation Bill tabled by the UPA government in March 2010, which provided for reservation of 33 per cent of the seats in Parliament for women. In concert with Lalu Yadav and Mulayam Singh Yadav, leader of the Samajwadi Party, Sharad Yadav declared he would not allow the passage of the bill until a quota for OBCs and Muslims was provided within the 33 per cent quota. Nitish said to the media: 'I am in support of the bill. It should be passed without delay in its present form. Quota within quota can be debated later.'

Nitish's stand earned him cheers from the UPA camp but raised concerns in the JD(U). I happened to be at 1 Anne Marg with Nitish on the day he received calls from Sharad Yadav who tried every argument to persuade Nitish to support an OBC–Muslim quota in the bill. Their debate went on for several minutes on the phone that ended in Sharad Yadav failing to make Nitish accept his viewpoint.

Nitish insisted that the awakening in women of all castes that he had witnessed in the state—as a result of 50 per cent reservation for them in PRIs and other women-centric measures—had convinced him of the need to promote women as a class. Politically, it suited Nitish because he had generated broad support for himself among women of all castes, including those of the upper castes. Nitish feared that if he supported quota within quota, the formidable female constituency he had built up by his assiduous efforts would get fragmented, leading to hardening of attitudes among the upper castes. Assembly elections were just six-odd months away and Nitish thought it would be suicidal for him to support the Sharad Yadav camp.

All Sharad's arguments about his stand being in tune with the principle of positive discrimination could not make Nitish change his position. For quite a few days in March 2010 the air was rife with talks of a JD(U) split. Nitish had conversations with his party MPs to convey his viewpoint. When the bill was introduced in the Rajya Sabha, Nitish was watching the proceedings on television in his office at 1 Anne Marg. Some MPs of the JD(U) expressed their opposition to it. One of them tore a copy of the bill to pieces. Only one MP, Shivanand Tiwari, spoke in its favour.

Nitish seemed to have mentally prepared himself for facing an early poll. Nitish told me that night:

> I will be extremely happy if my party expels me or my government is reduced to a minority owing to a split. That will work in my favour because first, the people at large will have sympathy that someone who was bringing about development has been pulled down from power unjustly, and second, women voters would massively rally in my support. I may even have the advantage of picking up good female candidates out of the hundreds of those who were elected to the PRIs.

The support of women for Nitish showed in the 2010 elections. The total number of female voters was over 5 per cent more than that of male voters. In several constituencies the difference was much more.

A serious cause for worry for Nitish was that his government's intervention for the marginalized sections of society—EBCs, Maha Dalits and women—had not brought about any significant improvement in their economic conditions. His initiatives to broaden the inclusion basket amounted in essence to carrying forward, with some refinements, the social justice revolution Lalu had engineered. Politics and society had further changed but not the economy. The EBCs, Maha Dalits and women had advanced politically but not economically. If there was no improvement in their economic conditions soon, the effect of their political advancement on the hitherto privileged classes would vanish and the privileged would be back at their game of dominating the scene, turning all efforts at social empowerment of the weak meaningless.

The performance of the Nitish government with regard to poverty alleviation was not good. Of the two key policies of the land reforms related directly to economic uplift—security of tenure for sharecroppers and distribution of cultivable land to the landless—the first one made no progress at all, and the other only routine progress.

The implementation of the MNREGA—whose objective is

to provide food security to the poor through wage employment at the village level for 100 days in a year—was very unsatisfactory. Only 2.62 per cent of the total number of households issued MNREGA job cards were provided 100 days of employment in 2008–09.

The biggest problem in MNREGA was fake muster roll. While the payments were siphoned off against fake names, the labourers who needed off-season work did not get any. The Nitish government failed to get a grip on this problem. The official machinery was too slow, and often collusive, to help the new government achieve results. At a later stage, the government decided to use technology—biometric cards with fingerprints for identification of a labourer—but this involved a search for a service provider to whom the job of preparing the cards could be outsourced. By the time Nitish's first term ended, little had been done in this direction.

A two-day workshop, organized by the state department of rural development for MNREGA review on 13–14 December 2009 in Patna found that although 117 lakh job cards had been issued by November 2009, only twenty-five lakh, or merely 20 per cent, of card holders were provided employment. Only 22 per cent of BPL job card holders had been given work. Only 32 per cent of women card holders were given employment, which was fairly low compared to the national average of 51 per cent. The state created employment of only twenty-six average person-days per household against the national average of forty-three, and the target average of 100 days. 'This reflects,' said the review, 'that either the MNREGA administration has not been able to reach poor people or poor people have not been able to reach MNREGA administration.'

Inter-district variations in employment generation were striking. In Madhubani, Supaul and Katihar, not a single job card holder was provided 100 days of work. In Khagaria, Lakhisarai, Purnea, Saharsa, Darbhanga, West Champaran and Sitamarhi, less than 0.1 per cent were provided 100 days' employment. The failure of the state government to plan and start works drove the lean-season unemployed out of the village to seek wage earnings elsewhere in the state or in other states.

A survey[15] found that labour migration continued to increase during the Nitish regime as in previous regimes. Even otherwise, the state's old and new migrants did not find MNREGA very alluring because it assured wage employment only for 100 days, roughly three months, in a year. And with the actual employment provided by MNREGA being much less, attraction for the programme was reduced further. No wonder the number of job card holders seeking MNREGA employment dropped. In Banka, Begusarai, Khagaria and Jehanabad, only 31 per cent of job card holders demanded employment in 2009–10 compared to 80 per cent in 2007–08. In Katihar, Purnea and Saran, less than 6 per cent job card holders sought work in 2009–10.

Fund utilization by the state for MNREGA was only about 63 per cent in 2009–10 (up to October). In Munger and Arwal, two of the poorest districts, fund utilization was less than 40 per cent, and in Nawada, Sitamarhi, Samastipur, Supaul, Madhepura, Purnea, Kishanganj and Khagaria, less than 50 per cent.

The implementation of MNREGA in the state was flawed all along the way. One of the basic ideas of MNREGA was social empowerment. The works to be taken up under the programme were to be debated and approved by a *gram sabha*, a village convention. In most cases a gram sabha was never conducted before making the Annual Action Plan (AAP) for the village. The powers of the gram sabha were misappropriated by the mukhiya. That left quite a bit of scope for works being chosen to suit private rather than public interest.

The mukhiya's choice of works could be influenced by any or a combination of the following factors: which caste habitations are going to be most benefited by the work, and whether their residents were the mukhiya's political supporters; whether a majority of *pancha*s, who had elected him as their leader, approved of the work; and whether he would be able to take along the engineers and officials to make a work plan and cost estimates (including the labour cost).

There were no regular meetings between the officials entrusted with MNREGA administration and the mukhiyas. Very often the government engineers drew up work plans and made cost estimates without visiting the site. One reason could be a deal with the mukhiyas; the other reason was that they were assigned too many villages. A junior engineer or a panchayat technical assistant had to look after about ten villages, and it was humanly impossible for them to devote time to visit each site either to design the project or to inspect the work in progress. They were also paid meagre allowances for travel.

The 2009 government review found that the works undertaken under MNREGA lacked vision and a holistic approach. Projects were taken up without any relation to the integrated development of the village. The whole idea of using MNREGA to transform the rural economy of Bihar was defeated.

Field reports found that even the quality and quantity of the works shown to have been executed were unsatisfactory in several places. Inadequate and poor supervision by the MNREGA administration allowed the mukhiyas to manipulate the making and distribution of job cards and measurement of work done by labourers (usually in terms of cubic feet of mud cut) and the amount of wages to be paid to them. In several cases, job cards were kept by the mukhiya or other elected members of the PRIs and filled by them at their convenience, not at the worksite but at their homes. The 2009 review found that cash books were not maintained on a daily basis: 'No dated receipts were given to workers. Consequently, the figures reflect a huge gap between allocation of work and application of work.'

A survey of MNREGA in ten villages in Jehanabad and Arwal districts in 2008 found:

None of the muster rolls were ever updated on the worksite. Worse still, the muster rolls were mostly in the possession of the mukhiya, and the beneficiaries were made to sign on blank muster rolls on the days they received their payments. The mukhiyas later matched and filled the same figures in both the muster rolls and the job cards.

Take for example [the] village Parasi in Arwal district. Of more than 15 people interviewed in Parasi, only one beneficiary had his card with him; all the others stated that their cards were lying with the mukhiya. We were witness to the payment for the recently completed work in Parasi being made by the mukhiya. We found that the mukhiya was making the beneficiaries sign on blank muster rolls. When confronted, he said he was doing the job for the Rozgar Sevak [employment assistant] who had fallen ill. Though he refused to take responsibility for the muster rolls being empty, he said it was because payments could not be made at the worksite as it was unsafe for the Rozgar Sevak to carry large amounts of money to the worksite.

In Saristabad in Jehanabad district—a fairly large village of 3,000 people, with a majority of Manjhi [traditional rat-eating community] households—job cards were in the possession of a zilla parishad member and her advocate husband. Construction of a canal undertaken in the village was completed three months earlier but the cards had still not been returned to their owners. Nor had they received any wages. Workers visited the zilla parishad member several times demanding their job cards and wages, but they received neither. They cannot apply for more work under [MNREGA] unless they get their job cards back.[16]

The 2009 government review recognized the problem: 'In some panchayats, mukhiyas have escaped with the funds. Strict action would be taken in cases where money has been blocked/siphoned. Instructions and disciplinary orders will be issued against defaulter mukhiyas. The programme officer should have some power to check the hegemony and misuse of power by mukhiyas in the villages.'

Poor MNREGA administration presented a stark contrast to the image of good governance under the Nitish regime. Considering that the key to the development of Bihar lay in the development of its rural economy, the haphazard, low-quality 'assets' built through MNREGA implementation ended up in sheer waste of resources with the most visible signs of prosperity coming to the homes of mukhiyas, other panchayat officials, contractors and government officials through a share of loot. 'No wonder every mukhiya today drives around in an SUV,' says Satish Kumar, elder brother of Nitish.

'MNREGA is an occasion to transform Bihar's economy,' said Vijay Prakash, principal secretary, rural development department, at the 2009 review. To make that happen, the state government decided on a phenomenal expansion of the programme; from just one scheme taken up by a panchayat in a month, the number of schemes would go up to twelve per panchayat per month in 2010–11 with the aim of covering all villages. That amounted to execution of more than 1,200 crore schemes across rural Bihar.

Such a huge expansion of works without any strengthening of MNREGA administration could be an open invitation to the mukhiyas to loot. On paper, the state government laid down certain preventive guidelines: the MNREGA district plan should be holistic and comprehensive, giving an integrated scope for convergence of relevant departments. The district authorities should exercise quality leadership in making the district plan. 'Convergence of minds is important.' All the line departments should be present during the planning stage. Also, in order to avoid haphazard and arbitrary works, 100 per cent irrigation was made the prime focus, substantively channelizing the MNREGA to schemes of canal construction and renovation and pond construction works.

For the first time, line departments were included as implementing agencies. The worst-performing panchayats were to be identified and inspected. BDOs or equivalent level officers were authorized to carry out inspection. After the cases were verified by BDOs, a charge sheet was to be issued. The mukhiya was to be given a chance to provide clarifications. If the clarifications were not satisfactory, strict disciplinary action would be taken against the mukhiya. If he was found guilty of misuse of authority he would be removed according to the provisions of law. It is yet to be seen how effectively these measures are implemented.

The delivery of the public distribution system (PDS)—which is aimed at providing food security to the poor through distribution of subsidized rice, wheat, sugar and kerosene—was also highly unsatisfactory under Nitish's first term. An important measure of the success of PDS is the percentage of amount of stocks lifted by licensed dealers from the government for distribution to targeted beneficiaries.

For the Antyodaya scheme, under which 'extremely poor BPL families' are provided thirty-five kilogrammes of foodgrains per month—twenty-one kilos of rice at Rs 2 a kg and fourteen kilos of wheat at Rs 3 a kg—the PDS dealers lifted only 79 per cent of the Central allocation of the commodities in 2008–09, compared to 95 per cent in 2005–06.

The drop was not sudden. The peak was reached in 2003–04 with 96 per cent; it was more or less maintained till 2005–06, then it dipped to 87 per cent in 2006–07, rose to 90 per cent in 2007–08 and then plunged to 79 per cent in 2008–09.

Under the BPL scheme, which entitles BPL families to thirty-five kilos of foodgrains, PDS dealers lifted much less of the Central allocation than in Antyodaya—46 per cent in 2005–06, 37 per cent in 2006–07, 57 per cent in 2007–08 and 65 per cent in 2008–09. In Saran, Sitamarhi, Madhubani and Banka only 10 per cent of the total allotment of wheat and rice was lifted in 2008–09. The lifting averaged 14 per cent in Nalanda, Vaishali, Supaul, Madhepura, Purnea, Araria, Bhagalpur, Lakhisarai and Jamui. Twenty-seven of the thirty-eight districts, or 70 per cent of the state, had lifted less than 35 per cent of Central foodgrain allocation.

Field reports suggested that even the lower amount of foodgrains that was lifted was not always distributed completely. In several fair-price shops, no foodgrains, sugar or kerosene were available for six to twelve months. The dealers would lift the quota allotted to them and sell it to traders in the open market to earn high profits. In some cases, a strong nexus existed between the dealers, traders and government warehouse officials, who facilitated direct transportation of the allotments to dealers to traders. A Planning Commission estimate in 2005 put leakage of PDS foodgrains in Bihar at 75 per cent.

For protection most of the dealers hid behind a political shield. Over 60 per cent of the 43,000 PDS dealers in the state were OBCs and SCs, most of whom were cleverly taking advantage of the political upsurge of their classes to indulge in profiteering. Often they switched their allegiance to the political party in power: in Lalu–Rabri raj they were with the RJD and in the Nitish years with the JD(U). In 2009 the CPI(ML) Liberation mobilized deprived ration card holders against thirty dealers in Patna rural district, twelve of whom were with the JD(U), ten with the RJD, six with the LJP and two with the CPI(ML) Liberation.

Party affiliation granted the dealers political and administrative clout: they could have their way with the influence of the local party leaders such as officials elected to PRIs and MLAs. A dealer could come to own a chain of fair-price shops and use 'ghost cards' (10–30 per cent of the total number of cards, according to the 2005 Planning Commission estimate) with the help of this clout.

Proxy licencees were not uncommon for a big dealer. And whenever these dealers were in trouble, local party leaders intervened on their behalf to force the local administration to act in their favour. This was the reason why most of the times when the deprived ration card holders went individually or in groups to the BDO or the SDO to urge him to take action against a dealer, they went back home with bags full of empty assurances. The BDOs and SDOs seldom exercised the powers vested in them to cancel the licence of such dealers.

In reaction to this situation, ration card holders organized themselves in several places and resorted to direct action against the dealers, laying siege to their houses, carting away the stocks hidden by them and forcing them to deliver the arrears of the quota of foodgrains, either in the form of foodgrains or as money in lieu of it. In the 2009 campaign against dealers indulging in diversion of lifted food stocks organized by the CPI(ML) Liberation:

At Kalyanpur Masaurhi (Dhanarua) when people shut RJD's Sadhu Yadav [dealer] up in his house for 12 hours in order to get 8 months of pending rations from him, his family called the police. But the dealer, fearful of people's wrath, denied any ill-treatment and distributed 5 months of rations. At Repura (Dhanarua), a People's Court was held against two dealers, Rajiv Singh and Akhilesh Thakur, both belonging to the JD(U), on the charges of having siphoned off 9 and 6 months' worth of rations respectively. When these dealers did not present themselves at the People's Court, enraged people surrounded their houses. Rajiv Singh managed to climb over the wall and escape, but Akhilesh Thakur was caught. People hung a notice announcing 'I'm a ration thief' around his neck and paraded him in three villages; then returned to the village to face the People's Court, which decided in favour of searching the homes of both dealers for rations. No grains were found at Akhilesh's house, but 9 sacks of grain were found at Rajiv's, which were confiscated by the people. Akhilesh asked [for] pardon of the people and distributed rations on 29 September, along with 2 kilos of grain per family by way of a fine. A TV channel happened to telecast some part of these events, and Patna being the capital-district, the issue gained a political dimension. As a result, the Government tried to crush the struggle, and the DM ordered an enquiry into the People's Court. But this came to naught as the dealers denied any ill-treatment.[17]

Residents of Chakfatte village in Vaishali district also organized themselves spontaneously and caught the local dealer selling kerosene at a price much higher than the fixed rate and selling foodgrains to traders in the open market. A video of the campaign was also put up online.[18]

During his first year in office Nitish had several meetings with his top officials to find ways to end corruption and inefficiency in the PDS. The conclusion he arrived at was that the nexus between the dealers, government officials, godown keepers, open market traders and transporters was so strong that it was impossible to plug all leakages and stop the diversion of foodgrains. He did not think his government machinery would ever be able to ensure food delivery to the poor through PDS. There had to be some other way to do that.

It was with that idea that Bihar followed the Rajasthan example to introduce food coupons to the poor in 2007. Every ration-card-holding household would be issued food coupons in lieu of subsidy every month, using which they could buy cereals, sugar and kerosene from any PDS shop. The PDS shop owner would charge the market price for the commodities, so a card holder would pay with coupons plus cash that would be the difference of the market price and the monetary value of the coupons. The dealers could change the coupons for money at a local bank and the banks in turn would be reimbursed by the government.

Nitish hoped that the food coupons system would reduce leakage and diversion of foodgrains between the godowns and outlets by letting the dealers sell commodities at the prevailing market price, but that did not happen. Nor did the state succeed in improving delivery of foodgrains to the poor under the old system, for the dealers of a particular area could act in collusion to make commodities unavailable as they would earn better in the open market. The state government agencies made it still worse by sometimes delaying the issue of coupons, sometimes not having adequate stocks to supply to dealers, making the coupons useless, and most of the time not taking penal action against dealers who were siphoning off stocks.

PDS allocation in the state up to 2007–08, that is, the year the food coupons system was introduced, totally depended on the Central government. From 2008–09, the state government also started making allocations to all the three schemes—Antyodaya, BPL and Annapurna—of the PDS. While the Central government allocated 27.58 lakh tonnes of rice and wheat in 2008–09, the state government allocated 35.53 lakh tonnes. The increased supply still did not improve availability of food to the poor. It only meant more of the food meant for the poor went into the black market.

A telling example was available in a civil society group's report on starvation in a drought-hit area:

> Acute hunger claimed lives of three in Rattu Bigha tola (Dhuriari village) of Ghosi block in Jehanabad district and Jhawantola village in Nursarai block in Nalanda district during August 10–14 [2009]. The deceased were Kunti Devi, Charittar Dom and Janardan Mahto. Two of them belonged to the dalit communities and one to the extremely backward caste (EBC). Both Rattu Bigha and Jhawantola are primarily dalit hamlets and [a] majority of the families are living below poverty line (BPL). They complained that government agencies have failed to provide any job to them [under MNREGA] . . . Of the deceased, Charittar Dom's MNREGA job card reads thus: card no. 0079, issued 2.02.2006, workday entries: 0. So Charittar Dom dies jobless on August 10 [2009] despite his job card being issued in February 2006 . . . Most of the villagers in the tola were malnourished and suffered from hunger-related diseases . . . Villagers stated they have not been provided subsidized food grains for the past several months by the local public distribution system (PDS) dealer . . . Since June 2008, not a single family has received regular supply of food grains under their Yellow (Antyodaya) cards, which entitle [them] to buy rice at Rs 2 and wheat at Rs 3 per kilo. The coupons continue to remain with the villagers, but the dealer claims 'shortage of food grains' and keep[s] the shop closed for most of the time.[19]

All new measures had failed. The nexus of the civil supplies bureaucrats, middlemen, transporters, food traders and PDS dealers had proven too strong to be broken. Nitish virtually accepted his defeat in the beginning of his second tenure when he started advocating direct delivery of food subsidy as cash to bank accounts of the poor. He was driven to think of cash subsidy by the roaring success of the Cycle Yojana (also known as the Balika Yojana) his government had introduced. In that scheme the government, instead of procuring bicycles through a tender and delivering them to school students, had distributed a cash award of Rs 2,000 to each student to buy a bicycle of whatever make and from whichever shop they wanted. The direct cash subsidy eliminated the scope of corruption by bicycle suppliers, government officials or school administrators.

Direct cash transfers for purchase of a bicycle and direct cash transfers for food subsidy were, however, two different things. Nitish had obviously not thought of its several implications. This would actually mean abolition of the PDS, which was designed with the twin purposes of providing incentives to farmers for increasing production and providing food security to the poor. The end of food procurement by the state could destabilize the country's agriculture and create a food crisis with major impacts on economy and politics. The end of PDS distribution could mean a loss of faith in the administration. If the administration could not manage PDS they could tomorrow declare the entire social sector (education, health, welfare) unmanageable and leave it in the hands of market forces.

## 14

## success as a journey

People who had given up on Bihar do not cease to be astonished by the 'turnaround' of the state. Nitish Kumar has achieved the status of a miracle worker in their eyes. How could he do it? How did he manage to resurrect the state? Or did he really do it?

Nitish Kumar is no professional manager. The only administrative experience he could count on was his six-odd years as a minister in the different departments of the Central government. But more than a minister or chief minister, Nitish considers himself a politician. A professional politician.

As a professional politician, he exudes an air of supremacy. He strongly believes that people are sovereign in a democracy, and hence the politicians they elect as their representatives are supreme. The politicians who run the government are above the bureaucrats who constitute the permanent arm of the executive. Even though they are there for five years, politicians represent the will of the people at that particular time, their aspirations for that moment in history—not the officers who are recruited for a lifetime to advise politicians and implement decisions.

When he took over as chief minister in November 2005, he would often remind officers that his ministry had the greatest stake in the performance of the government, not the bureaucracy. If the government achieved success, his ministry would get all the credit; if it failed, his ministry would have to bear all the blame. The bureaucrats won't lose their jobs. He will.

So, from the outset, he concentrated on driving the bureaucracy. During the fifteen years with Lalu at the helm, the bureaucracy had stopped thinking because the leader never provoked them, or taking action because it was not expected of them. Problems remained unresolved in the absence of ideas. Implementation of programmes lagged for lack of exertion.

The twin problems Nitish faced were of his people suffering and him having to propel a paraplegic bureaucracy to join him in his attempt to resolve that suffering.

One thing he was very clear about: he had to work with the existing bureaucrats. 'All you can do about the bureaucracy,' Nitish believes, 'is substitute A with B. If you have a hundred officers, say ten would be totally worthless; you can banish them to the corners where they can do the least damage. But you have to work with the rest. There will be good or average, more efficient and less efficient among the remaining ninety; you have to accept it. After all, no system is made of perfect men.'

In the initial few months of his first tenure Nitish held long meetings with officers of all departments. He tried to understand where things stood, where they were going wrong, and in the process also gauge the quality of senior bureaucrats: how much each bureaucrat understood his job, whether he had new ideas to offer, how much of a leader he was; who was a charlatan, who had a social conscience, who was earnest, who was a shirker.

The first challenge he threw at them was: Can we identify the problem? Once the problem was identified, brainstorming began to find a solution. Usually top officers of a department brought up issues that stood in the way of solving the problems. For instance, after 'fear of criminals' was identified as the gravest problem in Nitish's deliberations with home and police officials, they presented a long list of constraints the police faced in enhancing people's sense of security: the police force was severely short of manpower; recruitments to constabulary and subordinate officer cadre had not been done for years; police had outdated guns and inadequate transport; the average age of a policeman was thirty-eight.

'Let us not wait until all these problems are solved,' Nitish told them. 'We have to get going with whatever we have. We shall continue to search for a solution to each of these problems as we move.'

He emphasized movement, expecting the officers to take things forward step by step, rather than getting stuck in sceptical debates on a holistic solution through an unending exchange of files, which had become the bureaucracy's second nature. He drove them harder with his impartiality: they got no scope to glorify their escapism on grounds of 'political interference'. In his anti-crime campaign, Nitish acted even-handedly even where thug MLAs from his party were involved. That allowed the police no room to not pursue criminals.

And Nitish used a hands-on approach. That was his style. He would not be there just to make laws, frame policies and draw up programmes and leave the implementation to the bureaucracy. He did not believe in the conventional method of governance as it had come to be followed in post-Independence India. He believed implementation was the key. Governments usually faltered on implementation. Ministers would call officers to meetings and lecture them on policies and programmes, and there the involvement ended.

Nitish personally engaged himself with every programme. Once the officers saw the chief minister individually involved, they could not help being involved themselves. There was somebody monitoring them. Nitish regularly assessed the progress of the programmes. That kept up the momentum.

Nitish is obsessed with work. He has no extra-curricular activities, doesn't play any sport, watch television, go to movies or listen to music. Entertainment and fun away from work are seen by him as a waste of time. Working for fourteen hours a day, he cannot find much time for his family either, which was one of the reasons his wife did not stay with him at 1 Anne Marg.

'Do not consider work as a burden,' he would often tell his officers. 'Take work as your dharma, your duty, as inspiration for life.'

Sermons did not help much; what worked was the delegation of powers. Responsibility would still be considered a burden by officers if no authority was given to them. In the Lalu regime, any project above Rs 25 lakh needed cabinet approval. Nitish framed a policy delegating authority down the line from the minister of a department to the junior-most officer for approval of projects of a progressively declining amount. Only projects involving expenditure of Rs 10 crore and above would now come to the cabinet for approval.

Authority for approval of projects and freedom of action alone, however, could not have brought about the success Nitish was able to achieve in the four areas of his top priority during his first tenure: law and order, roads, education and health. There was a whole new driving force he had created that worked wonders. This new driving force was public pressure.

One of its best illustrations could be found in the revival of the primary health centres (PHCs), government's basic hospitals at the block level. Under the Lalu regime, PHCs were gloomy and forsaken. No medicines were available; doctors seldom attended duty. Patients had stopped coming.

These doctors were government servants. The new regime could have issued orders to them to attend duty. But the problem that was identified was not the dereliction of duty, but one of infrastructure. The new regime decided to provide adequate, regular medicine supplies to the PHCs. It gave incentives to private entrepreneurs to set up radiological, pathological and other facilities there.

With the news of improvements in infrastructure, patients started visiting the PHCs. This created moral pressure on doctors to be present to attend to them—not only be present, but to come early and leave late, until all patients had been examined. Doctors arranged shift duty among themselves: there would now be a doctor also on night duty for emergency. Since Nitish took over, disciplinary action has not been taken against a single doctor. Because public pressure had done the trick.

Nitish's innovative way of using double pressure on the bureaucracy—one from the ministry from above and the other from the public from below—could be called the 'squeeze formula'. The officers had no room for escape.

Using this formula, Nitish managed to increase school enrolments and improve education in schools. About 15,000 new schools were opened during his first tenure. Classrooms were added to the existing schools that needed them. Toilets were built. Sports activities were started. Children were given free textbooks and money to buy school uniforms and bicycles. Special centres were opened to prepare children from illiterate, disadvantaged sections—Taleemi Markazs for Muslims and Utthan Kendras for Maha Dalits—for admission in primary schools. All children who passed class ten in first division were awarded Rs 10,000 each by the government.

These incentives motivated poorer parents to send their children to schools. To create pressure on the parents, the ban on child labour was implemented more effectively. School enrolments (classes one to eight) in the state jumped from 10.9 million in 2004–05 to 14.6 million in 2007–08. In 2004–05 about twenty-five lakh children in the state were out of school; by 2009–10, the number dropped to 7.70 lakh. Huge enrolments created pressure on the officers in the human resource department as well as on principals, headmasters and teachers to work faster and more effectively to make resources available to children and improve education in schools.

Thanks also to the squeeze formula, Nitish was more successful in preventing the occurrence of communal riots than Lalu was. He made the district magistrate and the SP directly accountable for communal violence. He made it obligatory on them to rush to the village or town as soon as the news of trouble reached them. They had to camp in the village or town with a strong police force for as many days as it took them to start the process of reconciliation and establish peace. They had to act fair and book cases and arrest people on the basis of complaints from either side.

When such initiatives bore fruit at some places, wherever tension started to build up, Hindus and Muslims began to expect the concerned district magistrate and SP to hurry with a police force and camp amidst them until normalcy was restored. Public expectations created a pressure on officials to act with swiftness, sincerity and objectivity. People started judging a district magistrate or SP as good or bad depending on how rapidly they acted and how they interacted with them during their camping days.

During his many yatras, Nitish encouraged people to speak up from the dais about the lacunae and failures in the implementation of government schemes in the presence of the local officers and top officers from Patna. During his district tours, he visited sites of ongoing schemes with officers and heard beneficiaries on any issues they had with the execution of schemes.

The squeeze formula was most systematically applied in janata durbars. Janata durbars were not restricted to the chief minister. Every key officer, including the district magistrates and the station house officers, had to hear people's complaints at a janata durbar on a fixed day of the week. That kept the pressure on the field officers. They knew that if they did not resolve the complaints the aggrieved would go to the chief minister's janata durbar and their inattention would be exposed.

At the beginning of Nitish's second tenure, the state passed a Right to Public Services (RTPS) Act on the Madhya Pradesh model, under which a timeline was fixed for delivery of fifty services provided by ten key departments, including general administration, health, transport, commercial tax, home, human resource department, food and civil supplies, urban development, registration and social welfare. Earlier, people had to make several rounds of government offices for issue of a residential/income/caste/character certificate, ration card and driving licence or payment of scholarship and old age pension. Usually, they would not get it without paying a bribe. The new legislation set a time limit (seven to thirty days) for delivery of these services and provided for monetary fine (lump sum Rs 500 to Rs 5,000; in some cases Rs 250 per day up to a maximum of Rs 5,000) from an officer who failed to deliver within the prescribed period.

As though people were waiting for this, they inundated the bureaus of designated officers (BDOs, SDOs, SPs and DMs) with applications for services as soon as the RTPS Act came into effect on 15 August 2011. Within fifteen days 6.83 lakh applications poured in, the largest for residential certificate (2.50 lakh), followed by caste certificate (1.59 lakh) and income certificate (1.15 lakh). More than a lakh of the 6.83 lakh applications were disposed of during those fifteen days. In case of a designated officer rejecting someone's application for any service, they had the right to appeal. Fear of being penalized by the appellate authority was intended to keep officers from holding back certificates or denying other services arbitrarily. As officers depended on subordinate staff for speeding up disposal of applications, they set a time limit for them too, keeping the pressure on them and reducing scope for 'illicit private fees' that they demanded under the table.

However, government offices were an ancient habitat of the beast of corruption, one that refused to be driven out. It continued to stalk and grab its prey. Certificates were either not delivered within the timeline or until the last day of the timeline—the delay and maximal stretch seemed to be intended to force the prey to cave in. People often needed the certificates urgently for submitting it with their applications for jobs, college admissions or state welfare benefits. The officers, past masters of subterfuge, justified the delay on the plea that they were busy fulfilling the government's priority tasks. The touts, as before, operated outside the offices as extensions of the officers' claws. The state government had set up special centres in districts as a single window to receive applications for certificates, with financial assistance from the United Kingdom Department for Internal Development (DFID). The centres were manned by two to five educated, IT-trained youth, whose job was to send the applications to the designated officers of the departments concerned. The state government thought that by saving the citizens the hassle of going to the departments to submit their applications, it was saving them from the beast of corruption. But it was mistaken. The citizens had still to go to the government offices to collect their certificates, which is where the extended claws of the beast demanded its price.

In 2013, the government drastically reduced the timeline for the delivery of residence, income and caste certificates, for which most applications came, putting them under the *tatkaal*, or immediate, category. In the following years, web cameras were installed at the certificate-delivery counters to identify touts. District officials in disguises made surprise checks at the counters to catch them. The government started a district ranking system to rate the performance of district magistrates in the quick, transparent and corruption-free delivery of certificates. The beast could no more get its quarries as easily and abundantly as before, but it still found enough game to stay alive. By 2018, the government succeeded in moving the prey population away from the beast's habitat: citizens could now submit their applications online for the three-most-sought-after certificates of residence, income and caste online and also get these certificates digitally signed by the designated officers online. Thanks to the ease of getting certificates, the numbers of applications soared year after year. According to official statistics, from August 2011 to June 2020, the state government offices received 23.61 crore applications and satisfactorily disposed of 23.58 crore of them.

However, in other areas, the officials could still, as the Bihari saying goes, 'sit on the files'. A citizen might make a hundred rounds of an office, yet his or her petition would stay at the bottom of the pile of petitions on the table of this or that senior or junior official. The petition could leap up to the top the day he or she paid a bribe. That bribe was shared by the officials concerned.

Delaying had been the bureaucrat-devil's dateless device to get to its prey. It was to block this device that Nitish started the janata durbar. He held it continuously from 2006 to 2016. He heard petitions from citizens every Monday. All these years, he also welcomed petitions from citizens during his many yatras through different parts of the state. The chief minister's secretariat sent every petition to the department concerned, recommending prompt action. Nitish was playing his own game—the 'squeeze' game—to beat the beast of corruption: while he with his hands-on approach kept pressing the bureaucracy from the top, he encouraged the citizens to keep pressing from below. The grievances of a large number of citizens were satisfactorily addressed as a result of reference from the chief minister's secretariat, but the usual new fate of a petition was no different from its old fate: the bureaucrat came up with a dozen grounds, two dozen reasons and three dozen rules about why the application had not been entertained earlier and could not be entertained now. How often Nitish was bewildered to first receive a complaint; then, sometime later, another complaint from the same person about the earlier complaint not being addressed; then sometime later, yet another complaint about earlier complaints still not resolved! The whole pursuit of the bureaucracy seemed endless and fruitless. They seemed to have defeated Nitish in his own game.

Did he have no option then but to give up trying to tame the beast? Did the people have to reconcile with living under the bureaucrats who were as domineering and venal as the colonial administrators and not as sensitive, sympathetic and supportive as the public servants in a democracy are expected to be?

By the end of his second term, Nitish made up his mind to find a way to try and end *naukarshahi*, the servants' raj, as the bureaucrats are euphemistically known. Many ideas came to him. He finally picked the one that had the three key provisions—fixed timeline, appeal and penalty—that had made the right to public services a success. His experience was before him: during the ten years of janata durbars and yatras, he had succeeded in establishing a system for receiving petitions from citizens but failed in establishing a system for redressing them. If the bureaucrats realized that their potent weapon—delaying—had turned into a boomerang, they would change their behaviour. In June 2016, the Nitish government brought into force the Bihar Right to Public Grievance Redressal Act, empowering citizens with the legal right to seek redressal for their grievances related to all the schemes, programmes and services of all government departments.

In the following months, grievance-receiving centres were opened at the subdivisional, district and state levels: every centre would be a one-stop location for receiving grievances related to all departments. Citizens could also submit their complaints by email or through a dedicated mobile app, web portal or toll-free number to immediately get a receipt that carried the date and place of hearing. The hearing was conducted by a public grievance redressal officer who had independent authority with quasi-judicial powers. It was at such hearings that, for the first time, bureaucrats and citizens were seated at the same level, in similar chairs, in the same rows, as the quasi-judge heard the former's response to the latter's complaint. At least for the day of hearing, the power equation between the officers and the people changed. The bureaucrats could no longer ignore the citizens' pleas. They had to explain their inaction. As the time limit for redressal was 60 days, there could be hearings on other days too, when again the bureaucrats had to shed their aloofness from the hoi polloi. As the quasi-judge had independent authority, the judgment had every chance of going against the public servants. If the bureaucrat did not redress it within the time limit, the aggrieved party could appeal, which could mean more days of hearing and further erosion of their hubris.

According to official data, till June 2020, the quasi-judges had heard 7.56 lakh complaints and disposed of 6.86 lakh of them across the state. On an average, the quasi-judges received 525 complaints and passed orders on 476 of them every day since the redressal law came into force. Had the arming of the citizens with the two fundamental rights—the right to public service and the right to grievance redressal—really reformed the administration? Were all doors closed to corruption? In terms of petty corruption to an extent, maybe, but not to corruption in high places.

Bihar's GDP has maintained a higher growth rate than the national average, largely owing to high expenditure by the state government on building roads, bridges, power distribution and transmission networks, irrigation systems, hospitals, medical colleges, schools and other infrastructure. According to state finance officials, from an average of Rs 1000 crore during the Lalu–Rabri years, the annual government expenditure on projects rose to Rs 12,000 crore by 2010 and to Rs 45,000 crore by 2020. The Nitish years, which brought development, also proved to be a bonanza for businessmen of all kinds: the good, the bad and the ugly. There has arisen a whole new class of contractors who don political shirts or pay politicians for being their patrons and partners. There are many syndicates of businessmen, politicians and bureaucrats operating from the village to the state level to grab projects and make money. Most often they flaunt their illicit wealth without any fear or shame through opulent houses, land properties, apartments, luxury cars and jewellery.

People had given up believing that it was within any government's power to punish the plunderers among public servants. This is not to say that the Nitish government and the governments before had not arrested anyone under the Prevention of Corruption Act, but the judicial process was so slow, circuitous and never-ending that even if the culprits were penalized, it had no impact on the immediate environment. People did not get to see quick retribution. To give one example, in July 2007, a vigilance department team raided the house of Shiv Shankar Verma, secretary, minor irrigation department, and found him in possession of huge unaccounted wealth, including a bungalow, apartments, land, gold bars, jewellery, financial investments and cash. However, the case lingered on. It was for this reason that the Nitish government brought in a law in 2009, called the Bihar Special

Courts Act, to set up special courts for confiscation of properties and speedy trial in corruption cases. All through his election campaign for his second term, Nitish assured voters at every public meeting that he would confiscate the buildings of the corrupt and start schools there, receiving thunderous applause. The law came into force in 2010 and the Patna High Court quickly approved the opening of six special courts: two in Patna, two in Muzaffarpur and two in Bhagalpur. To prove that he meant business, Nitish got the properties of Shiv Shankar Verma confiscated. Verma challenged the confiscation in the Patna High Court and lost the case in August 2011.

No sooner had Verma lost the case than the government announced its decision to turn his stately bungalow in the Rukanpura locality of Patna into a school. Within a few days, the government primary school, earlier situated in a slum of Rukanpura, was moved to the bungalow. The slum was inhabited by penurious Dalit families whose co-breadwinners, men and women, did regular or odd low-paid jobs that nobody else in the world was ready to do. Perhaps their only consolation was that they were better-off than the destitutes: they had a hole for a hut and a small clay fireplace on which the pot boiled at least once daily. It was their children who went to the government primary school, a school whose conditions were not much different from those of the slum. So when these children, numbering about ninety, were taken to their new school housed in a luxurious, boundary-walled, three-storeyed bungalow with a forbidding heavy iron gate, they could not recover from their astonishment for months. One of the students (name withheld) recalled:

> Such a huge and dazzling house! I had never been inside one. To think that it was my school! Our school in the slum had no building of its own. It had a few rooms in a very old structure. We used to fear the building would collapse one day and we would be buried in the rubble. We were extremely fearful in the rainy season. The classrooms would leak and be damp. To make it worse, the open drains by the side of the building would overflow and fill our noses with stench. The classrooms had virtually no ventilation. Here, in the new school, every classroom has ceiling fans. In the old school

there were no toilets. In this palace, the bathrooms are bigger than our homes! There was no ground to play on during breaks. Here every floor has a terrace for us to gather on during breaks. Then there are spaces around the building inside the boundary wall.

The school was the beginning of the fulfilment of a dream Nitish had nurtured despite deep scepticism of several of his ministers and bureaucrats. Never before in the history of Indian democracy had the house of a corrupt public servant been seized and converted into a public school. Nitish told the *Hindustan Times* in Patna on 6 September 2011, after the school was inaugurated by a local Dalit leader: 'This is the beginning of a social change. If you have the will to fight corruption, you can take big steps. The people and I had been waiting for long for this to happen. Confiscation of property will have a far-reaching impact. Public servants will take a lesson.' His idea, he once told me, was also to send out a message to corrupt public servants that if they stole public money, it was not going to stay with them but would return to the public in the form of schools or shelters.

Buoyed by the success in the Verma case, the government confiscated the properties of some other bureaucrats, against whom a prima facie case of corruption had been established: Narain Mishra, former director general of police; Y.K. Jaiswal, former drug controller; and D.N. Choudhary, former director, state language department. The bureaucrats, having lost their cases in the Patna High Court in 2011, had challenged the constitutional validity of the Special Courts Act in the Supreme Court, which after many hearings rejected their pleas in 2015. The bureaucrats had argued that confiscation of properties was 'punishment before trial'. The Supreme Court said confiscation was 'interim' till the trial was decided, so it was not a 'punishment'. The bureaucrats argued that the act denied them the right to equality before law, as it treated them differently from the other accused. The Supreme Court said corruption among those occupying high public offices had become a 'social calamity' and that warranted a 'different control', which is what the act was intended to be.

That closed all the escape routes for corrupt public servants. The state government confiscated the properties of three other bureaucrats as well. It opened a school for differently abled children in the four-storeyed house of Narain Mishra; an orphanage in the bungalow of Raghuvansh Kunwar, a former motor vehicle inspector; and a residential school for girls from backward castes in the large house of Girish Kumar, a former clerk at the treasury office in Patna.

The Nitish government's pursuit of venality in high places continued through his third term. The government has been trying to establish prima facie cases against dozens of other officers in the special courts, so their houses too can be seized to open facilities for the underprivileged.

It would be highly erroneous to think that Nitish has won the war against corruption. The campaigns he mounted, equipped with the three new laws—the Right to Public Services Act, the Right to Public Grievance Redressal Act and the Special Courts Act—have brought him successes, but the beast is far from dead. The beast has veritably proved to be like the mythological demon who, even after being pinned down in one place, uses his illusory powers to become invisible in order to escape and find a new habitat. Between 2014 and 2015, its habitat was the office of the chairman of the Bihar School Examination Board, who took bribes to give merit ranking to examinees. It moved in 2016 to the office of an executive engineer of the public health engineering department, who embezzled funds meant for building toilets in villages. In 2017, its presence was detected in the offices of several bureaucrats and bank managers, and a non-government organization in Bhagalpur: together they had gobbled Rs 1600 crore of public money. By 2019, it had spread to the offices of 400 police executives who were promoting bootlegging and smuggling of liquor, after the Nitish government imposed total prohibition in 2016.

Nitish realized that corruption was like cancer. It spread silently inside the government and was detected only when the malignancy became visible in the well-developed stages.

epilogue i: economy

# the bird has begun to fly

In 2005, more than 90 per cent of the population of Bihar lived in the rural areas and 56 per cent of them were below the poverty line. In 2012, more than 88 per cent of the state's population lived in the rural areas, with 34 per cent of them below the poverty line. The rate of poverty reduction in Nitish's Bihar was faster than in India. Yet, the battle against poverty in the state has been like chipping away at a mountain. In human terms, even in 2012, more than 30 million of the 90 million men, women and children living in the villages and small towns of Bihar went to bed without enough food, wore old clothes, lived in a ramshackle shelter, had no electricity, cooking gas or piped drinking water, dropped out of or never went to school and died early for lack of good healthcare.

During 2010–20, much to everybody's amazement, the state consistently recorded high GDP growth (11.3 per cent in 2017–18 and 10.5 per cent in 2018–19, according to official data), but that did not rescue its vast masses from the swamp of poverty. Nitish has not been able to resolve the paradox of high economic growth and low poverty reduction. According to an analysis based on data from the National Statistical Office (NSO) on consumption expenditure, the overall poverty rate in Bihar rose from 33 per cent to more than 50 per cent between 2011–12 and 2017–18.[1] That meant 17 million more men, women and children in rural Bihar slipped into poverty, joining the 34 million people already there. It meant growth didn't create enough jobs. It meant the rural job-guarantee programme and other poverty-alleviation schemes were being poorly executed. It meant welfare benefits were hardly reaching the poor from government offices and panchayats.

In order to accelerate poverty alleviation, Nitish adopted the Andhra Pradesh model of creating self-help groups (SHGs) of the poor that would accumulate the savings of its members to give loans with interest, to either invest in agriculture or a new business, or to tide over food and health emergencies. The SHGs would be linked to banks. The banks would lend to the SHGs, the SHGs would distribute the loan among the members according to their needs and recover the money from them to repay the banks. Named Jeevika, this rural livelihood project has proved to be highly successful. Starting with a small number of SHGs and a few thousand families in four districts in 2007, Jeevika had set up 8.4 lakh SHGs with 99 lakh families as members across the state by 2019, according to a state government report.

Jeevika claims to have helped about 20 lakh families so far to enhance crop productivity and earn from non-farming activities such as poultry, goat-rearing and dairy. Ground reports suggest that the project has indeed helped a number of lower-caste families raise their incomes and gain social dignity. Nirmala, the forty-five-year-old female landless labourer from a lower caste who started a shop in her village with a SHG loan, says, 'Earlier, people would not even stand next to us. Now, they welcome me to their houses.'[2]

However, not many landless labourers like Nirmala have benefited from Jeevika. The project has played a very marginal role in the eradication of poverty. Figures can lie, but even if we believe that 20 lakh families have improved their earnings through Jeevika, it means that the remaining 79 lakh families enrolled have not. And 20 lakh beneficiary families constitute only 14 per cent of the total number of the state's poor families. Thus, in twelve years, Jeevika can claim to have raised the living standards of just 14 per cent of the poor. This surely is not mining the poverty mountain but just chipping away at it.

Landless farm labourers, who make up 30–40 per cent of the population in every village, continue to migrate in large numbers to towns both inside and outside the state for unskilled jobs. Even though these jobs are low-paid and insecure, the earnings are much higher than the farm work at home. The migrants can make savings, something they could only dream of as farm labourers. They can support their children's education, buy new clothes for members of their family, even buy a small piece of agricultural land. They owe their escape from poverty and social inferiority to the market and continue to have more faith in that redeemer than in the state. That is why the train of migration has not stopped in spite of the growth in the state's GDP. The landed castes just hate the train. A.K. Rai, a high-caste farmer from Naubatpur, said to me: 'The labourers just want to get out of the village. They may be cleaning sewers in Delhi or some town, but when they come home during some festival, they walk the village streets like high-ranking officers with a briefcase in hand.'

Sunil Singh, a large landowner in Jehanabad, echoes Rai's sentiments:

> Earlier I was god and labourers would gather in large numbers at my place to pray to me for favours, *Please give me work, please lend me a few rupees, please give me something to eat.* Today, most of them do not want to work in the fields. The few who do demand unaffordable wages, and even they might not be available when you need them if they are earning more elsewhere. Now, they are god and I have to go to their place and pray to them for favours.

An increasing number of Bihar's farmers are buying or hiring machines to bust 'labour arrogance'. Sudhanshu Singh of Bihta, who owns 20 acres of land, has bought every machine you can name: a tractor, rotavator, combine harvester, zero-till machine, thresher, chaff cutter, straw reaper and sprayer. He says:

> All my earnings come from my fields. With the coming of machines, farming has become very convenient. Unlike labourers, they work at all hours, without a break, with speed and accuracy. With technologies constantly improving, I am falling deeper and deeper in love with the machines. They are fantastic; they have just made my life heaven. Let the labourers go to hell!

The poor are happier too. In multiple surveys across 36 villages of Bihar, over a period of three decades (1980s–2000s), researchers from the Institute of Human Development found that only 30 per cent of working-age males still worked in the fields; the rest had moved to non-farming jobs inside and outside the state. The migrants sent Rs 20,000 every year to their families on average.[3] The poor families in the villages—whether they were engaged in farming or non-farming jobs—now had better meals, better clothes and better houses.

In a recent conversation with me, Nitish gave his own impressions of the changes in rural Bihar:

> Election campaigns are a crazy time for a candidate. He does not know where he would be at lunchtime. He has 20–25 people with him, if not more. Till the 1990s, if I landed in a village during an election, it would be hard to find a family that could fix lunch for 20–25 people on their sudden arrival. Now, many families can do so. Today, you go to a poor household in a village, they will have a cot for visitors. They have rice and cooking oil to fix lunch for at least two guests. Yes, true, Bihar even now gets the lion's share of the poverty pie chart. But tell me: Does anyone die of hunger in Bihar? Does anyone commit suicide?

The changes in a typical Bihar village are distinct. Until very recently, every village served a small number of large landowners, usually of a high caste, in their fields and at their homes. Not any more. Mobilization of backward castes and Dalits by political parties and militant communist groups unshackled their minds and the liberalization of the economy unfettered their feet. Their flight shook the foundations of the edifice of the power of the landlord. They did not know what to do with their fields. Their sons got attracted to high-paying private sector jobs in the big cities. There were divisions and subdivisions of property within the family.

Land ownership was losing its value as the sole marker of social status. The landlord had to reinvent himself if he had to maintain his high status. Big landowners like Sudhanshu Singh hitched their fields to the market: no wonder, the production and productivity of maize, coarse cereals, parboiled rice, vegetables, fruits, dairy and poultry have been growing at much higher rates in Bihar than the total foodgrain. Others used their capital, or sold parts of their land to start a 'respectable' business in the nearest town: a company showroom, an electronic goods store, a school, buses and trucks, even a pharmacy.

Vijay Singh of Kadilpur village in Vaishali district flung the vanity of his zamindar ancestry out of his window to set up a poultry house with 9,000 layer chicken on his land in 2016. In two years, he built another henhouse next to the first one. He says:

> Look, I am a Rajput, high-born, but who cares for your social status now unless you build it anew? I realized one thing very early. Unless you dirty your hands in the mud, you are not going to earn a good income. I grow potatoes, tobacco, vegetables and other commercial crops on 15 acres of my land. If you know your land, and if you know your market, there is nothing like agriculture. In six months, you get two rupees for one rupee of investment. Which bank doubles your money in six months? But I must tell you that I owe more to my hens than to my fields. They have made me what I am. And the beauty of it is that I do not have to go anywhere! The traders in local markets phone me, I quote my price, they come, pay and carry away the eggs. When the hens stop laying eggs, meat traders from other districts come buy them and cart them off.

It is not just the big landowners who have grabbed the opportunities offered by the market. Even the small landowners have done so. In Jasparha village of Vaishali, Mukesh Singh has capitalized on the growing demand for organic foods. He grows rice, maize, vegetables, mangoes and other crops, and has also dabbled in fisheries. The technologies he uses for sowing, irrigation, manuring and plant protection are borrowed from science but improved upon by him. He has no problem finding buyers for his goods.

Rakesh Kumar has been growing organic vegetables—potato, onion, bitter gourd and bottle gourd—in the 3 acres he has in Sohdi village of Nalanda district for the past ten years. For him, too, the market is the least of his problems. Traders from Nepal, Mumbai and Kolkata are ready to pay a premium for his produce. He says:

> My vegetables look close-textured and solid, have a rich taste and can remain in the kitchen basket for three to four days without the skin or flesh shrinking or loosening even the slightest bit. You don't need a fridge if you are eating organic. My cauliflower has densely packed florets and looks attractively white. My vegetables stand out from the ones produced using chemicals, which are anaemic and tasteless and rot quickly. Do you know the fun of it? People pay more for my vegetables, not because they are organic but because they are of better quality.

Still, farmers, small or big, who are profiting from the links they established with the market on their own are few. The majority, which is made up of small farmers, have no market intelligence and sell their produce at the farm gate, at the prices determined by local traders. They get a very small share of the price the consumer pays. In order to increase the bargaining power of small farmers, the Central government and NABARD (National Bank for Rural Development) have been encouraging them to organize as farmer producer organizations (FPOs). The idea is to increase the share of the producer in the ultimate price by aggregating small marketable surpluses of members to make up one large surplus that gets the best price from the market. The members would get market intelligence on their mobiles and payments would be transferred online to their accounts according to their share in the total produce sold.

The number of FPOs formed in Bihar in the last few years has been small. FPOs must become a special focus of the Nitish government if the lives of small farmers are to change. With electricity reaching every village and every home, FPOs can increase the bargaining power of the fishermen, weavers and artisans too. The government has achieved tremendous success in forming SHGs under the Jeevika programme. The Jeevika SHGs of small farmers, fishermen, weavers and artisans should be restructured as FPOs.

FPOs have enormous potential to revolutionize agriculture. Aggregation of small surpluses will spur the development of cold storages, where producers can keep their produce to sell it when the prices are high in domestic and export markets. Although the number of cold storages has grown phenomenally in the state in the past ten years, it is still inadequate in terms of the overall demand.

Aggregation will lure small and big investments in agro-industry, which can be a key potential driver of the state economy. Investments in other industries have eluded Bihar. Agro-industry can be its main industry. Agro-industrial units are few and scattered: the state needs to have more of them with organic and mutually profitable links with agriculture. It can happen only with aggregation under the FPOs. Today, even Nalanda and Vaishali, which are famous for the production of potatoes and bananas, respectively, do not have any agro-industry worth its name. In the absence of aggregation, the big brands that manufacture potato chips have not looked at Nalanda. Nor have the companies that process bananas for making flour and chips, and banana stem to make textiles, paper, bags and jewellery come to Vaishali. A few local entrepreneurs who set up small agro-industries gave up for lack of government handholding.

Anand Sharma, who started a banana-fibre unit in Nawanagar in Vaishali, says:

> The state government sent us to Tamil Nadu for training, but after that there was nobody to guide us. Me and two friends took a bank loan of Rs 12 lakh to buy six machines to produce banana fibre. The machines were of low quality, they had a complicated process, they took a long time before delivering the final product. We had planned for the cost of ten workers; we had to employ thirty. The market wanted regular supply in tonnes, we took two months to produce one tonne. In two to three months, our entire loan was consumed. We closed down.

FPOs alone can build the agro-industry, and the agro-industry alone can exorcise poverty by generating vast opportunities of employment both in agriculture and the industry based on its produce. In the coming years, the Nitish government—if it comes back to power—needs to mobilize all its resources to grow FPOs and the agro-industry statewide, if it wants to change Bihar.

On 20 June 2020, Prime Minister Narendra Modi launched a Rs 50,000-crore scheme named Garib Kalyan Rojgar Abhiyaan, or the Job Campaign for the Welfare of the Poor, to create jobs for the millions of migrant workers who had returned to the six major labour-supplying states of Bihar, Uttar Pradesh, Madhya Pradesh, Rajasthan, Jharkhand and Odisha from the big cities owing to the coronavirus-induced lockdown. 'The labour, talent and skills that were behind the rapid growth of cities,' Modi said in his inaugural speech, 'will now spur development in the villages.'⁴ Alas, the grandiloquence of Modi's oratory was not matched by any prodigiousness in the scheme. It was a temporary scheme, limited in purpose, to provide daily bread to the penniless, starving and angry migrant workers for four months by employing them in the government's ongoing rural road, housing, water, sanitation, underground cabling and railway projects.

Modi's critics saw a poll angle in the scheme directed at the Bihar Assembly elections due in November 2020. They claimed that he had launched it to win back the support of the migrant workers, many of whom had received no sympathy or support from the Central or state governments when they walked hundreds of miles on foot, in the scorching summer sun, with their wives and children in April–May 2020. Even if we were to dismiss the political criticism, it was hard to ignore that his campaign provided temporary, and not permanent, employment to them. At the end of the four months, the migrant workers would be forced to go back to the cities. The scheme, even in the economic sense, was intended to support them in times of hardship and distress, not to reverse outmigration. Even though the works to be undertaken were related to infrastructure, they weren't linked with the state government's high-priority areas of industrial development such as agribusiness and agro-industry, including food processing, which were aimed at the generation of permanent employment for local workers.

Most of the migrant workers were from rural backgrounds and quite familiar with agricultural and post-harvest processes. They could build a successful career in agribusiness and food processing. For instance, in the flood-prone Mutalupur village of Muzaffarpur district, there was a wetland spread over 87 acres that had never produced anything. A retired agricultural scientist from the village motivated twenty-two local small farmers to form an FPO to develop fisheries on the wetland. This became so successful that the youth of their families stopped migrating to other states for jobs.[5]

Bihar used to be a fish-deficit state. During the fifteen-year Lalu–Rabri rule, fisheries, like most other sectors, suffered neglect. Fish from Andhra Pradesh, where freshwater fisheries have developed into a gigantic agribusiness, filled the state's markets. Gradually, with the reanimation of fishermen societies by the Nitish government, fish production began to rise in the state. Import from Andhra Pradesh was progressively reduced. In 2005–06, the annual fish yield in the state was 2.79 lakh tonnes. By 2016, the state had begun to produce 5 lakh tonnes of fish against a consumption of 6 lakh tonnes. By 2020, it became a fish-surplus state and was exporting 30,000 tonnes annually to West Bengal and Nepal. It was not just fish production—livestock production too had increased substantially. In 2005–06, the state produced 1.75 tonnes of meat, by 2014–15, this went up to 2.94 lakh tonnes, and in 2018–19, it was 3.64 lakh tonnes. Egg production rose from 100 crore in 2005–06 to 176 crore in 2018–19.

Agriculture, which encompasses fisheries and livestock, is the cow whose udders feed the food-processing industry. It is the foundation on which stands the industry's edifice, to which the state is seeking to add further storeys. Bihar is blessed with fertile land, abundant water, good climate and great indigenous farming skills. The state is the country's largest producer of vegetables and the second-largest producer of fruits. In just a few years it has become the largest producer of honey— and behind the success story of beekeeping were landless peasants and women.

However, agriculture cannot employ the entire population of a village. By a rough estimate, it employs a third. Two-thirds work non-farming jobs. Mechanization of agriculture and migration of labour are proving to be the cause and effect of one another, scaling up the demand for non-farming jobs. Food processing can be the bridge to connect the farm with the labourers living away from it. These labourers are those who constitute the 30 million or more Biharis living below the poverty line, according to the World Bank, and include the 2 million or more migrant workers who returned to the state during the coronavirus-induced lockdown in April–June 2020. Agribusiness, combined with food processing, can reduce poverty at a rapid rate.

The 400 food-processing units set up in the state between 2008 and 2016 employed over 48,000 persons, making it an average of 120 persons per unit.

With its organic linkages to agribusiness, the food-processing industry can provide indirect employment to the primary producers. It is here that the aggregation of primary produce through cooperative societies, Jeevika SHGs and FPOs can play a very important role. Bihar produces 85 per cent of makhanas, or fox nuts, in the country. The annual yield of about 10,000 tonnes, commercially valued at Rs 500 crore in 2019, is cultivated by half a million fishing families grouped into cooperative societies and processed by hundreds of small units. The rising export of makhana to other states and countries has made the societies increase production by cultivating it even in fields, by filling them with water, in addition to ponds, lakes, tanks and wetlands in which they traditionally grew it.

The traditional makhana-processing industry used a very cumbersome and time-consuming process. Now, the Indian Council of Agricultural Research (ICAR) has developed a machine that can produce popped makhana, the final marketable product, in 20 hours instead of the average 60 hours. The state government has to develop as many clusters as possible to provide common facilities such as roads, power, technology and transport to the makhana-processing industry, with robust linkages to the primary producer cooperatives.

Dairy is a food-processing industry that has the potential to provide direct and indirect employment to millions of people. According to the Bihar Economic Survey, 2019–20, the state government's cooperative milk federation (COMFED), with its brand name Sudha, which collected milk from 7,750 cooperative societies in 2006–07, was collecting it from about 16,900 societies in 2018–19. In 2009–10, its procurement was 12 lakh kg of milk daily, by 2014–15 it was about 17 lakh kg and by 2018–19 it was over 19 lakh kg. Apart from milk, COMFED also makes milk products like a variety of sweets, ghee, curd and ice cream, and sells them through its retail outlets, whose number rose from 9558 in 2013–14 to 13,099 in 2015–16 and 19,238 in 2018–19. However, despite its rapid expansion, COMFED collected only 13 per cent of the state's total annual milk production of 98 lakh kg.

According to official data, between 2006 and 2015, the SIPB approved about 2,300 proposals, 1,400 of which were for food processing. After the state government placed food processing at the top of its priority list in its industrial investment promotion policy in 2016, backing it with alluring incentives, a stream of investment proposals has flown into the sector. Between 2016 and 2019, nearly 50 per cent of the 900 approved proposals were for food processing, with an investment of Rs 2,300 crore.

The Nitish government has not yet been successful in getting many large companies to invest in food processing in the state. There is an odd ITC dairy in Munger, and a Britannia biscuit factory and a Godrej Agrovet animal and poultry feed factory at Hajipur: most of the food-processing units fall under the MSME category and include papad, pickles, jam and jelly-making units to spice factories and rice mills. Maize is one of the main crops of Bihar, and yet only one-tenth of its total yield is processed within the state to make flakes, flour, starch or poultry feed.

The number of registered MSMEs in the state has slowly increased from 1.63 lakh in 2006–07 to 1.81 lakh in 2009–10 and 1.99 lakh in 2014–15. One in four of them was an agro-based industry, a category that included food processing. Between 2015 and 2019, the MSME ministry of the Government of India asked both proposed and existing MSMEs to register themselves through their Udyog Aadhaar web portal to be eligible for loan, subsidy and concessional land. 'Backward' Bihar beat all states with the registration of 8.73 lakh MSMEs. The elephantine MSME expansion, from 1.99 lakh in 2015 to 8.73 lakh in 2019, was astonishing. State government officials attributed it to two factors: one was the waiving of government inspection before registration, and the second was the offering of land at concessional rates, loans and subsidies. How many of them are real entrepreneurs and will survive, only the future can tell. Researchers Barna Ganguli and Debdatta

Saha, in their study of the food-processing industry of Bihar, found that 'enticed by the subsidies, some non-entrepreneurs with very low-risk appetite entered certain sub-sectors such as rice and wheat mills. These units, according to established players and bankers, lacked adequate information, skilled manpower and equity capital . . . and did not survive the pressures of competition'.[6] In another study, the same researchers found that 'small firms have tended to take advantage of the support schemes put in place by the government whilst not necessarily utilising them to grow their enterprises'.[7]

However, even if some of the 8.73 lakh MSMEs turn out to have been designed for fraud, it does not take away from the fact that MSMEs alone can give Bihar the wide industrial manufacture and employment base it so badly needs. Today, most of the state's demand for industrial goods is met by imports from other states. This is shown by the phenomenal increase in the share of the services (tertiary) sector in the state's economy—a sector that includes trade, repairs, hotels, transport, storage and communications—and near-stagnation in the share of the goods (secondary) sector, which includes manufacturing. While the share of the services sector rose from 55.5 per cent in 2011–12 to 61.2 per cent in 2018–19, that of the goods sector rose marginally from 18.8 per cent to 19.1 per cent during the same period.

One of the biggest challenges before the state government in the next few years is going to be to support, handhold, encourage and equip MSMEs to produce industrial goods and make profits by substituting imports in order to be sustainable and evolutionary in terms of technology and scale of production. The other challenge will be establishing strong bridges between the MSMEs in food processing and the FPOs of agricultural producers. The third challenge will be to develop labour skills, as it develops MSME entrepreneurial skills, in order to create enough jobs within the state to end or significantly reduce migration. In 2006–07, there were 5.36 lakh persons employed in 1.63 lakh MSMEs in the state. In 2009–10, there were 5.9 lakh persons employed in 1.81 lakh MSMEs. In 2014–15, 6.76 lakh persons were employed in 1.99 lakh MSMEs. Taking three jobs per MSME as an average, it can be projected that the 8.73 lakh MSMEs registered with the government—if we assume all of them to be genuine—can provide employment to 26 lakh persons, a number more than that of the migrant workers who returned to the state during the coronavirus lockdown in 2020.

The state economy Nitish inherited from Lalu–Rabri was a bird with a broken wing. During his first term, the wing healed and the bird began to flit about. During his second term, the bird began to glide. In the third term, it began to fly. Near the end of the third term, the bird has been flying but at low altitudes. Whether it soars higher or not, only the future will tell.

## epilogue ii: politics

# no gold, but glory

Even though the wheels of socio-economic change were moving slowly, people believed that only Nitish Kumar could accelerate them. He was voted in for the second time in 2010 with a mountainous majority—206 in a house of 243, 115 for his JD(U) and 91 for the BJP. His relationship with the BJP was going on fine, his allied governance was going on fine, until Narendra Modi cast his shadow over the national political scene a couple of years later. An epidemic of scams had struck UPA-II and the voters were looking for an alternative. The RSS saw a big opportunity there but decided not to bet on L.K. Advani again, or on any other star in the BJP galaxy—Nitin Gadkari, Rajnath Singh, Arun Jaitley or Sushma Swaraj. They picked Narendra Modi. He was an RSS preacher who had become a BJP election tactician. An election tactician who had become a chief minister. A chief minister who had become a legendary figure of Hindu machismo. A legendary figure of Hindu machismo who had then become an icon of economic advance. What more could Mother India want in her prime ministerial candidate!

But Nitish differed. In 2005, when the BJP had wanted to send Modi to boost the NDA's Bihar Assembly election campaign, Nitish had said no. In 2010, when Modi had advertised his Rs 40-million donation to the Bihar government for the Kosi flood victims, with an archival photo of Nitish and him holding hands on stage, Nitish had returned the cheque. The same evening, Modi, along with other BJP leaders who had gathered in Patna for a party national executive meeting, had been invited to a dinner by Nitish. However, Nitish called off the dinner. 'I feared the media would be on the prowl at the dinner to capture Modi and me laughing or eating together with the intention to "expose" my "hypocrisy",' Nitish said to me the following day. 'As the host, I would have to be pleasing to everyone.' To him, Modi was politically untouchable then.

None of the top BJP leaders publicly criticized Nitish for his undisguised hostility to Modi. There were three reasons for this. One was that each of them was a distant or close competitor of Modi's as the NDA prime ministerial candidate. They would have loved to see Nitish cut him to size: he would get their rival out of the way without any blood on their hands. Two, they knew that Nitish was opposing Modi to prevent the loss of support among the Muslims, which he had been building up over the years by taking strong positions on communally sensitive issues, despite being a partner of the BJP. The BJP could never get Muslim votes on its own. Three, the BJP had grown phenomenally in Bihar owing to the alliance with Nitish. From 37 Assembly seats in February 2005, they had 91 in November 2010, and had to follow him.

As the preference of RSS and BJP workers for Modi became more and more pronounced, Nitish sent out warnings through the media that he would never accept him as the NDA's prime ministerial candidate. As is his rhetorical style, he didn't name the person but he also didn't leave anyone in doubts who he was talking about: 'The NDA candidate must be one whose name does not generate fear in the society, one who can take everyone along'; 'The country cannot accept anyone espousing divisive politics'; and 'The BJP must consult its allies before deciding on the name.'[1]

Many believed that Nitish was opposing Modi because he wanted to be the NDA's prime ministerial candidate himself. That was not true. He was shrewd enough not to entertain such thoughts. He never lobbied for the candidature for himself within the NDA. Nor did his name ever figure in any of the discussions of the BJP top brass. He was very clear that the prime ministerial candidate had to be from the largest party in the alliance. His party was small and restricted to a state. He knew that if he embarked on such an adventure, he would end up a miserable fool. He said to me in an interview:

The lesson from history is very clear: never should the leader of a small party try to be [the] PM with the support of a large party. Charan Singh, Chandrashekhar, Deve Gowda, I.K. Gujral . . . they all fell with their faces down. The Congress did not even allow Charan Singh to face the Lok Sabha. Chandrashekhar quit before the trust vote, giving some absurd excuse. The boats of Gowda and Gujral were overturned by the Congress just a little way off the coast. How could I even think of taking such a route when there were these four self-destructive examples before my eyes? Coalition with a large party is okay. Leading a [Central] government with the support of a large party is a totally stupid idea.

So what was he trying to do by opposing Modi? 'To stop an icon of Hindu machismo taking over the BJP,' said a close associate of Nitish. He was not opposing the BJP; he was opposing Modi. He was also opposing Modi because he thought Modi had a domineering political style. In the past, the BJP's central leaders had never imposed themselves on their state units, allowing Nitish full freedom in policymaking and governance. Nitish feared the situation would change with Modi.

Modi had already cultivated a vocal group within the Bihar unit of the BJP to orchestrate support for his prime ministerial candidature. The group included some cabinet colleagues of Nitish. They sang praises of Modi daily, defying Nitish who had declared him unfit to rule multireligious India. Nevertheless, Nitish continued to oppose Modi, hoping the BJP would select someone like Advani, though he never suggested anyone's name to the party's leadership. 'Would you have stayed on with the BJP if the party had chosen Advani as PM candidate again?' I once asked him. 'Of course,' he said. 'Why, I supported Advani as the PM candidate in 2009 and campaigned for him.'

The BJP risked losing Nitish as an ally and, consequently, a number of Lok Sabha seats in Bihar if they endorsed Modi as the prime ministerial candidate. Eventually, they took that risk, venturing forth on the surge in support for Modi. They calculated that against the large gain Modi's popularity promised countrywide, the loss in Bihar would be small. At the end of their two-day meeting in Panaji on 10 June 2013, the BJP national executive declared Modi as the chairman of the party's national election campaign committee, a euphemism for the prime ministerial candidate. The BJP galaxy eventually concluded that if they did not hang on to Modi, they might hang together.

Nitish stormed out of the NDA, a scene that drew a big applause from the anti-BJP camp, triggering speculations that he could be the face of a joint front against Modi. That was the first time Nitish came close to fighting for the prime minister's office. In the following months, however, there were no talks between him and the rest of the anti-BJP camp. Each party in the camp was confined to its own tent.

He decided to go it alone. Though he could not be a prime ministerial candidate, he was at the peak of his popularity in Bihar. In the 2000 Assembly elections, he had been way behind the BJP and the RJD with just 8.65 per cent of the vote share. In the 2004 Lok Sabha elections, he had left the BJP far behind with a 22 per cent share, though he failed to catch up with the RJD. In the 2009 Lok Sabha elections, he took a clear lead even over the RJD, with a 24 per cent share, a lead he maintained in the 2010 Assembly elections with a 22.58 per cent vote share.

Nitish saw himself as a champion gladiator in Bihar politics. He had outplayed everyone in the arena. He had made JD(U) the number-one party. He had doubled its vote base from 3.2 million to 6.5 million in ten years, beginning in 2000. He had endeared himself to large sections of the poor and women. He had earned the appreciation of Muslims by restraining Hindu extremists from pursuing their vicious and violent agenda in Bihar and by expanding state patronage to the lower castes of Muslims despite being in alliance with the BJP. However, most Muslims had expressed their appreciation only in words thus far, not in votes. Now that he had dissociated himself from the BJP, he expected them to do so in a big way.

Though the anti-BJP camp denied him the opportunity to be a national challenger to Modi, Nitish decided to fight and defeat him in Bihar. He went to the battlefield with a pair of what he thought were his most potent weapons: the first, his campaign message that tore apart Modi's garb of a pluralist redeemer—bringer of good times *for all*—and the second, which pooh-poohed the 'Gujarat model of development'.

Both his weapons, however, veered way off target in the Lok Sabha elections of 2014. He was almost buried in the avalanche of the Modi cult. He won just 2 seats against 20 in 2009. In 2014, as many as 23 of his 38 candidates failed to get even one-sixth of the votes polled in their constituencies, forfeiting their security deposits with the Election Commission. His party's vote share plunged from 22 per cent in 2009 to 16 per cent in 2014.

He was stunned. Baffled. Heartbroken. He quit as the captain of the state government ship, picking Jitan Ram Manjhi, an ordinary seaman from the rear decks, to steer the vessel instead. 'I saw no point in continuing as chief minister,' he told me a few weeks later. 'I had expected the people would vote for me for all the good work I had done. But they bought the Modi utopia.'

Everybody, including his partymen, thought he would be back at the helm in a few months; after all, he had submitted resignations several times as a Union minister on 'moral grounds' and returned to the government. The selection of a nobody as his successor lent credence to such speculations. However, month after month, when the winds passing his house carried no murmurs of his return, Manjhi, who had been ready to move any moment, unpacked his bags and decided to settle down. A top JD(U) leader said to me anonymously:

> For three months, Jitan Ram Manjhi was okay. But then he started changing things. He started dismantling the systems Nitish Kumar had built for effective and transparent governance. He let the work started by Nitish stagnate or slow down. He did not have even one-hundredth of Nitish's vision and governing ability, but he started behaving like a CM forever. Most of us feared our party would fare badly in the Assembly polls in 2015 if Manjhi continued, but Nitish was not ready to take over as CM again. He was deeply hurt by the Lok Sabha defeat. He was also not keeping well. Manjhi and four or five other party MLAs were taking advantage of the situation. Manjhi began building a coterie of politicians and officers around

him. Corruption climbed to the top offices. This was something unthinkable when Nitish was CM. Now, the top guys were brazenly asking before approving projects, '*Isme mera kya*? [How much do I get out of this?]'

Manjhi caused a series of embarrassments to the party and Nitish Kumar. He told the media that though Nitish Kumar 'did a fine job by expediting development, at the same time it cannot be denied that the ugly face of corruption also manifested itself in good measure'. However, if Manjhi's intention was to convey to the people that the 'ugly face of corruption' no more 'manifested' under his government, it was defeated by his own public remark that 'small traders who indulge in black marketing should be condoned'. Manjhi was to make it even more obvious later with his admission in a public speech: 'Contractors and corrupt engineers paid bribes to several ministers, a part of which was given to me as well.'

Nitish gave Manjhi sufficient warnings, but he did not care as he now had the patronage of Sharad Yadav. Yadav, who had piggybacked on Nitish all these years, had not been allowed by him to exercise any influence over his government. His heart bore niggling pains of the paradox: he was the party president, yet he had no influence over his party's only government. With Manjhi in the CM's office, he broke free of his shackles to enjoy having his say in the government's decisions.

Nitish had quit as CM, but he had not quit his party, he had not quit politics. He planned to lead the party campaign in the 2015 Assembly elections and return as CM if the voters gave him a mandate. But Manjhi upset his plans. With Yadav's backing, he was trying to run away with Nitish's ship.

The BJP's battleship, with its 88 MLAs on board, cheered Manjhi on, offering him support. Nitish was in a dilemma: he had picked Manjhi because he was a 'mahadalit', one from the poorest of the poor castes, whose upliftment he had made an important mission of his government. With Manjhi as his government's face, he wanted to consolidate and expand his base among the mahadalits—by boosting their pride, the fact that one of them was CM and by making them feel indebted to Nitish for making it possible. If he removed him from the chief minister's office, he risked losing a section of his mahadalit constituency. But if he did not remove him, he risked losing a section of his party.


Indeed, the JD(U) in government had not been very stable since Nitish quit the NDA. The party depended on the Congress, the CPI and Independents for its majority in the Assembly. Its decimation in the Lok Sabha elections, followed by Nitish's resignation as CM, created an environment in which fault lines in the organization emerged and factions jostled for power. In this period of instability in the party, there were some MLAs who were tempted to switch over to the BJP, which they saw as the new powerhouse.

It started with the elections for 3 Rajya Sabha seats in the state, a month after the Lok Sabha defeat. With 115 MLAs, the JD(U) would have easily won all the 3 seats had the BJP not stoked the ambitions of some of them. The only way the JD(U) could foil the BJP's design was with the support of the RJD, which had 22 MLAs. Nitish had to choose between the ignominy of yet another defeat by Modi and the unappealing prospect of seeking Lalu's help, the villain of the Bihar story of which he was the hero. It was not an easy decision, but he finally told himself that the enemy in front of him was Modi, not Lalu. According to a top JD(U) source, Nitish had a conversation with Lalu on the phone. Badly hurt in the Lok Sabha elections himself, Lalu agreed to join him to keep the Modi juggernaut at bay, though he sold his fear-driven decision as magnanimity to the public: 'Nitish's house is on fire, so he called the fire brigade.'

The seed of the JD(U)–RJD engagement, sown during the Rajya Sabha elections, germinated during the by-polls to 10 Assembly constituencies a few months later, when the Congress too joined them. They held their fort in the four constituencies they had won in 2010 and drove the BJP out of 2 of their 6 seats, an electoral response that brought the necessity of an alliance home to Nitish and Lalu.

The Assembly elections were due towards the end of 2015. Both of them realized that alone they would not be able to block the advance of Modi and had to build an alliance—and to be still stronger, a grand alliance, a *mahagathbandhan*, that would take in the Congress. The mahagathbandhan was necessary as Bihar's electoral world had become tripolar, with the JD(U), the RJD and the BJP each agglomerating groups of particular castes around themselves, feeding on the silent and bloody mutinies against the old social order that had brought the lower castes into conflict with the higher castes. Every caste supported a party to retain or gain power in their village, and the party supported the caste to retain or gain power in the legislature. Caste–party relationships were enduring as social battles do not end in a day. Nitish and Lalu drew their strengths from such relationships. The JD(U) had got just 2 seats in 2014, but 5.6 million people had voted for the party. The RJD had got just 4 seats, but 7.2 million people had voted for it. If they combined forces, they would have 13 million voters, 3 million more than the BJP. If the Congress too came along, they would have 16 million voters with them, 6 million more than the BJP.

Though the arithmetic for their alliance attaining a majority in the next Assembly looked simple, the power equations between Nitish and Lalu were not so. Lalu was barred by court from contesting elections; so he could not be the chief minister. But he wanted to be the controller of the prospective alliance. According to a JD(U) leader, Lalu's position was:

I was Nitish's senior in the undivided Janata Dal. I became chief minister much before he did. I have a much larger constituency. I have Muslims with me; he never got them because of his alliance with the BJP. I got 20 per cent of the votes in 2014, he only 16 per cent. He desperately needs me to consolidate backward caste support and get the Muslim vote. He is needy; he must accept my superiority.

Nitish, however, was not ready to be controlled by Lalu. All the political capital he had accumulated was by making Lalu's bedridden Bihar walk. He was seen as a miracle worker. His innovative policymaking, effective governance, uncompromising commitment to pluralism and graceful speeches had earned him public respect countrywide, placing him on top in the list of politicians fit for the prime minister's office.

People voted for a JD(U)–BJP alliance government twice because they trusted Nitish as the chief minister. A small number of Muslims too voted for the alliance for this reason.

The alliance seemed to be slipping out of Nitish's hands as Lalu failed to resolve his dilemma: *to command or to conform.* Then both of them saw a streak of hope in the talks initiated by the Samajwadi Party president, Mulayam Singh, for the merger of the six splinters of what was once the Janata Dal—the Samajwadi Party, the RJD, the JD(U), the Janata Dal(Secular), the Indian National Lok Dal and the Samajwadi Janata Party—to make a single party that could challenge Modi and the BJP at the national level. But the talks stretched on endlessly: it was not easy to bring a divided family, each unit with its own kitchen, back under one roof to eat from a common kitchen. Most of these socialist parties had turned into family-owned political enterprises over the years, the mantle being passed on from generation to generation. They feared Modi, but they also feared losing their fiefdoms in integration.

Nitish worked spiritedly for a merger, not only because his JD(U) was not a family estate but also because he saw two clear results emerging from it. One, it would create a national socialist–secularist alternative to Modi, with a much larger social base than the Congress. Two, although Mulayam would be the new party's president, Nitish would have the opportunity to emerge as its prime ministerial candidate for 2019 based on the strength of his work and image. Three, the merger would leave Lalu with no option but to accept Nitish as the CM candidate for 2015, allowing him to take control of the party and government. Nitish had already become the CM again by removing Manjhi in February 2015, while the confabulations for a merger were going on and on.

It took two more months before Mulayam Singh announced the merger to the media in New Delhi, accompanied by Nitish, Lalu, Sharad Yadav and Deve Gowda. Beyond that announcement, however, the road for the new entity was not made clear. Mulayam Singh said the leaders of the six parties were going to hold discussions later to decide on the name, the flag, the symbol, the policies and programmes of the new party. This clearly suggested that there were problems, as some time back they had named the new party the Samajwadi Janata Dal and even adopted the Samajwadi Party's symbol, the bicycle, and said they would fight under '*ek jhanda, ek nishaan* [One flag, one symbol]'.

Apart from the other differences, what came in the way of a merger was Jitan Ram Manjhi laying claim to the JD(U) symbol, the arrow, saying his group was the 'real JD(U)'. Nitish refused to go to voters with the bicycle as the party symbol, as the arrow symbol would then go to Manjhi, giving a 'political nobody' a big advantage as any number of JD(U) voters could press the button for the arrow, unaware that it no more belonged to the party. Mulayam and other socialist leaders put the conglomeration on hold and decided to start with a JD(U)–RJD alliance at the state level, as a prelude to a formal national merger.

Lalu agreed to an alliance with Nitish but refused to accept him as the CM candidate. He said, 'We will select the leader after election results.' Nitish told Mulayam and the other leaders that the alliance could win only if he was projected as the CM: vagueness would only make people think that Lalu was going to have control and his 'jungle raj' would return. Mulayam and the other leaders spoke to Lalu again, but he resisted the proposal. He said Nitish and he had been political rivals. Their constituencies had crossed swords in many elections. The Yadavs, his primary base, would not easily agree to support Nitish, a Kurmi, as the CM candidate. The Muslims, his other base, would be even more reluctant to do so. If Nitish was announced as the CM candidate before elections, the Yadavs and Muslims might not wholeheartedly support the alliance. In order to get their full support, he argued, they should not name any CM candidate; they should choose one after the polls.

Nitish knew this was not the real reason why Lalu was refusing to name him the CM candidate. '*Woh chahate the ki humko mutthi mein rakhein, hum unki ichha se chalein* [He wanted me to be his puppet, to do what he wanted],' Nitish told me. After a few weeks, Nitish gave up. At that moment, he received a proposal from Rahul Gandhi to form an alliance with the Congress, independent of the RJD, for the Bihar Assembly polls. He had a meeting with Rahul, during which they agreed to fight the polls together. Nitish knew that with this alliance the fight was going to be triangular and that the BJP would profit from the division in the Opposition's votes. 'But I decided to take the risk,' he said.

Mulayam Singh and the heads of the other Janata Dal splinter groups were alarmed. A JD(U)–Congress alliance would be the last nail in the coffin of the yet-to-be-born Samajwadi Janata Dal. Mulayam called Nitish and Lalu for a discussion at his residence in New Delhi to resolve differences, but Lalu would still not agree to go to polls with Nitish as the CM candidate. Nitish came away from the meeting convinced that he had taken the right decision to go with the Congress. But after he left, Mulayam and Sharad Yadav warned Lalu of the risks Nitish's alliance with the Congress posed to his party and the Janata Dal merger. Lalu gave in with great reluctance. On 8 June 2015, Mulayam, flanked by Sharad and Lalu, announced to the media that Nitish was going to be the CM candidate of the JD(U)–RJD alliance. When Lalu was asked by the media why he agreed to it, he said, 'I am willing to drink all types of poison in order to crush the cobra of communalism.'

Nitish, who was back in Patna, was baffled and distressed by the news. In anguish, he did not come out of his house for four days, receiving no visitors, holding no meetings. He had closed the RJD chapter and made up his mind to go with the Congress. According to senior JD(U) leaders, he did really want to go with the Congress. He believed that would change the course of Indian politics. The alliance would have catapulted him into mainstream national politics, opening up the chances for him to be the PM, with several parties wanting to oust Modi joining it. The announcement by the three Goliath Yadavs threatened to shatter his dream.

Mulayam and Sharad kept urging Nitish daily to accept the offer. He was in a fix: if he accepted the offer, he would lose primacy in the alliance with the Congress, as the RJD had been a Congress ally for many years. Also, he would lose the direct equation and parity with Rahul Gandhi; he would lose the chance of emerging as the nucleus of the Opposition. On the other hand, an alliance with the RJD had its advantages: no scattering of backward-caste votes, zero waste of Muslim votes, higher chances of victory and the scope for a national political trajectory reduced but not closed to him with the Congress also in alliance. At the end of four days of mental churning, he accepted the offer.

In the Assembly elections five months later, the JD(U)–RJD–Congress alliance pulped the BJP. They captured 178 of the 243 seats. They wrested back their fort from Modi within a year. Nitish was celebrated as a hero, as a vanquisher of Modi, the giant. He had once again emerged as the fittest challenger to Modi in 2019. Things were going fine for him, until he realized, only a few months into his new tenure, that his alliance with the RJD might not last very long.

Since the time the JD(U)–RJD government was formed, Lalu had missed no opportunity to remark that even though his party had a larger number of MLAs (80) than the JD(U) (71), he had 'made' Nitish the CM because he had made that commitment before the elections. And he never forgot to add that he had to make that commitment as he could not fight elections owing to his conviction in the fodder scam, and since his two sons were too young to be claimants to the CM's office. That made it look like Nitish was the CM owing to circumstances and not because of his leadership ability or political strength. Some RJD leaders frequently echoed Lalu's views.

'Knowing Lalu's anarchic nature, I was prepared for some amount of *gadbad*, some disorderliness and confusion that he might cause in the administration,' Nitish told me. 'But things soon started going too far.'

A top bureaucrat recalled:

> Rogues who had enjoyed political patronage during Lalu–Rabri's fifteen-year reign started raising their heads again. They felt their government was back. Lalu would tell everybody, '*Ab hamara chalega* [My word will prevail now].' He got his two sons—Tejaswi Yadav, who was deputy chief minister and held several portfolios, including the Public Works Department, and Tej Pratap Yadav, who too held several portfolios, including health—as well as other ministers from his party to do his bidding. He would directly give instructions to the officers of the departments of his sons and other party ministers. He would even telephone police sub-inspectors to ask them to favour someone. The impression Lalu wanted to create was that Nitish was the king by his grace: he was senior, Nitish was junior; Nitish had the government, he had the power.

As a part of his campaign to speed up the prosecution of criminal politicians, Nitish had got murder convict Mohammad Shahabuddin transferred to the jail in Siwan, his native district where he had committed most of his crimes, to face a fast-track court. Shahabuddin had been the RJD MP four times. He was very close and important to Lalu for mobilizing the Muslim vote. One day, the RJD's Abdul Ghafoor, the minority welfare minister in Nitish's cabinet, went to meet Shahabuddin in jail. He carried his cell phone and some snacks with him, which is against jail rules. A photo of the meeting was posted on social media, obviously at the insistence of Shahabuddin. It came as a great embarrassment to Nitish. Ghafoor was unapologetic. He said, 'Shahabuddin is our party colleague. I was in Siwan and met him there. What's wrong with that?' Lalu backed Ghafoor saying, 'Every party in a coalition has its own leaders. They have a right to meet each other.'

The conflict between Nitish and Lalu on issues of governance only flared in the coming months. There was a dip in law and order owing to Lalu's interference, but Nitish did not allow him to influence policymaking and execution of programmes. At one point, Lalu proposed that a coordination committee of alliance partners be formed to 'advise' the government—on the lines of the National Advisory Council headed by Sonia Gandhi during the two UPA regimes—but Nitish rejected the idea outright. Lalu did not press for it. '*Usko maloom tha mera swabhav, main kisi ke niyantran mein nahi reh sakta* [He knew my nature, I am my own boss],' Nitish said to me.

However, a group of RJD men kept on making statements to the media to lionize Lalu and belittle Nitish. Nitish strongly suspected that they had Lalu's tacit approval, as he never publicly chided them. When Shahabuddin was released on bail after eleven years in jail in September 2016, he told the media, 'Lalu Prasad is my leader. Nitish Kumar is the CM owing to political circumstances [implying Lalu would have been the CM had he not been convicted].' He continued to mock Nitish in the following weeks, with Lalu never asking him to stop. The RJD leaders portrayed Shahabuddin as a 'popular leader' who had been 'falsely implicated' in criminal cases, a portrayal that was in total contradiction to Nitish's and the government's view of him. Ignoring the RJD's direct and indirect pressures, Nitish got his government to move the Supreme Court for cancellation of the bail granted to Shahabuddin by the Patna High Court in the Rajiv Roshan murder case. They pleaded that he had criminal antecedents and was a threat to society, a plea that was accepted by a two-member bench. Shahabuddin was sent back to jail less than a month after he was bailed out. He publicly swore to 'teach Nitish a lesson' at the next polls.[2]

The JD(U)–RJD alliance was bleeding so profusely from internecine wounds that it could not have survived for long. 'Even as the two parties were being welded,' Nitish said, 'I knew the welding would come apart in a year or two.' The alliance had serious difficulty breathing after the first week of July 2016, when the CBI registered an FIR against Lalu, Rabri Devi and Tejaswi Yadav on allegations of corruption in awarding a tender for the development, maintenance and operation of two Indian Railway Catering and Tourism Corporation (IRCTC) hotels in Ranchi and Puri in 2006, when Lalu was the railway minister. The CBI carried out raids at the houses of Lalu and Tejaswi. Nitish's clean image owed its sustenance to his personal integrity and untainted cabinet: he had sacked ministers when substantive allegations of corruption were made against them. He would have done the same with Tejaswi, but in order to avoid bitterness he wanted Lalu to ask Tejaswi to step down.

Lalu, Tejaswi and the whole family blew the case off like a bubble, saying that the FIR was not worth the scrap of paper on which it was written, as it was a conspiracy hatched by Modi, the BJP and the RSS to 'weaken the secular forces'. Nitish, according to sources close to him, took the opinion of lawyers and officers, who said the charges had substance; the CBI had done a primary investigation and found evidence before registering the FIR. So he refused to buy Lalu's conspiracy theory and insisted that Tejaswi 'explain it', i.e., present to him and the public convincing proof to refute the charges.

But the father and son kept on playing victims of a communal demon that intended to divide the secular forces and recapture Bihar. According to senior JD(U) leaders, when Nitish still insisted on an explanation, they said they could punch a thousand holes in the case, but they wouldn't do it as that would only help the 'communal forces and their tool, the CBI' to plug them and make a strong case against them!

Nitish was unimpressed and unrelenting. A top Congress leader advised Lalu to send Tejaswi to see Nitish personally. 'That would settle the matter,' the Congress leader told him. The suggestion was ludicrous; Tejaswi had been meeting Nitish almost daily as deputy chief minister. There was no special meeting needed if he wanted to speak to or 'explain his side' to Nitish. Nevertheless, Tejaswi sought a formal appointment with Nitish, which the latter quickly gave, hoping 'the boy' would come armed 'at least with something' to repudiate the charges. But Tejaswi came with nothing. He just mumbled what Lalu and he had been publicly saying: 'It is a design to weaken the secular forces.'

Nitish indirectly asked him to resign. He told him to take a decision looking at things from a long-term perspective. According to sources close to Nitish, he told Tejaswi, 'Your father and I represent the same socialist stream of politics. And neither of us will be there for too long. You are the future of our stream of politics. You have a long career ahead. You should make a proper decision seeing things in this light. As far as I am concerned, I have not compromised with corruption all my life, and I am not going to do it at any cost.'

The alliance now hung by a thread. No side was ready to budge. As a last resort, Nitish met Rahul Gandhi in New Delhi to seek his intervention to persuade Lalu to get Tejaswi to resign. He reminded Rahul how he had won national applause four years ago when he had torn up his own government's ordinance designed to negate a Supreme Court order barring convicted lawmakers from contesting elections, an ordinance meant to rescue Lalu. According to a top JD(U) source, Rahul said to him, 'Laluji often complains to me that he would have been the CM but for my tearing up of the ordinance!' Nitish began to sense Rahul's reluctance to intervene. He made another attempt to persuade Rahul. He pointed out to him that Lalu, in order to justify Tejaswi's refusal to resign, was citing the example of Virbhadra Singh, the Congress chief minister of Himachal Pradesh, who had not been asked by the party high command to resign even though he faced serious charges of corruption. '*Virbhadraji ko toh phansaya gaya hai* [Virbhadra has been framed],' Rahul said. Nitish was disappointed. 'Rahul Gandhi was talking like Lalu, not about internal corruption but about external conspiracy,' Nitish recalled. 'I came out of his house feeling dejected and alone. There is no help coming from anywhere, I told myself. I have to act on my own.'

Four days later, on 26 July 2017, he handed in his resignation to the Governor and told the media waiting outside, 'I tried my best to save the alliance. There were questions about someone in the government. I could not answer on behalf of him. What was happening was against my nature, contrary to the way I work. There was no point in running a government under such circumstances.'

No sooner did Nitish resign than Narendra Modi said in a tweet, '*Bhrastachar ke khilaf ladai mein judne ke liye Nitishji ko bahut badhai. Sawa sau karor nagarik imaandari ka swagat aur samarthan kar rahen hain* . . . [Many congratulations to Nitish for joining the war on corruption. One and a quarter billion citizens welcome and support honesty].' By the time Nitish returned from the Governor's house to his residence, the state BJP had announced support for him.

For Nitish, re-entering into an alliance with the BJP was the lowest point of his political career. He had to swallow his pride to accept the supreme leadership of the man who was the reason why he had broken off his decade-long relationship with the BJP in 2013. The warmth, applause and comradeship in Modi's tweet was like a scented kerchief passed to Nitish to wipe his eyes moist with shame and cheer up in 'the company of the pure'!

The BJP had seen an opportunity of reforging the alliance with the JD(U) as the crisis in the Nitish government deepened. Modi had kept his option of reuniting with Nitish open in any case. According to a senior JD(U) leader, months before the CBI filed the FIR against the Lalu family, a few BJP men from Bihar had gone to see Modi to persuade him to get the CBI to pin Nitish down in a Barh murder case dating back to 1991, in which he was an accused. Modi, according to the JD(U) leader, swatted away the suggestion, saying, 'I don't believe a man like him can ever do such a thing.'

The BJP had turned soft towards Nitish also because he had supported the party's candidate for the country's presidential office, Ram Nath Kovind. He had lauded demonetisation as a big step to curb black money. Further, most in the JD(U) core group preferred the BJP to the RJD as an ally. There were three reasons for this: one, they got important ministerial portfolios as the BJP was a junior partner. Two, BJP ministers did not interfere with their departments. Three, they were less greedy than the RJD ministers.

The JD(U)'s senior leaders had gone along with Nitish on the alliance with Lalu with great reluctance. What happened proved them right. Lalu secured creamy portfolios for his sons and party men. 'They audaciously behaved as though Lalu was their chief minister and not Nitish Kumar,' a JD(U) leader recalled. 'The RJD men touted a fallacy that Lalu was only mentoring his sons and partymen in the cabinet. Actually, he was trying to carve out a fiefdom of his own within the Nitish government,' he said. Apart from these factors, what alarmed the JD(U) was a series of reports about its members and supporters getting attracted towards the RJD. Lalu's party was seen as a more effective and useful instrument for 'getting things done' because its leader did not hang on moral strings like Nitish. For all these reasons, the alliance was coming apart at the seams even before the Tejaswi case happened.

Clearly, the ground for the JD(U)–BJP reunion was fallow but fertile.

Nitish's realliance with the BJP in July 2017 came at a high political cost to him. People close to him could see that he had done it out of compulsion and was not happy. Lalu nicknamed him 'Paltu Ram', a rank opportunist. The world that had praised him for good governance and the transformation of Bihar now ridiculed him as a seeker of power. His reputation as 'Mr Turnaround' was drowned in his infamy as 'Mr Turncoat'.

The secularist camp, whose respect he had not lost in the past despite his alliance with the 'communalist BJP', would not cease shooting poisoned arrows at the renegade. 'There were moments,' a close associate of Nitish recalled, 'when he felt really dejected. He felt that all his political life he had worked zealously to build his image as a "man of principles". But after he joined the BJP again—the BJP of Narendra Modi in particular—his image was bruised. "I have ruined myself," he would often say.'

The BJP as a whole, and the Bihar BJP in particular, saw Nitish's return to the NDA as one more big victory. Their equation with him had changed. Nitish's political discomfiture only increased when he found the Bihar BJP with Modi as the PM behaving differently from its pre-2014 avatar, with whom he had worked without much trouble for almost ten years since 2005. The hardliners had displaced the moderates at the forefront. What was 'extremist' became normal in the state BJP in the following months. More than 200 incidents of communal violence or tension took place in the state in the nine months since Nitish formed a government with the BJP again.³

A week before the Ramnavami festival in March 2018, BJP hardliner Arijit Shashwat the son of Union minister of state for health Ashwini Choubey, led a pre-festival procession through the streets of Bhagalpur town without the district authorities' permission, which ended in violence against the Muslims and damage to and looting of their property, according to police officials. That triggered similar processions throughout the state in the following week. State officials claimed that members of RSS-affiliate organizations marched through towns with swords in their hands—their edges glinting, fresh out of the workshop, all looking the same—threatening to crush any resistance to the building of a Ram temple. According to the police, never had so many Ramnavami processions been taken out, and never had so many naked swords been seen in the hands of the participants in the state before.

On the evening of Ramnavami, I happened to accompany Nitish when he went to Dak Bungalow, the central square of Patna, to watch the *jhanki*s, or tableaux, pass from a raised platform where the Union information technology minister, Ravi Shankar Prasad, and deputy chief minister, Sushil Modi, were already seated. There were many other BJP men sitting or standing there. All had saffron scarves round their necks. As soon as Nitish came up the steps, a saffron scarf was placed around his shoulders too. For about half an hour, we saw large numbers of men with unsheathed swords march past in processions, shouting war cries. The whole scene was chilling and awe-inspiring. Prasad and Modi responded to the greetings of the tableau leaders with beaming faces and a wave of their hands, and sometimes Nitish did so too. But we could notice the unease behind the veneer of Nitish's warmth. He was disturbed.

The BJP hardliners had been making attempt after attempt to mine Nitish's defences for communal peace. Police officials claimed that in several towns on the day of Ramnavami they tried to provoke Muslims into a fight by taking out processions through their settlements, pelting stones at their houses, playing derogatory songs, shouting derisive slogans, damaging mosques and private properties—ultimately succeeding in causing cross-violence. The district magistrates and police superintendents, forced to walk the tightrope as the hardliners belonged to a party in the government, did not take strong action against them until they received a firm instruction from Nitish 'to not spare anybody'. Over the next week, they arrested all those named in FIRs for violence, including BJP members. Even Arijit Shashwat surrendered after evading arrest for a few days. 'There was pressure on me to go soft on them,' Nitish recalled. 'But I said I can't compromise on communalism. The BJP leaders know me. If they try to play communal politics, I will quit the alliance.'

In order to keep Nitish on their side, the top BJP leadership— effectively meaning Narendra Modi and Shah—advised the state unit to desist from organizing any more activities with an aggressive Hindu accent. They did not want any disruptive antagonism with Nitish before the 2019 Lok Sabha elections. But at the same time they would keep shrinking him.

Nitish had been pleading with the Central government for central university status being granted to Patna University for years. He invited Modi to the centenary celebrations of the university and presented a strong case for making it a central university. But Modi did not accept his plea. Nitish had also been requesting the Central government for more special assistance in case of natural calamities. The Central government had made a rule that it would not grant more than 25 per cent of what a state spent on relief and rehabilitation as special assistance. According to sources close to Nitish, he met Modi in his office and urged him to raise the ceiling. 'Modi gave him an assurance but reneged on it,' they claimed.

In the matter of seat sharing for the 2019 elections, Shah played insensitive to Nitish's calls for distribution of the constituencies for months, leaving him with little time for the selection of candidates and preparations for the elections. Although Shah gave him an equal share, he did not give him the constituencies he wanted. In the elections, the BJP did not make special efforts everywhere to rally its caste blocs behind the JD(U) candidates. Consequently, the JD(U) lost Muslim-dominated Kishanganj and got much fewer votes than expected in Banka, Purnia and Jehanabad, which had a high share of upper-caste votes. 'Though the BJP gave us equal seats,' a senior JD(U) leader said, 'their game plan was to make us lose a few to make us unequal to them. Fortunately for us, Nitish's appeal worked in our favour and we ended up losing just one.'

The JD(U)'s suspicion that ever since Nitish had re-allied with the BJP, Modi and Shah had been trying to restrict him, weaken him and prevent him from getting bigger, only increased when they offered him just one ministry in the new Central cabinet after the NDA's massive victory in May 2019. Modi was to take oath with his ministers at the Rashtrapati Bhavan on 30 May. On 28 May, Shah called Nitish to say his party was going to get two ministries and requested him to come over to New Delhi so they could give it a final shape. When Nitish met him the following day, he was taken aback when Shah expressed his inability to give two ministries to his party. He could give him just one, he said.

The confinement hurt Nitish. The discrimination was explicit. The BJP got 17 MPs from Bihar and Modi had picked 5 of them for his council. The JD(U) got 16 MPs from the state, but he would take no more than one of them. Nitish told Shah to give his party proportionate representation. If the BJP was getting 5 ministers from Bihar, the JD(U) should get at least 4, if not 5. Shah was not willing. He was not even ready to give 3 offices—2 ministers of cabinet rank and 1 minister of state—which Nitish could have accepted as the middle ground between embarrassment and esteem. Shah stuck to one.

Nitish insisted on getting at least three offices, arguing that Bihar was important for him: the state was going to have Assembly elections the following year; a big representation of the BJP and a poor representation of the JD(U) from Bihar would send a message to the people of the state that the BJP, after winning 303 seats in the Lok Sabha, had decided to treat the JD(U) as an insignificant partner. It would also disappoint and demoralize the workers and supporters of his party; they might not engage themselves in the Assembly elections with the same enthusiasm as in the parliamentary elections. His party stood on the pillars of support of extremely backward castes and mahadalits; he wanted MPs from these castes to be ministers too, together with one from the upper caste. Under these circumstances, he said, just one office was too unequal, too unfair and too damaging to his party, and he would not accept it.

Shah politely refused to increase his offer, pleading that even other allies, the Shiv Sena, the LJP, the Shiromani Akali Dal (SAD) and the AIADMK were being given one ministry each. Nitish found the clubbing of his party with the LJP, the SAD and the AIADMK, which had won only 6, 2 and 1 seats, respectively, unjust and intentional. The Shiv Sena was the biggest NDA ally with 18 MPs, and it was up to the party leadership to negotiate with the BJP. Nitish was not concerned about Maharashtra, Tamil Nadu or Punjab. He was concerned about Bihar. His party had got a seat share equal to the BJP in the Lok Sabha elections in the state. He could not go home with a grossly unequal share in the ministry. It would amount to disgrace to him, his party, his workers, his voters.

When Shah refused to budge, Nitish took his leave, saying he would have to consult his senior partymen and see whether they were ready to accept just one ministry. As far as Nitish was concerned, he had made up his mind: his party would not be a part of the new Modi council. When he met the members of the core group of his party at his residence in New Delhi, they too expressed their unwillingness to accept just one ministry. On the morning of 30 May, Nitish conveyed his party's decision to Shah. But he did not tell this to the media. The swearing-in of the Modi council was scheduled in the evening. Nitish waited until early afternoon for any response from Shah. When there was no word from him, Nitish announced to the media that his party would not join the NDA ministry.

Although Nitish attended the swearing-in ceremony and told the media on his arrival in Patna that his party would continue to be a part of the NDA, political circles were abuzz about his supposed disenchantment with the BJP. What made the whispers louder was his emphatic declaration that his party's decision not to join the NDA council was final, leaving no room for speculation that his party would reverse its decision if the BJP offered more than one ministry. It set off rumours of his split with the BJP. Cartoons appeared in the print media and on social media ridiculing Nitish for making preparations for a 'Betrayal 2.0'. Voices from the Congress, the RJD and other parties invited Nitish to rejoin the grand secular alliance, to 'come back home'.

A few days after his return from New Delhi, he expanded his cabinet to include 8 JD(U) senior leaders (representing OBCs, EBCs and mahadalits) as ministers. He did not induct anyone from the BJP, which supplied further grist to the rumour mills. Publicly, Nitish explained the non-inclusion of the BJP on the ground that the 8 ministerial berths were from the JD(U) quota that had remained long unfilled. But the BJP leaders who knew Nitish's political style—*It is good to be clever, and even better not to be seen so*, as the saying goes—understood that it was intended to be his counterplay to Modi and Shah's imperious play. The rumour mills worked overtime when he announced sometime later that his party would contest the Assembly elections in 2020 in Jharkhand, Jammu and Kashmir, Haryana and Delhi without an alliance with any party.

Play and counterplay notwithstanding, Nitish had no plan of stretching it to the point of separation from the BJP. When he sat back and weighed what was good and bad, possible and not possible for him in the NDA and the mahagathbandhan, he would still prefer the former. For two years, between 2015 and 2017, he had attempted to build a Congress-led national alternative to the BJP—in Assam, in alliance with the Asom Gana Parishad and the All India United Democratic Front; in Uttar Pradesh, with Ajit Singh's group and other small parties; and in Gujarat with the Patidar community leader Hardik Patel—only to be disappointed by the cold, smug, short-sighted response of the Congress leadership. He had also not got any help when he had wanted the Congress to intervene and get Tejaswi Yadav to resign. He had lost faith in them.

Nitish's disillusionment with the Congress, his banishment of the 'other option' from his politics and the docility expected from his confinement to the NDA had proved advantageous to the BJP. In the following months, not only did they not try to appease him but they also introduced three bills in Parliament that were anathema to the JD(U). A very important part of the NDA covenant signed between the constituent parties was that the issues of the special status of Jammu and Kashmir, the uniform civil code and the Ram temple at Ayodhya—which were the core issues of the BJP—would be kept out of the alliance agenda. It was based on this covenant that the Samata Party (later the JD[U]) and the BJP had fought and won the elections in Bihar. It was by virtue of this covenant that Nitish could always claim to be a secular politician, despite being in the company of Hindu partisans. 'The alliance between us and the BJP is a tactical alliance, not an ideological alliance,' he would often say to the media. 'I will never compromise on communalism.'

A month into Modi's second tenure, beginning in 2019, the BJP-led Central government began to breach the covenant. It started with the triple talaq bill. All the JD(U) MPs could do was walk out in protest. Next came the Jammu and Kashmir (Reorganisation) Bill. All the JD(U) MPs could do again was walk out. The mild protests hurt Nitish's secular image. However, he could do no more, as that could mean walking out of the NDA. He did not want to lose power. He despised riches but loved power; he hated gold but loved glory. His explanation of his symbolic opposition was facile. 'At the moment, the BJP is a giant with the power to pulverize its allies,' Nitish said to a confidante. 'But it is not going to remain so always. When the situation changes, we will have our day.' It sounded like Don Quixote justifying his flight from an aggressive mob with the stance that courage is inseparable from wisdom and should wait for a favourable occasion to strike!

The compromise, the relenting, the acquiescence: those who trusted Nitish for his secularism were shaken. However, they would still not pelt a stone at the pennant of secularism he flew atop his political chariot. Their trust, however, began to sink when he supported the Kashmir bill after it was passed by Parliament a day after his party's walkout. He had abandoned the cause of special status for Kashmir. They were bewildered by the party's official position articulated by the national general secretary, R.C.P. Singh: 'We were opposing the bill, but opposing it is pointless once it has become a law. We should all accept the law. We are with the Central government on it. We have to also respect the sentiments of the people of Bihar and the rest of India who support the law, as they think it is in the nation's interest.'

The Muslims of Bihar and the rest of India were hoping Nitish would at least oppose the Citizenship (Amendment) Bill as it was widely considered to be of dubious intent.[4] He had opposed it when the Central government had introduced it towards the end of Modi's first tenure in January 2019, describing it as 'communal', discriminatory and dangerous for the country. But when the government brought up the same bill in December 2019, Nitish supported it, saying there was nothing communal in it, nothing that was contrary to the principle of secularism. His senior partymen almost parroted the BJP line: 'The bill is in accordance with the principle of secularism, as it intends to grant citizenship to persons who were persecuted on religious grounds.' The Muslims and Nitish's admirers could barely believe the U-turn.

The Muslims saw through the equivocation of the Central government and came out on the streets in large numbers in many parts of the country, demanding that the Citizenship (Amendment) Act (CAA) be scrapped and the follow-up National Population Register (NPR) and National Register of Citizens (NRC) be called off. The spontaneous protests, in which Muslim women took the lead, saying they were fighting for the future of their children, compelled Modi to declare that his government had never considered any proposal to build an NRC.[5]

The popular upsurge of the Muslims against the BJP's design at last forced Nitish to rethink his position on the CAA–NPR–NRC chain. In the elections he had fought, he had never got but a marginal share of the Muslim vote. But even though most Muslims voted for the RJD, they appreciated Nitish for his policies and actions for their educational and economic advancement, protection and welfare. Their admiration did not translate into votes because voting for him would mean voting for the BJP-led alliance. It was solely out of his secular convictions that he had taken measures for the development of the minorities, often contrary to the wishes and sentiments of the BJP. However, the peaceful protests of the Muslims made Nitish realize that he might lose even their admiration and respect. This was a political capital, a good part of which he had already lost. He could lose all of it if he did not try to break the chain. It meant risking the BJP's displeasure, but that was the gamble he had to make in order to redeem his secular image.

He finally declared in the state Assembly on 13 January 2020 that there was no need or justification for a countrywide NRC. But that alone would not bring back the Muslim esteem for him, because the NPR, its precursor, was still in existence. Two Opposition-ruled states, Kerala and West Bengal, had declared their objection to the new format of the NPR. The Congress and the RJD were speaking against it daily. There were murmurs against it within the JD(U) as well. Concerns about it were being raised in the media too. In order to avoid being found without valid documents to prove their citizenship, Muslims were queuing up at government and municipal offices to get certified papers of land titles, house ownership, birth, residence, education, marriage and what not. All this was like a terrible storm threatening to blow away Nitish's shrunken secular glory to obscurity. For weeks in January and February 2020 he studied the old and new formats of the NPR, held discussions on them with people inside and outside the party, who were close to him, and arrived at the conclusion that the requirement of new particulars—particularly the date of birth and dates and places of birth of parents—were going to sweep huge numbers of people into the category of doubtful citizens. He said to me in an interview on 24 January 2020, a few days after the discussions:

> People who are poor and illiterate cannot tell the date of their birth. They may mention a war, an epidemic or earthquake as the 'time'

of their birth, because that is what their parents will have told them. To expect them to tell us when and where their parents were born is to expect someone who doesn't know arithmetic to solve problems of algebra. Even many of us so-called educated people living in cities might not be able to tell the dates or places of the birth of our parents. I myself would not be able to say exactly whether my mother was born in my maternal grandmother's natal or marital residence. Ditto for my father's birth. The Muslims see the new particulars in NPR 2020 as wool-padded irons to fetter them as foreigners. But I have studied the whole thing and I am afraid the new particulars are bad for all communities, not just Muslims. How many of the OBCs, EBCs, Dalits and mahadalits will be able to give exact particulars to enumerators? If they do not, they can be marked as doubtful citizens, and harassed and detained or fleeced by corrupt officials. I see high political risks along with high human risks in the NPR exercise. The enumeration is slated for April–September 2020. This is the period when I will be campaigning to seek the popular mandate for the fourth time. I dread to imagine the environment: millions of people running from pillar to post for documents, distress, anxiety, disturbance and anger everywhere; the Congress and the RJD fuelling and fanning the fire. All this is going to generate hostility against me and my government, a hostility that might snatch even assured seats from the NDA bag. I just can't allow it to happen. It would harm both us and the BJP.

He brainstormed with the BJP leaders and told them that he was going to move a resolution in the Assembly, stating that NPR enumeration in the state would be done according to the 2010 format, which was designed by the then Congress government and required only simple particulars of individuals. The BJP leaders agreed in order to avoid a conflict with Nitish in the election year. The resolution was passed in the Assembly with the BJP's support on 25 February 2020.

The closer allies in power come during elections, the farther their bonhomie goes. They each fight for the maximum share of seats. It happened during the months preceding the 2019 parliamentary elections; it was happening in the months before the 2020 Assembly polls. In 2019, the JD(U) settled for an equal share with the BJP. In 2020, it demanded a higher share on the ground that while the BJP was the big brother in the alliance in national politics, the JD(U) was the big brother in state politics. In all the Assembly elections they had fought together, the JD(U) had got the larger share. Even in the 2015 Assembly elections, when they fought against each other, the JD(U) had won a higher number of seats (71) than the BJP (53).

The BJP tried to prick the JD(U)'s balloon by arguing that it had got a much higher vote share (24.4 per cent) than the latter (16.8 per cent) in the 2015 elections. And in the 2019 Lok Sabha elections, it had led in 97 Assembly segments and the JD(U) in 94. The BJP pressed for an equal share of seats in 2020, as in the 2019 Lok Sabha polls, if not a higher share. As per the JD(U)'s perception, giving a higher share to the BJP would be suicidal, but even an equal share carried a big risk. If the BJP won more seats than the JD(U), it could demand the chief minister's office. The JD(U)–BJP alliance was like beasts of two different species living in the same den: they prayed together but worshipped separately; they hunted together but ate separately; they fought together but weaponized separately. They acted to strengthen each other but worked to weaken each other. Senior JD(U) leaders said they were wary that the BJP, with the RSS grassroots organization behind it, was better equipped to ensure the success of the maximum number of its candidates, as well as to cause the defeat of some JD(U) candidates by undermining their support in order to come out with a larger number. And it was true: it has been the BJP's dream to have a chief minister of the party in Bihar. It had realized a similar dream in Maharashtra in 2014 by winning more seats than its ally, the Shiv Sena.

When Nitish insisted on a larger seat share, the national BJP leadership decided to handle the subject with care. Despite the desire within a section of the state BJP to fight elections on its own, the leadership has not been very warm to the idea, as there is nobody in the party's state unit who has the stature, worthiness and popularity to swing the electorate in the party's favour. The state's politics is dominated by backward castes and the BJP has no charismatic leader to choose from. The choice before the BJP's national leadership is limited to dependence on Nitish, and that tips the scale in his favour.

Bihar is currently divided into three political estates: the BJP, the JD(U) and the RJD. The BJP has farmed the plantations of upper castes and banias; the JD(U) of the EBCs and mahadalits; and the RJD of the Yadavs and Muslims. The JD(U) has its estate in the middle, with a flexibility to level up the fence on either side and emerge as the winner with a combined harvest. The BJP has no room for such flexibility. It could combine with the RJD only as self-destructively as fire could with water. It, therefore, has to stick with Nitish, and keep him in good humour by accepting him as the bigger partner in Bihar.

# notes

PROLOGUE

1. Published data of the Election Commission of India. See 'Bihar 2015', Election Commission of India, https://eci.gov.in/tags/ bihar%20assembly%20election%202015, last accessed on 21 June 2019.

## I. ON A SEA OF TURMOIL

1. *Samayik Varta*, 1–15 February 1978 (pp. 88–89).
2. *Samayik Varta*, 1–15 December 1977 (p. 89).
3. Arun Srivastava, Bihar state correspondent for the *Indian Express*, in an interview with the author (pp. 123–24).
4. Alakh N. Sharma, 'Political Economy of Poverty in Bihar', *Economic and Political Weekly*, 14–21 October 1995 (p. 126).
5. Indu Bharti, 'Bihar: Election-Eve Promises', *Economic and Political Weekly*, 17–24 February 1990 (p. 137).
6. Arun Sinha, *Against the Few: Struggles of India's Rural Poor* (London: Zed Books, 1991), pp. 20–21 (pp. 144–45).
7. B.G. Deshmukh, quoted in http://www.rediff.com/news/2003/ jul/10inter.htm, 10 July 2003 (p. 152).
8. Arun Srivastava in an interview with the author (p. 185).
9. Swapan Dasgupta and Farzand Ahmed, *India Today*, 13 March 2000 (p. 186).

10. Ammu Joseph, 'Rabri revisited', *The Hindu*, 9 September 2001 (p. 193).

11. Kalpana Sharma, 'Sita, Usha and Rabri', *The Hindu*, 26 August 2001 (p. 194).

12. Ashok K. Pankaj, 'Towards Changing Institutions for Governance and Development of Bihar', in Sachchidananda and B.P. Mandal (eds), *Crisis of Governance: The Case of Bihar* (New Delhi: Serials Publications, 2009) (p. 194).

13. 'Of deterioration and regression: An interview with Sushil Kumar Modi', *Frontline*, 10–23 May 2003 (p. 200).

14. http://indiainteracts.in/columnist/2007/09/06/Shahabuddin-The -epitome-of-criminalpolitician-Nexus/, 6 September 2007 (p. 208).

15. http://indiavikalp.blogspot.com/2008/06/indias-member-of -parliament-convicted.html, 26 June 2008 (pp. 208–09).

16. BPCC president Sadanand Singh quoted in 'Battles in Bihar' by Purnima S. Tripathi, *Frontline*, 30 July–12 Aug 2005 (p. 218).

17. Shivanand Tiwari in an interview with the author (p. 221).

## II. REINVENTING BIHAR

1. Nirmala Ganapathy, *Indian Express*, New Delhi, 5 January 2003 (p. 238).

2. Interview with the author, 26 November 2010 (pp. 257–58).

3. *Bihar Samachar*, Government of Bihar monthly, July 2010 (pp. 259–60).

4. Based on interview with V.K. Shashikumar of police officers who participated in the operation. http://www.indiandefencereview .com/homeland-security/Police-cannot-take-on-Maoists.html, 25 October 2010 (p. 264).

5. *The Times of India*, Patna edition, 19 December 2008 (p. 269).

6. Smita Gupta, 'The State at the Doorstep', *Outlook*, 26 April 2010 (p. 269).

7. Venkitesh Ramakrishnan, 'Soft on Maoists', *Frontline*, 25 September–8 October 2010 (pp. 269–70).

8. Jamal Kidwai and Juhi Tyagi, 'NREGA: Where is the people's participation?' http://infochangeindia.org/200807057205/

Livelihoods/Analysis/NREGA-Where-is-the-people-s-participation .html, InfoChange News & Features, July 2008 (p. 270).

9. The Vajpayee government (1999–2004) had instituted the programme as a special economic package for Bihar by way of partial compensation for loss of revenue from bifurcation in 2000 (p. 302).

10. Pratyaya Amrit, 'How We Turned Bihar Bridge Corporation Around', http:/www.governancenow.com/news/regular-story/how -we-turned-bihar-bridge-corp-around, 29 May 2010 (pp. 308–09).

11. Archana Masih, 'The Return of India's Lost State', http://www.rediff .com/news/slide-show/slide-show-1-bihar-the-return-of-indias-lost -state/20101027.htm, 28 October 2010 (p. 315).

12. Brajesh Kumar, 'Bridging the Gap between India and Bharat in Bihar', http://www.governancenow.com/news/regular-story/ bridging-gap-between-india-and-bharat-bihar, 22 October 2010 (pp. 315–16).

13. Saubhadra Chatterji, 'Bihar Voters in Dilemma', *Business Standard*, 28 October 2010 (p. 339).

14. http:/nitishspeaks.blogspot.com/2010/10/blog-post.html (pp. 339–40).

15. 'A Study of Bihari Migrant Labourers: Incidence, Causes and Remedies, 2009–10', Indian Institute of Public Administration, New Delhi (p. 346).

16. Jamal Kidwai and Juhi Tyagi, 'NREGA: Where is the people's participation?' http://infochangeindia.org/200807057205/ Livelihoods/Analysis/NREGA-Where-is-the-people-s-participation. html (pp. 348–49).

17. CPI(ML), 'Party Building: Letter from Patna', http://www.cpiml .org/liberation/year_2009/nov_09/party_building.html, November 2009 (pp. 352–53).

18. Varsha Jawalgekar, 'Villagers Expose Corrupt Dealer', http:// indiaunheard.videovolunteers.org/varsha/villagers-exposecorrupt-pds-dealer/, 30 August 2010 (p. 353).

19. Hunger Free Bihar Campaign, 'Poor service delivery causing starvation deaths in Bihar', http://asiapacific.endpoverty2015.org/ event/campaction/poor-service-delivery-causing-starvation-deaths -in-bihar-report, 1 September 2009 (p. 354).

## EPILOGUE I: ECONOMY

1. Pramit Bhattacharya and Sriharsa Devulapalli, 'India's rural poverty has shot up', Mint, 3 December 2019, https://livemint.com/news/india/rural-poverty-has-shot-up-nso-data-shows/11575352445478.html, last accessed on 31 July 2020.

2. Udit Misra, 'Poverty alleviation in Bihar', *Forbes India*, 19 May 2011, https://forbesindia.com/article/on-assignment/poverty-alleviation-in-bihar/25002/1, last accessed on 31 July 2020.

3. Gerry Rodgers, Amrita Datta, Janine Rodgers, Sunil K. Mishra and Alakh N. Sharma, *The Challenge of Inclusive Development in Rural Bihar*, Institute of Human Development, (New Delhi: Manak Publications, 2013).

4. 'Prime Minister Narendra Modi launches Garib Kalyan Rojgar Abhiyan', Press Information Bureau, 20 June 2020, https://pib.gov.in/PressReleasePage.aspx?PRID=1632861, last accessed on 31 July 2020.

5. Mohd Imran Khan, 'Bihar's Mutalupur farmers transform neglected wetland into integrated farm', Wire, 3 October 2017, https://thewire.in/agriculture/bihars-mutalupur-farmers-transform-neglected-wetland-into-integrated-farm, last accessed on 31 July 2020.

6. Debdatta Saha and Barna Ganguli, 'Food processing industries: Lessons from Bihar', Ideas for India, 29 November 2016, https://ideasforindia.in/topics/macroeconomics/food-processing-industries-lessons-from-Bihar.html, last accessed on 31 July 2020.

7. Debdatta Saha and Barna Ganguli, 'Study of Food Processing Sector in Bihar', www.igc.org, 31 December 2016, theigc.org/project/study-of-the-food-processing-sector-in-bihar, last accessed on 31 July 2020.

## EPILOGUE II: POLITICS

1. Janaki Fernandes, 'Nitish Kumar's 10 jabs at Narendra Modi', NDTV, 15 April 2013, https://www.ndtv.com/cheat-sheet/nitish-kumars-10-jabs-at-narendra-modi-519118, last accessed on

23 March 2020; see also, 'Country needs a leader who can unite, not divide', *Hindu BusinessLine*, 21 June 2013, last accessed on 4 August 2020.

2. Rohit Kumar Singh, 'My supporters will reply to Nitish Kumar in next polls: Shahabuddin before going back to jail', *India Today*, 30 September 2016, https://www.indiatoday.in/india/story/rajiv-roshan-murder-case-mohammad-shahabuddin-rjd-rjd-mp-lalu-yadav-nitish-kumar-344161-2016-09-30, last accessed on 6 May 2019.

3. Santosh Singh, 'How communal pot has simmered Bihar since Nitish Kumar's NDA return', *Indian Express*, 2 April 2018, https://indianexpress.com/article/india/bihar-nitish-kumar-communal-clashes-hindu-muslim-violence-bhagalpur-aurangabad-clash-bjp-5119972/, last accessed on 3 May 2020.

4. For the Lok Sabha debate on the bill, see Lok Sabha Secretariat, 'Citizenship (Amendment) Bill, 2019', Lok Sabha, 9 December 2019, https://loksabhaph.nic.in/Debates/Result17.aspx?dbsl=3993; and http://loksabhaph.nic.in/Debates/Result17.aspx?dbsl=4102&ser=&smode=t#4134*8, last accessed on 29 June 2020.

5. Jatin Anand, 'Pan-India NRC was never on the table, says PM Modi', *The Hindu*, 22 December 2019, https://www.thehindu.com/news/cities/Delhi/pan-india-nrc-was-never-on-the-table-says-narendra-modi-at-delhi-rally/article30372096.ece, last accessed on 1 July 2020.

# selected bibliography

Agrawal, S.P., and J.C. Aggarwal. *Education and Social Uplift of Backward Classes: At What Cost and How? Mandal Commission and After*. New Delhi: Concept Publishing, 1991.

Ahmad, Imtiaz. *Caste and Social Stratification among the Muslims*. Delhi: Manohar Book Service, 1973.

Alam, Jawaid. *Government and Politics in Colonial Bihar*. New Delhi: Mittal Publications, 2004.

Anwar, Ali. *Masawaat ki Jung* [in Hindi]. New Delhi: Vani Prakashan, 2001.

Barik, Radhakanta. *Land and Caste Politics in Bihar*. New Delhi: Shipra Publications, 2006.

———. *Politics of the JP Movement*. New Delhi: Radiant Publishers, 1977.

Bhalla, G.S. *Indian Agriculture since Independence*. New Delhi: National Book Trust, 2007.

Bhandarkar, D.R. *Asoka*. New Delhi: Asian Educational Services, 2000.

Brass, Paul R. *Language, Religion and Politics in North India*. Cambridge: Cambridge University Press, 1974.

———. *The Politics of India since Independence*. Cambridge: Cambridge University Press, 2004.

Byres, T.J., K. Kapadia and J. Lerche, eds. *Rural Labour Relations in India*. London: Frank Cass, 1999.

Chakravarti, Anand. *Social Power and Everyday Class Relations: Agrarian Transformation in North Bihar*. New Delhi: Sage Publications, 2001.

Chandra, Bipan. *In the Name of Democracy: JP Movement and the Emergency*. New Delhi: Penguin Books India, 2003.

Chandra, Bipan, Mridula Mukherjee and Aditya Mukherjee. *India after Independence, 1947–2000*. New Delhi: Penguin Books India, 2003.

Dayal, Shiv, ed. *Bihar ki Virasat aur Navnirman ki Chunauti* [in Hindi]. Patna: Sarokar, 2003.

Das, Arvind N., ed. *Agrarian Movements in India: Studies on 20th Century Bihar*. London: Frank Cass, 1982.

Desai, A.R., ed. *Agrarian Struggles in India after Independence*. Mumbai: Oxford University Press, 1986.

Desai, A.R. *Social Background of Indian Nationalism*. Mumbai: Popular Prakashan, 2008.

Dhavan, Rajeev. *Reserved! How Parliament Debated Reservations, 1995–2007*. New Delhi: Rupa & Co., 2008.

Doniger, Wendy, and Brian K. Smith, trans. *The Laws of Manu*. New Delhi: Penguin Books India, 1991.

*Era of Rapid Change*. New Delhi: Publications Division, Government of India, 1968.

Franco, Fernando, ed. *Pain and Awakening: The Dynamics of Dalit Identity in Bihar, Gujarat and Uttar Pradesh*. New Delhi: Indian Social Institute, 2002.

Frankel, Francine R., and M.S.A. Rao. *Dominance and State Power in Modern India*. New Delhi: Oxford University Press, 1999.

Jaffrelot, Christophe. *India's Silent Revolution: The Rise of the Low Castes in North Indian Politics*. Delhi: Permanent Black, 2003.

Januzzi, F.T. *Agrarian Crisis in India: The Case of Bihar*. Austin: University of Texas Press, 1974.

Jha, Jata Shankar. *Maharaja Lakshmishwar Singh of Darbhanga: Biography of an Indian Patriot*. Patna: Maharaja Lakshmishwar Singh Smarak Samiti, 1972.

Jha, Shashishekhar. *Political Elite in Bihar*. Mumbai: Vora & Co., 1972.

Jha, Usha. *Land, Labour and Power: Agrarian Crisis and the State in Bihar (1937–52)*. Delhi: Aakar Books, 2003.

Joshi, P.C. *Land Reforms in India: Trends and Perspectives*. Institute of Economic Growth. New Delhi: Allied Publishers, 1982.

Joshi, Hemant, and Sanjay Kumar, eds. *Asserting Voices: Changing*

*Cultural Identity and Livelihood of the Musahars in the Gangetic Plains*. Delhi: Dushkal Publication, 2002.

Kelkar, Indumati. *Dr Rammanohar Lohia: Jeevan aur Darshan* [in Hindi]. New Delhi: Anamika Publishers, 2009.

Kothari, Rajni, ed. *Caste in Indian Politics*. New Delhi: Orient Longman, 1970.

Kumar, Nitish. *Vikasit Bihar ki Khoj* [in Hindi]. New Delhi: Prabhat Prakashan, 2010.

Lohia, Rammanohar. *The Caste System*. Hyderabad: Samata Vidyalaya Nyas, 1964.

———. *Saat Krantiyan* [in Hindi]. Hyderabad: Samata Vidyalaya Nyas, 1966.

———. *Marx, Gandhi and Socialism*. Hyderabad: Nava Hind Publications, 1963.

Louis, Prakash. *People Power: The Naxalite Movement in Central Bihar*. Delhi: Wordsmiths, 2002.

Mandelbaum, D.G. *Society in India*. Berkley: University of California Press, 1970.

Mishra, Girish. *Agrarian Problems of Permanent Settlement: A Case Study of Champaran*. New Delhi: People's Publishing House, 1978.

Mishra, Girish, and Braj Kumar Pandey. *Sociology and Economics of Casteism in India: A Study of Bihar*. New Delhi: Pragati Publications, 1996.

Narayan, Jayaprakash. *Face to Face*. Varanasi: Navchetna Prakashan, 1970.

———. *Towards Total Revolution: Politics in India*. Mumbai: Popular Prakashan, 1978.

Nedumpara, Jose J. *Political Economy and Class Contradictions*. New Delhi: Anmol Publications, 2004.

Omvedt, Gail. *Ambedkar: Towards an Enlightened India*. New Delhi: Penguin Books India, 2004.

Pathak, Bindeshwar. *Rural Violence in Bihar*. New Delhi: Concept, 1993.

Patnaik, Kishan. *Vikalp-heen Nahin Hai Duniya: Sabhyata, Samaj aur Buddhijeevion ki Sthiti par Kuchh Vichaar* [in Hindi]. New Delhi: Rajkamal Prakashan, 2000.

Phadnis, Aditi, et al. *Business Standard Political Profiles of Cabals and Kings.* New Delhi: BS Books, 2009.

Prasad, K.N. *Bihar Economy through the Plans.* New Delhi: Northern Book Centre, 1997.

Prasad, Rajendra. *Autobiography.* New Delhi: National Book Trust, 1994.

Punit, A.E. *Social Systems in Rural India.* New Delhi: Sterling Publishers, 1978.

Purushottam and Jose Kalapura. *Hashiye Par Khade Bihar ke Nishad* [in Hindi]. New Delhi: Daanish Books, and Patna: Xavier Institute of Social Research, 2008.

Rai, Rambahadur, ed. *Vishwanath Pratap Singh: Manzil se Zyada Safar* [in Hindi]. New Delhi: Rajkamal Prakashan, 2006.

*Reservation Policy on Vacancies* [in Hindi]. Patna: Law Publishing House, 2009.

Sachchidananda and B.P. Mandal, eds. *Crisis of Governance: The Case of Bihar.* New Delhi: Serials Publications, 2009.

*Second Freedom Struggle: Chandapuri's Call to Overthrow Brahmin Rule.* Patna: Mission Prakashan, 2003.

Shah, Ghanshyam. *Protest Movements in Two Indian States: A Study of the Gujarat and Bihar Movements.* Delhi: Ajanta Publications, 1977.

Shah, Ghanshyam, ed. *Caste and Democratic Politics in India.* Delhi: Permanent Black, 2002.

Shah, Ghanshyam. *Social Movements in India: A Review of Literature.* New Delhi: Sage Publications, 2004.

Sen, Samar, et al., eds. *Naxalbari and After: A Frontier Anthology.* Calcutta, 1978.

Sharad, Onkar, ed. *Lohia ke Vichar* [in Hindi]. Allahabad: Lok Bharti Prakashan, 2008.

Sharma, Alakh N., and Shaibal Gupta. *Bihar: Stagnation or Growth.* Patna: Spectrum Publishing House, 1987.

Singh, Abhimanyu. *Development Administration Challenges.* New Delhi: APH Publishing, 2008.

Singh, Madhulika. *The Role of Peasantry in the Freedom Struggle in Bihar (1912–1947).* Patna: K.P. Jayaswal Research Institute, 2006.

Sinha, Arun. *Against the Few: Struggles of India's Rural Poor.* London: Zed Books, 1991.

Sinha, Indradeep. *Sangharsh ke Path Par* [in Hindi]. Patna: Anwesha Prakashan, 2002.

Sinha, Rajeev Ranjan Kumar. *Dynamics of Land–Caste Relations in India*. New Delhi: Manak Publications, 2009.

Sinha, Sushil Kumar. *Other Half of the Society: Backward Caste and Politics of Bihar*. New Delhi: Raj Publications, 2007.

Sohane, R.K., ed. *New Technological Innovations in Cereals, Pulses and Oilseed Cultivation*. Patna: Bihar Agricultural Management and Extension Training Institute, 2009.

Srinivas, M.N. *Social Change in Modern India*. Berkeley: University of California Press, 1966.

———. *The Dominant Caste and Other Essays*. New Delhi: Oxford University Press, 1987.

———, ed. *Caste: Its Twentieth Century Avatar*. New Delhi: Viking, 1996.

Suri, Surindar. *The Rise of V.P. Singh and the 1989 and 1990 Elections*. Delhi: Konark Publishers, 1990.

Thakur, Janardan. *V.P. Singh: The Quest for Power*. New Delhi: Warbler Books, 1989.

Thakur, Sankarshan. *The Making of Laloo Yadav: The Unmaking of Bihar*. New Delhi: HarperCollins Publishers India, 2000.

Thapar, Romila. *Ancient Indian Social History: Some Interpretations*. Hyderabad: Orient Longman, 1978

———. *The Penguin History of Early India: From the Origins to AD 1300*. New Delhi: Penguin Books India, 2003.

Tiwary, S.N. *Dynamics of Caste in Rural Bihar*. Darbhanga: Lalit Narayan Mithila University, Publications Department, 1989.

# acknowledgements

This book would not have been possible without Ranjana Sengupta, my commissioning editor at Penguin India. She sensed the potential of the book as soon as my proposal reached her and supported me through the researching, writing and revision of the manuscript in a very friendly and critical but non-invasive way. Thanks also to her colleague Richa Burman for her valuable suggestions.

I am grateful to my close friends Kaushal Mishra, Narendra Singh and Uday Kant Mishra for always being there. I owe thanks to Shaibal Gupta, P.P. Ghosh, Shashi Bhushan Prasad, Amitabh Sinha and a number of other social scientists, journalists and many others who provided me significant insights and inputs on the subject, as well as to all those young and bright friends who helped me with research.

Nitish Kumar's secretaries, R.C.P. Singh, Chanchal Kumar, S. Siddharth and Gopal Singh went out of the way to make official documents, materials on his personal life as well as his photographs available to me. My special thanks to them.

I owe a lot to my wife Purnima, daughters Nagma and Ruhi and their husbands Prateek and Rohit, who never ceased asking questions related to the book from time to time, helping me to fill gaps in the narrative.

# index